POLICING PATIENTS

Policing Patients

TREATMENT AND SURVEILLANCE
ON THE FRONTLINES OF THE
OPIOID CRISIS

ELIZABETH CHIARELLO

PRINCETON UNIVERSITY PRESS
PRINCETON & OXFORD

Requests for permission to reproduce material from this work should be sent to permissions@press.princeton.edu

Published by Princeton University Press
41 William Street, Princeton, New Jersey 08540
99 Banbury Road, Oxford OX2 6JX

press.princeton.edu

ISBN 978-0-691-22477-0
ISBN (e-book) 978-0-691-22478-7

Library of Congress Control Number: 2024935962

British Library Cataloging-in-Publication Data is available

Editorial: Meagan Levinson, Erik Beranek, and Rachel Levay
Production Editorial: Kathleen Cioffi
Jacket Design: Karl Spurzem
Production: Erin Suydam
Publicity: Kate Hensley and Kathryn Stevens
Copyeditor: Jennifer Harris

Jacket images: Thanate Rooprasert / Shutterstock; National Institutes of Health / United States Department of Health and Human Services

This book has been composed in Arno

Printed in the United States of America

10 9 8 7 6 5 4 3 2 1

To those who are suffering and those who want to help

CONTENTS

POLICING PATIENTS

Introduction

Prologue

THE PROBLEM IS PAIN. No one deserves to suffer—not people who face each day with debilitating pain nor people who use drugs to cope with trauma and other struggles. And yet U.S. drug policy pits people with chronic pain and people with substance use disorders against each other in a zero-sum battle over opioids. Too much opioid prescribing exacerbates addiction and overdose. Too little opioid prescribing leaves the pain unmitigated and sufferers with nowhere to turn. The U.S. overdose crisis[1] has taken more than 1 million lives, and overdose rates increase each year.[2] At the knotted center of this impossible situation, physicians, pharmacists, prosecutors, and investigators face few suitable choices for patient improvement. This book details America's misguided attempts to curb the overdose crisis and the professions hidden at the heart of the problem.

Chronic pain and addiction sit uncomfortably on the cusp of law, medicine, and morality. Pain is alternatively framed as a medical problem or insufficient moral fortitude while addiction is considered either an illness or a crime. Lacking an adequate social safety net, the powerful fields of medicine and criminal justice take control over social problems[3] they were never designed to address. People with chronic pain and addiction land in emergency departments and jails that have scant resources to help. As a result, these problems fall through the gap even as physicians, pharmacists, prosecutors, and investigators labor to resolve them. Ultimately, the tools at their disposal are ill-suited to the job. Do workers make things worse by using blunt tools on problems that require sharpened ones or is doing *something* better than doing nothing?

I began my inquiry into the overdose crisis with an overlooked set of professionals: pharmacists. Contrary to what many people think, pharmacists do not just dispense drugs that physicians prescribe. They have their own professional licenses that give them discretion over whether or not to dispense medications, and, in most states, pharmacists can refuse to dispense drugs they consider inappropriate. Their position as the ultimate gatekeepers to prescription drugs has propelled pharmacists into the crux of a national battle. Pharmacists, long considered healthcare's underdogs, like to operate in the background, to help patients without calling too much attention to themselves. The overdose crisis pushed them into the spotlight, where they found themselves grappling with competing forces: pressure to dispense drugs from patients, physicians, and managers and pressure to exercise caution from law enforcement.

Not long ago, I knew little about pharmacists and even less about the opioid crisis. As a budding sociologist, my interests centered on reproductive justice. When I learned that pharmacists were refusing to dispense emergency contraception (aka Plan B or the "morning-after pill"), I was troubled. What right did pharmacists have to refuse to provide drugs? Pharmacies, at the time, were the hottest battleground in the abortion debate that centered on whether healthcare providers could "conscientiously object" to dispensing medication. Delving into this debate taught me a lot about pharmacists and, to my surprise, helped me discover what was really troubling pharmacists.

From 2009 to 2011, I traveled to four states and interviewed ninety-five pharmacists. It was there, among towering shelves of medication in the recesses of chain and independent pharmacies, that I first encountered the havoc opioids have unleashed, and not just on patients but also on the professionals charged with helping them. Every interview began with the same question: What would you say are the key ethical issues pharmacists face in daily practice? For an answer, I expected emergency contraception, since the drug had captivated the media. Stories of pharmacists withholding the drug filled the newspapers. But emergency contraception was a minor concern for pharmacists. Across the board, their biggest struggle was opioids. And they had a lot to say.[4]

Their insights changed my entire focus. I was fascinated by pharmacists' stories about opioids—how they figured out which patients were misusing or selling medications and which patients needed them to treat pain, how they spotted "pill mills" and kept a blacklist of physicians for whom they would not dispense, how they managed complicated relationships with law enforcement who could be both friend and foe. I was struck by the Kansas pharmacist who kept a rifle on his counter after being robbed three times at gunpoint, by the Mississippi pharmacist who was frantically seeking guidance from law enforcement after he identified a suspected drug ring, and by the New Jersey pharmacist who told me that a federal agent waltzed into her pharmacy, gave her his card, and urged her to contact him.

These stories shed light on the complex relationships between pharmacists, physicians, law enforcement, and patients. And they revealed how the opioid crisis manifested in daily practice, on the frontlines of care. All of these elements fueled the perfect storm of law, medicine, and organizations. The pharmacist's dilemma promised to answer so many questions about professional might, about relationships between medicine and criminal justice, and about the cultural and organizational context surrounding frontline work. I was hooked.

My research expanded to include physicians and law enforcement. Initially, I envisioned a tussle between law enforcement and healthcare over who would control the opioid crisis, but the people I spoke with quickly dispelled that illusion. Far from a sought-after prize, one that healthcare or criminal justice leaders could use to make their mark on one of the country's biggest social problems, the opioid crisis in its infancy repelled all potential reformers, who tossed it quickly from one field to another. The battle for control would come once the crisis gained steam, but we weren't there yet.

I interviewed the head of a prominent enforcement agency in New York City in 2012 and floated the idea that healthcare and law enforcement were competing to stake their claims on the overdose crisis. She laughed. She insisted that she didn't want this problem but was forced to deal with an epidemic "created by doctors and by drug companies." Neither the Board of Health nor the medical board had acted quickly enough. By the time her agency caught wind of the problem, people were already dead. "Nobody has owned the problem," she told me. "Everyone else has dodged it because it is so complicated." She felt poorly equipped to intervene. "My tools are not well-crafted for dealing with this. It is like hitting a fly with a hammer." In her eyes, law enforcement should be the "call of last resort because we have the least tailored tools to fix it." She went so far as to note that if doctors were doing their jobs, law enforcement would not have to step in. "Doctors drop the ball and criminal justice has to clean up the mess." Hesitant, but compelled to intervene, law enforcement tackled the crisis early on using the tools at hand, those designed for identifying and punishing criminals.

One tool in particular caught my attention—a new surveillance technology designed to ensure appropriate opioid provision. Prescription drug monitoring programs (PDMPs) became popular in the mid-2000s. PDMPs are databases that track information about controlled substances dispensed in a state. Originally designed for law enforcement, the federal government has nudged this technology into healthcare.[5] State leaders, desperate to curb overdose rates, adopted this surveillance technology to help restrict out-of-control opioid prescribing, which, they hoped, would reduce overdose deaths.

Unlike other big data surveillance technologies that are generally used in a *single* field such as policing or social services, both healthcare *and* law enforcement use PDMPs. Physicians and pharmacists use PDMP data to assess signs of drug misuse or drug diversion before prescribing or dispensing opioids. Meanwhile, law enforcement uses PDMP data to root out patients who misuse or sell prescription drugs and to identify physicians and pharmacists who overprovide opioids.

When I first heard about PDMPs, I thought pharmacists would hate them. In my earlier interviews, pharmacists spoke with frustration about time constraints, managers who insisted they do more with less, working fourteen hours on their feet without a break, and dispensing prescriptions in four minutes or less. Surely, navigating a new technology would consume their time and detract from what they really cared about—treating patients. I was wrong. It turns out that what pharmacists hate more than time constraints is uncertainty. Pharmacists are exacting people. There is a reason they go into pharmacy, a precise science akin to chemistry, instead of medicine, which looks more like an art. Pharmacists like to do the right thing. The problem is knowing what the right thing is. The PDMP offers guidance.

Before the PDMP, pharmacists used gut feelings to make decisions about opioid care. If they felt like something was wrong with the patient or the prescription, they tried to gather more information, and often refused to dispense. They avoided confrontation by telling the patient that the drug was out of stock, a move that turned their unwillingness to dispense opioids into an inability to do so. This approach made them extremely uncomfortable, but they felt that it was all they had to go on. Some pharmacists lay awake at night wondering if they had made the right choice or if they had denied a pain patient medication they needed.[6]

Enter the PDMP. With this surveillance tool in hand, pharmacists can review patients' drug histories to see if they have gotten drugs elsewhere. Instead of resorting to the lie that it is out of stock, they have ammunition. They can tell the patient where and when they last received the medication and note that the patient should still have enough opioids to treat their condition. Doing so deters patients from trying to get drugs early and signals to patients that they are being watched. Pharmacists find that sharing PDMP data impedes confrontation and reduces the number of patients seeking drugs at their pharmacies. In the pharmacist's eyes, far from being a nuisance, the PDMP is a lifeline.

Physicians also use PDMPs, but they have additional strategies to vet patients, many of which look suspiciously like those used by law enforcement. Drug screens, random pill counts, and pain contracts all bear the imprimatur of the criminal justice system. Enforcement agents, meanwhile, use PDMPs to decide which providers to target and which to leave alone and to make their investigations easier and more convincing. At the same time, prosecutors use PDMPs to build airtight cases in preparation for battle with the high-powered, well-paid defense attorneys that physicians hire to represent them.

PDMPs are a hallmark of the digital age, a time when technology promises to make our lives better by providing solutions to a wide array of social problems.[7] Just as the digital age has transformed welfare, education, and immigration, so PDMP use has transformed healthcare and law enforcement.

Although the PDMP was pitched as a law enforcement *and* healthcare tool, it is really a law enforcement tool implemented in healthcare spaces.[8] PDMPs are rarely integrated into electronic health systems.[9] They do not diagnose or treat disease. They do not offer ways to refer patients to treatment. They are surveillance tools above all. Today, state-wide PDMPs exist in all fifty states. Moreover, forty-eight states participate in PMP InterConnect, a system designed to share PDMP data across states.[10] PDMP use enables law enforcement to expand its reach into healthcare and to track healthcare providers with an ease and accuracy never before possible.

These technological advances come at a cost. Healthcare providers who use PDMPs police patients in daily practice and consider enforcement central to their work. Providers' ready acceptance of enforcement technology lays bare how enforcement logics infiltrate hospitals, clinics, and pharmacies. We can think of PDMPs as *Trojan horse technologies*.[11] In the myth, the Greeks used a horse-shaped gift to convince the Trojans to let them inside the walls, a move that led to the destruction of the Trojan civilization. The opioid case, though not as extreme, bears striking similarities. Law enforcement's gift to healthcare ends up changing how healthcare providers understand their work in ways that threaten healthcare as we know it. Effective tools to treat chronic pain and addiction are sparse and diffuse. Many lie beyond the bounds of traditional healthcare. Without the right tools to treat pain and addiction, providers thrust patients out of the system, which exposes them to higher risk of arrest, overdose, and death. People who seek help face grave harm, and the human cost of the opioid crisis escalates unabated.

PDMPs changed the face of healthcare. Physicians and pharmacists police patients instead of treat them, actions that violate their professional oaths and that exacerbate instead of mitigate harm. But this policing is not entirely new and it does not result from cruelty alone. Healthcare has long been a site of surveillance and social control, where unruly bodies and behaviors are identified and treated to conform to society's norms.[12] Minoritized groups such as women and people of color along with people with moralized conditions such as addiction and mental illness have disproportionately felt the brunt of medical discipline.[13] They are all too familiar with the policing function of healthcare.

What has changed is that surveillance has grown wider and deeper—more people are being surveilled and the same person can be more easily followed across institutional boundaries.[14] Policing has also become easier, more systematic, and taken for granted. Healthcare providers can obtain information more easily and are more likely to trust the algorithms that produce it. They police more people and do so more efficiently than ever before. This shift speaks volumes about how social forces shape care and punishment. Policing by physicians and pharmacists is the predictable consequence of a healthcare system ill-equipped to handle pain and addiction, of a society saturated with myths about drugs and people who use them, of federal policy consumed by a half-century-long War on Drugs, of a society rife with race, class, and gender inequality. The first chapter of this book turns to this social context to explain why healthcare providers are policing patients and what we can do to stop it.

The Crisis That Shook America

After the surgeries, Quána never got better. . . . By early 2017, Quána was diagnosed with a number of chronic pain syndromes, including fibromyalgia and peripheral neuropathy,[15] as well as autoimmune diseases, depression, anxiety, and post-traumatic stress disorder. . . . Quána spent most of her days in bed crying, and she would vomit and feel dizzy. Pain often woke her screaming from her sleep. When she did go to the ER, nobody took her pain seriously: a nurse once accused her of being drug seeking and even called the police. Her white boyfriend, who was there with her, managed to talk them down and explain what had happened to her. But that trip to the ER left its mark: Quána is now afraid to seek treatment for pain. At its worst, Quána describes her pain as feeling like "hot pokers are stabbing through my hips."

At other times her hips and knees burn, or she has shooting pains that spider from one part of her body to another. Her skin hurts so badly that she can only shower for a few seconds because the pressure is extremely painful. For a long time, she had extreme fatigue, and could barely walk up a flight of stairs. "Even though I have learned to cope creatively with my pain," Quána said, "my life has immeasurably changed. My pain is poorly managed. I often struggle with food insecurity and to make ends meet. No one should have to suffer like this."

—QUÁNA MADISON, "PAIN STORIES,"
NATIONAL PAIN ADVOCACY CENTER

In 2005, I was living in Florida, directly in the path of Hurricane Katrina. News stations played nonstop warnings about staying inside. Normal people complied. By not *my* people. We were out in the storm. Because the thing is, drug addiction doesn't take a day off. A day before Katrina hit, I got a last-minute appointment at a pain clinic. The place was crammed with people, standing room only. I was rushed through a ten-minute "checkup" and given a prescription for the medication I desperately needed. Then it was on to the pharmacy. Clutching my script in my sweaty hand, I drove as fast as I could. My addiction gripped me so strongly that I didn't give a single thought to my own safety. The waiting area was crowded with people moaning, complaining, sighing, fighting, and just *waiting* for their number to be called. By the time it was my turn, I'd dissolved into a puddle of anxious sweat. *Hampton.* I couldn't get to the register fast enough. I dry-swallowed two pills on my way back to my car. I felt them stick in my throat. I swallowed hard again, willing my hands to stop shaking. I'd be fine now. In just one more minute, everything would be fine.

—RYAN HAMPTON, AMERICAN FIX[16]

Quána and Ryan represent two types of people who suffer from the opioid crisis: people in chronic pain who need opioids to treat searing, near-constant pain and people with opioid use disorders who take opioids to alleviate psychological pain or to avoid the agony of withdrawals. People like Quána and Ryan come into contact with four kinds of professionals who are tasked with combatting the overdose crisis: the physician, the pharmacist, the prosecutor, and the investigator. These workers devise various strategies to keep people safe, but sometimes their help hurts.

Physicians and pharmacists are supposed to ensure that only legitimate pain patients gain access to care, but things could have gone very differently for Quána if her boyfriend had not been there when the nurse called the police. Prosecutors and investigators are supposed to root out bad providers, but shutting down the pill mill where Ryan got his drugs could leave him and others suffering from opioid use disorder with nowhere to turn. Professionals face complicated questions on the frontlines of the opioid crisis: when to refuse to provide opioids, when to investigate physicians—and what will happen to patients if they do?

I traveled across the country to talk with these professionals in a quest to understand how they make difficult choices and how patients fare. These are the stories at the heart of this book. We begin with a snapshot of the U.S. opioid crisis, then learn a new story about what caused the crisis that is different from the one most Americans have heard. Next, we listen to stories from the four main professionals in this book, engage with a set of cultural touchstones that put their stories in context, and trace a roadmap of the book.

The opioid crisis changed everything, from how healthcare providers treat pain and addiction to how law enforcement conducts investigations, to how patients view painkillers, and so much more. The term "opioid crisis" is shorthand for the rapid rise in drug overdose deaths since 1999.[17] Opioid overdose destroys 136 lives per day.[18] This number is equivalent to a commercial airliner crashing, leaving no survivors, every day of the year. Many people mistakenly equate "opioid" with "prescription opioid" and believe that drugs like OxyContin, Vicodin, and prescription fentanyl are the leading causes of death. The truth is more complicated.

The opioid crisis has crested multiple waves over the past twenty years. Each wave has different drugs driving overdose death rates—first prescription opioids, then heroin, and now synthetic (not prescription) fentanyl.[19] Chapter 2 elaborates on the different iterations of the crisis, but for now it is important to know that the prescription opioids that once fueled the crisis pale in comparison to powerful, illicit drugs.

Prescription opioids entered the overdose scene with a bang and left with a whimper. In 2006, for the first time in U.S. history, prescription opioids accounted for more deaths than heroin, cocaine, and methamphetamine combined. Deaths from prescription opioids climbed steadily until they began to level off in 2010. That same year, heroin overdose rates began to rise until they surpassed prescription opioid overdose rates in 2018. In 2013, deaths involving synthetic opioids like fentanyl began to spike. By 2019, overdoses from fentanyl and other synthetics accounted for more than half of all overdose deaths and 1.5 times more deaths than either prescription opioids or heroin. Meanwhile, cocaine and methamphetamine deaths escalated until they each contributed to more deaths than prescription opioids in 2019.[20] After a small dip in overall deaths in 2018, the COVID-19 pandemic struck, and overdose rates hit an all-time high with 92,000 deaths in 2020, which jumped to 107,000 in 2021.[21] The majority of these overdoses involved fentanyl or other synthetic drugs.[22] Physicians were complicit in flooding drug markets with prescription opioids. When prescribing rates peaked in 2012, physicians were issuing 81 opioid prescriptions per year for every 100 Americans. Rates diminished after that, but did not return to baseline. In 2017, physicians still prescribed three times more opioids than they did in 1999.[23] The picture is bleak. Overdose rates increase year after year and the drugs driving those deaths change too quickly for anyone to fully grasp. What brought all of this on?

If you know anything about the opioid crisis, you probably think that Purdue Pharma is to blame. As the story goes, Purdue manipulated regulators and physicians to get patients hooked on their drug, OxyContin, a powerful opioid used to treat pain. When people started dying with OxyContin in their systems, Purdue ignored the warning signs, pushed their drug even harder, and made billions doing so. OxyContin devastated a nation and made the Sacklers, one of the richest families in America, even richer.[24]

But Purdue's reign would not last. In September 2019, while facing 2,600 state and federal lawsuits, Purdue declared bankruptcy.[25] For many families and activists, this was cause for celebration. The enemy had been vanquished, the dragon had been slain, and the people were finally liberated from twenty years of pain and loss.

Yet this victory over Purdue is only truly celebratory if we imagine that the driver of the contemporary U.S. opioid crisis can be reduced to a single causal factor—a bad drug company selling addictive wares to an unsuspecting public. A company that used shoddy science to convince physicians to carelessly prescribe its drugs, leaving a trail of destroyed lives in its wake. A company led by nefarious people who sold a drug so powerful and so addictive that people were helpless to escape its grasp.

This kind of fairy tale with easy-to-identify villains and victims resonates powerfully with Americans. After all, we have digested narratives about "good guys" and "bad guys" our entire lives. From stories read at our bedside, to religious texts, to blockbuster films, to an endless supply of legal dramas, we have been trained to spot good and evil.

But we are less prepared to deal with complexity, to recognize that the good guys do bad and the bad guys do good. We are woefully ill-equipped to critique bad systems, to unpack how an ecology of laws, norms, politics, economics, organizations, and relationships affect the decisions people make. We fail to consider that people do bad things because the systems in which they operate invite bad behavior. If systems are failing us, we can't just eliminate the so-called bad actor; we have to look at the rules of the game.

Painting Purdue as the villain in the opioid story does more than put a face to the crisis that has harmed so many Americans. It lets other, less visible perpetrators off the hook. If Purdue is a monster that intentionally set out to harm the American public, then slaying Purdue allows life to return to normal. What the Purdue narrative doesn't do is invite us to interrogate our social systems and ask what they did to invite this harm, how they let this monster breach our castle walls, and why our gatekeepers were asleep on the job. The opioid crisis, or, more accurately, the overdose crisis, is both a devastating tragedy for people whose loved ones are caught in its grip *and* a constructed social problem shaped by institutional power dynamics that affect how we define, elaborate, and respond to this issue. In other words, the so-called opioid crisis and our approaches to confronting it are distinctly cultural phenomena.

The Purdue story obscures more than it reveals; the truth is a far cry from this simple fairy tale. The true story of opioids is the saga of a society in which lines between illness and criminality are blurred, where punishers do the treating and healers do the punishing. A story in which the color of a person's skin and the substance that they use affects whether they receive care, punishment, or punishment disguised as care. A story in which suffering people are denied relief under the auspices of protection and support. For many, this story is a living nightmare full of impossible choices, one in which heroes die and in which villains, who are all the more powerful for being nameless and faceless, prevail. A chilling story, yes, but one necessary to unravel the tidy image knitted together by simplistic threads of blame so that we can finally understand this modern social problem's complexities and arrive at policy solutions that honor its subtleties.

We cannot understand the overdose crisis without understanding the people responsible for stopping it. That is why this book spotlights enforcement and healthcare workers on the frontlines of the opioid crisis, to ask what choices they make about providing opioids, targeting providers, and why. It invites readers behind the pharmacy counter, into the treatment room, and within the recesses of government bureaucracies to witness gatekeepers to medical resources and the enforcement agents who investigate and prosecute them. By looking at the opioid crisis through the lens of frontline work, we can see how strategies to curb the crisis affect the daily lives of workers and patients in powerful, but unexpected, ways. Particularly central is the use of shared surveillance technology called the prescription drug monitoring program (PDMP). This technology affects how workers interact with each other and how they treat patients. Broader cultural forces shape it all.

Drawing on a decade of research and 337 interviews in eight states (California, Florida, Kansas, Kentucky, Mississippi, Missouri, New Jersey, and New York), this book reveals how the overdose crisis and the surveillance technologies designed to combat it have fostered a punitive turn in medicine. I created a "nested maximum variation sampling strategy" (described more fully in the appendix) where I collected as many perspectives as possible across a wide variety of organizations. I also spoke to some of the same pharmacists before and after the PDMP was fully implemented to see how their work had changed. When it comes to punishment, the narrative isn't new, but the form is. Data-driven healthcare is the latest manifestation of the perpetual War on Drugs, a failed political experiment that has done more to fuel mass incarceration than to reduce drug use.[26] Criminal justice tools will not dismantle the opioid crisis. Placed in healthcare providers' hands, they are doing irreparable damage to patient care and public trust.

This book tells a story about the unprecedented surveillance capacity of the digital age. It is a story about how our society views social problems through a punitive lens. And it is a story about how shared surveillance technology has ushered criminal justice logics into healthcare and blurred boundaries between policing and treating. When policymakers ignore the complexity of the overdose crisis and instead view it through a singular punitive lens, they shut off the most promising avenue for addressing the crisis: healthcare.

On the Frontlines of the Opioid Crisis

In the opioid crisis, there are four groups who interact with patients: the physicians who prescribe opioids, the pharmacists who dispense opioids, the prosecutors who prosecute opioid cases, and the investigators who gather evidence. They have all received blame for the crisis, they all exercise discretion, and they all use technology at work.

Physicians and pharmacists have been blamed for overproviding opioids,[27] while prosecutors and investigators have been blamed for scaring physicians by creating a "chilling effect" on opioid prescribing that makes providers shy away from providing the drugs.[28] Each set of workers gets to decide how they allocate resources and punishment. Physicians and pharmacists decide who deserves access to opioids and who deserves to be turned away, while prosecutors and investigators decide which healthcare providers deserve to be investigated and prosecuted.

Over the years, all four groups have been given access to PDMPs. These systems were originally designed for law enforcement. Healthcare leaders later began to implement PDMPs to help providers decide whether to prescribe or dispense opioids.[29] Physicians and pharmacists use them to size up patients, while prosecutors and investigators use them to assess the legality of providers' and patients' behavior. To put it simply, PDMPs are two-tiered surveillance technologies shared by healthcare and law enforcement that allow healthcare providers to monitor patients and allow prosecutors and investigators to monitor patients and providers. I wanted to know how this new technology affected workers' decisions and patient care.

My quest to understand how workers fared during the overdose crisis took me across the nation into chain and independent pharmacies; into clinics and hospitals; into courthouses, statehouses, and federal agencies; into conference centers, coffee shops, and restaurants; and even onto a ferry. I sat down with physicians, pharmacists, prosecutors, and investigators and listened to their stories, the stories at the heart of this book, the stories that will make you question what you think you know about the opioid crisis. Their voices echo throughout the following chapters, but allow me to introduce a few of them now.

The Physician

Nobody in Florida wanted to talk to me. I spent hours cold-calling and cold-emailing physicians, pharmacists, and enforcement agents who, more often than not, ignored me or declined the interview. I chalked it up to exhaustion. Floridians had already had their share of research attention and media scrutiny. They were residents of one of the opioid hotspots, home to the "Oxy Express," a trip down I-75 that transported drugs from Florida pharmacies to small towns in Appalachia, a place where pill mills had popped up like weeds.[30] And here I was, late to the game, asking them to rehash old stories that they would prefer to let lie. But I was on a deadline and had only two weeks to gather data, so I decided to take matters into my own hands. Which is how I happened to meet Donna in an elevator.

Having had little luck with phone calls and email, I took a page out of the pharmaceutical rep playbook. I showed up at physicians' offices, left my card, and asked their staff to have the doctor contact me. On my way out of a medical office building, I found myself standing next to the very physician I had just tried to recruit. I recognized her from the photo on her website. She had barely pushed the button for her floor when I introduced myself, described my project, and requested a meeting. To my surprise, she agreed to meet at her office later that afternoon.

When I arrived, Donna escorted me through the drab, gray-green interior and into a room with two gurneys and a microwave (staff took breaks there). She offered me a tall metal stool, sat down across from me, and started talking. Donna was no-nonsense tough, having spent much of her career in pain management and seen the opioid roller coaster go from free-flowing prescriptions to austere restrictions. To hear her describe it, she never got on the ride. She set strict limits around opioids and urged her patients to reject them. But she had seen other physicians prey on vulnerable patients, a common practice at the height of the opioid prescribing boom. She described doctors who sold prescriptions or traded sex for drugs, and her frustration was so palpable she began to cry. "Why the tears?" I asked. She replied, "I've been feeling like I'm fighting an uphill battle for 30 years. . . . I really feel bad for the patients . . . because some of them I know they're going to die." That is when it struck me—how much most physicians struggled to do the right thing.

Donna was an early adopter of policing techniques. She had begun policing patients as soon as she opened her practice. She drug tested patients, required them to sign pain contracts that limited them to a single physician and a single pharmacy, and did random pill counts that required patients to show up at her office and reveal how many pills remained in their bottle. E-Forsce, Florida's prescription drug monitoring program (PDMP), made policing patients easier. She can now use the state's database to assess whether a patient is telling her the truth. If they aren't, if the PDMP report looks fishy, she fires the patient. But she tries to give patients every opportunity to improve. She prescribes vitamins, offers procedures, and requires specific exercises. Her goal is to prescribe as few opioids as possible. But she notes that many patients have a long way to go. "I will tell you, the patients I have that are chronic pain patients, they're scared. They're scared that one day they're not going to have any medications to treat their problem."

The Pharmacist

Halfway across the country in Kansas City, Missouri, Tracy faced similar challenges from a different perspective. As a pharmacist, she was the final gatekeeper to opioids, the person who ultimately handed over a small white bag of pills or sent the patient away empty handed. Like Donna, Tracy struggled to figure out which patients should get access to opioids.

Tracy was what pharmacists call a "floater." She worked for a chain pharmacy, but was not tied to any one store. She filled in at pharmacies that were short-staffed or needed extra help. In this role, Tracy saw how different pharmacies in the city operated, how those located in wealthy, white areas compared to those located in poor, minority neighborhoods. She tried to keep her practice consistent regardless of race or class. She checked the PDMP as often as she could, but not all counties in Missouri were covered. She felt pressure from her managers to work as quickly as possible.

Work piled up before she even arrived. Phone messages, electronic prescriptions, and faxes awaited her, so she started her shift already behind. She routinely put in extra, unpaid hours just to keep up. And her chain was so committed to filling prescriptions quickly that they had installed a computer program that turned prescriptions red on the screen when pharmacist didn't fill them fast enough. Despite her commitment to fairness, the pressure to work quickly required Tracy to cut corners, to scrutinize some patients more closely than others. She couldn't check the PDMP for every patient every time. "Often," she told me, "you don't even have time to log on. . . . Every second counts."

Her chain's policy was to call the police on fraudulent prescriptions, but she didn't always think that was the right choice. In part, she feared patient retaliation: "I'm not going to risk my life. I mean, I don't know what they're going to do if I call the police on them." And in part, she was sympathetic toward patients who were struggling: "they're not bad people, they're just people that got addicted to drugs somehow." She thought that calling the police might be the wake-up call her patients needed, but she simply didn't have the time.

Both Donna and Tracy closely monitored their patients to avoid coming under law enforcement scrutiny themselves. At the time I spoke with them, physician arrests were a regular occurrence and pharmacist arrests, though less common, were frequent enough to raise concerns. But prosecutors insisted that these healthcare professionals had little to worry about.

The Prosecutor

By the time I met Nick in the summer of 2016, he had already prosecuted a dozen physicians. He had only half an hour to spare, so he ushered me into a sun-filled conference room in downtown Los Angeles and began to share his war stories. It was a wild ride.

At the time, Nick was one of only a handful of prosecutors willing to go toe-to-toe with physicians and their well-paid defense attorneys. And he emerged victorious each time. There was the doctor who dealt pills from his car, the doctor who kept prescribing even after his patient overdosed in his office, and the doctor who had stashed millions of dollars' worth of pills in his clinic ceiling and at an off-site storage unit. All of these doctors destroyed lives with the stroke of a pen. One physician had thirteen deaths to her name. Was that unusual? Nick, new to the world of healthcare, wasn't sure, so he started asking around. He asked physicians he knew how many of their patients had died. They looked at him quizzically and replied "none." That's when he knew he was onto something.

Nick wasn't interested in gray areas, the physician who had prescribed a little too much OxyContin or the pharmacist who had dispensed a few too many pills. He was after the "worst of the worst," those physicians whose patients ended up dead from the pills they had prescribed, "the people that are literally drug dealers in lab coats." He doesn't go looking for cases; they come to him. "[We] just don't have the resources to look at a PDMP and be like, 'Hmm, this doctor's prescribing seems really high, let's sniff this out.' It's more like, 'We've received nine consumer complaints about this doctor; we need to go see if something's going on.'" He told me that CURES, California's PDMP, is "the Bible of prescription medication" and he considers it "indispensable" to his work. The database provides "footprints of what this doctor is doing. . . . You can see if they're dispensing a particular kind of medication. To whom? How often? What quantities? . . . It provides so much information to you as a prosecutor just from seeing the patterns."

When I caught up with Nick the following year at a conference in Atlanta, he took a riveted audience through the anatomy of one of his cases. Nick showed undercover surveillance video of the defendant's office that looked like no doctor's office I had ever seen. Files were thrown everywhere instead of neatly put away. Boxes of drug samples were scattered on the floor of the office area and stored in the bathroom. And when the doctor spoke to the patient, she asked him what he wanted, told him "I probably shouldn't write this for you," and handed over the script anyway. This case was career-defining for Nick—it was the first time a California physician had been convicted of murder for overprescribing drugs to patients.

Nick took on physician harm and emerged victorious, but the cases that he prosecuted were only the tip of the iceberg. Most physicians who harm patients experience no consequences, partly because they are difficult to prosecute and partly because law enforcement lacks motivation to do so. Prosecutors can complete several low-level drug cases in the time it takes to do a single physician case, so many of them choose the easy win over the gamble. Along the way, prosecutors frustrate investigators who devote time and energy to physician cases only to be told that there is not enough evidence to prosecute.

The Investigator

For Caleb, catching bad doctors was personal. When we met in 2017, he had spent three years on a task force with workers from agencies in Southern California, investigating prescription drug diversion (the sale of prescription drugs through illicit markets) as well as illicit drugs and organized crime. Asked the first time to join the task force, Caleb refused. He had considerable experience investigating narcotics cases, but his brother had recently died of a drug overdose and the pain of that loss was still raw. Addiction ran in the family, but Caleb's brother had never touched drugs until he was prescribed Vicodin to treat injuries from a car accident. When that wasn't enough, he was prescribed OxyContin, and he began smoking and injecting. He then transitioned to the heroin that killed him.

The second time his commanding officer asked him to participate, Caleb accepted. Time had healed some of his wounds and he had specialized skills that made him valuable to the task force. He became the PDMP expert. Tips from the public or from other agencies motivated him to search the PDMP to see what volume of opioids the physician was prescribing. "If someone was causing death, we would absolutely initiate an investigation to go after that individual." However, once he began the job, he faced stubborn barriers to investigating and prosecuting physicians. Despite his team's best efforts, he says that "there are doctors that are still practicing in a criminal capacity, providing pharmaceuticals to our streets that I can name right off of the top of my head." The biggest barriers are lack of respect, lack of resources, and unwilling prosecutors.

Caleb says that doctor cases are incredibly challenging. He finds that other officers and superiors look down on his work. They call it "kiddie dope" because "it's just a doctor prescribing, it's medicine, it's not real opioids." Misunderstanding the harm that prescription opioids can cause keeps prosecutors away. Caleb concedes "they're not sexy cases. They aren't cartel guys that walk around with guns; they're doctors. You're going after white-collar people, regular citizens, and nobody wants to have a part in it."

Some prosecutors don't take cases seriously and end up flushing years of investigatory work down the drain. Or Caleb's task force can't get the resources it needs. He described one physician who was still prescribing high volumes of pills because the task force couldn't get a confidential informant to work with it. In other cases, prosecutors lost cases that should have been slam-dunks. "It's disheartening to see that when you've put months and months and months of work into these cases and they're reduced to a ridiculous plea or the case is just not filed altogether. And we're talking cases that involved death, but the fear of taking on a doctor and a high-powered team of lawyers supersedes justice."

Donna, Tracy, Nick, and Caleb are just four of the workers trying to stay afloat in the wake of the opioid crisis. With different occupations and living in different parts of the country, these workers seem siloed, cordoned off from one another. But in reality, they are deeply interconnected in this crisis that threatens to drown them all. The choices they make affect their relationships with one another and have a profound impact on patient care.

Social scientists refer to workers like these as "frontline workers" or "street-level bureaucrats" because they do the client-facing jobs for the organizations in which they are embedded. Frontline workers exercise a great deal of discretion as they juggle heavy caseloads and reconcile conflicting laws and policies. However, they exercise far more power than one might expect. Even though they occupy the bottom rungs of the organizational ladder, their choices have such a great impact on clients that they are seen as bureaucrats in their own right, those who make law from the bottom up, hence the name "street-level bureaucrat."[31] Frontline workers in healthcare and law enforcement interact in spaces like hospitals and ambulances where norms of punishment and treatment jockey for position.[32]

It is tempting to hold frontline workers exclusively responsible for their decisions. When physicians or pharmacists deny opioids to a pain patient or when prosecutors and investigators scrutinize and charge an innocent physician, they make things worse instead of better. But frontline workers do not operate alone. They are embedded in cultural and organizational contexts that shape how they understand their legal and professional responsibilities and how they behave at work.

Cultural Touchstones

To truly understand workers' choices, we must also consider the context that surrounds them. There are four main touchstones that offer insights into the contextual factors that shape workers' responses to the opioid crisis: (1) the shortcomings of the U.S. healthcare system, particularly when it comes to treating addiction and pain; (2) the organization of society into social fields like healthcare and criminal justice that each have their own ways of understanding and responding to social problems; (3) the punitive turn that resulted in the criminalization of various social problems; and (4) the rise of the digital age that unleashed unprecedented surveillance capacity.

The U.S. healthcare system is notoriously inaccessible, expensive, and confusing. Compared to other Western, industrialized nations that treat healthcare as a right, 26 million Americans remain uninsured even after the Obama administration spearheaded the sweeping healthcare legislation that became the Affordable Care Act (ACA).[33] Insured Americans either get insurance from their employers or from government programs like Medicare and Medicaid. But having insurance does not necessarily result in access to care nor does it protect people from crushing medical debt. Waiting lists can be months long, particularly at Federally Qualified Health Centers (FQHCs) that treat the poor.[34] Insurance covers only specific facilities and specific providers and often requires authorization prior to a treatment or a procedure. For-profit corporations have a stranglehold on healthcare and the cost of procedures varies widely from place to place, resulting in what famed medical critic Dr. Arthur Relman called the "medical-industrial complex."[35]

At the same time, healthcare providers are typically siloed. They are experts in specific diseases or body parts, which makes it difficult to coordinate care for people with multiple conditions. There is a doctor for your skin, a different doctor for your feet, and yet another doctor for your bones, as if your skin, feet, and bones existed in isolation. And medicine has become heavily pharmaceuticalized, prioritizing drug-based treatment over hands-on treatment. With drugs available to treat all kinds of remedies, pharmaceuticals are globally a $1.5 trillion per year industry.[36]

This is the best-case scenario, what healthcare looks like for people who have insurance and who have diseases that are typically recognized as medical. Things look quite different for people with chronic pain and addiction, conditions that medicine keeps at arm's length. Chronic pain and addiction are heavily moralized and incompletely medicalized. Stereotypes of the "malingering pain patient" and the "manipulative addict" are used to justify refusing to provide adequate care to those who suffer. Not only that, but the healthcare system is ill-equipped to treat either condition. Most physicians receive little to no training on addiction or chronic pain. Chronic pain did not become a medical specialty until 1993,[37] and addiction medicine became a subspecialty in 2015.[38] Insurance companies are more likely to cover drug treatments like opioids for pain than hands-on therapies like massage, physical therapy, or chiropractic adjustments. And insurance companies often deny treatments that physicians order until patients try another, cheaper course of treatment. As a result, when it comes to addiction and pain, the healthcare system is practically unnavigable for even the savviest patient and the most well-meaning provider.

Healthcare's inadequacies are only one set of barriers that affect how workers contend with the opioid crisis. Another barrier lies in debate over whether the opioid crisis is medical or criminal in nature. Choosing one interpretation over the other affects what kinds of resources are brought to bear on the problem and which workers are put in charge of solving it.

Sociologists envision society as broken down into a set of "organizational fields" or organizations that, in the aggregate, belong to a specific branch of society.[39] Criminal justice and medicine are fields as are religion, art, and education. The field includes not only focal organizations like prisons, hospitals, churches, museums, and schools, but also government agencies that regulate them, resource suppliers, consumers, clients, and competitors.[40] What holds fields together and distinguishes them from one another are their core principles, what sociologists call "institutional logics."[41] For example, criminal justice operates on a logic of punishment, while healthcare operates on a logic of treatment. When faced with social problems—issues like crime, illness, and poverty—each field brings its own perspective, offers its own solutions, and fights to have its solutions realized. Social problems like the opioid crisis stoke tensions between fields that subscribe to different institutional logics, though sometimes these fields find ways to cooperate.[42]

Take, for example, the problem of excessive alcohol use. Three fields—religion, criminal justice, and healthcare—have spent decades battling over whether alcoholism is a sin, a crime, or an illness. Today, we consider it a form of sickness that warrants medical treatment, but for many years it was considered a form of badness that required atonement or punishment.[43]

How we treat social problems, then, depends quite a bit on who gets to decide what kind of problem it is, what logics they use to frame it, and what solutions they think are best. Framing the overdose crisis as a problem of over-prescribing and corporate greed suggests that solutions lie in the healthcare system. But framing the problem more broadly by pointing to the problems that arise from criminalizing drug use and the harms that result from a frayed social safety net requires new sets of logics and invites different types of solutions.

Not all fields are created equal. Some exert significantly more power than others. Today, one of the most powerful fields is criminal justice. Extremely well-resourced, especially compared to the associated fields of social services and public health, criminal justice enjoys not only financial power but rhetorical power as well. In a culture steeped in news of violent crime, often told from the perspective of the police, where investigators and lawyers play heroes on prime time, and a society whose impulse is to control minority groups and the poor, it is no surprise that so many behaviors from acting up in school to sleeping on a park bench are framed as crimes and the people who engage in them as criminals.[44] It was not always this way.

In the late 1970s, the United States began to experience a punitive turn.[45] Logics of crime and criminality ascended and overshadowed rehabilitative logics. This shift, especially pronounced in prisons,[46] occurred in a wide variety of fields, from social services to education to welfare.[47] Poor people and people of color disproportionately felt the brunt, entangled as they were in both carceral and social service arenas. Prisons and jails did away with rehabilitative programs in favor of punitive ones. Welfare offices prioritized rooting out welfare cheats over providing resources to needy families. These changes left poor, minority groups surveilled, disciplined, and punished, but they were not alone.

The punitive turn reverberated throughout the social strata, resulting in what socio-legal scholar Jonathan Simon calls "governing through crime."[48] That is, efforts to combat crime have become so politicized that they often serve very different purposes from the ones they purport to address. At the same time, "technologies, discourses, and metaphors" associated with crime and the criminal justice system have infiltrated other institutions.[49] To put it succinctly, we now live in a society where talk about crime and efforts to fight crime far outpace the actual crime rates. This is at least partly explained by the fact that invasive criminal justice logics have creeped into nonenforcement fields. What we don't yet fully understand is how technology affects how criminal justice logics infiltrate other fields, a central question for this book given that legislators are attempting to stop the overdose crisis by implementing law enforcement technology into healthcare.

Times of crisis make strange bedfellows. Contemporary approaches to the opioid crisis are dominated by two fields—healthcare and criminal justice—that bring very different worldviews, tactics, and resources to bear and that are independently inadequate to address a problem of this magnitude. These fields' leaders may disagree about the best course of action, but they do agree on one thing—the promise of technology. And they are in good company. Expansive computing power and the rise of the Internet have ushered in a digital age, one that makes it possible to gather, store, and analyze mountains of data and to deploy algorithms to make data analysis and decision-making easy and automatic.[50] Importantly, algorithms have become critical for allocating resources and punishment in social services, and policing and computers often take priority over individual workers for deciding who deserves resources or punishment.[51] Technology promises to solve social problems, even if it often fails to deliver. States have adopted big data algorithms to determine how they allot their shoestring social service budgets, which can perpetuate inequality.[52] With technology in the driver's seat, municipalities distribute resources in unfair or nonsensical ways.

Not only can new technology create and exacerbate social inequality,[53] but it also expands surveillance capacity of both law enforcement and of private businesses,[54] resulting in what Shoshana Zuboff calls "surveillance capitalism."[55] At a time when computing capacity is more powerful than ever before, we permit ourselves to be constantly surveilled by most of the technologies we use, even though some people are more heavily surveilled than others and surveillance is not always a choice. Most social science research on surveillance technology focuses on a single field like law enforcement[56] or compares surveillance technology across fields,[57] but we know little about how different fields use the same technology.

Technology built for use in one field often finds uses in other fields. Surveillance data, in particular, tends to creep across field boundaries.[58] This book addresses technology's migration by examining how surveillance technology shared across the fields of healthcare and criminal justice affects frontline work. It examines healthcare, rarely included in surveillance studies, and considers how shared surveillance technology links healthcare to criminal justice.

Our Journey Together

As this book unfolds, you will begin to grasp how these four touchstones—healthcare's shortcomings, the logics of social fields, punishment, and technological surveillance—help contextualize the frontline work to fight the overdose crisis. You also will notice how understanding what workers do and why helps us see these cultural forces in a new light. Healthcare and criminal justice are major sites of inequality, places where punishment and resources get distributed in ways that help some and harm others. This book explores how technology can intensify inequality by linking two unequal fields. How does giving law enforcement healthcare data affect the investigation and prosecution of healthcare providers? How does giving healthcare providers enforcement technology affect patient care? Most significantly, at the street level, how do patients with pain or addiction fare in this brave new healthcare world?

The answer to these questions lies in understanding how efforts to curb the opioid crisis have blurred boundaries between healthcare and law enforcement. Both healthcare providers and enforcement agents take professional oaths that commit them to helping others. Yet the ready embrace of PDMPs and other strategies to curb the opioid crisis threaten to undermine those commitments. People with pain and addiction need help, but providers lack the capacity to provide care. They have the wrong tools for the job. In short, the opioid story is far more complex and devastating than the story we have been told. An understanding of this complex ecosystem and a path forward begins here. I will show how PDMPs operate as Trojan horse technologies[59] as they usher enforcement logics into healthcare. Physicians and pharmacists who use them begin to accept policing patients as a core task, though they do not consider their actions policing. Instead, they embrace policing tasks while reframing them as treatment. This shift is possible because policing is already an aspect of healthcare work and because the technology that facilitates policing has become commonplace, easy to use, and, in some states, legally required.

PDMPs are widespread, but few people realize they exist. They have proliferated over the past decade, yet we know little about their social impact, particularly how they affect workers and patients. The book begins with a historical overview of the U.S. opioid crisis that explains how enforcement technology became a popular solution. Chapter 2 delves into specifics of PDMPs—where they came from and how they have evolved. In chapters 3–5, we see how PDMPs are used on the frontlines of three fields—law enforcement, medicine, and pharmacy—with a focus on how workers in each field use the same technology for different purposes and with different consequences. Changes in these fields raise questions about what happens to patients. Those questions are answered in chapter 6, which shows how efforts to curb overdose thrust patients out of the healthcare system, leaving them vulnerable to harm. Chapter 7 offers practical solutions for resolving the opioid crisis and zooms out to consider what this can tell us about frontline work, technology, and punishment. The methods used in this study can be found in the appendix.

Incomplete stories yield inadequate solutions. Current solutions that focus exclusively on doctors and drug companies won't curb the crisis and often do more harm than good. It is only by taking a systemic view of the healthcare and criminal justice systems and the social safety net that we might hope to disrupt the cycle of pain, addiction, and death that afflicts our nation. This book offers fresh policy interventions centered around treatment, harm reduction, and public health instead of surveillance, punishment, and incarceration. These approaches promise not only to stop the opioid crisis but also to prevent new crises from emerging in its wake.

From this point on, the story is ours. We decide whether we allow ourselves to be swept up in the rapids of moralizing and punishing that have claimed so many lives, or if we swim against the current and fight our way to a new river that offers a smoother and less treacherous journey. But before we can find solutions, we must reexamine the problem. We can only begin to understand how we got here, to a historically unprecedented moment where drugs claim over 100,000 lives each year, by venturing back to the turn of the twentieth century, when America's first drug law came into being.

1

Criminalizing Care

AMERICANS HAVE LONG BEEN at a crossroads when it comes to drugs and the people who use them. At times, we have conceived of addiction as a disease and have opted to treat those who suffer. At other times, we have conceived of addiction as a crime or a moral failing and have rushed to punish those who "offend" or "sin." In our current moment, we have chosen surveillance and punishment over care. This chapter shows how our present-day opioid crisis is yet another chapter in the history of our troubled relationship with drugs.

What we call the opioid crisis didn't happen suddenly. It didn't begin when Purdue Pharma started pushing OxyContin nor did it originate in the healthcare system. It developed over the course of decades, at the intersection of healthcare and criminal justice, shrouded in myths. Today, we see policy that criminalizes care and that results in the poor treatment of patients with substance use disorders and chronic pain that, to our eyes, looks new. To drug historians, however, this is all too familiar. These policies and practices hearken back to cycles of drug crises that date back over 120 years. Knowing something about that history helps to make sense of our current struggle and helps us understand the difficult position in which healthcare providers, enforcement agents, and patients find themselves. The policing of patients that you will witness in future chapters is not just a response to the contemporary opioid crisis. Physicians and pharmacists have been primed by 100 years of drug policy and 50 years of drug war.

A sociological lens gives us the broad perspective we need to understand the opioid crisis in all of its complexity. It offers a framework for examining the deep social, legal, economic, and interpersonal forces that shaped our current moment. Looking through this lens helps us see that the opioid crisis is really an outcropping of suffering and despair that emerges at the nexus of pain and addiction. This suffering is deeply rooted and goes back centuries. However, what sets the War on Prescription Drugs apart from the War on Drugs and from earlier iterations of drug policy is that it is taking place in a digital age, on the crest of a punitive turn, at a time when pain management activists have given us whole new ways of thinking about opioids and pain. This context helps explain why U.S. drug policy is in flux and why surveillance technology has been such an appealing solution to the opioid crisis.

More powerfully, viewing the opioid crisis from a sociological perspective reveals that what we are dealing with looks less like a crisis and more like a social condition, a pervasive, systemic problem of physical and emotional pain that we have come to accept as unchangeable. Our acceptance lies in the fact that we have viewed our problems so narrowly that we have overlooked the broad social systems at work and we have opted for ineffective shortcuts in place of enduring, systemic interventions.

Putting the opioid crisis in context dispels myths about who is suffering and who is to blame and draws our attention to the broader social structures and smaller social interactions that brought us here. This chapter lays out that context. We can begin to understand how this all unfolded by listening to a patient in chronic pain.

Maria's Story

Maria Higginbotham's pain was sudden and excruciating.[1] The forty-three-year-old was a bank manager in a town outside Seattle with no major health problems when a trip to the mailbox in 2003 changed her life. She found herself unable to walk and spent the next twelve years in and out of back surgery for a rare spinal condition. Maria's discs were degenerating rapidly, so each surgery that implemented metal rods and bolts to scaffold her spine was met by another disc collapse. The surgeries made things worse. They compounded the original pain with a condition called adhesive arachnoiditis in which the membrane around the spinal cord becomes inflamed. Higginbotham told Human Rights Watch, an international advocacy organization, that she has "constant pain in the middle of [her] back, and a sharp shooting pain when [she] move[s]."[2]

Maria tried a wide range of pain treatments. She did physical therapy, received steroid injections, and submitted to nerve ablations that destroy nerve tissue to stop pain signals in the body. She has organ problems that prevent her from taking ibuprofen and felt uncomfortable taking medical marijuana.

The treatments she tried and failed left her $2,000 in debt. While searching for more permanent remedies, Maria found some semblance of relief. She received a pain pump that transported opioids to her spinal cord as well as opioid pain patches that delivered opioids through her skin. These treatments helped her regain a portion of the life she lost to pain. She could cook for herself, care for her pets, and look after her grandchildren.

That is, until her physician decided to taper her medications. In 2018, his clinic implemented a new policy based on pain guidelines that the Centers for Disease Control and Prevention (CDC) issued in 2016.[3] The guidelines recommended keeping patients below 90 morphine milligram equivalents (MME). Maria's dose was almost twice that. The physician told Human Rights Watch that the clinic feared legal action for keeping patients on such high doses of opioids. The question that haunted him was: What if something happens to the patient while they are under my care? "It doesn't matter if you did everything appropriately [to prevent abuse]—and we do everything, urine drug testing, prescription monitoring, screening for mental health issues, pill counts. It doesn't feel like enough. We still feel like we're vulnerable to being held liable for patients if they're over that guideline limit, even when you know they're not addicted and they're benefitting [from opioids]."[4]

Cutting down the dose by only one-third catapulted Maria back into pain. Now, she has trouble standing and getting out of bed or using the restroom by herself. "Pain has a way of defeating you, taking away any pleasure you used to get. I'm 57 years old and I'm almost completely bedridden due to agonizing pain like torture," she explains. "I cannot hold my 15-month-old grandson. I cannot hold my beloved dogs, I can't bend over to touch them. I cry out in my sleep because I can't find a way to get comfortable."[5] Her doctor knows she is suffering, but feels he has no alternative. He thinks perhaps another surgery would help, but Maria is afraid to submit to yet another treatment that might fail. "I know I will never be free from pain but to subject me to even more pain is inhuman," she says. "How many times do I have to go through this to prove there isn't a fix? I can't be fixed."[6]

What choice does Maria have? Her life had been upended by debilitating pain and her clinic's policy has send her into a downward spiral. What should she do? These are questions pain patients face every day.

Millions of Americans live in pain, but healthcare's capacity to treat that pain is shrinking. Opioids that once flowed freely now face tight controls. Pain patients suffer as overdose deaths climb. While pain patients like Maria walk a tightrope pulled taught by invasive screening to receive a modicum of care, patients with opioid use disorders fare even worse. Blocked from the health-care system, they must fend for themselves, despite everyone from political leaders to police chiefs agreeing that addiction is a "disease." Note the difference between defining addiction as a medical problem and making punishment the solution. The tug of war between healthcare and law enforcement reveals our society's perpetual discomfort with illegal drugs and the people who use them. However, a growing number of experts consider health-care the better option to tackle the overdose crisis, regardless of why someone became addicted in the first place. Healthcare's disapproval of drug use reflects societal norms, and providers' ideas about how to help are culturally informed as well.

Twenty years of opioid law and policy have whiplashed healthcare providers. Healthcare leaders went from collaborating with drug companies to convince physicians to freely prescribe opioids to allying with law enforcement to root out bad providers. OxyContin, touted as a wonder drug, suddenly became a public scourge.[7] In the 1990s, at the behest of marketers and under threat by regulators, physicians measured pain consistently and prescribed opioids liberally for everything from cancer to broken toes. Prescribing rates soared.[8]

By the mid-2010s, everything had changed. As overdose rates skyrocketed[9] and the nefarious marketing practices of Purdue Pharma came to light, approaches to pain and addiction began to look different. Law enforcement arrested hundreds of physicians for overprescribing.[10] Several states implemented surveillance technology—prescription drug monitoring programs (PDMPs)—to track physicians who were running "pill mills" and patients who were "doctor- and pharmacy-shopping."[11] In this new legal landscape, physicians prescribed cautiously, fearful that one misstep could mean the end of their livelihood. And they imposed new rules on patients like Maria.

Today, patient surveillance is the standard of care. Physicians and pharmacists rely on enforcement tools to monitor patients and make treatment decisions. They require their chronic pain patients to sign contracts that specify the terms of their care.[12] Pain patients struggle to get opioids and some people with opioid use disorders have turned to heroin and synthetic fentanyl, illicit drugs that pose a higher overdose risk than prescription opioids. Yet we have not solved any of our opioid problems. Drug overdose rates continue to rise, chronic pain is no better managed, and the collateral damage to families, towns, and our whole society grows more destructive each year. These harrowing conditions have become a way of life.

How did we get here? How did healthcare providers get into the policing business and why do they routinely use surveillance tools? Why, in this historical moment, are prescription opioids instruments of crime when a few short decades ago they were instruments of treatment? Why has care become criminalized?

The answer to these questions is grounded in the history of drug policy and pain treatment. To understand this history, we must disentangle fact from fiction about the contemporary opioid crisis. The opioid crisis is not new. It is an outcropping of America's century-long struggle to assign medical, legal, and moral meaning to drugs and the people who use them. These meanings derive from racially biased political impulses and exaggerated ideas about drugs' power over human behavior. Putting the opioid crisis in context upends myths about who is suffering and who is to blame. It is to this context that we now turn.

Myths of the Opioid Crisis

If you are like most people, much of what you know about the opioid crisis is wrong. But you are not to blame. Two decades of best-sellers, news articles, and documentaries have coalesced into a single story about the opioid crisis that paints Purdue Pharma and the Sackler family as the villains. It depicts Purdue as a company that, "through greed and violation of the law, prioritized money over the health and well-being of patients,"[13] and "the Sackler family as the billionaire puppet masters who ignited the opioid crisis."[14] That story is compelling because it is simple, but it gets a lot wrong.

Four myths dominate the usual opioid story, and all have insidious consequences. They have invited law enforcement into our hospitals, clinics, and pharmacies, and given it access to the deepest recesses of our private lives. They have criminalized medicine by turning healthcare providers into either police or felons; they have subjected patients to surveillance and punishment. Do we want healthcare to become an extension of law enforcement? That is where these myths lead.

Myth #1: OxyContin Kicked Off the Opioid Crisis

Most people believe that the opioid crisis began when Purdue Pharma released OxyContin in 1996. They attribute hundreds of thousands of deaths to this powerful opioid alone. In reality, the opioid crisis is the latest phase of a century of punitive and rehabilitative shifts in drug policy and practice predicated on race and class.

Fact #1: The Opioid Crisis Is More Than a Century Old

Imagine starting a movie in the middle and thinking that you are at the beginning. You would reach the same ending, but you would only partially understand the events leading up to it. The popular story about the opioid crisis is truncated. It pegs the beginning of the crisis to the release of OxyContin and then tells a tale of a greedy drug company that sacrificed lives at the altar of profit. The problem is that this story starts in the middle of things, so it narrows our view of what happened and why. We get a better view of the opioid crisis if we put it in historical context—that is, if we consider the opioid crisis in light of a century of U.S. drug policy.

The opioid crisis is much older than people think. Starting with America's first drug law, the Harrison Narcotics Tax Act passed in 1914, the drug policy pendulum has swung repeatedly between punitive and rehabilitative approaches to addiction.[15] The modern opioid crisis is the latest oscillation of that pendulum. And the direction the pendulum swings—toward punishment or rehabilitation— corresponds with broader trends in racialized drug policy.

The history of drug policy is a history of race and class. Time and again policies that criminalize drugs have been used to criminalize people, particularly those who belong to poor, minority groups. White lawmakers' concerns about immigration, interracial relationships, and economic insecurity have frothed into moral panics that purport to be about drug harm but are in fact about social control and fear of social change. When one surveys the drug policy landscape, it is easy to spot how laws to prevent Chinese laborers from smoking opium and (as lawmakers at the time put it) luring virginal white women into opium dens[16] resemble laws to prevent Black and Mexican migrant workers from using marijuana in the 1930s. It is also easy to see how those laws paved the way for harsh restrictions on crack cocaine aimed at African American drug users in the 1980s. In each case, drugs were criminalized along with the racialized groups who used them.[17]

Politicians and mass media played a critical role in linking minoritized groups to drugs and stoking public fear about drugs and the people who use them. Politicians engaged in blatantly racist fear mongering and journalists uncritically regurgitated their toxic cocktails into facts for public consumption. In the early part of the twentieth century, Harry Anslinger, the commissioner appointed to the freshly minted Federal Bureau of Narcotics (an agency that would eventually become the U.S. Drug Enforcement Administration, or DEA), led the charge. Anslinger worked with powerful legislators to get drug criminalization onto the political agenda and to link racial threats to drug threats throughout his thirty-two-year tenure at the bureau. His political machinations helped criminalize marijuana in the 1930s by capitalizing on anti-Mexican sentiment, which paved the way for anti-heroin laws in the 1950s. After Anslinger's retirement in 1962, other politicians such as Presidents Ronald Reagan and George H. W. Bush along with like-minded members of Congress followed in his footsteps to criminalize crack cocaine. Democrats and Republicans alike supported harsh drug laws. When the opportunity arose to reverse racially discriminatory mandatory minimum laws, President Bill Clinton opted in favor of the status quo. Clinton also signed into law the 1994 federal crime bill that prompted harsher laws and more punitive penalties for drug use and that initiated a bipartisan race to see who could be toughest on crime. Anti-drug politicians fomented fear by drawing on class, race, and gender divides and painting politically expedient pictures of urban residents sowing mayhem in suburban communities. Of particular concern was men of color "preying" on white women, which served as a handy racist trope to justify harsh drug laws.[18]

White people have always consumed drugs, but their drug use has received relatively lax treatment in law and policy.[19] Consider, for example, the white, rural housewives who ate opium prescribed by their doctors at the turn of the twentieth century without causing a scandal. How different their experiences were from those of Chinese railway workers whose opium smoking raised a public outcry. Users of the same drug—ingested or inhaled—faced very different consequences.[20] Partly due to the demographic shift in opium use from white women to Chinese men and partly due to international political posturing, Congress passed the Harrison Act.[21] The new law required all opium prescribers and dispensers to register with the state so their revenue could be taxed. However, its consequences were far-reaching. A few years after the law's passage, three court cases—*Jin Fuey Moy v. United States* (1916), *Webb et al. v. United States* (1919), and *United States v. Doremus* (1919)—made it illegal to "maintain" an addict (meaning to prescribe opioids to keep a patient comfortable on their current dose), a common practice at the time. Law enforcement arrested thousands of doctors and pharmacists, sending a chill through the healthcare community.[22] Since that time, U.S. drug policy has swung between more punitive and more rehabilitative approaches to drug use. The oscillator must be broken, though, because the pendulum keeps getting stuck on the punitive side.

Throughout the past century, the lens through which addiction has been refracted—whether one of "badness" or one of "sickness"[23]—has been formed through notions of moral worth linked to race and class. Government officials have used fabricated ideas about how drugs affect poor people of color to justify harsh drug laws that double down on punishment while white people who use the same or similar drugs manage to escape the grasp of the criminal justice system. You have already seen one example, opioid use by white housewives versus Chinese immigrants in the early 1900s. Several decades later, during the Vietnam War, white soldiers returned from war hooked on heroin. President Richard Nixon insisted that those veterans receive treatment, and many recovered.[24] Less than twenty years after that, under the Reagan administration, Black people who used cocaine faced a very different fate. Cocaine had two main variants: powder and crack. They were used by different people—whites gravitated toward powder cocaine, while Blacks gravitated toward crack. They were the same drug; powder cocaine was simply a more refined version of crack, but reading the news at that time, you would never know it. Crack became enrobed in a cultural narrative that stoked fear about the (predominately Black) people who used it. Journalists suggested that crack gave people outsized strength and framed people who used the drug as "superpredators" who could easily overpower police.[25] These kinds of stories helped to justify extensive surveillance and hyper-policing of Black communities as well as mandatory minimum laws that established lengthy prison time for felony convictions.[26] They also justified setting prison time for the possession of crack cocaine at the same rate as 100 times the amount of powder cocaine. The result? Incarceration rates soared and mass incarceration was born.

Drug policy and enforcement have done more to increase rates of incarceration than any other type of crime.[27] Incarceration rates quintupled from 1972 to 2007 and racial disparities increased in tandem. In 2012, the United States incarcerated 2.23 million people.[28] The number dropped to 1.8 million in 2020, but the United States still incarcerates far more people than any other country in the world.[29] In 2017, the rate of Black adults in prison was six times as high as that of white adults and twice as high as that of Latino adults.[30] Almost half of federal prisoners and 13 percent of state prisoners are currently incarcerated for a drug crime.[31] People incarcerated for drug crimes are disproportionately Black and Latino despite the fact that whites use and sell drugs as often or even more often than these groups.[32] If the goal of the War on Drugs is to eradicate illegal drugs, it has been a complete failure. However, if the goal is to control poor, minority groups, it has been an unmitigated success.

It is against this backdrop of hyper-criminalization that the opioid crisis emerged. The opioid crisis initially differed from these earlier iterations of drug use and drug policy in two puzzling ways: first, the people dying from opioids were disproportionately white, and second, the opioids they used were legal. This gave lawmakers pause, not when deaths were confined to impoverished areas of Appalachia, but when they popped up in wealthy suburban refuges. Urgency to solve the crisis mounted, and the solutions proposed looked quite different from those implemented twenty years earlier. Gone was the trope of the superpredator unleashing hell on terrified communities. In its place was the trope of the patient victimized by a doctor who had turned an injury into an addiction.[33] Parents, police, and lawmakers agreed: addiction was a disease, and sufferers deserved care, not punishment.

This rehabilitative moment gave rise to new forms of assistance. Police departments armed their officers with naloxone, an opioid overdose antidote. They also created programs in which police referred people who used drugs to care. Drug courts expanded to permit people with substance use disorders to expunge their criminal records as long as they successfully completed treatment programs. Blame relaxed its grip on drug users and glommed onto the physicians and drug companies who got them hooked. These changes were not entirely therapeutic. Access to care required contact with the criminal justice system and the stakes for failure were high. Still, the narratives surrounding prescription opioid use contrasted sharply with those that had plagued heroin and crack use.

This rehabilitative moment would not last long. The narratives and programs would remain in place, but the policy pendulum would swing back toward punishment. Surveillance tools would infiltrate healthcare spaces and change the face of healthcare practice. Surveillance technology would make it easier to prosecute physicians. Drug-induced homicide laws would criminalize those who gave or sold drugs to people who overdosed. And law enforcement would tighten its grip on treatment.

Events dating back almost a century lay the groundwork for today's opioid crisis. And the pendulum is still swinging. Knowing this history leaves us better positioned to evaluate other popular myths of the opioid crisis such as the idea that doctors are to blame.

Myth #2: "Bad Apple" Doctors Are to Blame

Most people believe that bad doctors bear most responsibility for overdose deaths. The American public has seen news articles that spotlight "pill mill" physicians who sell prescriptions for cash[34] and has seen TV segments about suburban teens who overdosed on pills their doctor prescribed.[35] Many Americans think that opioid deaths are due to iatrogenic (physician-caused) addiction. In reality, addiction is far more complicated.

Fact #2: Doctors Are Not the Only Culprits

The dominant story of the opioid crisis frames physicians as perpetrators. It describes how physicians—"drug dealers in white coats"—collaborated with Purdue to spread deadly drugs across the nation.[36] This story tells us that, with the stroke of a pen, physicians released a flood of opioids that left our loved ones gasping for air. Doctors chased profit and power: some sold prescriptions for cash, others rose to fame as thought leaders backed by Purdue. Liberal opioid prescribing got patients hooked, so when overdose deaths began to rise, doctors were blamed.

This tale makes us believe that if physicians had resisted Purdue's lies, if they had taken their duty to protect the public seriously, if they had interrogated the science, if they had sounded the alarm, the opioid crisis would never have happened. Much of this is true. Doctors certainly fell for Purdue's line and helped fuel the overdose crisis. But there are pieces missing from this story, important and glaring omissions. What has been overlooked is that addiction is a complex condition that is caused by more than a physician's prescription and that illegal drugs play a bigger role in overdose death. A closer look at these factors puts doctors' culpability into context.

Addiction is far more complex than the dominant story would have us believe. The common narrative is that simply encountering an addictive drug is what drives addiction—one hit of heroin, one snort of cocaine, and a person is hooked for life. In reality, drugs alone are not that powerful. We now know that various social and psychological factors drive addiction. Once considered "badness"—a moral failing or a crime—today addiction is understood as "sickness"—a brain disease or a learning disorder.[37]

To understand the social underpinnings of addiction, let's turn to a miniaturized version of our own social world—the world of rats. In the 1970s, psychologist Bruce Alexander and his colleagues conducted a series of experiments to determine how community integration affected addiction.[38] The researchers put one set of rats in cages with two water bottles, one with pure water, the other water laced with heroin. They found that rats isolated in cages with only the two water options at their disposal quickly got hooked and drank themselves to death on the opioid-laced water. The researchers exposed a second set of rats to a social community and a rat amusement park full of tunnels, cedar shavings, small boxes, a climbing pole, and other stimulating things that rats enjoy. To the researchers' surprise, very few rats in "rat park" were drawn to the opioids. Those that found it appealing used the drugs only occasionally and never overdosed. The researchers concluded that social interaction and community belongingness protected rats from addiction.

Now, rats are not people, but this study sheds light on human behavior. It tells us that substance use disorders are produced by a wide variety of social factors, not drugs alone. U.S. history offers a powerful illustration. During the Vietnam War, many soldiers became addicted to heroin. The drug was readily available and soldiers used it to cope with the atrocities of war. However, when veterans returned home, many stopped using heroin, even with no formal treatment. Psychiatrist Lee Robins discovered why: they feared arrest, social disapproval, and negative health outcomes.[39] Being part of a community was more important than the drug.

Fast forward to the twenty-first century. We know more about addiction than ever before. We know that addiction is a "disease of despair," which means that it occurs more often among people with poor social and economic prospects.[40] We also know that addiction often occurs alongside other mental health disorders and is closely linked to childhood trauma.[41] Substance use disorder is relatively rare. The latest National Survey on Drug Use and Health shows that, in 2021, 16.5 percent of Americans twelve years of age and older had a substance use disorder in the past year. Most of those people (64 percent) had an alcohol use disorder rather than a drug use disorder. Many people who are exposed to addictive drugs—even drugs as powerful as heroin and cocaine—do not get hooked. The survey shows that 61 percent of the 9.2 million people who misused prescription opioids and heroin in the past year met the criteria for an opioid use disorder. That number, while high, means that 39 percent of people who misused opioids did not have a disorder. Research also shows that most pain patients who take opioids show no signs of addiction.[42] Taken together, this evidence shows that the mere introduction of a drug, even by an authority figure like a physician, is not the only factor that drives addiction.[43]

A second major problem with the dominant story is that doctors are no longer prescribing the drugs that are killing people. Prescribing rates have declined to pre-crisis levels even as overdose rates have risen sharply. Figures 1.1[44] and 1.2[45] show that prescribing rates have gone down each year since 2012 while overdose rates kept going up, but for a slight dip in 2018. If prescribing was to blame, less prescribing should lead to fewer deaths. It does not. That is because prescription opioids are rarely the sole cause of death, prescription opioids are not obtained exclusively from doctors, and illegal opioids have flooded drug markets.

A trick of statistics makes it look like prescription opioids cause more deaths than they do. And the word *cause* is misleading. Most deaths involve multiple substances. According to the CDC, almost 80 percent of deaths attributed to "synthetic opioids" (aka prescription opioids) involved another drug such as "another opioid, heroin, cocaine, prescription opioids, benzodiazepines, alcohol, psychostimulants, and antidepressants."[46] However, when overdose deaths are reported by the National Center for Health Statistics, this complexity disappears. The agency categorizes each death according to all of the drugs involved, so if a person dies with OxyContin, heroin, and illicit fentanyl in their system, that counts as a prescription opioid death, a heroin death, and an illicit fentanyl death, which masks the role of drug interactions.[47] Even those deaths that involve prescription opioids are not necessarily due to reckless prescribing. There is a thriving market in illicit opioids, and the most recent data show that people who misuse painkillers are slightly more likely to have gotten the drugs from a friend or family member (44.9 percent) than from a physician (43.2 percent) (figure 1.3).[48]

The impact of illegal drug use has eclipsed the impact of prescription drugs used illegally. What is often framed as a single opioid crisis is in fact three waves of a drug crisis, distinguishable by different drugs accelerating overdose rates for a given time (figure 1.4). Wave 1 was prescription opioids; Wave 2, heroin; and Wave 3, synthetic opioids like fentanyl. In 2021, nearly 107,000 Americans lost their lives to overdose. Fentanyl and its analogs contributed to 66 percent of these deaths, but prescription opioids contributed to only 16 percent. Even at their peak in 2017, prescription opioids contributed to just over 17,000 deaths, less than a quarter of the more than 70,000 deaths fentanyl precipitated in 2021.[49] In 2021, 23 percent of overdose deaths involved cocaine and 30 percent involved methamphetamine, each more than prescription opioids (figure 1.5).[50]

Did physicians' overprescribing contribute to opioid overdose death rates? No doubt. Is overprescribing still the major driver of overdose deaths?

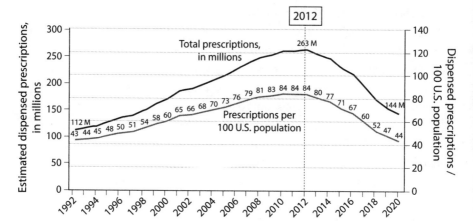

FIGURE 1.1. Estimated opioid analgesic prescriptions dispensed from U.S. outpatient pharmacies, total and per 100 U.S. population, 1992–2020. Data extracted July 2021. M = millions. Outpatient pharmacies included retail and mail-order pharmacies. Data included opioid analgesics only, excluding cough–cold products and medications to treat opioid use disorder. Any changes over time must be interpreted in the context of the changes in methodology, specifically during two trend breaks between 2016 and 2017 and between 2018 and 2019. *Source*: IQVIA, National Prescription Audit, time period 1992–2020. fda.gov.

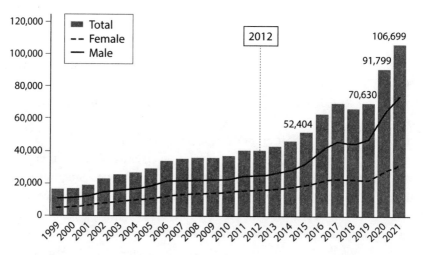

FIGURE 1.2. National drug-involved overdose deaths, 1999–2021. *Source*: Centers for Disease Control and Prevention, National Center for Health Statistics. Multiple Cause of Death 1999–2021 on CDC WONDER Online Database, released 1/2023. http://nida.nih.gov/research-topics/trends-statistics /overdose-death-rates.

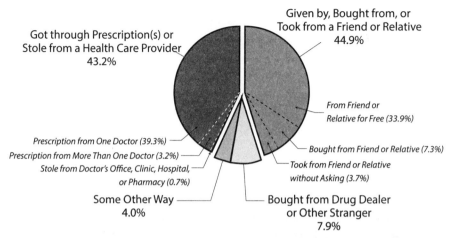

8.7 Million People Aged 12 or Older Who Misused Pain Relievers in the Past Year

FIGURE 1.3. Source where pain relievers were obtained for most recent misuse: among people aged 12 or older who misused pain relievers in the past year (2021). *Source*: 2021 National Survey on Drug Use and Health. https://www.samhsa.gov /data/sites/default/files/reports/rpt39443/2021NSDUHFFRRev010323.pdf.

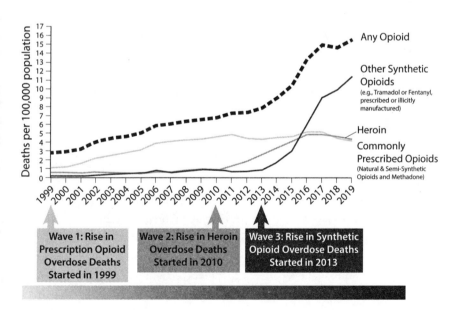

FIGURE 1.4. Three waves of the rise in opioid overdose deaths. *Source*: National Vital Statistics System Mortality File. https://www.cdc.gov/opioids/basics /epidemic.html.

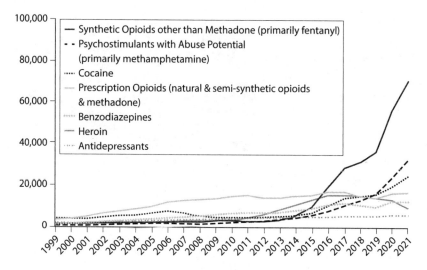

FIGURE 1.5. National drug-involved overdose deaths, number among all ages, 1999–2021. *Source:* Centers for Disease Control and Prevention, National Center for Health Statistics. Multiple Cause of Death 1999–2021 on CDC WONDER Online Database, released 1/2023. http://nida.nih.gov/research-topics/trends -statistics/overdose-death-rates.

Decidedly not. Fentanyl has been a game-changer. Blaming physicians for today's overdose deaths is tantamount to prosecuting yesterday's criminals for today's crimes. Yet many popular policy solutions aim to stop doctors from prescribing opioids. Whether those solutions are prescription drug monitoring programs that track physicians' prescribing practices, hospital- or clinic-wide rankings that compare physicians' prescribing rates to their peers, opioid-free emergency department policies, or opioid stewardship programs that closely guard opioids in hospital settings, there is no reason to believe that stopping physicians from prescribing will reduce overdose death rates. In fact, there is good reason to believe that tamping down on prescribing could result in more lives lost.

As a thought experiment, let us, for a moment, ignore polysubstance deaths and assume that every death that involved a prescription opioid was caused by that opioid alone. And let's assume that the overdose rates this year were the same as 2021. Even if every physician stopped prescribing opioids right now, we would still have almost 90,000 overdose deaths due to other drugs.[51] But evidence suggests that we would see even more.

People who previously got drugs from their physicians would not stop using drugs just because the physician stopped prescribing them; they would turn to the far riskier illicit drug market. They would encounter drugs that were too strong, whose purity they could not surmise, and many people would die. Also, pain patients who could no longer access their medications might find the pain unbearable and take their own lives. We are already seeing tragic evidence of that. Physician Thomas Kline has documented forty-one cases of pain patients ending their lives after being denied pain medication,[52] and a group of international pain leaders has called for an urgent review of policies that mandate tapering patients down to lower opioid doses.[53] These experts contend that forcing patients off of opioids can catapult patients into pain and motivate them to seek relief in illicit drugs or resort to suicide.

Together, these findings suggest that blaming doctors for the opioid crisis can blind us to other powerful factors. Careless prescribing is one of many factors that ignited the opioid crisis, but other factors stoke it today. These deserve consideration. Another key issue warrants attention: racial disparities in how substance use disorders are talked about and treated. Opioid use is racialized, but in different ways than many people believe.

Myth #3: White People Are the Only Ones Affected by the Opioid Crisis

Media coverage of the opioid crisis has led many people to believe that the opioid crisis is a white crisis that has devastated middle-class, suburban communities.[54] Because of this, they think that responses to the crisis constitute a kinder, gentler War on Drugs. In reality, the opioid crisis affects people of all races, but in different ways than we might expect, and the responses that look kinder and gentler on the surface are still punitive underneath.

Fact #3: The Opioid Crisis Affects People of All Races, but in Different Ways

The iconic image of opioid overdose, the one pasted across newspapers from Seattle to Miami, is that of a young, white teen, clad in a football or cheerleading uniform, their innocent smile a sharp contrast to the grim details of their death. This image conveys a powerful story—one of a young person struck down in their prime while their entire life lays ahead of them. Unable to realize their full potential, their deaths constitute a loss to their families and to society. But this image also communicates a more subtle, but equally powerful, story—a story of whiteness.[55] It is a short leap from believing that the opioid crisis is a white crisis to believing that law enforcement treats people who use opioids better because they are white.

A second popular story reinforces the idea that white people who use opioids manage to escape enforcement by virtue of their race. This story documents police officers and judges who treat addiction like a disease and help people instead of punishing them. These stories highlight people whose lives have been saved by police officers with naloxone or feature drug court graduates grateful for a second chance.

There is certainly truth to these stories. Black people who used crack and heroin in the 1980s and 1990s were stigmatized and severely punished. White people who use opioids are framed in a more positive light and have more options for treatment. Yet this disparity is not as stark as it initially appears.[56] Not only does punishment reign today, but what many see as a kinder, gentler, war on drugs is in many ways a more insidious, more comprehensive War on Drugs.

The opioid crisis is not a white crisis, but it is easy to understand why so many people believe it is.[57] When we look at opioid overdose deaths overall, it is clear that many more whites have died from opioids than Blacks. Early in the crisis, non-Hispanic whites and non-Hispanic Blacks had a similar rate of overdose deaths (3.7 and 3.3 in 2001).[58] White overdose deaths rose until 2014, when the rate of overdose deaths for non-Hispanic whites grew to more than twice that of non-Hispanic Blacks (12 versus 5.6).[59]

But these statistics do not tell the whole story. They miss the fact that overdose deaths were devastating Black communities even at a time when white overdose rates were soaring. Yale psychologist Ayanna Jordan and lawyer Keturah James note that "the current opioid epidemic is the largest drug epidemic in recorded U.S. history, for all racial groups," and that "opioid deaths, in particular heroin overdoses, have nearly doubled among Black Americans since 2000."[60] Statistics that show national trends also fail to account for geographic variation. There are several jurisdictions, including West Virginia, Washington, DC, Wisconsin, Missouri, Illinois, and Minnesota, where the Black overdose rate is higher than the white overdose rate.[61] Synthetic fentanyl, today's leading cause of overdose death, has hit Black communities hard. Between 2014 and 2017, the death rate for non-Hispanic Blacks went up by 818 percent, making their rate the highest among all races and ethnicities.[62] Racial disparities have increased during the COVID-19 pandemic. At a national addiction conference in

2021, Dr. Nora Volkow, director of the National Institute on Drug Abuse, noted that "the highest increase in mortality from opioids, predominantly driven by fentanyl, is now among Black Americans."[63] In short, overdose is everyone's problem. But that does not mean that everyone receives equal care.

Efforts to combat the opioid crisis certainly look more compassionate when you compare strategies used to curb the opioid crisis to those used to curb the crack cocaine crisis in the 1980s and 1990s. Black crack users were "addicts"; white opioid users have a "disease." Police arrested crack users, driving up rates of mass incarceration, particularly for Black men. Police assist opioid users: They revive them with naloxone (an opioid overdose antidote), refer them to treatment, and route them into drug courts where they get a chance to complete treatment with no jail time and no criminal record. At first glance, this looks like a kinder, gentler War on Drugs. But looks can be deceiving. If we scratch the surface of this treatment-based approach, we find punishment lurking below.

Drug enforcement has expanded during the opioid crisis, and enforcement agencies have tightened rather than loosened their grip on people who use and sell drugs. Police capacity for tracking drug use is more robust than ever before, and enforcement agencies have doubled down on their commitment to focus on the drug supply (the movement of drugs across and within U.S. borders) while continuing to overlook drug demand (the psycho-social reasons that motivate people to use drugs). Law, too, is oriented toward punishment. Many states have passed or revived drug-induced homicide laws that make it a crime to provide drugs that result in death.[64] These laws are often used against friends and families of overdose victims—facing a criminal charge compounds their grief over losing a loved one.

Even those approaches like drug courts, naloxone distribution programs, and police-assisted recovery programs that look like treatment have problems. Drug courts offer people who are arrested for drug crimes a second chance. They can avoid jail time and a criminal record by completing treatment to a judge's satisfaction. If they fail, they serve their entire sentence—the time they spent in drug court doesn't count in their favor. Experts disagree about the benefits of drug courts. Proponents consider them promising vehicles for keeping people out of prison and getting them the help they need. Skeptics argue that the programs are highly coercive and unequally distributed. They ask why judges, rather than doctors, decide when treatment is complete. They also note that drug courts tend to rely on less effective forms of treatment for opioid use disorders such as abstinence-based programs and mutual support groups like Narcotics Anonymous. They believe this sets participants up to fail, which can mean spending far more time involved with the criminal justice system due to layering the time spent trying to complete drug court onto the time served when they fail. Sociologist Rebecca Tiger, whose book *Judging Addicts* explores the world of drug courts, critiques these systems for linking two forms of coercion. Says Tiger, "[F]orce is not the best medicine. The marriage of punishment and treatment is a failed one; it is time for a divorce."[65] With all of their flaws, drug courts do wipe the slate clean for those who succeed, which is no small thing—the mark of a criminal record can have a devastating impact on job and housing prospects.[66] This raises another issue—white people are disproportionately selected into drug courts, which makes existing racial disparities in drug sentencing even worse.[67]

For their part, naloxone distribution programs make getting a life-saving drug contingent upon calling the police, inviting enforcement agents to a scene where people have been using drugs. Laws called "Good Samaritan Laws" are supposed to encourage people to call the police by promising that people will not be arrested for doing so, but they don't always work, and many would prefer not to take the risk. Similarly, police-assisted recovery programs, through which police officers refer people to treatment either before or after they have been arrested, also require engagement with law enforcement to get access to care. Each of these approaches centers law enforcement as "fixers," helping enforcement agents morph into treatment specialists, healthcare providers, and referral conduits, roles for which they lack training.[68] Law professor Taleed El-Sabawi explains that these programs help law enforcement stay relevant even as the idea that addiction is a disease gains popularity. Law enforcement retains authority by shape-shifting from punisher to helper. El-Sabawi and her colleague, anthropologist and public health scholar Jennifer Carroll, warn that communities of color are harmed when police take over public health tasks. They insist that "We must be intentional about creating institutions that will not replicate the racist and oppressive systems of the past.... Instead, we must fundamentally reimagine what public safety can look like, creating systems that are useful, dignifying, and equitable for all people who need care."[69]

What all of this suggests is that strategies to combat the opioid crisis that appear at first glance to facilitate treatment in fact create opportunities for punishment. People who use and sell drugs face punishment on two fronts: through the traditional criminal justice system that has spent half a century mired in a federal War on Drugs, and through the healthcare system that has ceded much control of addiction treatment to police and the courts and that has welcomed law enforcement workers, logics, and tools into hospitals and clinics.[70] Far from pushing the pendulum toward treatment, these efforts help to refashion punishment in treatment garb. While it is true that politicians and police chiefs call addiction a "disease" and support some treatment options like drug courts and naloxone distribution programs, it is also true that they continue to invest significantly in expanding enforcement capacity, particularly in the realm of surveillance and big data analytics. Enforcement agents have used new surveillance technology to enter the realm of healthcare to identify and punish doctors and pharmacists.

Perhaps the best example of dressing up punitive strategies in the trappings of healthcare are prescription drug monitoring programs (PDMPs). Discussed in detail in chapter 3, PDMPs are surveillance technologies implemented in healthcare spaces. Purportedly designed to help healthcare providers identify people who go to multiple doctors and multiple pharmacies to accumulate drugs, these systems gather information about all controlled substances dispensed in a state and feed that information back to healthcare providers and to law enforcement. PDMPs track far more than opioids. They contain information about drugs as wide-ranging as benzodiazepines like Xanax and sleep aids like Ambien. Most people who use these drugs have no idea that their information is being gathered and shared.

Unprotected by healthcare privacy laws like the Health Insurance Portability and Accountability Act (HIPAA), PDMPs are dragnet surveillance technologies that capture sensitive data on patients nationwide.[71] PDMPs expand enforcement capacity in the healthcare realm by capturing information about patients of all races, so more people's healthcare information is monitored by law enforcement than ever before. Nevertheless, PDMP use disproportionately affects Black patients.[72] As we shall see, it is through PDMP use that surveillance has become a medical standard.

There is a striking mismatch between popular narratives that frame addiction as a disease and popular enforcement strategies that treat addiction as a crime. We might call addiction a disease, but we are certainly not treating it like one. To believe that the opioid crisis is a white crisis and that it has ushered in a kinder, gentler War on Drugs is to overlook the ways that Black communities suffer from opioid overdose and to ignore how efforts to combat the opioid crisis have normalized punishment in the guise of treatment.

The War on Prescription Drugs bears a striking resemblance to its predecessor, the War on Drugs—both are racialized and both rely on punitive strategies to stop drug use. What sets the War on Prescription Drugs apart is its emergence during a time of unprecedented surveillance capacity and computing power when tracking, storing, and analyzing billions of prescriptions each year is feasible. It has also fostered new "treatment" strategies that position care in the criminal justice system.

These facts do not erase the fact that rhetoric surrounding the opioid crisis differs dramatically from rhetoric surrounding the crack epidemic. Nor do they suggest that white people who use opioids are being treated as poorly as Black people who used crack were treated decades ago. But they do undermine the notion that opioid users are being treated as patients and are escaping punishment because they are white.[73] In reality, approaches to drug use have changed little even if the rhetoric surrounding them looks different.[74] Only by recognizing these aspects of the contemporary crisis can we fully understand the real racial dynamics at work. Says sociologist Doris Marie Provine in her book *Unequal under Law*, "The war on drugs is likely to remain invulnerable to reform until people seriously begin to discuss its purpose and its racial and class impact."[75] If it is surprising to learn that the opioid crisis is not a white crisis, it is perhaps even more surprising to learn that the opioid crisis involves more than just prescription drugs.

Myth #4: The Opioid Crisis Is All about Prescription Opioids

Most people believe that we are dealing with a prescription opioid crisis. They think that drugs themselves are the problem and that if we eradicated prescription opioids, we would save lives. In reality, illegal opioids drive most overdose deaths and prescription opioids have an important role in treating pain.

Fact #4: The "Opioid Crisis" Is Really an Overdose and Pain Crisis

If opioids are the problem, if they kill tens of thousands of people each year, then why isn't restricting opioid prescribing the answer? Many people grapple with this question. The answer is easier to understand if we first recognize that the term "opioid crisis" is really misleading. It is misleading for two reasons: one, people confuse the term "opioid" with "prescription opioid" and two, the concept of an "opioid crisis" obscures a second, related crisis: the pain crisis.

When we focus narrowly on the "opioid crisis," we do ourselves a disservice by distilling the problem into a single class of drugs instead of addressing drug use more generally. This flattens the complexity of the problem at hand and leads us astray when it comes to developing solutions. We overfocus on prescribing rates and underfocus on what motivates people to use drugs in the first place.

Further, what is commonly called the "opioid crisis" is really the confluence of two crises—an overdose crisis and a pain crisis—that shape how opioids are provided in the United States. A broader perspective invites us to acknowledge that people are dying of drug overdose at staggering rates and that people in pain can't get access to care. It also invites us to recognize that those with substance use disorders and those in chronic pain are not enemies, but suffering people who have been pitted against each other in the battle over opioids. The overdose crisis and the pain crisis are inextricably intertwined.

Broadening Our Perspective:
From "Opioid Crisis" to "Overdose Crisis"

The term "overdose crisis" more aptly captures our situation because, one, many nonopioid drugs drive overdose deaths, and, two, the social conditions that motivate people to use drugs in dangerous ways pack a bigger punch than drugs themselves.

What comes to mind when you hear the word "opioid"? For many Americans, that word conjures up images of prescription opioids, drugs like Oxy-Contin, Vicodin, and Percocet designed to treat pain. They are surprised to learn that heroin and synthetic drugs like fentanyl are opioids too. The difference is that the first three opioids are regulated by the federal government, tested for safety and efficacy,[76] used in hospitals, and sold at community pharmacies, while the last two opioids are unregulated, untested, and sold in illegal markets. Fentanyl gets even more confusing because there are two types—prescription fentanyl, which is regulated and prescribed, and synthetic fentanyl, which is made and distributed illegally.[77]

Illegal opioids like synthetic fentanyl and heroin are now driving the overdose crisis even though prescription opioids claimed more lives when the crisis began.[78] Synthetic fentanyl, a particularly potent drug, has spread across the country and tainted the illegal drug supply. Sometimes it is pressed into pill form so that it resembles a prescription opioid and sometimes it is sold as heroin, but it is much more powerful than either.

If you take a 20-milligram OxyContin pill, you know that you are getting 20 milligrams of oxycodone. If you inject heroin or buy a prescription pill on the street or on the Internet, you don't know what is in it and could easily get a stronger drug than you intended. The same way that people who drink alcohol know if they can have one drink or four, people who use drugs know their limits. However, while hard drinks contain a set amount of alcohol by volume, illegal drugs can contain anything. If you plan to use heroin, but wind up with synthetic fentanyl, you are at serious risk of overdose.

As the contours of the crisis change, one fact endures: overdose claims many lives too soon. Using the term "opioid crisis" to describe the broader overdose crisis jumbles together the very different types of fuel that have stoked overdose deaths for the past twenty years. Focusing narrowly on prescription opioids also misdirects our attention toward the healthcare system when the biggest threat lies outside of it in unregulated, illegal drug markets.

Drugs occupy vast space in our cultural imagination. Drugs capture the public's attention and receive a disproportionate share of blame for social ills. Elected officials in the United States tend to zero in on the drug du jour. News media and public health research follow their lead and give outsized importance to the power of a single drug.[79] Drugs have been implicated in everything from joblessness to homelessness to violent crime, from low-birth-weight babies to fractured neighborhoods to poor educational attainment. One drug at a time does the heavy lifting. In the 1980s and 1990s, it was crack cocaine, in the early 2000s it was methamphetamine, in the mid-aughts it was prescription opioids, and now it is synthetic fentanyl. Can drugs really be to blame for so much of what is wrong with our society?

What researchers, politicians, and journalists miss is what historians and social scientists have known all along: drugs, like fashion, come in and out of vogue and overdose deaths come in cycles. What persists, however, are the underlying factors that motivate people to use drugs in the first place. The situation is complex. On the one hand, overdose deaths are "deaths of despair."[80] Substance use disorders manifest due to economic decline, poor job prospects, and a frayed social safety net,[81] and the treatment system has never been adequate to meet need.[82] Some people use drugs to self-medicate in the face of trauma or other mental health conditions like depression or anxiety.[83] If we normally think that drugs do harm, these facts make us consider if, instead, harm causes people to do drugs.

Then we pause and realize that drug use is not just about harm. It is also about pleasure.[84] People use drugs to have fun (as well as to navigate a tough time). As Columbia neuroscientist Dr. Carl Hart details in his controversial book *Drug Use for Grown Ups*, drugs can help people feel closer to their partners and more in touch with themselves. Like alcohol, they alleviate the stressors of daily life and offer a way to relax with friends or lovers.[85] Plus, most people who use drugs do not develop substance use disorders,[86] and only a small subset of people who use drugs chaotically tend to fare the worst.[87] Suddenly, you wonder if drugs are driving this issue or if the underlying motivations are the culprit. Perhaps the opioid crisis is more a crisis of trauma, mental illness, and unmet need.

The topic of need brings us to the other side of this crisis—the pain crisis. If you don't know how terribly pain was once treated in this country, then you may think that the opioid crisis came out of nowhere. In fact, it was an overcorrection to a devastating problem. Pain is rampant in the United States. In 2011, the Institute of Medicine reported that at least 116 million Americans suffered from chronic pain,[88] defined as pain that lasts three months or longer.[89] For decades, chronic pain sufferers have struggled to get their pain taken seriously and to find physicians willing to treat them.[90] We live at a time when pain medication is largely available. This is the result of hard-fought battles on the part of pain patients who mobilized for access to care. Together, social movement efforts buoyed by the pharmaceutical industry released a flood of opioids into illicit markets beginning in the late nineties.[91]

To understand how we got here, let's go back to the beginning. The long reach of physician and pharmacist arrests that occurred after the passage of the Harrison Act maintained a stranglehold on late twentieth-century pain treatment. For decades, physicians hesitated to prescribe opioids—even to relieve suffering at the end of life—out of fear that they would get patients addicted. They also worried that drugs used to relieve pain such as morphine would hasten death, making them culpable for taking a life. Their fears were well-founded. Opioids like morphine slow the respiratory system, so providing patients enough to treat pain without stopping their breath is a delicate balance.[92]

Opioids were underutilized for decades. In the 1950s, anti-opioid sentiments were so strong that cancer patients were dying in pain while the drugs that would have relieved their suffering were available but inaccessible.[93] People who watched their loved ones endure these horrors were fed up and decided to take action. Two tandem social movements sought to end these inhumane practices.

First, the British hospice movement insisted that people should not have to die in pain. In 1967, Dame Cicely Saunders, a nurse, social worker, doctor, and writer founded St. Christopher's, the first modern hospice, in the London suburbs. Saunders offered a revolutionary new perspective on death and dying. She insisted that dying people should be removed from hospitals and returned to their homes, where they should receive holistic treatment that addressed their physiological, psychological, and emotional needs. Her research showed that using morphine to relieve patients' pain did not foster addiction. Saunders's work inspired hospice advocates in the United States, who based their approach on hers.[94]

The U.S. pain management movement followed quickly on the hospice movement's heels. If people should not have to die in pain, activists reasoned, why should they have to live in pain? The pain management movement spurred a series of policy changes that set the stage for rampant opioid prescribing in the first decade of the twenty-first century. Purdue financially supported some of these groups, and their release of OxyContin in 1996 made activists' efforts even more impactful.[95]

In the halcyon days of pain treatment, doctors took pain seriously and treated it with gusto. The legal context that had once frightened them had changed so much that failing to prescribe opioids was considered the greatest offense. Purdue and pain management activists convinced regulators to take pain seriously and insisted that clinicians did so as well. Pressure to treat pain and the relaxation of federal scrutiny went hand in hand. The American Pain Society, an organization funded by Purdue, initiated a campaign called "Pain, the Fifth Vital Sign" that was eventually taken up by the Veterans Health Administration in 1999. In 2001, the Joint Commission, an organization that accredits hospitals, issued patient satisfaction surveys to evaluate pain treatment and required clinicians to adequately assess and treat patients' pain in order to receive federal funds.[96] Hospitals that failed to tackle pain lost money and status. Meanwhile, in 1998, the Federation of State Medical Boards, an organization that oversees medical boards nationwide, stated that physicians who prescribed excessive opioids would be free from inquiry. In 2001, the U.S. Drug Enforcement Administration (DEA) adopted a "balanced policy" in which they promised to reduce physician scrutiny to encourage the use of opioids to treat pain.[97]

Opioid prescribing soon began to escalate. Prescribing rates quadrupled from 1999–2010.[98] Bear in mind that what looked like unbridled prescribing was, at least in part, a corrective to the lean years when people couldn't get opioids even in the most dire circumstances. For pain patients, opioids were not a crisis. They were a godsend. By 2015, physicians were prescribing enough opioids each year to keep every American medicated around the clock for three weeks.[99] Not everyone benefited from this opioid windfall, however.

A strict racial divide persisted even in the heyday of opioid prescribing. When it came to Black and Latino patients, physicians continued to closely guard their prescription pads. Influenced by myths dating back to slavery that Black people could withstand greater amounts of pain, they took these patients' pain less seriously and prescribed them less powerful opioids in lower doses with fewer refills.[100] Still, opioids flowed freely through American cities and towns as physicians handed over opioids to white patients without a second thought.

Racial discrimination in prescribing helps to explain why whites saw higher rates of overdose deaths at a time when prescription opioids contributed to most overdose deaths. Some researchers have dared to suggest that discrimination in pain care protected Black patients against the worst fallout of the opioid crisis,[101] but their optimism is misguided. True, Black patients received opioids from their physicians less often than white patients, but because the opioid crisis is not an artifact of physician prescribing alone, Blacks have been equally if not more subjected to the illicit pathway than whites.[102] Add to that the fact that Black pain patients have suffered without relief, and the benefit these researchers propose looks dubious.[103] Indiana University law professor Jennifer Oliva puts it best when she critiques these researchers for suggesting that "Black people should be grateful for the day-in, day-out racism in medicine that ensures that they—and their children—will always suffer more than everyone else because such rampant racism spared them the absolute worst of fates: opioid use disorder."[104]

The pain crisis lives in the shadow of the opioid crisis. Efforts to stop overdose deaths often fail to consider the impact on patients with chronic pain.[105] Opioids of course have a place in medicine. It is unthinkable going into surgery or recovering from a car accident without them. Their role in chronic pain is less clear, but some people legitimately require high doses. Imagine being well-managed on opioids for years, then suddenly having them yanked away.[106] Pain patients and patients with substance use disorders are caught in a zero-sum game. Restricting opioid prescribing hurts pain patients by making a powerful source of relief unavailable, but prescribing them liberally hurts people with substance use disorders because it creates a glut of opioids available for nonmedical use. An easy solution eludes at every turn.

There are no good guys and no bad guys in the opioid crisis, just a lot of people suffering. Still, popular policy solutions pit them against each other in a game that nobody wins. In fact, both sides typically get framed as bad guys— people with substance use disorders as manipulators who will say and do anything for a hit,[107] and people with pain as malingerers who use pain as an excuse to get out of work and social obligations.[108] This tells us that, in many ways, pain and addiction are flip sides of the same coin—both groups are cast as undeserving and struggle to access care they so desperately need.

Philosopher George Santayana warned that "those who cannot remember the past are condemned to repeat it."[109] An overcorrection to the pain crisis may have birthed the overdose crisis, but now we risk overcorrecting the overdose crisis and catapulting millions of people into pain. Our efforts will be for nothing if we end up exactly where we started. Today, the pendulum is swinging away from opioid treatment for pain and toward the criminalization of opioids and the people who prescribe, dispense, and use them. Meanwhile, chronic pain patients who need opioids can't get them and are left with few effective options to manage their pain. We can't stop the pendulum without knowing all of the factors at stake, which is why the term "opioid crisis" is insufficient. It is also why we must upend opioid crisis myths in favor of the facts.

From Busting Myths to Examining Frontline Work

The story of the opioid crisis is more nuanced and complex than the simple fare we have been fed. Distracted by the big, bad drug company and the harm it has inflicted, political leaders, researchers, and journalists tell an incomplete story about the crisis we face. They lob criticism at a single drug, place blame on physicians' shoulders, locate the problem in white communities alone, and misname the crisis a prescription opioid crisis. As we have seen, these myths truncate our understanding of the crisis and lead us toward policy solutions that barely make a dent.

Myths so easily become construed as facts. And they are barbed. Once they embed themselves into our cultural imagination, they are terribly difficult to dislodge. We repeat these myths because they serve a purpose. They reinforce what we believe to be true about the world—that single companies and single professionals do irreversible harm, that each problem is unique and new, that people who have privilege receive kinder treatment. In this way, myths become facts. They seem true, so they must be true. Once established, it is so easy for myths to silence those voices that question their veracity. We must not fall prey to these temptations. We must not take the easy route.

The rest of this book encourages us to dig deep, to excavate the complex realities of the overdose and pain crises. We will unearth how efforts to resolve these crises have blurred boundaries between healthcare and criminal justice and we will witness the process by which care becomes criminalized. We will see how changes in law enforcement spill over into healthcare and prompt healthcare providers to police patients. One way that criminalization happens is that social problems move into the criminal justice arena—problems like being unhoused or misbehaving at school become criminal activity. The opioid case reveals a different process of criminalization: the transportation of enforcement logics into healthcare. Surveillance technology is the vehicle.

2

Trojan Horse Technologies

IT WAS THE SUMMER OF 2013 and everyone I interviewed was talking about prescription drug monitoring programs (PDMPs). Questions I asked about opioids were met with answers about surveillance technology. This caught me by surprise. When I began my research five years earlier, almost no one had mentioned PDMPs, even though many were in use. What was it about this technology that had captivated enforcement agents and healthcare providers alike? I did not yet know that PDMPs were rapidly becoming standard tools for law enforcement, physicians, and pharmacists. I did not realize how these technologies had evolved into sophisticated risk tools. I did not understand how PDMPs fused two tracks of social change: the rise of punishment as an answer to social problems and the use of digital technology across all areas of social life. It had not occurred to me how much PDMPs resembled the mythic Trojan horse in that they were a gift presented with ulterior motives. I was about to find out.

My journey into the world of law enforcement began in California, where I managed to secure interviews with a handful of officers who investigated opioid crimes. These were professionals who targeted physicians and pharmacists suspected of overprescribing and overdispensing opioids. Some worked for federal organizations like the U.S. Drug Enforcement Administration (DEA), the primary agency that oversees controlled substance distribution. Some worked for the Office of Inspector General for the U.S. Department of Health and Human Services (HHS), an agency designed to root out Medicare and Medicaid fraud. Others worked on narcotics task forces in local sheriffs' departments. They had one goal: to stop opioid diversion. And they all used the PDMP to do so.

By then, policing technology had become incredibly sophisticated because exponential growth in computing power made it cheap and easy to collect, store, and analyze vast amounts of data. The big data revolution was a boon to enforcement agents who could now link all kinds of data to identify crime patterns. Doing so enabled them to hone in on specific suspects and locations and devote their attention to the most pressing needs. As rivers of data flowed into enforcement agencies, PDMPs became another tool in the law enforcement toolkit, one particularly useful for investigating doctors and pharmacists.

In a conference room overlooking the Bay Area, I sat across from DEA agents Abby and Brandon. I was there to interview them, but first they had questions for me. Abby thumbed through my curriculum vitae and asked pointed questions about an article I had written. They both wanted to know if I planned to expose or embarrass the DEA in some way. I must have passed the test because they started talking.

When I decided to interview federal enforcement agents, I had no clue how to find them. Pharmacists were easy to approach, you could just call them on the phone or show up at their pharmacy. Federal agents were elusive. I remembered a nurse I interviewed years earlier who mentioned that her husband was a narcotics agent, so I started there. After several unanswered phone messages, he finally agreed to meet at a coffee shop in downtown San Francisco. He mostly worked on street arrests and mail fraud, things that had very little to do with healthcare. But when I asked if he knew anyone who worked for the DEA, he put me in touch with Brandon. That serendipitous connection would be the critical link I needed to reach enforcement agents nationwide.

Once Abby and Brandon had vetted me, they were ready to talk. If I asked you to picture a DEA agent, the image that pops to mind is probably that of a large man in a navy blue jacket emblazoned with "DEA" in yellow capital letters. You might think of someone toting a gun, kicking down doors, or cuffing a perp. That Hollywoodesque image is inspired by one type of DEA agent known as the Special Agent (SA). Special Agents fight the illegal drug trade by helping to build prosecution, partnering with local law enforcement, and seizing assets connected to drug trafficking. They carry guns and issue arrest warrants.[1]

However, the DEA has another face, that of the reserved, thoughtful number-cruncher known as the Diversion Investigator (DI). These unarmed investigators are responsible for guarding the prescription drug supply—making sure that there are enough controlled substances to meet public need, but also ensuring that those medications do not find their way into illicit markets.[2] DIs receive less airtime and less glory than SAs, but they are no less important. I was fortunate to be talking to one of each.

Abby and Brandon worked together on a Tactical Diversion Squad, a type of working group first created by the DEA in 1996.[3] A strict hierarchy at the DEA historically placed DIs on the bottom rung. They were responsible for stopping drug diversion, the sale of prescription drugs through illicit markets. They investigated doctors, not kingpins. They seized pills, not heroin, drugs other agents dismissed as "kiddie dope."[4] However, once the overdose crisis revved up, DIs enjoyed an elevated status. Their deep understanding of the healthcare system was critical for rooting out bad doctors and pharmacists and they were experts in topics that SAs knew almost nothing about. The DEA combined DIs' knowledge with SAs' muscle into collaborative teams known as Tactical Diversion Squads. In the throes of the overdose crisis, the number of Tactical Diversion Squads nearly doubled from 37 in 2011 to 66 in 2014.[5]

Tactical Diversion Squads consist of SAs, DIs, and Task Force Officers (TFOs) who are police officers from state and local precincts. Their goal is to stop the illegal distribution of prescription drugs, and the PDMP helps them achieve it. Abby explained that most of their cases start from a complaint. "We will get some kind of call from the public, medical professionals, or law enforcement that a doctor's practice is suspicious," she says, "then we start to look at them."

CURES, California's PDMP, is their first stop.[6] They use CURES to assess the physician, which means sifting through data, looking for patterns, and second-guessing assumptions. Sometimes, they search CURES to identify facilities with the top prescribers, but, Abby warns, even that information requires context. She explains that when she identifies heavy prescribers, she might think "he is doing all of this himself." But then she explores further and asks, "What if that physician is the head of a surgical center? What if he shares prescribing with other practitioners?"

The PDMP is one digital tool that can be combined with other information to paint a fine-grained picture of a physician's actions. DEA agents collaborate with other law enforcement agents like fraud investigators who have access to Medicare and Medicaid data. They can see whether a prescription paid for by Medicaid has a corresponding office visit, also paid for by Medicaid. If not, they need to dig further. Abby describes her group's job this way: "We are not SWAT, we are Columbo."

To make the difference clear, Abby throws a book she is holding down on the table. "This is a kilo of cocaine. It is illegal." These cases are easy. "But in another case, the doctor gives a patient a prescription. What is illegal?" She digs deeper and finds "The doctor didn't do an exam. The patient paid cash.

The patient said 'I have a headache; I like Percocet. Can you give me 100.'"
That's a case. PDMP data make the arduous task of investigating physicians
and pharmacists much easier.

PDMPs enable enforcement agents like Abby and Brandon to venture
deeply into healthcare territory. Using the database, investigators can easily
spot physicians who are prescribing egregious amounts of opioids. With the
click of a button, they can analyze physicians' prescribing histories and compare them to their peers.[7] PDMPs are even more useful when paired with
sources like the Automation of Reports and Consolidated Orders System
(ARCOS), a drug reporting system that tracks controlled substances from the
point of manufacture through distribution to the point of sale.[8] Together, they
offer comprehensive information about providers' behavior, since they show,
for instance, what drugs pharmacies ordered in what amounts, which can be
linked to their dispensing patterns. PDMP data gets investigations off to a
good start and helps investigators devote their energy to promising cases.
PDMP use makes enforcement work efficient and effective—investigators can
target physicians quickly using more information than ever before.

PDMPs equip enforcement agents with information that makes them better investigators. But healthcare providers use PDMPs too. Do PDMPs help
them to be better doctors and pharmacists? The answer to that question depends on how one defines good medicine and good pharmacy.

A few days later, in a clinic across town, Omar managed to squeeze in a
phone call with me between patients. A chronic pain specialist, Omar takes
a holistic approach to pain. He works in a multidisciplinary clinic that houses
physicians, psychologists, physical therapists, acupuncturists, pain pharmacists, and a nurse case manager. Omar describes the PDMP as a "very helpful
tool" and explains how it has changed his interactions with patients.

Omar had begun using CURES three years earlier, largely because it was so
easy to sign up. "The Department of Justice came to one of our regional meet-
ings of pain specialists and they signed you up right there." He also got on
board because he realized how helpful the PDMP could be for finding patients
who did not exhibit other "red flags" (indicators of misuse). "A lot of times you
get surprised. You do a CURES check, and it turns out patient is getting the
narco[9] from other providers. And then you have to approach them and find
out why they are doctor shopping."

Omar uses the PDMP alongside various other screening tools such as urine
drug screening and assessments that track risk factors for addiction. He also
requires his patients to sign an opioid agreement that limits them to a single

doctor and a single pharmacy. "We do the opioid agreement on every single patient. And we do the urine drug screening," he told me. His team uses these indicators to put patients in color-coded categories. Patients with no red flags go in the green box, patients with some suspicious activities or signs of abuse potential go in the orange box, and patients with both a substance use disorder and chronic pain go in the red box. The team monitors patients with greater risk factors closely and checks their PDMP reports frequently.

I asked Omar how he uses the information in the PDMP when he discovers that patients are seeing multiple physicians. He gives them an opportunity to explain. "We actually approach them and say, 'We did the check, and you have Drs. X, Y, Z selling you narcos and you never told me about it.' Most patients don't have a good explanation, but some say 'Well, yeah, I did see a dentist but I didn't feel like I needed to tell you.'" In those cases, Omar gives patients a warning and tells them they must tell him if they are taking opioids from other providers. However, "If the behavior continues, then we would have to make a decision to taper them or refer them to chemical dependency. I mean, that is a clear-cut case of abuse."

Later that day, I caught up with Anthony at a coffee shop down the street from his chain pharmacy in San Francisco's Castro District. This was our third interview. He had been generous with his time and forthcoming about his experiences, so I made a point to check in with him each time I found myself in the city. When we met the previous year, he had just begun using CURES. Now, it was central to his work.

He noted that using CURES was time-consuming and resulted in some pushback from patients and physicians, but "overall, it's been a blessing." His chain initially required him to check CURES and photocopy IDs for all patients getting certain drugs. Later, they relaxed the ID requirement so that he only needed to get an ID if the patient was not known to him. Anthony sometimes goes a step further and checks other controlled substances in CURES, especially when he has a feeling that something isn't right. His chain also created a checklist that he uses to identify red flags that include a patient paying cash,[10] going to more than one prescriber, or attempting to fill the prescription early, but those are not the only things he uses to decide whether or not to dispense medications.

He acknowledges, "those red flags have kind of helped me in my decision making," but in the end, "it's still your professional judgment, should you dispense." In the beginning, patients were frustrated that they had to wait longer since Anthony and his staff required extra processing time to check the PDMP.

But now patients are used to it. Getting more information makes Anthony feel better about dispensing. He looks for red flags and says he has "caught a few patients" who were "doctor shopping" or "pharmacy shopping"—bouncing between clinics and pharmacies to stockpile opioids—by checking CURES. "Generally speaking, CURES is a great thing," he says. "It still requires extra time, but I'm okay with that, because I think it's for a good reason that we're doing it."

After talking with Omar and Anthony, it hit me: these providers were policing patients. I struggled to understand how professionals tasked with caring for others so readily policed them. Even harder to comprehend was how unremarkable it seemed to them. Omar reported testing his patients' urine and requiring them to sign a legalistic pain contract as if it were the same as taking X-rays or filling out a patient history. Anthony proudly stated that he "caught a few patients" who were misusing drugs. Both praised the PDMP and considered it an essential tool for doing their jobs.

I knew from talking to pharmacists just a few years earlier that this was a major departure from business as usual.[11] The pharmacists I interviewed from 2009 to 2011 resisted policing patients. They knew that they had a role in regulating opioids, but they were uncomfortable with any tasks that required them to move into policing territory. Several told me outright, "I am a pharmacist, not a police officer." In later conversations, that earlier discomfort had been resolved and policing patients had become central to pharmacy practice. What I didn't know was why.

PDMPs: A New Tool for an Intractable Social Problem

I would soon learn that PDMPs were part of a sea change in how opioids were handled in the United States. They swept the nation at a time when prescription drug overdose rates soared, when drug overdose became the leading cause of accidental death, when deaths involving prescription opioids exceeded deaths from all other illicit drugs combined.[12] OxyContin had gone from wonder drug to public scourge and physicians were cast as the villains.[13] Against the backdrop of this mounting public health crisis, government officials searched desperately for ways to curb deaths in their communities, and the PDMP offered a solution.

The reasoning at the time was that reducing opioid prescribing would limit the number of drugs available for nonmedical use, which, in turn, would cut overdose death rates. To that end, states adopted PDMPs, surveillance technology that served two purposes: they helped healthcare providers monitor patients by providing them with comprehensive information about the medications patients received, and they helped law enforcement monitor providers by giving them prescribing and dispensing information. The thinking went that physicians and pharmacists would be less likely to prescribe and dispense opioids to patients who were "doctor shopping" or "pharmacy shopping" if they could spot that behavior in the PDMP. Meanwhile, law enforcement could use PDMP data to identify physicians and pharmacists who were prescribing and dispensing inordinate amounts of opioids and to locate "pill mills," shady operations where physicians sold prescriptions for cash.

PDMPs consist of aggregated pharmacy data. Pharmacists routinely submit information about all the controlled substances (not just opioids) they dispense. Controlled substances are a subset of drugs deemed medically useful but also prone to abuse[14] by the Federal Comprehensive Drug Abuse Prevention and Control Act of 1970, better known as the Controlled Substances Act (CSA). At one extreme are Schedule I drugs that include illegal drugs like marijuana[15] and heroin that, to the federal government, have no medical use and high abuse potential. At the other extreme are Schedule IV and Schedule V drugs, prescription drugs like Tramadol and Lyrica that the government classifies as having medical use and low abuse potential. In the middle are Schedule II and Schedule III drugs with medical use and high abuse potential; opioids fall in these categories along with stimulants like Ritalin and Adderall, barbiturates, and anabolic steroids.[16]

PDMPs are the product of a public–private partnership. They are situated in various state agencies such as boards of pharmacy, departments of public health, departments of justice, and consumer protection agencies.[17] In most states, these agencies collaborate with a private company called Bamboo Health[18] that compiles and analyzes PDMP data and gives it to the state. The state provides those data to healthcare providers and law enforcement. Bamboo's offerings include PMP AWARxE, the basic PDMP platform; NarxCare, a data analysis and visualization tool; PMP Gateway, which integrates the PDMP into electronic health records; and PMP InterConnect, which links PDMPs across states and territories, a system that currently includes fifty-one of fifty-four PDMPs across the country.[19]

PDMPs are expensive. They cost between $450,000 and $1.5 million to set up and between $125,000 and $1 million annually to maintain.[20] Knowing that limited state budgets were likely to impede expensive PDMP implementation, in 2003 the U.S. Department of Justice (DOJ) established the Harold Rogers

Prescription Drug Monitoring Grant Program. These grants, provided by the DOJ's Bureau of Justice Assistance and named for Kentucky Congressman Harold "Hal" Rogers, offer funds to states who wanted to create, implement, or enhance a PDMP, and they have been critical for PDMP expansion.[21]

Purdue Pharma also pitched in to help but did so a decade later after weathering expensive lawsuits. In 2011, the OxyContin manufacturer offered a $1 million grant to Florida to fund a statewide PDMP and another $1 million grant to the National Association of Boards of Pharmacy to support PMP InterConnect.[22] The rest of the money comes from state budgets. Public funds helped establish these programs and pay to maintain them, but states do not own the data. Bamboo does. And it is not easy to transfer the data to another system. States either foot the PDMP bill or risk losing their data.

PDMPs were new to me, but they were not new to law enforcement. New York created the first PDMP in 1918 and California has the oldest, continuously operating PDMP in the nation, developed in 1939 under the authority of the state's Bureau of Narcotic Enforcement.[23] However, today's PDMPs look almost nothing like their predecessors. For starters, the original PDMPs were paper, tracked only Schedule II controlled substances, and were used exclusively by law enforcement. Early PDMPs amassed data by gathering duplicate or triplicate forms that physicians were required to use to prescribe Schedule II drugs such as opioids. In states that required three copies, physicians, pharmacies, and the state each got one. In states that required two copies, they went to pharmacies and the state. The state agency that housed the PDMP entered the information into a database. Law enforcement used PDMP data to track prescribing patterns.[24] Like any paper-based system, early PDMPs—the beta versions—were clunky and difficult to analyze.

Fast-forward to the early 2000s. when PDMPs began to crop up across the country. These systems—PDMP 1.0—were far more sophisticated.[25] They were automated, not paper, so they could be easily sorted and analyzed. They were shared by healthcare and law enforcement, so they enabled two tiers of surveillance: providers could track patients and law enforcement could track patients and providers.

With all their bells and whistles, PDMPs were still clunky. Healthcare providers had to log on to the PDMP through a separate interface because it was not integrated into electronic healthcare records or into pharmacy records. This process consumed their already limited time. The PDMP interface was difficult to read, let alone use to make quick decisions about patient care. The data looked much like a Microsoft Excel spreadsheet with columns for prescriber, address, medication, volume, and so on that providers could use to sort the data. However, providers couldn't process PDMP information quickly enough for it to be useful. Nor could they be assured that they were using the same criteria to make prescribing and dispensing decisions each time, so the specter of bias against patients loomed large.

PDMP 2.0 helped to solve some of these problems. Branded "NarxCHECK,"[26] these systems that were implemented in the 2010s use algorithms to determine a "Narx Score" from 000 to 999. A higher score indicates that prescribing opioids to the patient is more likely to harm them.[27] Newer PDMPs also offer charts and graphs depicting the number of prescribers and the amount of opioids received.[28] PDMP 2.0 makes it fast and easy for healthcare providers to assess patients and determine whether to give them opioids. All PDMPs offer pull mechanisms—workers can fish around for information—but the best versions also offer push mechanisms that automatically analyze the data and flag heavy prescribers. This information is then reported to either law enforcement, the professional board, and/or the physician or pharmacist, depending on the state.[29]

Today, PDMP 3.0 is on the horizon. PDMPs in Kentucky and Wisconsin now contain drug arrest and conviction data so that healthcare providers can see whether a patient has been arrested for a drug crime before giving them opioids.[30] Bamboo has also expressed interest in incorporating data into the PDMP from systems as far-flung as the auto industry, banking, and real estate.[31]

PDMPs are evolving at a time when surveillance technology on the whole is getting better. Black box algorithms—recipes for sorting people and making decisions whose details are known only to their creators—fuel technologies that do everything from housing the homeless to policing citizens.[32] These technologies are certainly efficient, but their use raises concerns about fairness, justice, and transparency. Black box algorithms conceal their origins. A person who uses them cannot determine how decisions about placing people into one category or another or calculating a risk score was done. They must trust the algorithm to be accurate and fair. Too often, they are not.[33]

There is a common belief that numbers don't lie. Math exists outside the realm of human influence, which seemingly makes it more objective than other ways of measuring and sorting information. Decisions made using algorithms should be fairer than those made by human beings.[34] Consider the pharmacist who uses PDMP 1.0 to decide whether to dispense opioids to a patient. That pharmacist has to scan a spreadsheet, determine whether the patient's behavior is out of the ordinary, and make a decision in a few short minutes, all while hoping that they are treating patients equally and fairly.

Now, consider the pharmacist who uses PDMP 2.0. The algorithm has done the work for them. In seconds, the algorithm has calculated a risk score and charted the patient's record in comparison to others that the pharmacist can read at a glance. And the algorithm uses the same kind of information to create risk scores and charts for every patient, which should eliminate the biases to which pharmacists fall prey. That makes algorithmic decision-making superior to the choices that workers make unaided by technology, doesn't it?

Social scientists are not convinced. They remain skeptical that algorithms yield more fair, more transparent mechanisms for making decisions about people's lives. First, they note that technology does not replace discretion but rather shifts discretion to an earlier process. People decide how to train the algorithm and which variables to include, choices that are informed by people's biases about what matters.[35]

Second, they warn that algorithms can bake in discriminatory practices from the past. Most algorithms are trained on preexisting data. When those data are systematically biased—when they reflect racism, sexism, classism, and unconscious biases—the use of algorithmic technology reinforces rather than uproots inequality.[36]

Third, they point out that what workers who use algorithmic technology see is not you, but rather your "data double." Your data double is a portrait of you painted in digital traces, those bits of information gathered about us continuously as we go about our daily lives. Your data double includes information about where you have traveled, what websites you have visited, what purchases you have made, what services you have used, and so much more. Aggregated, they provide a picture of you, albeit a distorted and incomplete one.[37]

You have little to no power to fix a data double that is inaccurate. Unlike credit reports, much of the data private companies collect offer no mechanism for individuals to correct inaccuracies. This includes information like arrest records maintained by third-party websites such as mugshots.com and prescription data maintained by PDMPs. A data double tells a partial and sometimes misleading story about who you are. Therefore, using a data double to make decisions about a person's life—whether to give them opioids or offer them a job or a loan or an apartment—can result in discrimination.[38]

These problems are endemic to algorithmic technologies writ large, but PDMPs raise serious privacy concerns. Even though PDMP data come from healthcare, they lack the legal protections that shield healthcare data. The Health Insurance Portability and Accountability Act (HIPAA) restricts how healthcare providers and healthcare organizations use and share patient information. Yet PDMPs lie beyond HIPAA's reach. Legislatures and courts do not treat PDMP data as if they are healthcare data. Instead, they treat the data like trash . . . literally.

Consider how the third-party doctrine has been used to justify giving PDMP data to the DEA. Legal doctrines are frameworks that judges use to determine the outcome of a case. The third-party doctrine states that a person has no reasonable expectation of privacy with regards to information they have disclosed to a third-party, including items that they have discarded such a garbage. If you leave your trash out by the curb and someone goes through it, you have no recourse because you "abandoned" your trash. In high-profile PDMP cases in Utah and Oregon, the DEA claimed that the third-party doctrine applies to PDMP data. The argument goes that by giving prescription data to the pharmacist, the patient has "abandoned" their health information and it can therefore be used for any purpose (never mind that the patient has no other choice). Part of this hinges on the public–private partnership between states and Bamboo Health described earlier. PDMP data does not stay in the healthcare system. It goes to a private corporation that amasses and analyzes the information, so the DEA argues that once it leaves the healthcare system and goes to Bamboo, it is no longer patient data. By this reasoning, the DEA does not need a warrant to access PDMP data and doing so does not undermine a person's constitutionally protected right to be free from unreasonable searches as seizures as guaranteed under the Fourth Amendment.[39]

Legal scholars disagree. Indiana University law professor Jennifer Oliva contends that "DEA warrantless searches of PDMP prescribing information violate the Fourth Amendment." She says that the third-party doctrine does not apply because health information is extremely sensitive and revealing and because people do not share it voluntarily, conditions spelled out in the *Carpenter* decision that set limits on the third-party doctrine.[40] Northeastern law professor and public health scholar Leo Beletsky concurs. According to Beletsky, lack of privacy could deter the most vulnerable patients from seeking healthcare. In his opinion, "we should advocate that privacy protections be *expanded* to shield PDMP data from unfettered law enforcement access at state and federal levels."[41] As fights over PDMP data rage in the courts, the fact that there is even a fight to begin with suggests that PDMPs are particularly valuable to law enforcement.

By virtue of writing prescriptions, physicians permit themselves to be monitored by the PDMP. Unlike police officers who have developed strategies to resist being monitored—strategies like breaking off police car antennae and turning off body cameras—healthcare providers cannot easily handicap the tools that monitor them. Surveillance tools are too deeply integrated into their daily work. By virtue of filling prescriptions, pharmacists amass data that they are legally required to send to the PDMP. The alternatives—not writing or filling prescriptions—would bring healthcare to a grinding halt. Providers are stuck contributing to the very database that monitors them. Not that they mind. Providers appreciate PDMPs because they help with workflow and provide information not easily obtained elsewhere. However, providers overlook how PDMP use shifts their priorities from treatment to surveillance, from helping patients to policing them.

Electronically Policing Patients: A New Iteration of an Old Practice

I was surprised to find healthcare providers policing patients, but I should not have been. Policing socially disadvantaged patients was the norm long before PDMPs came along. The impetus to police patients comes from multiple sources, not the least of which is stigma. Patients who suffer from addiction, chronic pain, and other incompletely medicalized conditions fit uncomfortably into a healthcare system that was not designed to treat them, a healthcare system suffused with cultural narratives about bad life choices that render people with pain and addiction undeserving in providers' eyes.[42]

At the same time, pernicious tropes of the Cadillac-driving welfare fraud, the crack addict, the violent patient, and the unfit mother hound women, patients of color, and poor patients as they navigate a healthcare system largely controlled by upper-class white men. Poor women of color, in particular, have found themselves policed at an alarming rate, particularly if they struggle with substance use disorders.[43] Physicians have no qualms about reporting these women to social services or calling the police, bringing the full weight of the criminal justice system down on women they deem unfit to parent.[44]

No, policing patients is not new, and it did not start because of the PDMP. But policing patients does look different since the PDMP arrived on the scene. Two striking changes have occurred: (1) policing patients has gotten easier and more systematic, resulting in larger numbers of patients being policed; and (2) policing patients has come to be seen as a legitimate aspect of patient care, not an unusual behavior grounded in discrimination. In the first instance, PDMP implementation has made possible a form of dragnet surveillance that did not previously exist in the hospital, the clinic, or the pharmacy and, in the second instance, providers increasingly take for granted that policing patients is a core part of their job in a way that previously seemed foreign to them.

PDMPs provide a partial answer to a baffling question: How did policing become a fundamental component of patient care? The answer lies in skyrocketing overdose deaths, cultural trends toward punishment and digitization, increased capacity of law enforcement, and an ineffective healthcare system. Together, these forces supercharged healthcare criminalization by giving healthcare providers new tools to police, but not treat patients, and by surrounding them with cultural justifications for doing so.

Why would healthcare leaders embrace criminal justice surveillance technology? If the goal of healthcare is to heal, why implement a system whose main purpose is to surveil and enforce? Healthcare leaders are not alone in falling prey to the technology's seduction. When considered in light of broader social changes, PDMP adoption looks reasonable if not inevitable.

PDMPs appeared at the crest of two broad social trends: the punitive turn and the rise of the digital age. The hallmark of the punitive turn—a growing trend toward punishment in all areas of social life—began in the prison system. In the 1950s and 1960s, prisons were guided by philosophies of rehabilitation and reform. Political leaders believed that prisons could be sites for transforming criminals into productive citizens—indeed, they believed it was prisons' responsibility to do so. Prison leaders tried to achieve this goal by implementing education programs, job training, and counseling. Their strategy seemed to work. Prison rates remained relatively stable from the 1920s to the 1970s, with just over 100 incarcerated people for each 100,000 American residents.[45]

This success would prove short-lived, due in no small part to the War on Drugs.[46] Like Richard Nixon who declared a War on Drugs in 1971 while he dubbed illegal drugs "public enemy number one," Ronald Reagan declared a War on Drugs in 1982. But unlike Nixon, Reagan scrapped all efforts at rehabilitation and diverted funds to ramp up enforcement. Starting with the Anti-Drug Abuse Act of 1986, the Reagan administration instituted federal mandatory minimum sentences for cocaine distribution. They doubled down two years later by introducing new civil penalties for drug offenders such as eviction from public housing, denial of federal benefits such as student loans, and, more onerous, expanded the use of the death penalty for drug-related offenses. States followed suit by instituting "three-strikes" laws that imposed a life sentence on those convicted of a third drug offense.

Not only did the War on Drugs help to usher a "get tough on crime" attitude into American politics, but it was a thinly veiled attempt to stigmatize and control the Black population, one that complemented anti-welfare (read: anti-Black) policies of the 1980s.[47] Driven by the Republican Party's commitment to small government and deep skepticism of social programs, Reagan cut federal spending for anti-poverty programs such as food stamps and school lunch programs that had tripled under Nixon. He used the fabricated image of the Cadillac-driving "welfare queen" to justify gutting social programs.

It soon became evident that criminalizing drugs and the poor had bipartisan appeal. While campaigning for president, Bill Clinton "vowed that he would never permit any Republican to be perceived as tougher on crime than he."[48] Clinton simultaneously decimated welfare funds while radically expanding budgets for prisons and police. He transformed welfare by introducing "welfare-to-work" programs that required recipients to hold down jobs and limited the amount of aid families could receive. The policy empowered states to create even more restrictive requirements and permanently excluded those convicted of a felony drug offense, including marijuana possession.[49] Law professor Michelle Alexander observes that "Clinton escalated the drug war beyond what conservatives had imagined possible a decade earlier."[50]

Under Reagan, Bush, and Clinton, rehabilitative prison programs eroded as punishment became the de facto mission of the prison system.[51] Drug cases sent hundreds of thousands of people to prison each year, stretching prisons' resources beyond their capacity. In the thirty years from Reagan's first term to Clinton's last, the number of Americans incarcerated went from 300,000 to over 2 million.[52] Drug convictions drove most of this increase and helped to further exacerbate racial disparities in imprisonment.[53] Scholars call this process the "punitive turn," a time when U.S. policy doubled down on punishment at the expense of rehabilitation and care.[54]

Today, the United States has the highest incarceration rate in the world. Compared to other Organisation for Economic Co-operation and Development (OECD) countries,[55] the United States is literally off the charts, with 698 people imprisoned per 100,000, a rate five times higher than the runner up, the United Kingdom.[56] The racial impact of the War on Drugs is evidenced by the fact that 56 percent of the incarcerated population is Black or Latino, while these groups comprise only 32 percent of the population.[57]

But prison was not the only institution that moved punishment to the top of its agenda. Punitive logics escaped the prison system and made their way into public services such as education, welfare, housing, policing, and healthcare, eclipsing their missions and putting surveillance and punishment front and center.[58]

Cast in the warm glow of the dawn of the digital age, the punitive turn has taken on a new appearance. In our current moment—characterized by new technologies with unprecedented surveillance, analytic, and storage capacity—punishment has become woven into the fabric of the vast array of social institutions that use big data systems to track people.[59] These technologies promise to sort people into categories of deservingness—those deserving of resources and those deserving of punishment—and to do so seamlessly without the messy problems that plague human decision-making.

One can almost believe that big data algorithms can eradicate inequality by substituting digital tools for human decision-makers, but only if one ignores the fact that technology itself is a social product, one fashioned by human decisions about what data to collect, how to collect it, and what thresholds separate the deserving from the undeserving.[60] Yet leaders in fields as wide-ranging as finance, housing, welfare, law enforcement, and healthcare seem to believe that big data algorithms provide substantial benefit given that they have rushed to implement big data surveillance technology into their work.[61] The fact that leaders know little about the algorithms themselves does nothing to dampen their enthusiasm.

From our current vantage point, on the crest of the punitive turn, at the dawn of the digital age, PDMPs are not an anomaly, but a product of trends toward punishment and automation that have impacted social institutions writ large. PDMPs did not come out of nowhere; they are part of a broader zeitgeist that considers punishment the best approach to social problems and that vaunts technology as the best way to identify the punishable.

Emphasis on punishment and algorithms has collectively paved the way for the punitive strategies enlisted to combat today's opioid crisis, particularly states' widespread adoption of PDMPs. More proximate trends also spurred PDMP use. Enforcement agents had begun to zero in on healthcare providers who handed out opioids as if they were candy, and healthcare lacked the tools necessary to stop overdose.

Managing Uncertainty under Law Enforcement's Gaze

Healthcare providers face significant uncertainty about opioids. It comes in two varieties: uncertainty about law and uncertainty about clients. Struggles to follow the law and struggles to decide which patients really need opioids go hand in hand.

The same law that schedules controlled substances—the Controlled Substances Act (CSA)—sets legal standards for physicians and pharmacists. The law requires physicians to prescribe "in good faith" meaning for a legitimate medical condition for a patient with whom they have a formal relationship. It assigns pharmacists a "corresponding responsibility" to avoid "knowingly" dispensing drugs to a patient who is addicted or diverting. It all but prohibits physicians from dispensing drugs to people with substance use disorders.[62] State medical and pharmacy practice acts typically mirror the federal statute.

However, the law is not as clear as it seems at first glance. The terms "good faith," "legitimate medical purpose," and "knowingly" are ambiguous.[63] Judges and healthcare providers have interpreted these terms unevenly, sparking heated political and scholarly debate.[64] Compounding the lack of legal clarity is the fact that providers have been legally charged for both overproviding and underproviding controlled substances. Providers must walk a legal tightrope as they make consequential decisions—for their patients and themselves.[65]

Not only is formal law ambiguous, but the true test of law is how providers interpret, make, and deploy law in daily practice. Socio-legal scholars tell us that law is not simply dictates that workers follow, but that workers have a hand in creating law as they make decisions in the day to day. This results in a gap between the "law-on-the-books" or formal, written law, and "the law-in-action" or law as it is constructed in daily practice.[66] What passes for law in work settings may be unrecognizable to those who created it.

The interaction between workers and clients is where law truly comes to life, but uncertainty looms over these interactions. Healthcare providers are unsure about the roles they should play and the kinds of patients they should care for. Healthcare providers are supposed to be *medical gatekeepers*. That is, they are supposed to use science and patient information to make diagnostic and treatment decisions. At the same time, healthcare providers are supposed to be *legal gatekeepers*. That is, they are supposed to follow the law as they make decisions about patient care.[67] In an ideal world where law was clear and information about patients complete, decisions would be a breeze. In real life, they are not.

Three kinds of patients show up at clinics, hospitals, and pharmacies seeking opioids: patients in pain, patients with opioid use disorders, and patients who sell opioids illegally. Many are some combination of the three.[68] Healthcare providers can only legally provide opioids to pain patients,[69] but they have a difficult time distinguishing those patients from the other two. In the first place, pain is subjective. It cannot be measured with an X-ray, a blood test, or an MRI, so the provider has to trust that the patient is telling the truth.[70] At the same time, patients with opioid use disorders and patients who sell opioids are motivated to invent physical pain to avoid the horrors of withdrawal or to turn a profit. If patients either can't or won't tell providers the truth, how can providers possibly determine the appropriate course of action? Pharmacists are at a particular disadvantage because they don't know the patient's diagnosis, so they are stuck trying to evaluate a prescription's legitimacy with very little to go on. Still, they have to make a decision knowing that law enforcement can punish them for making the wrong one.

What happens to physicians and pharmacists who fall off the tightrope, who fail to perfectly balance their medical and legal gatekeeping roles? They face dire consequences. A single misstep could mean (1) losing their ability to prescribe or dispense controlled substances if the DEA yanks their registration; (2) losing their ability to bill Medicare and Medicaid if fraud agencies restrict their National Provider Identifier[71]; (3) losing their capacity to practice medicine or pharmacy if the state board revokes their license; and/or (4) losing their freedom if they are criminally sentenced for dealing drugs. Unlike the safety net designed to rebound tightrope walkers, the net of punitive consequences traps providers like fish caught in a net.

Antonio, a New Jersey lawyer, is all too familiar with this scenario. He defends pharmacists who are brought before the DEA, the Board of Pharmacy, Medicare, and Medicaid with their licenses and livelihoods on the line. According to Antonio, "The loss of your license is the big issue. Because if you lose your DEA license at a federal level, the state will take away your state DEA license. When you lose your state DEA license, every third-party provider of Medicaid and Medicare will not allow you to participate in their network. So you'll lose all that business. And it's very likely if you lose your DEA license, then the Board of Pharmacy will come in and take away your regular license and your store license. So it'll become a house of cards and you'll basically lose everything."

Pharmacists also suffer financial loss when the government claws back funds they paid out for medications dispensed illegally. Antonio describes it this way: "Medicaid or Medicare will come back and reclaim all the money for all the prescriptions that they paid you for, even though you dispensed them. But if it turns out they were dispensed for a nonlegitimate medical purpose, they're no longer a valid prescription, so Medicaid, Medicare, and all the third-party payers will take back all that money." For pharmacists stripped of their licenses and plunged into debt, "these cases become a multiple nightmare."

Healthcare's New Normal

If it wasn't enough for healthcare providers to practice in a stricter, more threatening legal environment under the watchful gaze of law enforcement, they have also begun to practice in a new healthcare environment, one transformed by the glaring spotlight of blame shone on healthcare providers for fueling the opioid crisis. Physicians and pharmacists had to do something. Peering into their healthcare toolkits, they found the wrong tools for the job. Pressure to resolve an enormous social problem motivated them to search elsewhere. They found what they were looking for in an unlikely place, a law enforcement surveillance technology. Little did they know, this technology would not solve their problems, but rather create more. At the time, though, PDMPs seemed like perfectly reasonable remedies to complex social ailments, so healthcare leaders latched on and held tight.

The opioid crisis took root in a healthcare system plagued by meager resources to treat addiction and chronic pain, rampant fragmentation, and persistent power struggles. Not only that, norms about opioid provision are inscrutable and constantly changing. These realities primed healthcare to adopt law enforcement technology and, with it, punitive logics that undermine care.

The U.S. healthcare system excels at many things, but when it comes to addiction and chronic pain, it flounders. Medical schools overwhelmingly fail to train students on either condition despite the fact that 20.5 percent of Americans have chronic pain[72] and 7.4 percent of Americans have a substance use disorder.[73] Most U.S. medical schools do not offer a single class on pain (80 percent) or addiction (92 percent).[74] A handful (less than 4 percent) require a pain course, and a few more (16 percent) offer a pain course as an elective.[75] Advanced training is also limited. There are only 55 addiction medicine fellowships and 100 pain medicine fellowships in the United States, a number that pales in comparison to other fellowships. To put those numbers in perspective, there are 235 fellowships in sports medicine, 258 in general surgery, and 1,445 in pediatrics.[76]

You read that right. Lucky physicians receive a single class, in four years of medical school, for conditions that afflict millions of Americans. Most receive none at all. This leaves physicians poorly equipped to diagnose and treat two exceedingly common conditions and helps explain why opioid prescribing became so popular.

Physicians are problem-solvers. They like to figure out why someone is hurting and help them get better. The journey from diagnosis to treatment is a short one for many medical conditions. People with bacterial infections need antibiotics. People with viral infections need anti-virals. People with diabetes need insulin. People with a broken leg need their leg cast. This is, of course, a gross oversimplification, but it does capture quite a bit of medical practice and it throws the treatment of addiction and chronic pain into sharp relief.

Addiction and chronic pain are both persistent, relapsing conditions. Their root causes vary and many of the most effective treatments lie beyond physicians' reach. Addiction is particularly difficult to diagnose and treat because it often arises out of trauma and co-occurs with other mental health conditions such as depression, anxiety, attention-deficit and hyperactivity disorder, bipolar disorder, schizophrenia, and personality disorders.[77] Meanwhile, standard tools in physicians' toolkits such as X-rays, blood tests, and MRIs do little to pinpoint the origins of chronic pain.[78]

Some of the most effective treatments for addiction and chronic pain are housed in organizations far afield of mainstream medicine. For example, methadone, one of the most effective treatments for opioid use disorders, is available only in methadone clinics that are disconnected from other hospitals and clinics. The isolation of these clinics is a result of the policies that originally established methadone as a treatment for heroin after World War II. Similarly, alternative treatments for chronic pain such as cognitive behavioral therapy, chiropractic, and massage are provided by practitioners who work separately from their mainstream medicine counterparts.

Physicians in mainstream settings generally have two choices for treating chronic pain: drugs such as pain medications and muscle relaxants, and surgery. As a result, their capacity to treat chronic pain is severely restricted. The lack of alternatives helps to explain why opioids became so popular—physicians could prescribe opioids to treat pain and, if they weren't enough, could increase the dose. Pharmaceutical reps and physician thought leaders taught doctors that there was no such thing as prescribing too many opioids to treat pain and that people in pain were at low risk of getting hooked.[79]

Physicians have more options when it comes to treating addiction. At the time of my interviews, they could do a little extra training (about four hours' worth) to get an X-waiver, a special addendum to their DEA registration. They could complete the training online or in person to obtain a certificate that they would submit to the federal government. The X-waiver allowed them to prescribe opioids like buprenorphine to treat opioid use disorders. However, less than 10 percent of primary care providers chose to obtain one.[80] As of January 2023, the X-waiver is no longer required to prescribe buprenorphine, but it is not yet clear how this change will affect the number of physicians who provide it.

Without the proper tools to treat addiction and chronic pain, patients suffer. When they return to their physicians still complaining of pain or still using drugs, physicians feel frustrated. They are there to help, but their efforts keep failing. In those circumstances, it is easy to project frustration onto the patient. They assume that the patient doesn't want to get better or is using them to get opioids. These negative views of patients as "malingerers" or "manipulators" helps to breed stigma about chronic pain and addiction and compounds other stigmas grounded in race, class, and gender biases.[81] Add to that the fact that physicians have very little time with patients, nowhere near enough time to explore the root causes of long-lasting conditions, and it is easy to see why physicians are so eager to get rid of these patients. It is far easier to fire the patient than to try to fix medicine's shortcomings.

Pharmacists must make decisions even faster than physicians. Busy pharmacies dispense hundreds of prescriptions a day, which translates to roughly one every three to four minutes. Pharmacies are chronically understaffed and overburdened, continuously required to do more with less. Pharmacists must follow the law and appease their employers, a difficult task. The law urges them to be cautious, to check every prescription carefully. Employers urge them to dispense prescriptions as quickly as possible. Figuring out why a patient needs opioids takes longer than four minutes, especially given that pharmacists lack patient information. Before the PDMP, they could get information only by calling physicians, talking to the patient, calling other pharmacies, or contacting the insurance company. All of this takes time that pharmacists do not have.[82]

Meanwhile, pharmacists exhibit the same biases physicians do against people with addiction and chronic pain. They are on the lookout for "drug seekers" and "pharmacy shoppers," who might dupe them into giving out opioids for nonmedical purposes. It is not just pills that concern them. They don't want people who use drugs in their store. They are wary of patients who could inject heroin in their bathrooms and leave unsanitary syringes around that could harm others. From the pharmacist's perspective, these patients take time away from their "real" patients.

Like physicians, pharmacists have very few tools to treat chronic pain and addiction. They can choose to dispense the pain medications that physicians prescribe. However, many pharmacies do not carry buprenorphine or Suboxone, medications that physicians with an X-waiver prescribe for opioid use disorders.[83] And many pharmacists refuse to sell syringes to patients who do not have a prescription for an injectable medication like insulin.[84] Research shows that sterile syringes prevent the spread of diseases like HIV/AIDS and hepatitis C among people who use drugs, which makes them an important harm reduction resource.[85] However, some pharmacists fear that selling syringes enables drug use. This leaves pharmacists in a position to tell patients "no," something that might lead to a heated discussion or an altercation that, again, robs them of time. Without the resources to treat pain and addiction, U.S. healthcare providers have received hefty criticism from journalists, policy makers, and the public for harming those in pain and driving up rates of overdose.

One reason that physicians are blamed for the overdose crisis is because they doled out an astounding number of opioids. There were some bad actors, to be sure, such as those who ran pill mills or traded drugs for sex. But for the most part, what appears to be carelessness or callousness on the part of physicians is in fact an indictment of the healthcare system. The U.S. healthcare system is so fragmented that poor communication is the norm rather than the exception. Each physician keeps their own set of records, and physicians who see the same patient rarely communicate with each other unless they work for the same healthcare system and share an electronic health record. On the whole, physicians do not know how other physicians are treating their patients (or even *that* they are treating them), and they have no reason to know that other physicians are prescribing opioids. Proprietary software used by labs, clinics, hospitals, and pharmacies gums up communication between them, and electronic healthcare records have reinforced walls between providers at different locations instead of dismantling them.[86]

Consider what happens when a patient overdoses and is brought to the emergency department. In most cases, that overdose is never reported to the primary care physician, so the physician might continue to prescribe opioids without realizing the patient is at risk.[87] Of course, that assumes that the patient has a primary care physician. Many do not. At the same time, emergency medicine physicians rarely receive information about the patient from other physicians.

Luke, an emergency medicine physician in Kansas City told me, "There's no interlinking between primary care, ER, pharmacies." He doesn't have access to notes from primary care physicians in his hospital, let alone those outside his system. "There's a bunch of general practitioners throughout the entire KC area and there's like maybe 10 percent of them that we have any access to their notes and they have access to ours."

As a result, he says, "We fly blind. I mean, we have no idea what the patient has been doing or seeing. If I really want to track down the truth, I have to get ahold of that specific doctor and then they might be off. It might be nighttime, so their clinic's closed. Or they might be in surgery and they might not be having clinic. And then if you do get ahold of them, who knows whether or not they'll remember that patient? It makes it very tough." Luke is not alone. A nationwide study found that 91 percent of patients continued to receive opioids after they had overdosed.[88] Poor communication is at least partly to blame.

A related problem is that most emergency departments do not have a way to help patients with opioid use disorders get treatment. They might revive a patient with naloxone, monitor them, or help them begin to detox, but they rarely provide the most effective treatments for opioid use disorder—medications like buprenorphine and methadone—and they have no systematic way to refer patients to care.[89] Again, fragmentation is the culprit. The mental health system is cordoned off from the traditional healthcare system and tends to be expensive and difficult to access.[90] Without established lines of communication between emergency medicine physicians and addiction specialists, and without adequate insurance to cover treatment, patients who overdose get caught in a vicious cycle—they leave the hospital only to overdose again.

Pharmacists face similar communication difficulties because they, too, are separated from other parts of the healthcare system. However, their difficulties are compounded by insufficient patient information and power struggles with physicians who push them to the bottom of the professional hierarchy. This subordinated position makes it hard for pharmacists to follow the law.

Recall that the CSA requires physicians to prescribe in good faith and assigns pharmacists a corresponding responsibility to ensure that the prescription is legitimate. The CSA provides checks and balances by making physicians and pharmacists gatekeepers to controlled substances. At the same time, the CSA makes pharmacists gatekeepers to physicians. They are responsible for ensuring that physicians are prescribing opioids legally.

Pharmacists' role as gatekeeper clashes with their low position in the interprofessional hierarchy. They lack critical information that they need to make decisions about opioids. Pharmacists do not have access to patient charts, so they don't know the diagnosis or the treatment plan. They don't know what other remedies the patient has tried and failed. Much of this information needs to be obtained from the physician. Yet, when pharmacists reach out for additional information, they often receive pushback from physicians who are sensitive to having their power questioned, especially from a subordinate like a pharmacist.

Anthony, the San Francisco chain pharmacist described earlier, said he faced a lot of resistance from physicians when he first started using the PDMP. He described one especially bad encounter. "There was this one doctor that was kind of rude to me, and he was like, 'I don't see why you need to know this—I'm just going to send my patients to another pharmacy.' And I was like, 'okay.' Because it frustrated me that some providers just see us as dispensing pharmacists, and why do we care why a patient's on [a drug]? 'I wrote the prescription, you should dispense it,' pretty much was the attitude that I got. But at the same time, I'm a healthcare practitioner too, so it's a little bit frustrating."

Pharmacists find themselves in a bind: they cannot easily fulfill their legal obligation without accessing information that physicians tend to withhold. That is if they can reach the physician at all. Carter works for a pharmacy in a big box store in Kansas City. He describes what happens when he tries to get in touch with a physician to question a prescription. "You have to make a phone call and hope that you get someone agreeable enough to talk. Everyone's busy and probably not enough prescribers consider pharmacists as an equal or part of the healthcare system that deserves their time. And doctors work in an environment where they're not questioned for the most part. So any questions feel like an affront to their authority." He usually gets a nurse instead. "Like one out of twenty times do you ever actually talk to a doctor." And the nurse will say, "This is what the doctor wants."

Part of PDMPs' appeal lies in how they improve access to information, upset power dynamics, and serve as robust tools where resources are scarce. Physicians and pharmacists like PDMPs because they help them categorize patients more effectively and efficiently while also helping them obey the law and please their employers. Bear in mind that providers don't opt for law enforcement tools while discarding healthcare tools. The lack of healthcare tools is what makes enforcement tools like the PDMP attractive.

Changing Healthcare Norms

Another factor that has enhanced PDMPs' allure is shifting norms around opioid provision. In the late 1990s, everyone from thought leaders to government agencies to pharmaceutical reps encouraged physicians to prescribe liberally with no regard for patient consequences which, they assured doctors, were minimal.[91] PDMPs became popular in the mid-2000s at a time when physicians were pressured to exercise caution when prescribing opioids. The rules of the game had changed dramatically from those just a decade earlier.

Government agencies helped to spur liberal prescribing practices and to stop them. Key policies bookend the liberal and conservative prescribing eras. In the late 1990s, Veterans Affairs and the Joint Commission[92] required physicians to treat pain as the "fifth vital sign," as essential to human health as body temperature, pulse rate, respiration rate, and blood pressure. They got physicians on board by linking pain treatment to reimbursement rates—hospitals where doctors failed to treat pain adequately received less money than those that succeeded.[93] In 2016, the Centers for Disease Control and Prevention (CDC) released the "CDC Guideline for Prescribing Opioids for Chronic Pain," which discouraged overprescribing and set parameters around pain treatment.[94]

The CDC guidelines recommended that physicians check the PDMP, annually test their patients' urine for illicit drugs, prescribe for short durations for chronic pain, and avoid prescribing at or above 90 morphine milligram equivalents (MME) for new patients.[95] Some providers were enthusiastic to receive official guidance around opioid treatment, but many providers, activists, and scholars pushed back.

Critics worried that legislatures, insurance companies, pharmacy chains, pharmacy benefit managers, and law enforcement were interpreting the guidelines as law. Shielding themselves behind the CDC guidelines, these entities limited the number of days a physician could prescribe opioids for acute pain, used standards designed for new patients to limit opioid prescribing for existing patients, and used prescribing rates over the recommended amount to criminally target physicians.[96] The guidelines, critics claimed, motivated physicians to rapidly taper patients on high doses of opioids down to 90 MME, sometimes with deadly consequences.[97] They undermined physicians' ethical duty to "do no harm."[98] Still, the guidelines remained a powerful force shaping opioid provision for years to come.

Even before the CDC issued its guidelines, pharmacies, drug companies, and drug distributors could sense the tides turning. Major lawsuits against Purdue Pharma, Walgreens, and Cardinal Health culminated in settlements that reached $600 million, $80 million,[99] and $34 million,[100] respectively. Shortly after the settlement, Walgreens adopted a "good faith dispensing program," the name a riff on the good faith prescribing requirement spelled out in the CSA. The controversial policy required pharmacists to call physicians to request additional information such as the diagnosis, duration of treatment, and previous failed remedies before dispensing opioids. It met with swift backlash from physicians, who viewed pharmacists' requests as intrusions into medical practice.[101]

Healthcare leaders sought shelter from the onslaught of lawsuits peppering their industry. The CDC guidelines promised refuge. Hospitals and clinics took the CDC guidelines as gospel and rushed to integrate them into policy and practice. Opioid stewardship programs designed to closely monitor opioids cropped up in hospitals nationwide, and hospitals and clinics began to issue reports that compared physicians' opioid prescribing rates to those of their peers.[102] As critics feared, physicians began to taper patients on opioids down to 90 MME (the highest rate the CDC endorsed) and below, even for patients who were well-managed on high doses.[103] Policies that required physicians to check the PDMP before prescribing opioids grew in popularity. Emergency departments proudly declared themselves "opioid-free."[104] Many hospitals incorporated PDMPs into their electronic health records.[105] Pharmacies—less focused on the CDC guidelines than hospitals and clinics but equally concerned about lawsuits—also urged pharmacists to exercise caution when dispensing opioids and pressured them to use PDMPs.[106]

Of course, the CDC guidelines were true to name—they were guidelines, not laws—and the CDC had no formal power to sanction organizations that refused to comply. However, even guidelines can take on undue power when adopted in an enforcement environment rife with uncertainty. PDMPs offered a way to navigate volatile norms and shifting requirements, but PDMPs came with their own set of challenges.

PDMPs as Trojan Horse Technologies

PDMPs transport punitive logics into healthcare. Two linked processes make this happen. First, PDMP use helps law enforcement get better at targeting healthcare providers. Second, healthcare providers use PDMPs to avoid law enforcement scrutiny and, in the process, start to morph into police. In other words, the *extension* of law enforcement capacity prompts the *transformation* of healthcare fields into hybrid spaces oriented toward both treatment and enforcement. Context matters. Where technology is implemented shapes how it is used. That explains why we see such different PDMP uses in law enforcement and healthcare.

The looming threat of arrest raises the stakes for overprescribing and over-dispensing opioids. In response, physicians and pharmacists have become hypervigilant and use the PDMP to protect themselves from enforcement agents who have become more efficient and more skilled. Healthcare providers don't fully embody enforcement; they don't put on a badge. Instead, they embrace policing tasks but reframe those tasks as healthcare duties. They now consider surveillance, profiling, and punishment part of their jobs. PDMP use helps them to perform these tasks and to justify doing so.

The technology alone does not set this process in motion. The changes we see are only possible because of the legal and medical landscape in which the PDMP is implemented—one characterized by enormous pressure to address a mounting crisis paired with inadequate tools to do so. Against this backdrop, PDMPs have massive appeal because they promise to resolve problems that have no easy answer.

This all might seem a bit abstract. It is easier to understand if we view it through the lens of a metaphor—that of the Trojan horse. Written over two millennia ago, Virgil's *The Aeneid* remains relevant today. On the eve of their victory celebration, the Trojans were surprised to find a generous gift waiting outside their city walls—an enormous wooden horse. "How delightful!" the Trojans thought. They were horse people, so this gift was the perfect symbol to commemorate their military prowess.

As the Trojans wheeled the horse into the city center, they had no idea that hidden inside were Greeks who planned to kill them. When night fell, the Greeks leapt from the horse and slaughtered the Trojans, bringing an end to the war and felling the Trojan civilization. This legendary tale reveals subterfuge at its best.

The Trojan horse remains a cultural touchstone, as relevant now as it was two thousand years ago. Why do we keep telling ourselves this story? We rehearse this tale as a reminder to keep ourselves safe, to protect our cities and other precious things from obliteration. The story ends well for the Greeks but badly for the Trojans, who lost their entire civilization because they couldn't imagine the horse as anything other than what it appeared to be.

In a similar way, reorganizing healthcare to reflect the values and advance the goals of law enforcement threatens to obliterate healthcare as we know it. The Greeks and the Trojans came from different cultures and battled over whose version of civilization would prevail. The fields of healthcare and law enforcement have different goals, values, practices, and "logics," or ways of making sense of the world. These fields fight over whether problems society faces should be categorized as medical or criminal and dealt with by treatment or punishment. Problems deemed medical belong to healthcare, while problems deemed criminal belong to law enforcement. Often, the same problem receives different designations over time—alcoholism, HIV/AIDS, and childhood deviance have all been treated as both "sickness" and "badness."[107] Whether a problem is medicalized or criminalized reflects the power of a field and the actors within it to impose their worldview on society.

When it comes to the opioid crisis, these two powerful fields are at an impasse: Healthcare wields treatment logics and tools, and law enforcement wields punitive logics and tools. Both are hungry to gobble up the social problems that lie in their path and both enjoy cultural power and vast resources, which makes them worthy opponents. Though each field was initially hesitant to tackle the problem, now they jockey for control. But the opioid crisis is too big for a single field to handle alone, so they have each gotten a foothold on the problem and staked their claim. They don't want to cede power, but that doesn't stop them from trying to pull workers from the other field into their territory.

Healthcare has attempted to convince law enforcement to engage in healthcare work, and has succeeded on some fronts. Some police chiefs now concede that addiction is a disease and declare, "We can't arrest our way out of this problem." Police in many cities now carry naloxone, an opioid overdose antidote, which they can administer to save lives. Some prisons and jails now provide medications for addiction treatment, medications like buprenorphine and Suboxone that stabilize people with opioid use disorders. Police have even taken their own initiative to connect people to treatment through programs like the Law Enforcement Assisted Diversion (LEAD) program and Police Assisted Addiction and Recovery Initiative (PAARI). People who use drugs go to police stations, surrender their drugs, and instead of being arrested, get immediately referred to treatment, or they opt for treatment after arrest. Criminal justice has also conceded to healthcare by offering diversion programs such as drug courts that provide people with substance use disorders an alternative to jail.[108]

Even if law enforcement engages in healthcare practices, it does so without fully relinquishing power. Police-based naloxone provision programs put a life-saving drug in the hands of police officers instead of the general public. Addiction treatment in prison requires people to be arrested and convicted before they can get access to care. Police-assisted recovery programs require people to seek help from law enforcement when they are at their most vulnerable. Drug courts leave it up to judges, not doctors, to determine whether someone has sufficiently recovered. Law enforcement can have its cake and eat it too—it can reframe addiction as a disease while still positioning enforcement agents as the best workers for the job.[109]

Law enforcement has used a different tack to entice healthcare, a far more covert and successful one. Instead of trying to convince healthcare providers to police patients, law enforcement made them a gift. It was a technological tool designed to help them root out patients misusing medication. Providers who used this tool—the PDMP—to track patients could rest assured that they were making the right decisions, following the law, and warding off enforcement action.

Much like the wooden horse appealed to the horse-loving Trojans, healthcare providers, too, were enamored by the shape of the gift. It arrived at a time when electronic health records (EHRs) had become standard fare and when monitoring patients electronically and sharing information with other providers was taken for granted, not contested as it was when EHRs first entered the scene.[110] To add icing to the cake, EHRs were expensive and PDMPs were free (at least initially). Through this generous offering, law enforcement agents wooed healthcare administrators, who marched their gift into healthcare spaces and pressured healthcare providers to use it.

What healthcare administrators did not realize was that embedded within this technology lay enforcement logics that were at odds with healthcare's core goal of treatment. When legislatures rapidly began adopting PDMPs in the mid-aughts, the prevailing narrative was that PDMPs were both enforcement tools and healthcare tools, but this was not entirely accurate. PDMPs are fundamentally enforcement tools that have been implemented in healthcare settings. This has been true since their inception. PDMPs do nothing to diagnose or treat disease. They are surveillance technologies through and through.

For law enforcement—whose logics are embedded within the PDMP Trojan horse—the goal is not to murder, but to co-opt. Healthcare providers wield untapped enforcement potential as they interact with potential criminals every day. The PDMP provides a way for law enforcement to harness healthcare's potential and, in doing so, overcome one of their own shortcomings—the tendency to respond to crime reactively instead of proactively.[111]

Most investigative strategies are reactive. Tip line calls prompt investigations only after bad doctors have done irreparable damage to unsuspecting communities. According to a California sheriff's deputy, one Florida doctor put "90 million Vicodin on the street in three years' time," hundreds of thousands of which surfaced in Southern California, where officers tried in vain to get pills back in their bottles and off the streets. A sheriff in a nearby department equates this work with leaving the door to the bank vault open all night and then spending the next morning trying to figure out who took the money.

By contrast, healthcare providers can be proactive. They can use the PDMP to surveil every patient who walks in the door and alert officers to suspicious behavior. Meanwhile, law enforcement can use the PDMP to identify bad providers because it tracks every controlled substance prescription they prescribe or dispense. Co-opting healthcare extends law enforcement's reach without taxing its budget.

Not everyone has embraced the PDMP. Primary opposition came from the American Civil Liberties Union (ACLU), whose lawyers argued that PDMPs impinged on patients' privacy rights. They sued the DEA in Oregon, Utah, and New Hampshire, to prevent the DEA from obtaining private health information without a warrant, effectively casting their spear against the horse.[112] But their warnings went unheeded. Nevertheless, the PDMP's true colors have begun to shine through as it helps to usher healthcare providers into law enforcement territory.

Healthcare providers who use the PDMP have begun to think and act differently. They endure pressure from lawmakers, employers, and law enforcement to closely monitor patients and restrict opioid provision, but primarily see themselves as healthcare providers who should care for patients. Pulled in two directions, healthcare providers experience a fundamental tension between treating and policing patients. This tension calls into question what kind of work they should do, whom they should align themselves with, and even who they are. They begin to resolve this tension as they use PDMPs in daily practice. Routine use of this technology teaches them that policing is normal and necessary. Where once they felt conflicted about policing patients, they now consider policing central to their work. Even more insidious, they now think that policing patients constitutes treatment.

To put the metaphor in the starkest possible terms, healthcare is the Trojans, law enforcement is the Greeks. The PDMP is the Trojan horse, embedded with enforcement logics. These logics creep out slowly as healthcare providers use the PDMP on a regular basis. The technology, paired with legal, cultural, and organizational pressures, results in a reorientation of healthcare work away from treatment and toward punishment. These changes have a profound impact on patient care.

The Trojan horse is a useful metaphor for understanding how PDMP use extends enforcement reach and transforms healthcare practice. The value of envisioning PDMPs as Trojan horse technologies will become evident as we investigate what workers on the frontlines of enforcement and care do while fighting the biggest drug crisis the United States has ever seen. To get there, we must journey behind the pharmacy counter, into the hospital and clinic, and gain special admission to some of the most powerful enforcement agencies in America. We begin with law enforcement to find out how they decide which providers to target and how the PDMP helps them do so.

3

White Coat Crime

SHE MURDERED HER PATIENTS. At least, that's what the prosecutors said. All it took to get powerful opioids from California internist Lisa Tseng (figure 3.1) was a brief conversation. No X-rays. No lab tests. No medical exam. Video surveillance shows an undercover officer posing as a patient who asks Dr. Tseng for methadone (an opioid) and Xanax (an anti-anxiety medication), drugs that can form a deadly cocktail when combined. He tells her that he is in recovery and takes the drugs at night with alcohol to "take the edge off." He makes clear that he is not in pain and does not plan to use the medications to treat a medical condition. Tseng writes the prescription—after the agent hands over $75 cash.[1]

Did she know what she was doing was wrong? Tseng received desperate calls from patients' family and friends concerned that their loved ones were hooked on the meds she prescribed.[2] She did not stop. Coroners and law enforcement agents called Dr. Tseng each time a patient died—fourteen in total.[3] She did not stop. Perhaps she thought the financial perks outweighed the risks. Dr. Tseng's reckless prescribing raked in $3,000 a day and exceeded $5 million in three years.

Dr. Tseng's prescribing spree ended in 2015, when a jury convicted her of three counts of second-degree murder.[4] In 2016, Superior Court Judge George G. Lomeli imposed a prison sentence of thirty years to life in prison. The trial lasted eight weeks. It included seventy-seven witnesses and 250 pieces of evidence. Families of overdose victims praised the judge's decision and concluded that "justice has been served."[5]

Dr. Tseng was the first California physician ever convicted of murder for overprescribing opioids and one of the first in the United States (figures 3.1 to 3.4). Her case was a turning point for law enforcement because it created a playbook for subsequent prosecutions and because it sent a clear signal to physicians across the nation: *you* could be next. "The message this case sends

FIGURE 3.1. Dr. Lisa Tseng. Osteopath. Rowland Heights, California. 3 counts of second-degree murder. 30 years to life in prison. *Source*: Photo by MediaNews Group / The Riverside Press-Enterprise via Getty Images.

FIGURE 3.2. Dr. Rolando Lodevico Atiga, Internal Medicine. Glendora, California. Multiple counts of unlawful prescription of a controlled substance. Never stood trial. *Source*: Photo by Liz O. Baylen / Los Angeles Times via Getty Images.

FIGURE 3.3. Dr. Xiulu Ruan. Pain Management. Mobile, Alabama. 7 counts of conspiracy. 21 years in prison. *Source*: Photo by jmartinie courtesy of Wikimedia Commons.

FIGURE 3.4. Dr. Stephen Schneider. Pain Medicine. Wichita, Kansas. 21 counts of conspiracy, fraud, unlawful distribution. 30 years in prison. *Source*: Photo courtesy of Alamy.

is you can't hide behind a white lab coat and commit crimes," declared Deputy District Attorney John Niedermann. "A lab coat and stethoscope are no shield." Medical experts warned that Tseng's case could scare physicians away from prescribing opioids and leave chronic pain patients to suffer without care.[6]

Doctors are hard to investigate and even harder to prosecute. It is difficult for judges and juries to wrap their minds around the idea that physicians perpetrate crime. The image of the "dirty doctor" sits uncomfortably with the popular image of "doctor as savior." And many overdoses involve multiple drugs, making it hard to pin a death on a single drug or a single doctor.[7] Still, over the past decade, judges and juries have put physicians behind bars. Law enforcement arrests scores of physicians for opioid crimes each year. They charge physicians with the same counts as illicit drug dealers: fraud, unlawful distribution, racketeering, manslaughter, and murder.[8] Doctors are legally required to keep extensive records that investigators use to prove criminal activity. Physicians who avoid arrest still face steep penalties such as losing their medical license, losing the ability to prescribe controlled substances, or paying a hefty fine.

It was not always this way. As early as the mid-1990s, evidence showed that physicians were generously doling out opioids, but the first murder conviction did not occur until 2016.[9] What happened over those twenty years that unleashed prosecutors' power and helped them win cases against providers? The answer lies in organizational change, education, and technological innovation. New organizations centered on criminal healthcare providers cropped up, enforcement agents came together to share strategies, and PDMPs spread across the country which made targeting physicians a far easier task.

To understand how this happened, we need to go *inside* law enforcement agencies. We need to hear about their struggles firsthand to see how new organizations, new education, and new technology made their work easier. Witnessing these changes in enforcement strategy will make clear why healthcare providers' legal terrain has grown rockier and riskier over time.

Drug-Dealing Doctors

Law enforcement is responsible for making sure that doctors prescribe opioids legally, which is no easy task. However, some physicians make it easy when they engage in behavior that is explicitly and undeniably criminal. These are the cases that make headlines. Opioids are illegal by default. Federal law gives doctors a special exception to prescribe for legitimate medical purposes like pain. But how can a physician be legitimate if he has a parking lot full of out-of-state license plates and a line of patients snaking around the building like they are waiting to buy concert tickets? If he asks the patient to state his blood pressure while a brand-new blood pressure cuff hangs on the wall, unused? If he can't tell the difference between a dog X-ray and a human one?

It sounds far-fetched, but in July 2012, Glendora police arrested physician Rolando Lodevico Atiga (figure 3.2) for prescribing powerful opioids to an

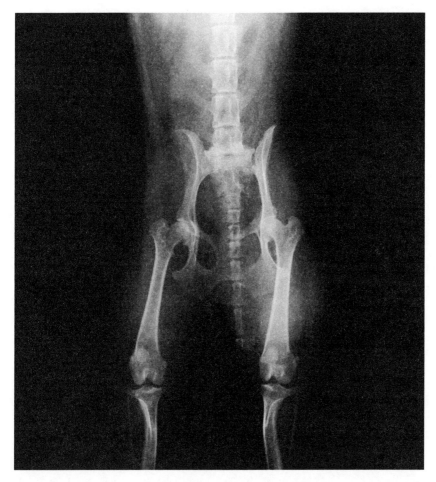

FIGURE 3.5. An X-ray of a dog similar to the one that undercover officers brought into the office of Dr. Rolando Lodevico Atiga. *Source*: Photo by choja / Getty Images.

undercover officer. The officer used a dog X-ray—with the tail clearly visible—to prove he had a bad back (figure 3.5). Police Captain Tim Staab told CBS, "either Sparky the dog really needs Percocet or this doctor is a drug dealer masquerading as a physician."[10] The medical board suspended Dr. Atiga's license in August 2012.[11] Criminal proceedings were suspended in 2013 due to Dr. Atiga's poor mental health and inability to stand trial.[12]

The dog X-ray was legend among law enforcement. Word had traveled as far as Florida, where, in a beachside community overlooking the Atlantic

Ocean, Brenda told me she had tried a similar strategy with a cat MRI. When I met Brenda, a federal agent, she had been pursuing doctor cases for more than 20 years.

Florida was a hotbed of illegal opioid activity in the 2000s and early 2010s. The state attracted fly-by-night clinics and pill mills because its law placed very few restrictions on who could open a business and permitted physicians to dispense opioids out of their offices instead of sending the patient to a pharmacy. People from the Appalachian region that spans West Virginia and Kentucky traveled to Florida for pills so often that flights between Huntington, West Virginia, and Fort Lauderdale, Florida, as well as stretches of Highway I-75 from Lexington to Miami earned the nickname "the OxyContin Express."[13]

Brenda told me that a common scheme was for organized criminal groups to take a tour bus full of people from Appalachia down to Florida to get pills. They would target desperate people—those with severe substance use disorders and no jobs—and offer them pills in exchange for their participation. The groups would meet in a grocery store parking lot at 6:00 am to begin the drive south. Once in Florida, they were divided into two groups: those with MRIs, and those without. Those with MRIs were sent to the doctor. Those without were sent to see a man called Parking Lot Pete who, for $250 cash, would perform an MRI in his trailer located in an alley behind a strip club in Palm Beach. This was no ordinary MRI. Pete would have the patient lie on tennis balls to disfigure the spine in a way that indicated bulging discs in their low back.

Pete was sloppy. He found shortcuts to process people as quickly as possible. That caught Brenda's attention. "We would see these MRI reports all from the same place. When we would look in the patient files, often the sex of the person wasn't changed." Men would come in with X-rays that said "female" and vice versa. Instead of writing a new report for each patient, he did a "very ugly job of cutting and pasting. Sometimes in paragraph one, they would talk about the bulging discs, L4–L5.[14] Sometimes they would talk about their knee in the next paragraph."

Doctors running illegitimate businesses did not care. "The doctors' offices didn't even read them. They just needed something to put in the file." With presumptive evidence of injury in hand, doctors would engage in what Brenda calls "robotic prescribing," giving the same prescription to every patient. Law enforcement dubbed the modal prescription "240-90-90"; it consisted of 240 thirty-milligram OxyContins, 90 fifteen-milligram OxyContins, and 90 two-milligram Xanax, 420 pills in all. "It didn't matter if you had been on pain medicine for two days or ten years. It didn't matter if you were a twenty-two-year-old female who weighed 95 pounds or if you were a fifty-year-old male who weighed 325 pounds; you got the same prescription," Brenda said. To put that in perspective, she told me that most people who are new to opioids would feel out of sorts after receiving one 5 milligram tablet of Percocet.[15] These physicians doled out the equivalent of fifty-one Percocets per day.

When her ailing cat, Mittens, received an MRI to pinpoint cancer pain, Brenda was investigating a physician in Hollywood, Florida, just south of Fort Lauderdale. The physician lived in a trailer, but drove a Ferrari. That was one of many red flags. She wanted evidence that he was not practicing legitimate medicine, so she sent an undercover officer into the clinic with her cat's MRI. Brenda changed the name Mittens to a human name, but left the rest of the document untouched. It listed the physician as a veterinarian and the patient as a "feline." The target of the investigation was unfazed. He gave Mittens his standard prescription: 240-90-90.

Good Doctors in a Bad Situation

Even legitimate physicians had trouble navigating this territory. When Gerard Pasquier moved to Tampa from Buffalo, he couldn't find a legitimate clinic in which to practice. "I found out that Florida is a joke. Every single place that was advertising was nothing more than a pill mill. I was shocked because coming from New York, all we heard was Florida's horrible with drugs, but they got it all straightened out." This was in 2018, long after Florida had adopted a PDMP, changed the law to prohibit physicians from dispensing out of their offices, and made the process of opening a clinic more difficult.

Practices that appeared legitimate were also skirting the law. After encountering five or six pill mills, Gerard went to colleagues for help. The practices they referred him to only gave people opioids if they consented to expensive procedures for which the physicians could bill insurance. These include epidurals (an injection of steroids around the spinal nerves) and spinal cord stimulators (implanted metal devices that send low levels of electricity into the spine). Gerard said these doctors told their patients, "You've got to get this, you've got to get that. And if you don't want to get it, we're not going to see you. And if we're not going to see you, who is going to write your opioid prescriptions?"

This kind of medical practice was both coercive and ineffective. Gerard explained how patients told him that the procedures "never helped. 'I just get them so I can keep coming here.'" "Wow," Gerard thought. "Not only are you basically extorting people to stay here for these procedures, but you're lying on the medical record." To top it all off, "you're one of the good places. You're, quote, unquote, 'well respected,' in this community. Insane." Pain management physicians like Gerard find themselves stuck between "pill mills" that broker in pills and "drill mills" that broker in procedures.

From law enforcement's perspective, Gerard is right to avoid dodgy practices. Enforcement agents are after "the worst of the worst." The physician's motivation holds the key to building a case. On one end of the spectrum are naïve physicians who are easily duped by patients who are "doctor shopping." These physicians might be fresh out of medical school or have a soft spot for people in pain. At the opposite end of the spectrum are nefarious physicians, those who know they are doing something wrong and do it anyway for money, sex, or power. In between are negligent physicians—those who are disorganized, bad at recordkeeping, and struggle with time management. These might be older physicians near retirement age, or they might be compromised because they themselves struggle with addiction to alcohol, narcotics, or sex and use their prescription pad to meet their own needs. I devised these categories after talking to several enforcement agents. When I shared them with other agents, they agreed that these four categories—the naïve, the nefarious, the negligent, and the compromised—reflected their experiences.[16]

Enforcement agents I spoke with emphasized that the nefarious physicians are their main targets. They have neither the time nor the resources to go after the other types. Beyond that, it would be difficult for investigators to convince prosecutors to take a borderline case and it would be difficult for prosecutors to convince a judge and jury that a negligent or naïve physician intended to break the law. Enforcement agents consider naïve and negligent behavior educational problems that belong with medical boards, not law enforcement.

Today's physicians practice in a new enforcement landscape[17] that differs dramatically from that of two decades ago. The reason is that law enforcement has gotten better at targeting physicians. Investigators and prosecutors have finely tuned their skills so they know what questions to ask, what behaviors to look for, and what charges to bring. These changes are most striking when we compare law enforcement's early experiences to what happens today.

Chasing Physicians without a Roadmap

Early on, cases against physicians for prescribing opioids were so rare as to be almost nonexistent. The investigators who wanted to pursue doctors found themselves without the necessary resources to pursue such complicated cases.

One barrier was their superiors who were unwilling to devote time and money to cases that would most likely go nowhere. Another barrier came from prosecutors who had a hard time buying the notion that healthcare providers could be criminals. They did not believe that legal drugs could be as deadly as crack or heroin. Nor did they have the skills to take on a physician. These shortcomings hamstrung law enforcement and shielded doctors from legal consequences.

Randi worked her first doctor case in 1997 as a detective in a Florida sheriff's department. For years, she was the only one willing to do these cases. She got pushback from her sergeant, who thought doctor cases belonged to the DEA, and from others in her department, who thought her cases took too long. Eventually, she convinced her sergeant that the doctors were as bad as the heroin dealers, and as overdose rates continued to rise, she was free to pursue doctor cases. Then, prosecutors became roadblocks.

Randi used law creatively to pursue doctors. At the beginning of her career, she was the first to charge a physician in Florida under the Continuing Criminal Enterprise Statute, a law designed to take down large-scale drug traffickers.[18] She charged fourteen defendants with committing 122 crimes. The state prosecutor resisted. "He looked at me and said, 'No way. Nobody charges these cases, it hasn't been done.'" Randi pushed back: "Don't tell me it's not drug trafficking." The argument got heated and she finally asked him, "What do you need?" He told her, "I need something so blatantly obvious that a jury can't miss it."

That was her cue. She sent a confidential informant and an undercover officer in with a wire. The informant was an established patient, someone the doctor trusted and did not realize was working with law enforcement. The doctor conducted no exam. He just pulled out his pen and pad and started prescribing. The informant received three prescriptions in his name all written for the same date.[19] The undercover officer received two prescriptions in the bogus name he had given the doctor. Each prescription was for 100 tablets of Percocet. Each cost $100 cash. The doctor asked the confidential informant if he brought any cocaine. Randi took this evidence to the prosecutor, who was outraged. "Get me a search warrant." Vindicated, she looked at him and said, "Now you are hungry. Now you want this." Eventually, she became the gatekeeper. The prosecutor was willing to take doctor cases, but only if Randi cleared them first. Randi's experience fighting her sergeant and then the prosecutor shows the kind of opposition trailblazing investigators faced in their quest to stop criminal doctors.

Prescription opioids like OxyContin occupy a legal gray area. Physicians can legally prescribe opioids—drugs that are illegal in other contexts—as long as they are registered with the DEA and act in "good faith." When the opioid crisis began, investigators had experience pursuing drug dealers who were selling drugs like cocaine and heroin that were illegal in all circumstances. Physician cases raised the bar. Now, investigators had to prove that doctors were prescribing opioids outside the bounds of their professional practice, thereby violating the Controlled Substances Act (CSA) or its state equivalent.

Investigators had to show a pattern of behavior. Their best bet was to amass physicians' prescriptions and show that they fell far outside the standard of practice.[20] The problem was finding evidence. Pharmacies keep duplicates of physicians' prescriptions, so investigators would delineate an area such as a five-mile radius around the doctor's office and drive from pharmacy to pharmacy to gather prescriptions. Not only was this strategy time-consuming, it yielded partial results. Patients could easily fill prescriptions close to their home or work, far away from the doctor's office, so investigators struggled to gather enough prescriptions to show criminal activity. Their time was better spent on other, more promising cases, which meant doctor cases were few and far between.

Some investigators persisted and built solid cases but found it difficult to get prosecutors on board. Prosecutors hate to lose, so they usually take only those cases they think they can win. They guard their limited time and resources fiercely.[21] Physician cases are unappetizing on both counts. Prosecutors are used to illicit drug cases against low-level drug dealers whose public defenders steer them toward a plea bargain. Doctors have money and won't go down without a fight, so their cases consume significant resources. They require undercover surveillance and expensive expert witnesses who spend a lot of time on chart review. Conflicting experts muddy the case and confuse juries. No matter how good the expert witness is at showing that the physician's behavior violated professional norms, the defense team will inevitably have its own expert who affirms that the physician was practicing well within professional boundaries.

So much can go wrong with physician cases that prosecutors have historically shied away from them. Prosecutors who pursue physicians must walk a razor's edge, knowing that one misstep could undermine their case and flush months of work down the drain. These cases often hinge on undercover surveillance—photographs, videos, and tape recordings are powerful evidence to convince a jury that a doctor is a criminal. However, undercover surveillance is difficult to get. Prosecutors have to show a pattern of illegal behavior. That requires undercover investigators or confidential informants to make several visits to the doctor over a prolonged period and requires the physician to continue behaving illegally. This process is easily disrupted—doctors get skittish and stop prescribing, informants disappear, and other agencies get in the way.

The first problem is that criminal physicians are skeptical of new patients, which makes it difficult for law enforcement to get an undercover officer into the practice to start gathering evidence. Undercover officers must gain their trust by having an existing patient—someone who has become a confidential informant—introduce them to the physician. Once the officer has forged a relationship, they have to show a pattern of illicit prescribing. Patients usually see their doctors monthly, so it can take months or years to gather sufficient evidence.

Officers must also be careful not to entrap the physician. If the patient says he is in pain and brings in legitimate-looking X-rays, the doctor has no reason not to prescribe. Instead, the undercover officer must say things that make it clear that they are using the drugs illicitly, things like "I'm getting it off the streets," or "I owe somebody some pills back because I got some from a friend." Prescribing in these circumstances clearly violates the law, and this is what prosecutors want documented. "We're not trying to trick the doctor," undercover officers Tyler and Ben told me. "If we're going in there screaming pain, we don't have a case. They have a defense."

The second problem is that other investigators can tank an undercover case. Think back to the "house of cards" that New Jersey lawyer Antonio described in chapter 2. A physician who practices outside the standard of practice risks losing their medical license, their DEA registration, and their ability to bill Medicare and Medicaid. These losses might, to an outsider, look like a precarious structure tumbling down, but in reality, each one is the result of a separate investigation that is conducted by a different agency.

Tension simmers between criminal investigators working for the DEA, sheriffs' departments, and local task forces on one hand and administrative investigators working for the Board of Medicine on the other. Criminal investigators aim to put bad doctors in prison, while administrative investigators aim to take away their license to practice medicine.[22] Criminal and administrative agencies can pursue the same physician at the same time. However, they have different motivations, legal requirements, and strategies. Administrative cases move faster than criminal cases because they have shorter statutes of limitation and lower burdens of proof. The legal standard for administrative cases in most states is *preponderance of the evidence,* meaning that it is more likely than not that the person violated the law. By contrast, the legal standard for criminal cases is *beyond a reasonable doubt*, meaning that "there is no other reasonable explanation that can come from the evidence presented at trial."[23]

Administrative investigators have a tool that criminal investigators do not—the audit—that poses particular difficulties for undercover surveillance. Undercover cases thrive in secrecy—the key is making sure that the doctor doesn't know they are being watched so they keep prescribing illegally. This pattern of illegal behavior is the evidence necessary to put the physician in prison. Otherwise, there is no case. Administrative investigations are an open book. When medical board investigators conduct an administrative audit, they seize all of a physician's records and search them for evidence of illegal prescribing. The moment his records are seized, a smart doctor knows he is under investigation and changes course, fast. This can tank an undercover investigation happening at the same time because the doctor is no longer committing a crime. This frustrates criminal investigators who have spent months on a case but don't yet have enough evidence to convict.

Mike, a federal agent in Missouri, described a case ruined by a board investigator who "went to a practitioner and said 'You're so bad that the DEA is looking at you. You need to knock off what you're doing.'" The physician did an about-face. He "fired the bulk of his patients," some of whom were working with law enforcement as confidential informants, "and he became far more cautious in his dealings with the undercover investigators that were posing in a role as a patient." Mike and his team did not yet have sufficient evidence to prosecute the physician, and the board investigator's actions ensured they never would. "They're basically tanking everything for us." I asked Mike why a board investigator would behave that way. He offered a generous interpretation: "I think it's typically a lack of experience. And I think they get so excited with information that, you know, 'by gosh I've really got you now!' They just can't wait to go and confront somebody and try and shut them down."

Of course, this is only one side of the story. The mismatch in investigatory strategies—covert undercover versus overt audit—is compounded by extremely different timelines. From the perspective of administrative investigators, criminal cases take too long and prevent administrative investigators from doing their jobs. They simply can't permit a physician to harm patients for five years while a federal case is pending. Schisms among enforcement agencies make undercover surveillance a risky tool. Why would a prosecutor invest outsized resources in a case that could be destroyed in a flash?

Nick, a criminal lawyer in Southern California, has won plenty of doctor cases, but he can see why other prosecutors avoid them. "They're going to have a high-powered attorney. It's going to be a complicated case. The case is going to rest on some pretty subtle arguments. And face it, they aren't really sexy charges. I mean, it's not murder. It's not a gang member. So there's a lot of downside but not much upside." For all of these reasons, prosecutors have historically found doctor cases unattractive.

Even when prosecutors took the case, juries and judges presented new hurdles. Juries see doctors as good people, as helpers, not criminals. And most jurors have been to a doctor, so they have an image in their mind of what a doctor's office should look like. A smart prosecutor can use this to his advantage. Nick has a near-perfect record for prosecuting physicians. The secret to his success? Every case has a "holy cow moment," meaning "one circumstance that any juror, as skeptical as they wanted to be, would have to say there is just no way that person is practicing medicine."

Nick described a litany of holy cow moments: the strip mall physician who was the number two prescriber of opioids in the country, the physician who called 911 when a patient overdosed in her clinic ("they're actually overdosing at your feet!" Nick exclaimed), the doctor who was hiding over $2 million worth of pills in a storage unit and even more in the ceiling of his office, the doctor who texted his office manager who was selling drugs on the street and encouraged him to "go be the drug dealer that you are." And who can forget the physician who accepted a dog X-ray as proof that his patient was in pain? Criminal intent is clear. "It's not 'Whoops! I gave you a little too much medication.' Or 'You came in a little early and I prescribed to you.' It's like 'What are you doing dealing out of the trunk of your car?!'"

Despite damning evidence, judges still resist punishing doctors. Nick knows from experience. "I've had judges vacate a jury's conviction because they don't want this doctor's livelihood to be taken away, regardless of how bad the conduct was." Some prosecutors speculate that judges refuse to punish physicians out of professional courtesy because they comingle in society's upper echelons. Others think that judges see physicians' lack of a criminal record—a sharp contrast to the records of most federal defendants—and wonder if they are really criminals or just smart businesspeople who skirt the rules to make profit. Whatever the motivation, physicians who overprescribe opioids historically enjoyed the same benefits of other white-collar criminals— they flaunted the law, caused egregious harm, and got off scot-free.[24] Not anymore.

Reshaping the Enforcement Landscape

A lot has changed since the days when pill mills popped up like weeds and law enforcement had no way to stop them. Enforcement agencies have responded to the opioid crisis with three strategies: (1) organizing task forces, (2) educating investigators, and (3) using prescription drug monitoring programs (PDMPs). Together, these efforts have made physician cases easier and faster, even if some challenges persist.

Task forces are subunits of enforcement agencies that bring together individuals who have different resources and expertise to address a common goal. Remember Randi, the detective who fought a lonely battle to investigate physicians? Today, she would have company. Federal agencies like the Drug Enforcement Administration (DEA) and local agencies like sheriffs' departments have devoted themselves to physician cases by creating task forces centered on prescription opioids. DEA task forces do much of the heavy lifting, a major shift from decades ago.

The DEA plays the biggest federal role in regulating opioids. The DEA's Office of Diversion Control oversees registrants—physicians, pharmacies, hospitals, manufacturers, wholesalers, and drug distributors—who must register with the agency in order to provide controlled substances. The Controlled Substances Act (CSA) designates these registrants as part of a "closed system of distribution," which means that the DEA tracks everyone who handles opioids along the supply chain and accounts for every transaction. The DEA monitors opioid transactions using the Automation of Reports and Consolidated Orders System (ARCOS), a database that tracks controlled substances all the way from manufacture to public distribution.[25]

For decades, the Office of Diversion Control[26] was considered a lesser part of the DEA, and the agents who worked for it—known as Diversion Investigators (DIs)—were treated as less important than Special Agents (SAs), who work for the Operations Division. The position of DI was originally created to relieve SAs from the burden of inspecting and auditing manufacturers and distributors of controlled substances as mandated by the CSA. Handing off those tasks to DIs freed SAs to focus on heroin and cocaine trafficking. This hierarchy persisted into the late 1990s, the heyday of opioid prescribing, when physicians treated pain as a fifth vital sign and were urged to aggressively treat pain. With physicians and regulators on board with generous opioid prescribing, the diversion office found itself underfunded and understaffed. Laura Nagel, who was appointed head of the DEA's Office of Diversion Control in

2000, led DIs who struggled to get resources and respect. Unaware of the giant opioid wave poised to crest a few short years later, SAs thought prescription opioids were nothing more than a child's version of the hard drugs they pursued.

That all changed in the early 2000s when, for the first time in U.S. history, Americans were more likely to overdose on prescription drugs than illegal ones.[27] Suddenly, DIs were in high demand. In late 2006, the DEA created task forces called Tactical Diversion Squads like the one that Abby and Brandon participated in. Recall that these included DIs, SAs, and Task Force Officers (TFOs). DIs understood healthcare norms; SAs could arrest people; and TFOs had fine-grained knowledge of their communities. This created the organizational synergy needed to pursue doctors.

Local agencies like police departments and sheriff's departments also created narcotics task forces that enabled them to exchange information with other local agencies. Joe runs a task force out of a sheriff's department in Southern California exclusively dedicated to prescription drug and heroin cases. Members of the task force represent various police departments, the highway patrol, the district attorney's office, the department of healthcare services, and the medical board. Joe's group also allies with the FBI, the DEA, and the Food and Drug Administration (FDA).

Joe lists the kinds of work his task force does: "We work all overdose death cases in the county from death back and try to find the source of supply and then arrest them and prosecute them for manslaughter or drug dealing resulting in death, which is kind of a new, innovative way of going after drug dealers." This is known as a "drug-induced homicide" case.[28] Joe's team also works any crime that involves a pharmaceutical drug "whether it's international trafficking of prescription meds, counterfeit meds, or dirty physicians who are overprescribing and not conducting good faith exams for their patients."

Provider cases constitute only a small share of the cases these task forces conduct, but they are among the most important. Says Joe, "A bad doctor is like a cartel leader because the amount of drugs that one dirty doctor can put on the streets is the same amount as a cartel leader can put on the street with a typical cocaine case."

Federal and local agencies have complementary resources. Local police departments have insufficient funding to do provider cases, so they collaborate with federal law enforcement either formally by sending one of their officers to the DEA's task force or informally by working cases together. Federal agencies have more money and equipment. They can do federal wire taps, which are expensive and require specialized technology. They can also afford expert witnesses, who are crucial for building a doctor case. Local agencies, on the other hand, have more agents, so they are better equipped to conduct under-cover investigations and process the mountains of paperwork that a doctor case generates.

Task forces are only one site of information exchange. Enforcement agents have found various ways to break down silos and distribute knowledge. Years of failed attempts have taught investigators and prosecutors what works, and what doesn't. They know what questions to ask, what behaviors to look for, and what charges to bring. Task force members eager to share what they had learned with others lacked formal venues to do so, so they got creative.

Joe cited the lack of cross-pollination as one of the reasons that physician cases were so hard in the early days. The California Narcotic Officers' Associa-tion (CNOA), a nonprofit that has trained enforcement agents since 1964,[29] did not offer training on prescription drugs. "It was all meth and heroin and cocaine and marijuana, so we had to write a lot ourselves also because it's context specific to each case in each state." As investigators traveled into new legal territory, they had to create their own roadmap.

Joe and his team took their cue from investigators in other states who had attempted doctor cases. In 2002, they flew to Pensacola, Florida, where a judge sentenced a physician to sixty-three years in prison for killing his patients. "We met with the case agents and the state's attorney and had them walk us through how they did that investigation."

They also learned from failed cases. "There was another case against a doc-tor in Tahoe that fell apart because they didn't have the support of the district attorney up there, but we walked through the case with them and found out why their case didn't go." They dissected investigations and learned how law operated in different states. "We had to understand that in California when you go into a physician's office why that's different than going into somebody's home to search for regular drugs." Then they found ways to use the law to their advantage and get others on board. "We had to write our own templates for search warrants. And then slowly, over the past fourteen years, getting buy-in from other people to investigate these as well. We've kind of written the book on how to do that."

In addition to Joe and his team's bottom-up approach, national organizations began training investigators how to do doctor cases. Notably, the National Association of Drug Diversion Investigators (NADDI) brought together en-forcement agents across the country to share strategy. There, Joe learned "what a dirty doctor looks like, what a good doctor who maybe just doesn't understand looks like, and why pharmacists are so important." Today, Joe says his task force members "will talk to anybody that will listen to us, whether it's social workers or probation or parents or law enforcement groups or attorneys or doctors, we will educate anybody and we do quite a bit of that as far as traveling the country and talking to different groups."

Together, new organizations, new knowledge, and new technology expand law enforcement capacity. These changes are evident when we consider what investigation and prosecution look like today. I have already described how task forces and education improve enforcement. Now, let's turn to the PDMP.

PDMPs have dramatically transformed the ways that investigators and prosecutors conduct cases against providers. New organizational developments paved the way for monitoring programs to have the greatest impact. Enforcement agencies' impetus to investigate providers coincided with the arrival of technology that made those investigations easier and faster. Enforcement agents find both provider and patient data useful—provider data because it shows patterns of providers' behavior and patient data because it helps law enforcement convince patients to become confidential informants in exchange for leniency in their own cases.

Healthcare providers have direct access to the database, but law enforcement access is more complicated. State laws restrict which enforcement agencies can get access and how. Some states give law enforcement direct access to data. In those states, enforcement agents have their own login to the system but can only legally access the data in the process of an active case, meaning that they are already investigating a specific crime. They can't just go searching through the database to see what they find. Other states require law enforcement to request access from the agency that houses the PDMP, and the agency returns only information relevant to the case. Still other states require enforcement agents to obtain a warrant or a subpoena to access the data.[30] Regardless of how they get the information, PDMPs are a boon to law enforcement because they make tasks easier and more efficient.

Physician cases are reactive instead of proactive, which creates a barrier to starting an investigation. Enforcement agents say that they do not go out looking for bad doctors but find them through tips they receive from a patient, a parent, a healthcare provider, or another agency. They use information from tips to gather evidence and determine whether the case is worth pursuing. For a provider to come under law enforcement scrutiny, someone has to notice their behavior, feel compelled to do something, and know who to call.

The legwork necessary to investigate a physician traditionally posed a second barrier because investigators had to travel from pharmacy to pharmacy to gather the physician's prescriptions. Now, thanks to the PDMP, that legwork has become deskwork. Instead of spending time on a potentially fruitless pharmacy expedition, enforcement agents simply look up the physician in the database or request access to information from the agency that controls it. Investigators can obtain a physician's prescribing history, analyze prescribing patterns, and link findings to other databases without setting foot outside the office.

Ken works as a federal agent in Kansas City, a city that spans across the borders of Kansas and Missouri. He finds himself doing more provider cases in Kansas and attributes that to the fact that Kansas has a PDMP and Missouri does not.[31] He gets more calls from pharmacists who spot questionable physician activity in Kansas than Missouri and he can more easily act on that information because of K-TRACS, Kansas's PDMP. "It's easier for us to make a determination on the front end like what's this guy doing?" he says.

Information from the database helps his team to decide whether the case is worth its time, especially because his group has very limited resources. He told me about a physician he arrested after receiving some phone calls from a pharmacist. "We did a little bit of surveillance to sort of corroborate what the pharmacist was telling us"; then they got a grand jury subpoena to access K-TRACS data, a legal requirement in the state. "Anyway, you look at the PDMP and we're like 'Whoa, okay!' Because this guy's practice was erectile dysfunction and he was the third leading prescriber of opioids in the state of Kansas during the period of time. Like that's nuts, right?"

PDMPs help investigators learn the norms of healthcare practice. Caleb says that looking at CURES[32] reports helped him "obtain a mental picture of what a reasonable doctor would be prescribing versus a doctor who is practicing illegally." When he is unsure, he asks a medical expert. The expert's answer along with information from the database helps him spot illegal behavior and show that the physician is prescribing out of bounds. Mike, a federal agent in Kansas City describes his strategy for using the monitoring program. First, he acquires a grand jury subpoena to obtain information. Then, he receives a Microsoft Excel spreadsheet. "I'll just start going through that Excel sheet and ordering it by different criteria. How many people with the same address are getting narcotic prescriptions from the same practitioner? How many individuals are getting just obscene amounts of oxycodone?" Once investigators like Mike identify problematic trends, they use the PDMP report like a treasure map to get the actual prescriptions from the pharmacies, because prescriptions, not reports, are the best evidence to use in court.

PDMP data are a starting point. They do not make a case alone. Investigators examine the data from various angles and try to come up with alternative explanations for the patterns they see. Quinton, a DI in Missouri and Kansas, explains why this is so important. Just because a pharmacy is dispensing more opioids than anyone else doesn't mean it should be investigated. It might be located near a major pain clinic or a cancer center. A doctor who writes the most opioid prescriptions "may be the only pain management doctor in that county." Quinton doesn't just go by the numbers. He is cautious about who he chooses to investigate, partly because he lacks resources and partly because he doesn't want to do harm. "I don't want to subject someone to a criminal investigation who doesn't deserve it. And there are plenty of crooks out there for us to spend our time investigating. I got six investigators to cover a state and a half. I don't want to waste time looking at that doctor just because he happens to have written more prescriptions than anybody else in the neighborhood. Because I got this guy over here that I know is just doing crazy things and needs to be locked up."

Most enforcement agents are quick to note that they pursue providers for cause. They do not go on "fishing expeditions" in the PDMP, looking for people with minor infractions. Joe says he is "very sensitive to overstepping bounds from a law enforcement side when it comes to the practice of medicine." When it comes to the monitoring program, "we don't want get too deep into the weeds with that stuff because there's usually a good explanation for why physicians are doing what they're doing." They have neither the time nor the resources to do minor cases, and prosecutors would not take them anyway.

PDMPs also have their drawbacks. Investigators can use the database to track physicians, but a smart criminal physician also uses the database to monitor their patients and identify potential undercover investigators. People who are addicted to or diverting medications usually have a long PDMP report because they are actively trying to obtain opioids from various physicians. Undercover agents do not have a report at all, so running a report is a way to root out narcs. Knowing this, law enforcement finds ways to create fake reports so that they blend in with other patients. Overall, PDMPs benefit law enforcement because they improve the speed and accuracy of investigations. Better investigation leads to better prosecution.

For many years, Nick felt like the only one willing to prosecute physicians. Even though he won nearly all of his cases, convincing other prosecutors that these cases were worthwhile proved impossible. "Maybe I'm a masochist, maybe I have a death wish, maybe I'm a kamikaze," he told me in his colorful way. His goal was to train other prosecutors how to do doctor cases. To that end, he traveled to other jurisdictions to share his strategies, without success. "I have been marching across the country singing the Lord's praises and no choir will respond! I've been lecturing on this for two years now, probably once every six to eight weeks, all over the place. And it's thunderous applause and then crickets."

Today, more prosecutors follow in Nick's footsteps and pursue doctor cases without hesitation. Some even consider it a moral obligation. These prosecutors are equipped with savvier investigators, blueprints from successful prosecutions, and PDMP data.

In 2017, I spoke with two young prosecutors in Northern California who had recently begun to prosecute doctor cases. Sylvia had just completed a training from the National Advocacy Center, the training arm of the Department of Justice (DOJ). The focus of the training was doctors and pharmacists who were diverting, and, to her knowledge, it was the first training of its kind. She chose to prosecute physician cases because she considered it a challenge and because she wanted to have a positive impact on public health.

Sylvia acknowledges that "they're hard cases to make," especially compared to illicit drug cases. "They're not as straightforward, as you know, I just pulled someone over and they have a pound of methamphetamine in the back seat. It's more of a puzzle to work through and to figure out which doctors are doing what they're supposed to and which clearly know that they're doing something that they shouldn't." Her colleague, Julie, came to this work with a background in healthcare, white-collar defense, and criminal investigation.

Both women use CURES, California's PDMP, to build their cases. Sylvia looks at "the volume the doctor is prescribing, the percentage of that volume that is commonly diverted controlled substances, whether the doctor is prescribing the holy trinity,"[33] and whether the doctor is prescribing the same thing to each patient. Julie initially looks at drug, dosage, and volume, and if she thinks she has found something, she turns the data over to a medical expert and asks, "What does this look like to you?"

These prosecutors believe that the data accurately reflects a physician's prescribing practices. Julie says, "I rely on it to be a hundred percent accurate," but she corroborates with pharmacy records to be sure. Unlike prosecutors who avoid doctor cases to keep up their win rates, Julie believes she has a moral obligation to do these cases or risk becoming a "member of the chickenshit club." The term, coined by former FBI director James Comey, refers to prosecutors who fail to take risks, who only file charges on which a jury will convict.[34] In Comey's mind, and in Julie's, prosecutors who behave this way are "not enforcing the law to its full extent."

Despite their commitment to pushing the envelope, enthusiastic prosecutors like Sylvia and Julie face difficulties navigating complicated doctor cases. It is still hard to convince judges and juries to convict physicians. It is hard to put a respected professional with no criminal record behind bars. The PDMP helps make their case.

Drug cases capture media attention for a reason. Whether on popular TV shows or the evening news, drug cases are sexy. Towering bags of confiscated drugs and arrays of automatic rifles captivate audiences. This stagecraft also justifies the War on Drugs. Props like drugs and guns show that the "bad guys," the drug dealers, are armed and dangerous. They also show how desperately we need the "good guys," the investigators and prosecutors, to keep the bad guys off the street.

By comparison, physician cases are decidedly unsexy. There are no drugs. There are no guns. There is paperwork. Stacks and stacks of paperwork. Not only do prosecutors have to prove to judges and juries that doctors—professionals revered as pillars of our society—are criminals, but they have to do so using something as uninspiring as paperwork. It's a tough sell.

Peter prosecutes federal crimes in Missouri, where he specializes in fraud. He has taken on more doctor cases recently but admits that they lack the jury appeal of other drug cases. He explains: "You have to present the evidence differently and it's harder to imagine, if you've never done it before, how to turn the paper into an exhibit that will be interesting to the jury and how to manipulate it on the screens the jury looks at." Peter compensates for this lack of appeal and his lack of props by choosing his battles wisely and developing airtight cases. His background prosecuting fraud cases has made him agile in using paper trails to tell a compelling story. He knows how to work with expert witnesses. However, he is at a disadvantage because Missouri's county-based PDMP offers incomplete data compared to state-level programs like California's, so he lacks all the information he needs.

By contrast, Tyler, a federal prosecutor in Southern California, has full access and routinely uses CURES data. His case rests on what he calls "three tentpoles": undercover investigations, data analysis, and expert review. Undercovers help identify "red flags" that show that the provider is prescribing beyond the limits of standard practice, data analysis traces patterns of prescribing or dispensing, and expert review confirms that the physician's behavior violates the standard of care. Tyler analyzes CURES data alongside Medicare/Medicaid and ARCOS data to paint a detailed picture of illegal medical and pharmacy practice. It is largely the discrepancies between these databases that make his case.

When we spoke in 2013, Tyler was prosecuting a pharmacy that was under-reporting its dispensing data to CURES. Failing to report was illegal, but the pharmacy owners claimed it was an "accident." Tyler had a different take. He thought that the pharmacy owners knew that law enforcement could see their CURES data, so they selectively reported to evade enforcement scrutiny. What they didn't count on was ARCOS, the tracking system controlled by the DEA. When Tyler looked up the pharmacy in ARCOS, he discovered that this "small mom and pop pharmacy" was "the number one purchaser of oxycodone in the entire county of Los Angeles," more than UCLA Medical Center, more than Cedars-Sinai. These data showed a troubling pattern in the ARCOS data and depicted "massive discrepancies between ARCOS and CURES." They helped Tyler convince a judge and a jury that the pharmacy owner's actions were intentional.

In another of Tyler's cases, a physician began working for a clinic that his team was investigating after she was fired by Kaiser, a health system in California. Her prescribing at the new clinic was suspicious because it differed dramatically from her prescribing at Kaiser. Tyler and his colleagues used the CURES data to highlight the contrast. "1.3 percent of her patients got an opioid and Xanax at Kaiser compared to 98 percent at the clinic." (This combination is known to increase the risk of overdose.) "No 2 milligram Xanax prescriptions at all at Kaiser compared to like 90 something percent at the clinic." (Two milligrams is a hefty dose of Xanax and can be readily misused.) This "before and after snapshot," made possible by CURES, helped him win the case.

The PDMP also helps prosecutors locate current or former patients who are willing to serve as witnesses against their physician. Nick described how he used the monitoring program to find witnesses: "I looked at CURES and I'm like 'I'm going to find every person that was going to her for a regular period of time and then dropped off.' Why? Because either they died or they went into rehab because you don't get 120 Vicodin for three years and then suddenly just stop. So I could have my investigating officer run the names and say 'Hey, go out and pound the pavement and see if these people are willing to talk.' And I think we got six or seven former patients of hers who had gone into rehab and were now willing to be witnesses."

Even with PDMPs, barriers persist. Provider cases are still resource intensive and they still disproportionately go to trial where prosecutors spar with top defense lawyers. They are also reputationally risky and easy to lose. Prosecutors, it seems, have not benefited from the same kinds of education that investigators have. Caleb told me about a case his co-worker investigated that a prosecutor "fucked up." It was "the most prolific doctor shopping that we had. Slam dunk case. I mean no question about it and the prosecutor lost the preliminary hearing." Caleb's task force colleague, Nate, sums up the mismatch this way: "It's like you have a varsity team of investigators and a middle school prosecutor." From Caleb and Nate's perspective, there are too many bad doctors out there practicing for law enforcement to handle. They wish they could do more, but do not have the resources.

Investigators are not the only ones frustrated. Prosecutors also find themselves waiting a long time to get their cases on the docket. Ben works for the Statewide Prosecutor in South Florida. The office is responsible for all cases that cross county lines, as drug cases often do. Ben completed four high-profile cases against providers in 2013 when Florida's pill mills were in full swing. When I spoke with him in 2019, all but one was still pending.

The cases take so long for two reasons. One is that discovery takes, in Ben's words, "forever." The defense "gets to take the deposition of every witness. They get to review every document." These are normal practices, rights of the defendant enshrined in the Constitution, but they take years in pill mill cases with several defendants and several attorneys. The second is that Ben is caught in a pickle between the division court and the trial court. Division court judges don't want long trials to "clog up their court room," so they send the cases to the trial division, whose judges don't want the cases either. "The trial divisions are created in order to try people who have been incarcerated for over 700 days or something of that nature." Physicians, who are usually out on bail, don't qualify. With no courtroom and no urgency to try the case, "they drag on." Foot dragging benefits physician defendants because cases atrophy over time. Prosecutors "lose witnesses and people lose interest," which makes these cases even harder to win. Task forces, shared knowledge, and PDMPs make it easier to build cases against physicians. Court dynamics create roadblocks. But is prosecuting physicians a good thing?

The Downside of Prosecution

What enforcement agents consider a victory—putting bad doctors out of business—pain management advocates bemoan as grave harm. Enforcement agents cast themselves as heroes who keep the public safe by stopping drug dealers who parade as physicians. Meanwhile, advocates cast them as overzealous "drug warriors" who destroy the lives of pain patients by ruining the livelihoods of compassionate physicians.

One of the biggest problems, advocates claim, is that no clear standard of care exists for when to provide opioids. A standard of care is a medical term that describes what a reasonable physician would do in a given circumstance. Standards of care are generally quite flexible because physicians enjoy significant discretion over how they practice. Yet the lack of a standard with regard to opioids means that physicians are flying blind, expected to follow rules they don't know exist.[35]

When Wichita, Kansas, physician Steven Schneider (see figure 3.4) and his wife and office manager/nurse, Linda Schneider,[36] were arrested for "causing the deaths of three people through the unlawful distribution of controlled substances" a week before Christmas in 2007, Siobhan Reynolds leapt into action.[37] Reynolds had been a leading pain management activist since 2003 when she founded the Pain Relief Network, an organization designed to defend wrongly accused doctors and patients.[38]

Reynolds had seen firsthand the harm that physician prosecutions could do. Her husband, Sean Greenwood, lived with chronic pain due to a congenital connective tissue disorder. The disease was rare, which left him in pain and without a diagnosis for decades. Opioids helped him function, but the doses he needed were so high that he struggled to find physicians who were willing to prescribe his meds.[39] Physicians balked at treating him even though he was using the medications for their intended purpose.

The first physician Reynolds fought for was one of Greenwood's physicians, William Hurwitz. Dr. Hurwitz was charged with forty-nine crimes including drug trafficking and running a criminal enterprise. According to *New York Times* journalist Maia Szalavitz, "the sheer number of charges in this and similar cases is designed to intimidate doctors into accepting plea deals and avoiding trial: with that many counts, jurors will naturally think that the physician must have done at least something wrong."

Szalavitz dismisses this as misleading and points out that when a doctor exceeds the bounds of "legitimate medicine," even ordinary events become criminal. Writing a prescription becomes drug dealing or distribution. Mailing a prescription become mail fraud. If a patient sells a prescription to someone else, the doctor has participated in a drug conspiracy. Depositing a paycheck becomes money laundering. "Instantly, every action is transformed into one or more crimes."[40]

Reynolds refused to let that happen to Schneider. She moved from New Mexico to Wichita, where she worked with the family to hire a defense team and staged a vigil for one of Schneider's patients who had been admitted to the emergency department. One of Reynolds's most visible acts of resistance was buying a billboard along a major Wichita highway that read "Dr. Schneider Never Killed Anyone."[41]

Dr. Schneider became a magnet for poor patients who suffered from pain largely because he was one of very few physicians in the greater Wichita area who was willing to take Medicaid. Other physicians refused to accept Medicaid because it offered paltry payments compared to private insurance. According to *New Yorker* writer Rachel Aviv, who profiled Schneider in 2014, Schneider stood up at a meeting to ask members of the Sedgwick County Pain Society to take some of his Medicaid patients. No one volunteered. The meeting's moderator, addiction specialist Gregory Lakin, said he felt "embarrassed about it." In Lakin's eyes, "Steve had a little bit of the martyr in him. He's isolated, being in a small town, and he saw himself as a rescuer, a savior of the downtrodden, and that overrode his ability to assess the warning signs."[42] Advocates like Reynolds used Schneider's compassion to paint him as an innocent victim caught in law enforcement's net.

Prosecutors disagreed. To hear them tell it, Schneider was a drug dealer who ran a criminal enterprise from his office. They linked his prescribing to sixty-eight patient deaths and brought thirty-four charges against him and his wife, including one count of conspiracy to commit healthcare fraud, four counts of unlawful distribution of controlled substances resulting in the death of a patient, and three counts of healthcare fraud resulting in a death.[43] And they went after Reynolds herself.

According to Szalavitz, the lead prosecutor was so angered by Reynolds's tactics that she "got the court to impose overwhelming fines, claiming that Reynolds had obstructed justice. Before long, this bankrupted her and her organization." She appealed all the way to the Supreme Court, but the fines were upheld.[44] Judge Monti Belot sentenced Dr. Schneider to thirty years in prison and Linda Schneider to thirty-three. He justified giving them longer sentences than illicit drug dealers because, unlike physicians, those dealers have "no duty or obligation, legal or otherwise, to do no harm to their customers."[45] Szalavitz notes that a handful of physician prosecutions can have an outsized effect as fear reverberates throughout the medical community. One expert told her that "each local prosecution led at least fifty or sixty other doctors to stop prescribing."[46]

In 2015, five years after Schneider's arrest, I sat down with Jennifer Campbell, a nurse who runs a pain service in a Kansas City hospital. Her job is to work with patients and providers to set a course for pain care. She told me that shortly after Schneider's practice closed, she began to see patients who drove almost three hours from Wichita to Kansas City in search of opioids. Schneider's arrest created a vacuum of pain care in the state, turning his patients into what Jennifer called "Schneider refugees." She told me that writing opioid prescriptions is an easy, but largely ineffective way to treat pain, and that "when [patients] find you are a 'writer,'[47] everyone comes out of the woodwork."

How can we make sense of someone like Schneider? Did his offenses rival those of physicians who doled out the "holy trinity" as if it were candy? Did they surpass those of Lisa Tseng who left fourteen patients dead? Were patients better off with Schneider's clinic open or closed? There is no simple answer to these questions.

Schneider was certainly naïve; he believed what his patients told him about their pain even as patients sat in his waiting room trading tactics for getting him to prescribe. He believed the patients who claimed that they were going out of town or that their pills had fallen in the sink—common tricks for acquiring more meds—and provided early refills when asked.[48] Schneider was also negligent. His office was cluttered and his charting disorganized. He had so many patients that they waited for hours in his parking lot in lawn chairs brought from home. During busy times, medical assistants would copy vital signs from previous visits instead of taking new measurements. Linda Schneider failed to convey news from the coroner's office that a patient had died because Dr. Schneider "didn't want to hear bad news."[49]

The question is, was he nefarious? Was he intentionally reckless with patients' lives, or was he an overwhelmed physician who lost control of his practice? The other question is what happened to his patients after he was arrested? He treated some of the poorest, most desperate patients who other doctors refused to touch. Some of Schneider's patients misused their medication, not all. Those who saw him to treat pain had to try to find someone new while weighed down by the stigma of a high-dose opioid prescription and a previous physician who was now in prison. Who would help them now?

Many enforcement agents with whom I spoke acknowledged that they risk creating a pain desert[50] when they arrest a physician. They pointed out that many physicians run both a legitimate and a criminal practice at the same time. They might run a legal business on weekdays and sell prescriptions for cash on weekends. Others adjust their treatment from patient to patient. Quinton explained that when doing a doctor case, "You have to remember that you're going to be disrupting a lot of people's lives. And even dirty doctors, doctors pumping drugs out there knowingly and intentionally, aren't necessarily bad doctors for those legitimate patients." He described one such physician. "I had a doctor that was writing Dilaudid[51] prescriptions for anybody and everybody that would have sex with him. But during the course of the investigation, talking to a lot of folks that were legitimate patients of his, all I heard was what a great doctor he was."

Was Dr. Schneider, like those physicians, a modern Jekyll and Hyde? Or was he a good doctor who fell prey to an overzealous team of investigators and prosecutors hell-bent on proving their worth? The answer depends on who you ask—the pain patients who claim that Dr. Schneider saved them from chronic and interminable pain, the parents who lost a child to drugs that Schneider provided, or the investigators and prosecutors who brought him to justice.[52] Tanya Treadway, the assistant U.S. attorney who prosecuted the Schneider case, put it like this: "There were patients who absolutely loved Dr. Schneider and thought he was a wonderful doctor, and there were patients who thought he was the devil incarnate."[53]

The Schneider case raises a number of questions that legal experts are still grappling with a decade and a half later. At issue is whether prosecutors must prove that physicians violated the CSA by prescribing outside the normal course of practice *and* that the prescriptions were not medically necessary, or if simply proving that their prescribing was out of bounds is enough. The reason this matters so much is that it affects whether a physician who unknowingly prescribes opioids to someone without a medical need is criminally culpable. In legal terms, this is the difference between *actus reus* and *mens rea*, a "guilty act" versus a "guilty mind." Criminal law often requires both—someone must intentionally and knowingly commit a crime to be held criminally accountable.[54]

Circuit courts have interpreted the CSA differently; some have required both elements, while others have allowed the bad act to suffice. Legal scholars warn that relying on the act alone amounts to criminalizing malpractice. A recent Supreme Court case promises to resolve this issue. *Ruan v. United States*[55] concerns a Mobile, Alabama, pain management specialist, Dr. Xiulu Ruan (see figure 3.3), who was sentenced to over twenty years in federal prison in 2017 for running a "massive pill mill" with his business partner Dr. John Patrick Couch.[56] Did Ruan knowingly engage in illegal behavior? Does it matter if he did? Advocates insist that it does matter. In December 2021, legal scholars Kelly Dineen and Jennifer Oliva spearheaded an amicus brief[57] in the Ruan case. They and their co-signers urged the Supreme Court to take the case to clarify the legal standard under the CSA.[58] Dineen, a Creighton law professor, told Fox 10 News, "Our position is that the most, the harshest, penalties ought to be reserved for those that really are engaged in knowingly criminal conduct."

Ultimately, the Supreme Court agreed. In the summer of 2022, the Court held that "if a defendant produces evidence that his conduct was authorized, the Government must prove beyond a reasonable doubt that the defendant knowingly or intentionally acted in an unauthorized manner."[59] The opinion stated: "With few exceptions, wrongdoing must be conscious to be criminal."[60] The Ruan case now imposes a steep roadblock for prosecutors who plan to use the CSA to convict physicians. They have to prove that the physician not only acted outside the confines of the law but also did so knowingly or intentionally, a fact much harder to prove.[61]

It remains to be seen whether the findings in this case will shield physicians who cause harm or protect innocent physicians unfairly targeted by law enforcement. A pharmacy law expert I spoke with thought that law enforcement oversold the idea that they only pursued bad providers. He thought it was more complicated, especially when a case doesn't bear out the way they expect. "There are false positives where they go after what they believe to be the most egregious bad actors and then discover 'Gosh, we missed it. This guy's not a bad actor.'" Then, they can't stop because they have invested so many resources. "So we really need to go after this guy for a couple of minor things, otherwise, we're going to have to explain to someone, somewhere that we've wasted our time."

Practicing Medicine in a Changing Enforcement Terrain

The legal terrain that physicians must traverse has changed in the wake of the opioid crisis. Enforcement organizations have set their sights on healthcare providers and have gotten better at identifying, investigating, and prosecuting them. They owe their success to three trends: the growth of task forces, the spread of education through national organizations and informal social networks, and the availability of PDMP technology.

Most people can agree that bad doctors need to be stopped. There is far more debate about how to distinguish the good from the bad and what punishment should look like. Is it enough to prosecute bad providers, or are there other aspects of the healthcare system that require attention? There is also significant concern that punishing criminal physicians will prevent good physicians from prescribing opioids and leave their patients without care.

Absent clear legal standards, physicians practice in a legal gray area. Enforcement agents claim that they only go after the worst of the worst, but what counts as "worst" is in the eye of the beholder. According to pain advocates, some enforcement agents make mistakes. They misinterpret evidence or see illegal behavior where there is none. They take innocent physicians through a grueling process. Even if physicians are cleared of all charges, the damage—to their reputations and their practices—has been done.[62]

How does prosecution affect doctors writ large? Physicians don't know the ins and outs of the legal system or the strategies used to investigate and prosecute providers. They are not aware of the roadblocks enforcement agents face when building and trying cases. All they know is that more physicians are going to prison for something they themselves do—prescribe opioids. Physicians protect themselves by policing patients.

4

Surveilling Patients in the Hospital and the Clinic

PHYSICIANS ARE CAUGHT in a contradiction. On the one hand, they are trained to care for patients, and on the other, they are blamed for the most harrowing drug crisis the United States has ever faced. They must strike a balance, treat patients without making the problem worse. Yet many tools at their disposal are more useful for policing patients than treating them. In the fast-paced world of medicine where physicians have only a tiny window of time to juggle law, policy, insurance coverage, and patient need, it can be very difficult to put the patient first. Add to that pressure from federal agencies like the Drug Enforcement Administration (DEA) and the Centers for Disease Control and Prevention (CDC), and it is clear why physicians venture into enforcement territory. What is not clear is whether these changes in medical practice are good for patients.

I asked Jessica, a family medicine doctor in Kansas City, how she could tell the difference between a patient in pain, a patient with a substance use disorder, and a patient who is diverting drugs. She told me it was "impossible to tell," because "they all look the same. They all behave the same." Still, she has to decide whether or not to provide opioids. Like most physicians I interviewed, Jessica uses a variety of tools such as pain contracts and the PDMP to separate patients into categories for whom she will and will not prescribe. "You set expectations; you have them sign the expectations; you check up; you follow through on checking up; and you make sure they're following your prescribing as directed." She finds this frustrating because "doctors have caused this problem to a certain extent, but we're also stuck with that impossible task. There is no good answer."

She longs for the clarity about opioids that she thinks physicians had before the 1990s. At that time, "opioids were very much reserved for specific causes and we were a little bit more clear about pain." Now, she thinks that "everybody expects to be pain free," which she considers "unreasonable." "You can't tell the difference between somebody who is in pain or somebody who is frankly selling drugs on the street so that they can eat food." She says that the problem is so immense that the simplest action has a lot of appeal. "Sometimes it's just easier to turn a blind eye, write a prescription, and go home to your family and eat dinner." Dealing with uncertainty and working with patients who want opioids is extremely taxing. Says Jessica, "you only have so much emotion to give." So "at the end of the day, you're, like, fine; here. I just don't have the bandwidth to fight with you. So, good luck." She knows that other primary care doctors refuse to prescribe opioids at all. She and her colleagues are not ready to take that step; "we just do the best we can."

Jessica's struggle over opioid prescribing reflects larger hardships in medical practice and in professional work in general. The medical profession has lost quite a bit of its authority to powerful forces like insurance companies and legislatures who have a vested interest in how healthcare is practiced. Insurance companies have positioned themselves as for-profit mediators between doctors and patients.[1] Legislators try to reshape medical practice to suit their political agendas, as we have seen recently with abortion, guns, COVID, and trans care.[2] Sociologists once held medicine up as a model of professional power and authority.[3] No longer. Constraints on healthcare practice have simply become too great to afford physicians the independence they once enjoyed.[4]

An undeniable force that has transformed medical practice is the pressure to work efficiently. According to professor of medicine Saul Weiner, physicians have become "efficient task completers" instead of healers, which isn't good for them or their patients.[5] Moving quickly from one case to the next makes it difficult to connect with patients in meaningful ways, resulting in corner-cutting and burnout.[6] Efficiency struggles also invite moral beliefs to creep into professional practice. Inadequate time to make decisions can prompt workers to rely on stereotypes, cognitive shortcuts that make working fast easier. Workers who control resources and punishments have to triage, and their choices are frequently influenced by ideas about moral worth. In their book *Cops, Teachers, Counselors*, professors Steven Maynard-Moody and Michael Musheno reveal how professionals in each field use ideas about "worthiness" to determine whether clients get more than the law allows, less than the law allows, or exactly what the law allows.[7] Notions of deservingness also seep into decisions made by other professionals with heavy workloads and inadequate resources such as judges, emergency medical technicians, nurses, and social workers.[8]

Interviews I conducted with physicians mirror this larger body of research. They reveal how they decide who deserves opioids and who does not, how they treat "deserving" and "undeserving" patients differently, and what happens to the patients they refuse to treat. The language of deservingness comes from sociology, not medicine, but it provides a useful way to think about how patients that some physicians consider undesirable are treated. I interviewed three types of physicians who prescribe opioids: primary care doctors (including internists and family medicine doctors), pain specialists, and emergency medicine physicians. They grapple with the same problems in different ways. However, at some level, physicians in each field police patients. We can begin to understand how by entering the hospital and the clinic to witness physicians' struggles, see how they reconcile them, and consider the social and cultural forces that shape their choices.

Physicians Are Powerful and Conflicted

Physicians have a great deal of power in the healthcare system. They have expert knowledge derived from years of training; they control valuable resources that improve people's lives; and they have discretion to decide who gets those resources.[9] Physicians are also fiduciaries tasked with making decisions for patients when patients are unable to decide for themselves.[10]

As noted earlier, physicians normally act as *medical gatekeepers*.[11] That is, they use medical knowledge to decide what a patient needs and use medical tools to treat them. Physicians run tests, make diagnoses, and devise treatment plans.[12] In the usual practice of medicine, screening leads to more treatment, and physicians make referrals when the patient has a problem they can't handle. Let's say you slip on some ice and land on your arm. Your arm is tender, swollen, and difficult to move. You suspect it might be broken, so you go to your general practitioner. They order an X-ray, which is read by a radiologist. If the injury requires a procedure that the primary care physician cannot do, they will refer you to an orthopedist, who will set your arm and follow up until you heal. This is an idealized version of medicine, what we think physicians *should* do. Keep this idealized version of medical care in mind as you learn how physicians treat patients with opioid use disorders and patients with chronic pain. The differences are striking.

One critical difference between treating a broken bone and prescribing opioids is how closely the physician is monitored by law enforcement. Law enforcement polices physicians with the same tool physicians use to police patients, the prescription drug monitoring program (PDMP). Few physicians I spoke with knew that law enforcement uses the PDMP, but they hesitate to prescribe opioids because they sense that someone is watching—if not law enforcement, then certainly their employer or medical board.

Some physicians also feel guilty for their profession's role in the opioid crisis and see restricting opioids as a way to atone. Guilt arises for Matt, an emergency medicine physician in Kansas City, when he sees a patient on high doses of opioids. "The way that our country has dealt with chronic pain in the past has always been opioids," he says. "Patients know when they take their pain pills, they will feel better." However, patients develop tolerance to their dose over time, so doctors have historically increased the dose to keep pace with the pain. "So when people come and say, 'I'm not addicted to my pain medicines,' I say, 'No, you are, and I'm not saying that's a bad thing. We've done that to you. Some doctor has addicted you to opioids, because that's all they've done for your chronic pain.' So yes, they're dependent on it and they're drug seeking, but they have chronic pain."[13] Previous doctors did what seemed right at the time, and Matt is left to pick up the pieces.

Shannon, a lawyer who works for a physicians' association, explains: "Doctors are in a tough spot because now they have to be on the defensive. If they don't treat the pain, they're at risk of being liable for not treating the pain." On the other hand, if the patient develops a tolerance to the drug and the physician gives them a high dose that's "accurate for whatever level of pain they have and what tolerance they have," the physician is "at risk of law enforcement action." Doctors want to treat their patients, but they do not want to lose their license or end up in prison. Therefore, they must find a way to protect themselves from law enforcement while also prescribing opioids. This predicament pulls physicians beyond their normal role as medical gatekeeper into the role of *legal gatekeeper*, where they make decisions about patient care while highly attuned to law and law enforcement. Physicians act as legal and medical gatekeepers when they decide who deserves opioids.[14]

Legal gatekeeping is a defensive strategy. In physicians' minds, they protect themselves by tightly restricting access to opioids and meticulously documenting their decisions. Doing so shows that they are obeying the law by prescribing opioids appropriately. Most physicians prescribe to a small set of "deserving" patients, create strict rules by which those patients must abide, and use enforcement tools to check compliance. Decisions about which patients deserve care are informed by cultural ideas about moral worth that come

from law and medical education. Making decisions this way amounts to policing patients.

Three intertwined constraints motivate physicians to police patients:
law, uncertainty about the patient, and time limits. First, federal and state
laws require physicians to prescribe opioids in "good faith," which means
that the physician must have a relationship with the patient and the patient
must have a "legitimate" medical condition.[15] From a legal standpoint, the
"deserving" patient is the one with pain and the "undeserving" patient is
the one with an opioid use disorder or the one who is diverting medication
to sell.

Second, following the law is hard when it comes to chronic pain because
physicians have no objective way to measure it. Pain is highly subjective. X-rays
and MRIs might show bone or tissue damage, but they cannot show the
amount of pain a person is in.[16] One popular approach is asking patients to
rank pain on a scale of 1–10.[17] Patient reports are not always reliable, though.
Chronic pain patients might exaggerate their pain because they are afraid
physicians will not give them sufficient medication. People with opioid use
disorders might fabricate physical pain to get opioids because they want to
escape the painful process of withdrawal. And people who sell opioids might
lie about pain to protect their revenue stream. To make things even more complicated, the same patient might fall in multiple categories. The pain patient
might also be selling their meds. The person with the opioid disorder might
also be in physical pain.

Third, physicians rarely have enough time or resources to figure out what
kind of patient they are working with. They have less than twenty minutes on
average to make the complicated and consequential decision of whether to
prescribe opioids.[18] All of this leaves physicians at a loss.

Under-resourced and under the gun, it seems reasonable for physicians to
seek out other ways to differentiate "deserving" patients from "undeserving"
ones and to ensure that their prescribing meets legal standards. "Is this patient
in pain, struggling with an opioid use disorder, or diverting medications?"
physicians ask. Enforcement tools provide an answer. Nestled in the enforcement toolkit are pain contracts, PDMPs, urine drug screens, and random pill
counts that operate in tandem to help physicians decide whether or not to
prescribe. Almost all of the physicians I interviewed used some combination
of these tools.

What sets enforcement tools apart from medical tools is their purpose. Medical tools are used to screen and diagnose patients with the purpose of providing

care. Enforcement tools are used as lie-detector tests with the purpose of denying care to patients who, in physicians' minds, shouldn't get it. The same tool can fall in both categories. For example, a urine test can help diagnose diabetes or show that a patient has taken an illegal drug. In the first instance, the results prompt a referral. In the second, the physician refuses to prescribe opioids or fires the patient. Use of enforcement tools takes physicians far afield of their standard practice and into the realm of policing patients.

Policing Patients

Physicians have become very conservative about opioids. Prescribing rates have plummeted since 2012,[19] and today's physicians take several precautions to ensure that they are treating only those patients deemed deserving in the eyes of the law.[20] Physicians police patients when they use enforcement tools to determine whether a patient deserves opioids. The choice is as much moral as it is medical. Physicians find opioid patients difficult to treat. One pain specialist in Missouri called these patients "emotional vampires" because they require a lot of time listening and negotiating. "It's exhausting," she told me. "Every single one of them is an exhausting encounter." Patients must prove they are worth the trouble.

The first precaution is limiting the patient panel. Many physicians take on only those patients that they think are good candidates for opioids and who they think can follow the rules. In their minds, these are the "deserving" patients, though they don't use that term. They use more coded language like "difficult" and "challenging" to describe patients who seem risky. These physicians avoid "undeserving" patients by screening them out or by refusing to prescribe.

Kristen, who works as a pain management specialist in Kansas City, instructs her front office staff to screen patients before she sees them. When staff see red flags in a chart such as "this is the sixth pain clinic they're coming too, they were fired from the last provider and had a drug screen that was not good," they tell the patient that they are "not a good candidate to come to our clinic." Kristen has limited time, so she wants to devote her energy to patients she thinks she can really help, not those who present challenges from the outset.

Not all troubling patients are easily screened, so physicians build in an extra safeguard—they refuse to prescribe opioids on the first visit. Physicians see this as a way to identify problematic patients and protect their own reputations. Darren is an internist in Kansas City who never prescribes opioids on an initial visit. He is very selective about the patients he takes but says that patients who are seeking opioids do get in sometimes. "Of the new patients coming to see me, I would say about 30 percent to 40 percent are seeking opioids." I asked what his interactions with those patients looked like. Patients are explicit about what they want. "They're like, I have chronic pain. I want Percocet. Some of them are legitimate in that they have chronic pain and they really feel like this is what will help them. And some of them are trying to get high, and it's hard to know who's who." Making the patient wait is one way to tell the difference. Darren says when patients come to their first appointment, "they shouldn't be so desperate that they need a script right then. Because it doesn't make sense. What were you doing before you saw me?" He suspects patients who exhibit excessive and immediate need of buying the drug on the street.

It is also common for physicians to use policy to stop addicted and diverting patients from coming to their clinic. Autumn, a family medicine physician in Saint Louis, works at a university hospital with a policy that does not allow opioids on the first visit. She says this is standard in academic settings; the hospital where she did her residency had one too. The goal is to avoid patients who go from doctor to doctor to get opioid prescriptions. Autumn thinks that having the clinic manager share the policy up-front keeps drug-seeking patients away. "Because patients talk to each other, especially if you have a group of them that's diverting their medication. 'Hey, I found this doc so and so, you can get them right on the first day.' Or, 'Hey, I saw this doc the other day and she was mean, and she wouldn't give me any of blah. We're not going there.'" Whereas some physicians dole out opioids like candy, restrictive policies tell patients, and those in their social networks, that "you're not a candy factory."

Screening strategies don't work for everyone. Sometimes physicians have no choice about who they see. They inherit patients when another physician retires or when a physician in legal trouble leaves patients behind. Physicians who inherit patients known as "legacy patients"[21] struggle to reconcile their own prescribing preferences with those of past physicians. Prescribing norms have undergone a sea change in the past 20 years with newer physicians far less willing to prescribe opioids. Shocked by the volume of opioids their patients are taking, new physicians try to limit patients to an amount they find acceptable and that conforms to the CDC guidelines.

When I met Jennifer, a Saint Louis pain management specialist, in the summer of 2019, a physician in her practice had just retired, which left her team of twelve physicians to absorb 650 of his patients, all of whom were on opioids for chronic pain. This was a huge shift for Jennifer, who normally did not prescribe opioids. Now, around 10 percent of her patients are on opioids, all from the retired physician.

I asked Jennifer how she dealt with patients on opioids that she would never have prescribed. Her approach was standard: she tapered. Jennifer tried to reduce the dose as compassionately as possible, but she emphasized that "my goal, regardless of whether or not it makes the pain slightly worse, is to come down on this number, and we're going to do it slowly." She expects the elevated pain that occurs with tapering to diminish over time. She restricted all patients "unless they're on a pretty low number already."

Another reason physicians sometimes take patients that they would usually screen out is financial—they want to maintain a good relationship with the physicians who refer to them. Take pain specialists, for example. Those who work in private practice get many of their patients from internists and family medicine physicians. The real money in pain medicine comes from interventions—things like cortisone or steroid injections, nerve blocks, and spinal cord stimulation. Opioid prescribing is neither profitable nor desirable, but physicians in primary care need a place to send the patients they can't (or won't) treat.

Scott, a pain specialist in Kansas City, told me he attracts referrals by taking difficult patients off these practitioners' hands. "I know that if I take care of some of their nightmare patients, when they get the fifty-year-old who's got a herniated disc who needs a cortisone injection, who are they going to send that patient to? The provider whose name they know, who they know that they can send their pain patients to." This quid pro quo creates a political economy of care—doctors take undesirable patients to secure desirable patients in the future. Physicians try to limit themselves to deserving patients, but usually wind up with a mix.

The second precaution physicians take is establishing the rules of engagement. Many require patients to sign a pain contract[22] that sets restrictions around their care. Standard pain contracts state that the patient will receive opioids from only one physician and one pharmacy. They will submit to urine drug screens. They will not get early refills. They will not go to the emergency department to get opioids and they will not give their medications to other people. Any violation of this contract can result in termination from the practice.[23] "It's good to lay out all the rules," Darren says. "Because when somebody's breaking the rules then you can look back at it and say, look, you are not following the rules. We have to change this. Because if you don't, people would be like, I didn't know. You need to do that at the start."

Pain contracts also help keep physicians in line. Physicians who practice in the same group may prescribe quite differently. Some are more comfortable with stronger opioids in higher doses and others shy away. Deb's group of internists in Missouri has created a policy that requires all opioid patients to be on pain contracts. She explains, "I have some partners who I would be a little uncomfortable practicing how they do or taking on the burden of some of their patients." The pain contract relieves this tension because it makes her feel like they "are all practicing up to the same standard."

The third precaution is tight monitoring. If the pain contract sets the rules of engagement, PDMP reports, urine drug screens, and random pill counts ensure that the patient follows the rules. Knowing that opioids are desirable and profitable, physicians hesitate to take patients at their word. They ask patients if they have gotten opioids elsewhere and if they are taking illegal drugs, then they use other evidence to confirm the patient's statements. Don, a family medicine physician in Southern California, advises to "trust, but verify." He adopted that mantra because, according to him, "addicts will tell you anything to get their drug of choice."

Enforcement tools seem to indicate whether or not a patient is deserving. Patients have to continuously prove their worth. Like a tightrope walker who must place each step perfectly, patients struggle to stay aloft in the physician's mind. The deserving patient is the patient who follows all of the rules: their PDMP shows one physician and one pharmacy; their urine contains prescribed opioids and nothing else; and the right number of pills remain in their bottles.

These screening tools are so powerful that they can make physicians second guess their first impression. Gerard, who works on Florida's Gulf Coast, had a patient, a white guy in his early thirties, whose story was so outlandish that it could have been a movie plot. He was fixing up a house when he and his partner got shot, which catapulted him into pain. When he showed up at Gerard's clinic from a town an hour and a half away, he "looked squirrely, very thin, a little shaky," and he had this crazy story to tell. Gerard immediately labeled the patient undeserving. "There's no way I'm buying this." Gerard decided to drug test him. To his surprise, he found nothing illegal. "OK," he thought, "you've given me a story that, though incredible, is consistent. So I have no reason to not take you on as a patient." He remained suspicious, but every time he tested the patient, "it was perfectly fine."

It may seem counterintuitive, but patients who don't want the pills or who are not using all of their prescription are considered particularly deserving. They contrast sharply with undeserving patients who are adamant about getting opioids or who run out of pills before a refill is due. Colin, a Kansas City family medicine doctor, says "The ones that you know are probably spot-on are the ones that come in somewhat reluctantly. They have pills left over. They're saying geez, I really still need these, but is there anything else that we can do?" This is an odd twist on medical norms. Usually, the deserving patient is the "compliant" or "adherent" patient, the one who takes all of their meds as prescribed. A diabetic patient who doesn't use all of their insulin is considered a problem; a pain patient who doesn't use all of their opioids is considered worthy.

The deserving patient receives opioids. The undeserving patient faces further scrutiny. Perhaps they got a prescription from another physician or their urine drug screen comes back positive for marijuana. This sets off alarm bells. The physician's response depends on the offense.

Physicians first respond to troubling news by sitting the patient down for a talk. The physician presents the patient with the evidence and offers a chance to explain. Kristen tells her patients, "We check this drug monitoring program and according to this, it says that you're getting opioids from at least two other doctors. You've gotten them while you were under an agreement with me and that's not a situation that we can allow." Some violations are more serious than others. A patient who had a tooth extracted or an operation and received medications from the dentist or orthopedist has technically violated the pain contract, but most physicians simply remind those patients that they should not receive opioids elsewhere. If the behavior continues, it results in a warning. Kristen cautions, "If I see anything like this in the future, then our agreement will be discontinued and you will not get any more pain medication here."

Physicians' second response is to ramp up policing. They check the PDMP and screen patients' urine more frequently or require them to submit to random pill counts. Gerard doesn't do random pill counts often but considers them an option "for people we are unable to really get a handle on." These were patients whose stories didn't quite fit and whose drug screens did not always show the prescribed drug. Gerard says that "unfortunately, it became a sting operation."

When physicians decide they can't trust the patient with opioids and the patient is on a high dose, the physician tapers. I asked Danielle, a Saint Louis pain specialist, how she navigated circumstances in which the patient was seeing multiple doctors. She said she responds by "pulling out the old tried-and-true opioid contract." She tells the patient, "You have a contract saying you're only going to get your medications from one prescriber. Since you are getting medication from multiple providers, we're going to talk about weaning you. I don't know where the medication is going. I don't want to give you more medicine that I can't trace. Are you selling it to your friends? Are you giving it to kids in the street?"

To an outsider, tapering sounds easy, but those who have been through it say it is a grueling process.[24] If you've ever been on a diet, you understand something about tapering. You are used to a certain number of calories a day, and suddenly you have to cut those calories by a quarter or a half. Only with tapering, instead of feeling hungry and cranky, you feel all of the symptoms of withdrawal—the anxiety, the diarrhea, and the body cramps.

Travis Rieder, a bioethicist who took opioids to recover from a gruesome motorcycle accident, describes his experience trying to taper himself off like this: "The early stages of withdrawal felt, for the most part, like a terrible case of the flu. It ramped up sort of slowly, with nausea, runny nose, and the sweats." This was after he reduced his opioid intake by 25 percent. These initial symptoms later gave way to trouble sleeping and a feeling of being "caffeinated." By the time he tapered another 25 percent, he found himself sweating in the air-conditioning and covered in goosebumps in the sun. When people ask him what withdrawal symptoms are like, he tells them to "imagine the worst case of the flu you've ever had, and then multiply it by a thousand."[25] Patients stay with doctors who taper them because it is difficult to find another physician who will prescribe, and some opioids are better than none.

There are physicians who don't even taper; they just refuse to prescribe. Colin says he "investigates" patients when he spots red flags. "If they're truly shopping around, I say 'Look, I don't want any part of this. I'll see you for your hypertension, but I'm not going to give you opioids anymore.'" Gerard does the same thing. He had several patients test positive for cocaine; "I said I'm happy to treat you, but under no circumstances will you get opiates." Most patients left the office and never came back.

Some physicians take it a step further. Not only do they refuse to prescribe, but they try to stop their colleagues from prescribing too. Matt tells patients who visit his emergency department (ED) in Kansas City that he is going to look them up in the PDMP and "find all of their dirty laundry." When he finds something suspicious, he confronts the patient. He prints out the PDMP report as proof that they lied to him. "'You told me that you don't take any opioids but I see that you got thirty,' I'll show [the report] to them, 'thirty oxycodone filled at this pharmacy from this doctor.'" The patient might try to explain it away, "Oh, well that was for my back or that was for my hip, that's not for this," but Matt will not back down. "You told me you don't have *any*." He asks the patient what is going on. "Are you abusing these pills? Are you selling them? Do you feel like you need help?" He considers this a form of counseling. If the patient responds, "No, I am just in a lot of pain," Matt says, "Well, I worry about that for you. I'm going to mark the chart so we're not going to give you any more opioids from our health system." He flags the patient in the system so that the next time they come to the ED, "there will be a note that says they have been untruthful about their opioid usage." The new doctor could choose to prescribe, but the note is a big red flag.

In the most extreme cases, physicians fire patients. This happens when a patient is "doctor shopping" or their urine doesn't have the prescribed medication in it, which suggests that they are selling the drug instead of using it. Kristen had a patient on a pain contract who kept getting opioids in the ED. She considered them a risk. "I feel like your behavior demonstrates that you will potentially be found dead of an overdose, so I cannot, in good conscience, write you medication." She let this patient go because "they're not capable of following the agreed upon terms."

I asked Gerard why he uses a pain contract since he could fire patients at any time without a contract in place. He told me, "It's an easier sell to a patient" because "you're no longer telling the patient, 'I can't see you because I choose not to.' It's 'I can't see you because you broke the contract.'" This approach leaves the physician blameless by transferring blame onto the patient. Gerard shrugs: "I kept my end of the bargain up. You didn't keep up your end of the bargain. You can't be mad at me. Be mad at yourself."

Firing a patient could result in retaliation. Doctors mitigate this possibility by firing the patient by mail or by ramping up security. When Gerard confronts patients, they react in one of three ways: "You get absolute denial, and they would go to their grave denying it all. You get the complicated explanation, which makes no sense. Or you get the 'yeah, you got me,' and they just quietly walk out of the office." The deniers, he says, could get violent.

He handles that possibility by using security cameras, having a plan for his staff, and de-escalating the situation by saying that the decision is out of his hands. His standard response to patients is "'I totally believe you. But I have no choice, because otherwise I'm going to end up in jail. So I'm stuck.' They know you're bullshitting them, but it doesn't escalate the problem, usually." He says that avoiding confrontation and giving patients an out made things better. "They're really bummed that they're not getting their medication, but they'll usually go peacefully. Maybe a door slam or clog the toilet up. We've had that multiple times."

Some patients save the physician the trouble of firing them—when confronted, they leave on their own. Gerard had a white patient in her late forties.

She was a nurse on workers' comp and well-educated and "presented really well." There were never any red flags, and she was "the perfect patient" until she came in one day with her grandchild. His secretary was the first to spot it: "There's something off with her, something bizarre." He decided to drug test her. "Holy crap. Everything came up. Heroin, meth, you name it." He confronted her and "she just walked out. She knew she was busted." That experience taught Gerard never to let his guard down and fail to screen a patient who seems to be doing the right thing. "I mean, you are the poster child for what a good pain patient should be, and you are the worst."

Physicians know that they could find themselves in legal trouble if a patient overdoses on a drug they prescribed. However, few were explicitly concerned about law enforcement using the PDMP. I asked physicians how they felt about law enforcement. I noted that physicians can use PDMPs to monitor patients and asked if they thought that law enforcement could use PDMPs to monitor them. Many had never considered the possibility, but none were particularly concerned. Their standard response was, "I don't care about being monitored because I am not doing anything wrong." They also feel like they are doing a lot of things right. Documentation is the main way that physicians protect themselves from law enforcement. Closely detailing their decisions alleviates concerns about being investigated or losing their licenses. Because they are so cautious, they do not worry about what law enforcement might learn about them from the PDMP.

Policing patients is a form of defensive documentation that creates a paper trail. It shows that the physician did everything possible to ensure that the patient had a legitimate need for the opioid. That means surveilling patients and following the CDC guidelines. Different specialists use different tools. They all use the PDMP on a regular basis, but general practitioners and pain specialists are more likely than emergency medicine physicians to use pain contracts, urine drug screens, and random pill counts. However, the purpose of the tools—surveillance and enforcement—remains the same.

Omar, who practices pain medicine in San Francisco, says he is not concerned about law enforcement or the medical board because he has equipped himself with enforcement tools. He estimates that the pain specialists in his group are probably among the top three prescribers in the state. "That doesn't bother us, as long as we are doing an opioid agreement, the urine drug screen, and making the documentation." As long as physicians note the rationale for their prescriptions, he says, "I don't think any of our doctors have fears." Kristen points out that policing patients frees physicians from culpability. If a patient for whom she was prescribing were to overdose, she says, "It would be like, 'Well I was conforming to the CDC guidelines.'" Doctors' behavior calls to mind the old adage: "If you can't beat 'em, join 'em." Physicians don't fear law enforcement because they are policing patients themselves.

Deserving patients must run a gauntlet to get opioids, but they still fare better than undeserving patients. "Undeserving" patients are deserving patients who fall from grace or patients who were never deemed worthy in the first place. Some patients cannot comply with the physician's strict rules because they have an opioid use disorder. Some patients are in the wrong place at the wrong time—they have a lot of pain on a Saturday and go to the emergency department, which violates their pain contract. Patients like these find themselves tossed from one physician to the next.

The Patient "Hot Potato"

Faced with a patient deemed undeserving, physicians are caught in a dilemma. They can prescribe opioids and risk legal action, or they can dismiss the patient and fail to help someone in need. Providing help is difficult because most physicians have not been trained to treat opioid use disorders and the vast majority lack the certification necessary to do so.[26] Physicians cope with this impossible situation by passing patients along to other physicians they think can provide better care. The result is an endless cycle. Because everyone hands the patient off, the patient ends up without treatment.

Physicians protect themselves by drawing a firm boundary around their professional expertise and sending patients who fall outside that boundary to someone else. What this means in practice is that patients find themselves in a liminal space, untethered to a specific provider who can give them long-term care. Patients literally cannot find help to save their lives.

Physicians' scope of practice consists of the treatments and procedures they are educated, trained, and legally permitted to provide. When it comes to opioids, each type of physician narrows their scope of practice to place undeserving patients out of bounds. General practitioners (GPs) say that they are ill-equipped to provide opioids for chronic pain, so they limit opioid care to 90 days. According to the CDC guidelines, 90 days is the transition point at which pain goes from acute to chronic,[27] so GPs want to send those patients to a pain management physician. Pain specialists emphasize that they are specialists, trained to handle complicated cases, not basic opioid prescribing, so they resist patients whose cases are simple. Emergency medicine physicians limit themselves to emergencies, so they see only patients who are in crisis and do so for a brief period. No specialty is eager to treat chronic pain patients on high doses of opioids. And physicians are especially resistant to treating patients they suspect have an opioid use disorder.

The core tension between general practitioners and pain specialists arises from the question of who will prescribe opioids long term. Both types of physicians resist this task. General practitioners believe that pain specialists should be the ones to provide opioids because chronic pain falls within their scope of expertise. Pain specialists believe that general practitioners are perfectly capable of managing patients on opioids and prefer to spend their time doing procedures that are fast and lucrative compared to opioid prescribing, which is slow and unprofitable. Pain specialists are willing to evaluate patients on opioids or consult with their primary care physician, but then they want to hand the patient back.

At her internal medicine practice in the San Francisco Bay Area, Seema rarely prescribes opioids herself but sometimes inherits patients who are already on them. When that happens, she uses a common strategy—she tells the patient that she will prescribe for three months, but then they must go to pain management. Seema's expectation is that the pain specialist will taper. She stays involved a bit. She asks the patient how things are going and says, "If pain management is not reducing it the way I'd like, I tell them how I would prefer they do it." Other physicians expect the pain specialist to continue prescribing the current dose.

Pain specialists balk at these scenarios. Scott, who works in private practice, feels backed into a corner by general practitioners who promise patients he will do something he won't. "The primary care says, 'I don't write for opiates. The pain specialist does.' Then they come to me with that expectation. And I want them like I want a freakin' hole in my head."

Jennifer, who works in a hospital, wants to use her specialized knowledge and perform procedures. "That's really our primary goal, to try to do the things that we're fellowship-trained to do." Seema's cases don't meet these criteria. Jennifer considers what Seema is doing "dumping" patients. Even sending a patient along with the goal to taper is a dump "because of the time-consuming nature of it. It's a lot of work, actually."

Pain specialists are specialists above all, and they expect to be treated that way. Jennifer doesn't consider opioid treatment unique to her specialty: "We aren't any more equipped to prescribe opioids than anyone else just because we're pain management." Kristen draws a parallel between pain management and other specialties and wants to tell general practitioners: "You don't expect the gastroenterologist to write their proton pump inhibitor once they get started on that. You don't expect the cardiologist to write their hypertensive once they get started on that. Why is it that you expect the pain management specialist to take over management that you've already initiated because you don't feel like it?"

Kristen's comments highlight the differences between how medicine usually works and how opioids are treated. The drugs she mentions—those used to treat acid reflux and hypertension—can be prescribed by either a primary care physician or a specialist. Regardless of who prescribes them, they are usually managed long term by primary care in consultation with the specialist. The 2016 CDC guidelines that were developed to help primary care physicians with opioid prescribing support a similar dynamic. They suggest that primary care physicians should consult a pain specialist when patients whose doses are above 90 morphine milligram equivalents (MME) do not show improvement or require escalating doses.[28] However, this does not mean that they should hand off the patient to the pain specialist for long-term care. As Kristen notes, primary care providers are permitted to manage patients on long-term and high-dose opioids, but legal risk motivates them to hand them off to specialists. She doesn't want to take on simple tasks just because the general practitioner is uncomfortable. "Sometimes I feel like they view me as a way to get rid of their undesired situations."

If the simplicity of the task is one reason pain specialists resist opioid patients, the effect on productivity is another. Kristen's employers measure her productivity using something called a "relative value unit," or RVU.[29] Her compensation depends on how many RVU targets she meets. It works like this: "If I do an established patient visit for 15 minutes, the RVU is just under one. If I do an epidural, like a cervical epidural, that's almost two." Interventions are desirable because they take little time and have high RVUs, especially compared to prescribing opioids. "If I end up taking a patient that's going to spend an hour in my office sobbing and crying the whole time, if that's what I end up getting every single time the general practitioner sends someone to me, and I get nobody that I'm going to do intervention on, it's reducing my ability to reach my RVU targets." Efficiency is key. Working with opioid patients makes Kristen look less productive to her bosses, which can affect her paycheck, so she has no incentive to see them. Some general practitioners are transparent about handing difficult patients off to pain management. Says Deb, who works in Kansas City: "I have an out. I sit down with you and say, 'I'm going to send you to a pain specialist. So bye-bye.'"

Deb makes it look easy. It is not. Pain specialists have their own strategies for avoiding "dumps" from primary care. Some, like Scott, simply refuse to treat the patient. "I don't want them," he says. "I tell them, 'I'm not taking you on. I mean, I see all kinds of red flags. You're on benzodiazepines. Your urine's dirty from marijuana. You're not showing up to work.'" The combination of opioids and benzos escalates overdose risk. Patients respond, "Well, what am I supposed to do, doc? I have one pill left, and my primary care doc won't write for me." Scott tells them "I don't know" and walks out, leaving the patient "irate."

Others, like Jennifer and her colleagues, adopt policies that state they don't "take over opioid prescribing." They will not continue the dose of opioids that another physician prescribed; they make their own independent decisions. Both the referring physician and the patient are informed of this policy and the pain physicians follow it even when the patient is in a great deal of pain. That doesn't always stop patients from expecting a refill. Jennifer blames misinformation spread by the GP. "They've been told that once we see how much pain they're in we will change our minds. But we pretty much don't ever take over opioid prescribing."

A third way pain specialists push back is by having a frank conversation with the general practitioner. They attempt to educate the GP about the kind of work they do while also setting boundaries around their practice. For example, Kristen, like many pain specialists, does not consider it her responsibility to prescribe a small number of opioids for chronic pain. However, she encounters resistance from general practitioners when she points this out to them. "I've said, 'You know, the patient's on three Hydrocodone a day,' and the primary care provider's like, 'Well, I am not going to write opioids for this patient; they need to go to the pain clinic for their pain medication.'" Kristen tries to invoke the CDC guidelines to make the GP understand. "I say, 'This is well below the CDC's recommendations for primary care physicians. I don't see anything that looks like a red flag. The patient's been on it for quite some time. I see no reason why this cannot be maintained in a primary care setting.'" After all, she reasons, "we cannot take every single patient that needs three Hydrocodone a day." Doing so would create such an influx of patients that she would never get to the work that she is board certified to do. "I can spend my whole day doing nothing but writing prescriptions for people but that's not really why I come to work." Sometimes her explanations fall on deaf ears. GPs balk at her refusal to prescribe opioids by insisting "that's your job." Interactions like these reveal a serious mismatch between how general practitioners see pain management and how pain specialists see themselves.

Kristen is willing to make a deal: She will evaluate opioid patients with the understanding that they must go back to primary care. "I'll give them options, I'll assess risks, I'll do a drug screen, and I'll make a recommendation." But she insists that they work together in partnership. "It's not just you send them to me and they never come back to you for this problem. If it's not a highly complicated high-dose situation with high risks, I should feel comfortable saying, 'Now you're going to go back and see the GP.' And you should be willing to accept those patients back." This collaborative approach aligns with the 2016 CDC guidelines.

Some GPs take her up on it. Most patients, however, are caught the middle. The GP sends them to the pain specialist and the pain specialist sends them back to the GP. Where do patients refused by these doctors end up? Some go to the emergency department, but that's not a solution either. Emergency medicine is structured around emergencies, not ongoing medical problems, so it is not an option long term. Besides, some hospital administrators have begun to declare their EDs "opioid free," which makes them a poor short-term option as well.[30]

Seema and her partners have a policy: they don't prescribe opioids on weekends. Other providers do the same. Standard pain contracts require patients to promise "I will not call between appointments, or at night, or on the weekends looking for refills."[31] From Seema's perspective, "Opioids are never an urgent prescription. Because if it's that urgent you're going to the ER or you're going to an urgent care setting." Seema's policy works well for her—she teaches her patients where her boundaries lie—but her policy creates a burden for emergency medicine physicians who see her patients when she won't.

Emergency medicine physicians don't think of chronic pain as an emergency. They expect patients to be established with either a GP or a pain specialist who prescribes their opioids. They might give out a few pills in the emergency department but are reluctant to offer more. Toby, who works in Kansas City, says he would be unlikely to prescribe opioids for chronic pain because "we expect them to already be in a relationship with a provider who is managing their pain." In the rare cases that he does give the patient a day or two's worth of a prescription, the patient still needs to return to their primary provider.

Some emergency medicine physicians acknowledge how hard it is to get opioids from pain management and primary care. Matt sums up the game of hot potato that lands so many patients in his lap. "A lot of primary care doctors nowadays are saying, 'I won't prescribe opioids. You need to go see pain management.' And what does pain management say? Pain management will say,

'We're a procedural specialty. We don't prescribe opioids.' Then these people are back to the ER a couple of days later, saying, 'I'm still in a ton of pain.'"

Matt says he is "stuck in a pickle" asking whether he should give the patient more meds. He finds the PDMP "exceedingly helpful" in those cases. He looks up the patient, and if he sees no red flags, might try to get them help. But patients still get stuck, especially if they don't have insurance. He describes uninsured patients as "even more screwed because you don't have a primary care doctor. And you're not going to get in to see a pain management specialist if you don't have insurance." These patients, he says, "get bumped around, emergency department to emergency department. They're going to get these onesie, twosie prescriptions of pain pills, and we'll say, 'Hey, follow up with a safety net clinic.'" However, he admits that he has no idea how long it will take the patient to get in.

Like many emergency medicine physicians, Matt ends up with patients who have been fired by their GP or pain specialist. Some patients are fired when the doctor finds out they are using illegal drugs. "If they have THC in their urine, they're going to get fired from the pain clinic and now what are they going to do?" Matt asks. Of course, he knows the answer. They will come to his emergency department. He considers firing patients for "dirty" urine drug screens a form of patient abandonment. He sees it as "a slippery slope" of physicians imposing their morals on patients, especially at a time when marijuana is becoming legalized. "Where are we in society now that I'm going to terminate them because they use drugs?" The firing, however dubious, creates more work for him. "I think patient abandonment is a big issue because then it pushes them back in my lap."

Stuck with patients they believe someone else should care for, emergency medicine physicians also want to avoid "frequent flyers," patients with opioid use disorders who return to the ED again and again. Hospital policy helps. Physicians like working in "opioid-free EDs" because it takes the decision out of their hands. They don't have to tell the patient "I *won't* prescribe you opioids"; instead they tell them "I *can't*." According to Matt, putting formal rules in place "has made it easier for several of the physicians to state that this is a system policy and not just me saying this." That gives him a ready answer when patients use popular excuses like their medication was missing, destroyed, or stolen. Matt tells them, "It's in our policy; we can't replace lost or damaged prescriptions." The patient must get the new prescription from the original prescriber. The fact that the response is so consistent also helps prevent patients from coming back again. They understand that it's not just one doctor refusing, the whole hospital system is a dead end. From general practice to pain medicine to emergency medicine and back again, patients are trapped in an endless loop.

You may have noticed one player conspicuously missing from the game: the addiction specialist. If a physician suspects that the patient has an opioid use disorder, why don't they send them to someone who can treat them?

The short answer is they don't know how. And even if they knew, it would be a struggle. The structure of healthcare is the culprit. Hot potato is a game played in a tight circle. Participants sit knee to knee as the music plays and the potato circulates. Mainstream medicine is also a tight circle that excludes practitioners who fall outside narrowly defined categories. Physicians who work in long-established fields such as oncology, orthopedics, family medicine, and internal medicine are in. Addiction specialists are out.

Addiction specialists are excluded from mainstream medicine for several reasons. One, it is a relatively new specialty. The American Board of Medical Specialties did not recognize addiction medicine as a subspecialty until 2015.[32] Certification exams were created a few years later. Although residency programs were available as early as 2011, the Accreditation Council for Graduate Medical Education did not legitimate these programs until 2018. Doing so enabled addiction medicine programs to receive federal funding enjoyed by residencies in other specialties.[33] Another factor is that practitioners typically work in clinics that are physically isolated from other practitioners. They work with stigmatized patients, so some of that stigma spills over onto them.[34] And, most importantly, addiction treatment is a vast and largely unregulated field. Its workers range from physicians who are certified in addiction treatment to people with no formal training at all. Facilities range from hospital-based clinics to freestanding opioid treatment programs, from church basements to expensive resorts. As a result, it is very difficult for an outsider to distinguish between places that provide excellent treatment and those that provide no treatment at all.[35] Add to that the fact that the average physician receives little to no addiction training[36] and the fact that facilities are chronically full, and it is clear why physicians struggle to find help for their patients.

In a perfect world, physicians would refer patients to addiction specialists the same way they refer patients to other kinds of specialists. In the real world, they rarely refer at all. Physicians who want to send patients to addiction treatment must navigate the Wild West of addiction territory without a map. Most have neither the time nor the desire, so patients must fend for themselves.

Some physicians fire patients outright. "To me, an addiction is a legal problem," says Scott, the Kansas City pain specialist. "They're lying, cheating, stealing to get the drug. So I don't deal with them. They're fired from my practice." Other physicians question patients' motivations for wanting treatment. Luke, who works in a Kansas City emergency department, thinks that patients manipulate the system. They pretend to want treatment, but "really what they want is some food and a place to stay." Once released, "they go back out and they start using again."

More compassionate physicians offer resources that are likely to be fruitless. A common strategy is to give patients phone numbers of treatment centers and have the patients call in the hopes of getting in. Blake, a pain specialist, says, "I'll offer them phone numbers for methadone clinics or other places that can help with coming off of opioids." He knows their efforts are futile. "Let's be honest. Most of those places are either full or expensive."

Toby and Matt, emergency medicine physicians in Kansas City, told me that they have patients call detox and rehab centers in the local area. Says Toby, "We can't call for them. They have to call themselves to get accepted." This shows motivation. Still, most places are full. They ask the patient to call back in two weeks and they will try to get them in. Toby knows that is unlikely. "You have a window of an hour or two hours to get some of these people into treatment and there's just not enough in-patient resources for these people." These physicians send patients on a road to nowhere; it should be no surprise that they keep coming back.

From a legal and medical standpoint, physicians don't have to refer out for addiction treatment. They can provide one of the most effective treatments—buprenorphine—themselves. At the time of these interviews, all it took was a few hours of training and an application for physicians to get an X-waiver that permits them to see 100 patients in the first year and 275 patients after that.[37] Now, any physician with a DEA registration can prescribe bupe. People who take buprenorphine have a 59 percent lower risk of overdose and a 26 percent lower risk of opioid-related acute conditions.[38] However, only 5 percent of physicians currently have an X-waiver, and many who have them do not prescribe to capacity.[39] Failing to get an X-waiver is a missed opportunity to treat patients.

I asked Neil, a Kansas City internist, what prevents him from getting an X-waiver. He responded, "The better question is what would motivate me to do something like that? I mean, you certainly are taking on some really difficult patients." He told me he was content with the care he already provides and preferred to refer out. To him, referral means telling patients to go to a psychiatry group that specializes in addiction medicine. Some patients don't want to go. They tell him their bus doesn't go there. He says "I'm trying to empathize, but not enough. I think if people want something, they can figure out a way." He isn't sure what kinds of treatment they provide but thinks it is detoxification and other standard forms of rehab like talk therapy. He doesn't think they provide buprenorphine.

Neil's approach—which stands in sharp contrast to typical medical referrals—highlights how segregated addiction treatment is from other forms of care. Usually, referrals take the form of a warm handoff. Let's say that you have stomach problems that your primary care provider can't address. They might send to you to a gastroenterologist that they know has a good reputation. They are also likely to have some sense of the kinds of procedures that the specialist offers even if they don't know all of the details. What often happens with addiction treatment looks more like a cold handoff. Neil knows where to send the patient but can only guess at what kinds of treatments they provide. Those he mentions—detox and talk therapy—tend to be far less effective than medication treatment like buprenorphine and methadone.[40] A patient could take his advice, go to great lengths to get treatment, and be no better off for it. This is not entirely Neil's fault; the problem is systemic. With addiction medicine cordoned off from mainstream specialties, most physicians have few opportunities to learn about addiction treatment in school. Unless they independently seek out the information, those knowledge gaps persist.

Other physicians don't prescribe out of fear of law enforcement. After Kristen had gotten an X-waiver but before she began prescribing, "DEA agents came into our office one day and said we want to audit all your Suboxone and charts. Well, like we don't have any, but that's scary. I mean, you're under scrutiny and, am I going to be walked out of here in cuffs if you don't like what you see?" With so few physicians prescribing the medication, even if addiction specialists were included in the game, the results would be no better. Those at capacity would simply toss the patient away.[41]

The New Face of Medicine

Think back to the idealized version of medical practice I described at the beginning of this chapter. By now, you have probably concluded that the way physicians treat patients with chronic pain and patients with opioid use disorders is dramatically different. The contrast is partly due to physicians' attitudes, partly due to their fear of law enforcement, and partly due to a healthcare system that is not designed to treat chronic pain or addiction. Physicians have learned a lot about opioids in the past decade, and they are genuinely concerned about doing more harm than good. However, the tools available push them toward enforcement.

Like the mythic Trojan horse that distracted the Trojans with its shape, enforcement tools have the same contours as healthcare tools. They have been billed as healthcare tools. They can operate as healthcare tools. In fact, they look so much like healthcare tools that physicians can convince themselves that they are using them to treat patients. However, these tools have a pernicious quality that becomes evident when we see patients policed out of treatment and shuffled between practitioners. Physicians can't do what they normally do—screen, diagnose, and treat—because they don't have the training or the resources. Forced to straddle the line between treatment and enforcement, physicians police patients and call it care.

Physicians rarely acknowledge that they are using enforcement tools to police patients. I asked several if they thought these tools were enforcement tools and most said "no." They said that they used these tools to provide better care for their patients. However, as we will see in chapter 7, what they call care looks dangerously like abandonment. They taper patients to lower doses, refuse to provide opioids, shove patients off on other providers, and fire them from their practices. Sometimes they give the patient a chance to explain; often they do not. No one stops to ask what happens to patients who can't get help. Patients who are lucky enough to get a prescription must run another obstacle course, this one at the pharmacy.

5

Surveilling Patients at the Pharmacy Counter

SUSAN WORKS IN A FAMILY-OWNED PHARMACY located eleven miles outside of Jackson, Mississippi. When we met in the spring of 2010, she had worked at Gerald's Drugs[1] for over twenty years and had been a pharmacist for fifty. Full of laughter, she greets each patient by name as they walk in the door. She asks about their families, their jobs, and their injuries, and they seem happy to see her too, chuckling as they walk out the door with a white paper bag of medication. But not all interactions are as friendly. Susan has struggled with some of her patients, particularly those looking for opioids. I ask how she can tell that a patient is addicted to or diverting opioids.

Susan grows serious as she explains. She keeps an eye out for "red flags." Behavior and appearance are dead giveaways. "It's the way they walk up to the counter and it's their demeanor and it's also their vocal tone. They walk in and they say, 'Hey, Susan! How are you today?' and I look at them and think, 'I've never seen them before in my life.' But they're smart. They read the name up here, see?" Susan points to the name plate above the counter. "And they start talking—chatter, chatter, chatter, chatter, chatter, chatter, chatter. They pace. The whole time you're filling, you're going crazy because they're pacing up and down, okay?"

Patients who ask for specific colors or shapes of medication raise concerns as do patients who get multiple opioids at once. "Do you have the blue Xanax?[2] Do you have the pink Lorcet?" "They ask for the bar of Xanax," her technician chimes in. "Yeah," Susan nods. "And you get more on the street for the bars." Different colors fetch different prices too. Some patients come in with prescriptions for Hydrocodone and Xanax and either Dilaudid or Percocet. This sets off alarm bells; "people don't get those three drugs at the same time."

Patients who must travel several miles to get to the pharmacy are also suspect. As much as anything, it is a gut feeling that tips her off. Susan tells me,
"I wish one would come in and you wouldn't have any trouble." She admits
that she treats these patients differently. "I don't feel much compassion for
them at all. I'm sorry." And she isn't afraid to tell them no. "I don't have any
trouble turning them down even knowing that they may pull a gun out of their
pocket and shoot me. If they do, then I'm gone, okay?"

When I began interviews in 2009, most pharmacists had a lot in common
with Susan. They had quite a few patients who they thought were misusing
opioids, but no way to prove it. They made decisions based on red flags and
gut feelings. However, while Susan was confident in her choices, other pharmacists were haunted by the possibility of making a mistake, and unlike Susan,
who was ready to confront violence head on, other pharmacists tried to avoid
confrontation by telling the patient the drug was out of stock.

Pharmacists realized that the overdose crisis was mounting—they saw evidence every day—but it would be a few years before the problem made national headlines. Pharmacists made decisions with little guidance. They knew
one thing, though. It was not their job to police patients. Yalena, a chain pharmacist in New Jersey, summed it up: "The main reason why I love this profession is that I have the opportunity to help people. I would never want to be
involved with hurting them."

When I returned to some of those same pharmacies in 2011, pharmacy work
was beginning to change. The overdose crisis was on the front page of every
newspaper, the death toll had risen to over 40,000,[3] and the federal government had adopted a four-pronged attack.[4] Every state except Missouri and
New Hampshire, had created a statewide prescription drug monitoring program (PDMP),[5] and pharmacists were using them more often.

By the time I wrapped up my research in 2019, PDMP use had become
standard practice. PDMPs made it easier for pharmacists to deal with difficult
patients. With a few keystrokes, they could amass hard evidence of where patients had gotten opioids, which doctors had prescribed them, and how much
they had received. They didn't have to lie to patients and tell them that the
medication was out of stock. They could tell the patient that their own behavior made them undeserving of opioids. If they thought a patient was diverting
drugs, they could call the police. Something else had changed, too. Pharmacists now thought that policing patients was essential to their work. Most told
me they were helping patients by policing them.

What happened in the decade between 2009 and 2019 to make hesitant pharmacists enthusiastic about policing patients? PDMPs became more popular, and employers encouraged (sometimes required) pharmacists to use them. For some chain pharmacies, Walgreens in particular, enthusiasm for the monitoring program came after the Department of Justice (DOJ) sued them for failing to adequately monitor opioid provision.[6] Others saw the tides turning and tamped down preemptively.

New requirements brought pharmacists into foreign territory. Everyday use of the PDMP helped to change pharmacists' *routines*—whether or not they liked policing patients, they were doing it. Policing patients went from haphazard, case-by-case decision-making to a streamlined process. Pharmacists who performed new routines developed new *relationships* with physicians, law enforcement, and ultimately patients. All of these shifts helped pharmacists reimagine their professional *roles* such that policing became central to their work. As we shall see, these changes have had a powerful impact on patient care.

A Word about Pharmacy

Before we dive into how pharmacy practice has changed, let's take a step back and consider what pharmacists actually do. Most people give little thought to pharmacists, even though patients see them on average nine times more often than they see physicians.[7] Doctors, on the other hand, loom large in our cultural imagination. Countless TV shows dramatize medical life; almost none features a pharmacist.

Could it be that pharmacists are just not that interesting? Many people believe that pharmacists are glorified store clerks who obey physicians' orders without question. They think, as comedian Jerry Seinfeld once quipped, that pharmacists do nothing more than "take drugs from a big bottle and put them in a little bottle."[8] Public ignorance of the pharmacy profession makes sense. Many of us approach the pharmacy counter, hand over a piece of paper, and see it magically transformed into a bottle of pills without ever encountering a pharmacist. This might lead us to believe that pharmacists are powerless or unimportant. Nothing could be further from the truth.

Pharmacists are the "ultimate gatekeepers" to opioids.[9] They are the final barrier standing between patients and their medication, so they exercise significant power over patient care. Pharmacists make their own decisions. They have their own licenses and answer to their own professional boards. Pharmacists can refuse to dispense medications they deem inappropriate, and it's a good thing, too. Pharmacists serve as an important check and balance on physicians' prescribing. They spot medical errors like the wrong medication or the wrong dose that could injure or kill patients.[10]

Pharmacists are legally obligated to refuse to dispense in some cases. The federal Controlled Substances Act (CSA) that requires physicians to prescribe in "good faith" assigns pharmacists a "corresponding responsibility" to ensure that the medication is used for a medical purpose.[11] In the eyes of the law, the "legitimate" purpose of opioids is to treat pain. Failing to fulfill their legal responsibilities can land pharmacists in hot water with the DEA. Over the past twenty years, many pharmacists have been charged with overdispensing opioids and other crimes. Pharmacists' decisions matter. And, more importantly, *how* they make decisions matters. Conversations with pharmacists taught me how much pressure rests on their shoulders and how they grapple with difficult decisions. Even if we take for granted that pharmacists are professionals, the question remains what kind of professionals they are supposed to be.

Pharmacists as Gatekeepers

Like physicians, pharmacists struggle over whether to be medical or legal gatekeepers.[12] Most got into pharmacy to help patients, but law requires them to make sure that patients are getting medications for the right reasons. Pharmacists face another challenge. They work in stores that make money by dispensing medications. Refusing comes at a cost, literally. Choosing not to dispense doesn't affect chain pharmacists' base salaries,[13] but they know that it can result in a confrontation with management if the patient complains. Independent pharmacists know that they must dispense medications to keep their business afloat.[14]

Pharmacists are also strapped for time. Pharmacies are chronically understaffed, and workers are expected to do more with less. Many pharmacies have only a single pharmacist working at a time.[15] The other people in white coats behind the counter are technicians with less education and training. At many stores, a single pharmacist and a single technician must juggle prescriptions that arrive via phone, drive-thru, walk-in, and text, and they are expected to dispense a prescription every 3–4 minutes. Some stores have a countdown clock on the computer that turns red as soon as they exceed their optimal dispensing time. All of this adds up to a high-pressure environment where consequential decisions must be made fast.[16]

To add another layer of difficulty, pharmacists contend with a great deal of uncertainty. They do not have the medical chart that shows the patient's diagnosis and course of treatment.[17] If they work for a chain, they can see the prescriptions that the patient has filled chainwide, and they do keep notes on patients, but that information is incomplete. Their blind spots are huge. They don't know the patient's medical history or the justification for the course of treatment they are on. These limitations make it especially hard for pharmacists to fulfill their duties under the CSA. How can they know that a physician's decision is sound when they know so little about the patient? They can call the physician for more information, but physicians are difficult to reach and sometimes balk at questions from pharmacists, who occupy a lower position in the healthcare pecking order.

The pharmacists I interviewed in the days before the PDMP did the best they could to follow the law and appease their employers, but they struggled mightily. They did not want to police patients, but felt they had no choice. I remember talking to Richard, an independent pharmacist near Jackson, Mississippi, who thought he was caught up in a drug ring. Patients were coming "out of the woodwork" from clinics as far as Houston, Texas, to his tiny pharmacy to fill opioid prescriptions. His biggest concern was the volume. "I've got people coming to this little podunk town from Louisiana and Mississippi by the dozens for thousands of units of hardened narcotics: oxycodone, other stuff, too." He did everything he knew to do. He called the clinics to verify the prescription. They confirmed they wrote them, but he couldn't shake an eerie feeling that "something's wrong there." When we spoke, Richard was eagerly awaiting a call from the Texas Medical Board, the organization responsible for licensing and disciplining physicians. "I'm hoping that the board says, 'Yes, it's all on the up and up. These guys are all clear.'" In the meantime, he couldn't find clear answers and had no idea what to do.

When I caught back up with pharmacists starting in 2011, they had been thrown a life preserver of sorts: the PDMP. The PDMP solved a lot of problems. It made their work easier and faster. What they didn't anticipate as they clung tightly to this life preserver was how using it would change their profession. Observing pharmacists with and without the PDMP reveals how using this technology changes pharmacists' *routines, relationships,* and *roles.* What will first become evident is that PDMP use helps pharmacists decide who deserves opioids. Next, we will see how new routines for making decisions dislodge entrenched relationships with physicians and law enforcement. Then we will witness how pharmacists begin to envision policing patients as central to their professional roles. These changes are subtle, but impactful, so watch closely.

Bear in mind that policing patients is not new. The CSA that assigns pharmacists a corresponding responsibility to ensure that a prescription is being used medically is half a century old. Pharmacists had ways to police patients before the PDMP.[18] And communities of color have reported being policed by healthcare providers for decades.[19] However, three evolutions are worth noting.

First, the tools that pharmacists previously had to police patients (described in detail later) were not terribly effective. Second, pharmacists only had the bandwidth to police a subset of patients, so they had to be choosy. And third, pharmacists did not think that policing patients was their job. They insisted that their goal was to treat patients and felt very uncomfortable with any push to act like police. It is also important to recognize that pharmacists' greatest power lies in refusal. They can refuse to dispense a drug that a doctor prescribed, but they cannot do the opposite—dispense a drug with no prescription. Refusal can impact patients differently depending on where they live. Patients who live in cities or suburbs can simply try another pharmacy, but a single obstinate pharmacist can block access for patients living in urban cores or rural areas who cannot easily reach another store. Patients who need opioids must convince pharmacists that they deserve them. However, the processes pharmacists use to decide who deserves what—their routines—have changed.

Routines

Pharmacists' choices about whether to dispense opioids depend on how they categorize patients, a process sociologists call "social sorting."[20] Pharmacists sort patients by posing the same questions physicians ask: What kind of patient is this? Is this a patient who is in pain, has an opioid use disorder, wants drugs to sell, or is some combination of the three? "Deserving" patients have physical pain; "undeserving" patients do not. Pharmacists must figure out who they are dealing with and act accordingly.

Awash in uncertainty, pharmacists find themselves pulled in two directions—toward careful and cautious dispensing by law enforcement and toward fast, efficient dispensing by their employers. Yet they must decide, again and again, day in and day out, who deserves opioids, knowing that one misstep could place them in law enforcement's crosshairs. Potential errors are twofold: (1) they might overdispense to patients who are addicted to or are diverting medications, which could result in the loss of their pharmacy license or an arrest; or (2) they might underdispense to patients in pain, which could cause trouble with their employers and harm the very patients they have sworn to serve.

Despite having so much at stake, pharmacists spent years without the tools to make the right decisions. The PDMP offered insight where they had once been flying blind. Pharmacists welcome monitoring programs because they resemble healthcare technology, but they don't see that PDMPs sneak policing into pharmacy. Like the ancient Greeks who crept out of the gift horse when the Trojans were asleep, pharmacists' regular use of PDMPs invites enforcement logics into their practice. In the past, pharmacists made haphazard, time-consuming, and ambivalent decisions about who got opioids. Today, that process is far smoother. Policing patients has become routine.

The main differences in pharmacy work before and after the PDMP lie in how pharmacists decide who is deserving, how they protect themselves from law enforcement, and how they communicate their choices to the patient.

Before the PDMP, pharmacists lacked information about patients and acquiring more was a slow, painstaking task that risked angering physicians, pharmacy managers, and patients.[21] They did not have time to closely scrutinize hundreds of prescriptions a day without falling impossibly behind. Pharmacists made decisions based on the patient they saw in front of them and how those patients made them feel. They drew on stereotypes about people who looked unclean or unkempt and relied heavily on their intuition. None of this made pharmacists feel confident about their decisions.

Most pharmacists relied on a set of "red flags," social cues that signaled that patients might be using drugs for the wrong reasons. Pharmacists observed appearance and behavior; they noted when patients paid cash or asked for specific colors or shapes of drugs. They reasoned: "Who, except people who sell drugs, cares if their pill is a rectangle or an oval?"[22] Patients who looked bedraggled or had track marks on their arms were considered suspicious, as were patients who were overly friendly. "Honestly, when you've been in the business as long as most of us have at my age, it didn't take long just to watch the person, listen to him to know whether this is something that we really want to be pursuing," a sixty-three-year-old pharmacist who worked outside of Wichita, Kansas, told me. "I mean when they come in and they've never been here before and they want to know your life history and they're talking and just Mr. Chitty Chatty, the flags just start waving." Pharmacists were skeptical when the pharmacy was a long distance from the patient's home. How many pharmacies did they have to pass to get to me?[23] they wondered. They knew which physicians made a habit of overprescribing and watched their patients closely.

Pharmacists also sorted patients based on a gut feeling. Eric, a Mississippi chain pharmacist, explained: "Sometimes you get kind of a gut feeling that something's not right. . . . Later on, you kind of go . . . 'I hope to God that was a legitimate prescription.' . . . You don't want to lose your license or get in trouble in general for doing something wrong."[24] Gut feelings raised questions that pharmacists like Eric attempted to answer by gathering more information about a patient. They called physicians and neighboring pharmacies. When patients who had insurance on file wanted to pay cash, pharmacists would run the script through insurance anyway to see if they were trying to refill the prescription too soon. And if the pharmacist worked for a large pharmacy chain like Walgreens or CVS, they checked the patient's history through the chain-wide patient records system.

Investigating every person with an opioid prescription was untenable—any one of these strategies took time away from other tasks—so pharmacists chose which patients to scrutinize. The result was uneven, haphazard policing through which pharmacists monitored some patients very closely but gave others a pass, conditions ripe for discrimination. Indeed, some pharmacists admitted to unfair treatment. One independent pharmacist in Northern California only called the doctor on some opioid prescriptions. I asked him how he decided which ones warranted calls. He responded: "The same disgusting profiling that cops do. You know, what do they look like, what kind of vibe you're getting. There's a gut feeling or something that just doesn't feel right about it." Most pharmacists I interviewed were not this overt about discrimination, but statements like these confirm that patients were profiled at the pharmacy counter.[25]

Pharmacists might dispense a prescription that they thought was iffy when the physician encouraged them to do so. In those cases, pharmacists tried to protect themselves from law enforcement by documenting their phone call with the doctor. One pharmacist explained that in borderline cases, "It behooves us to have a conversation with the doctor and document the prescription." That way, the patient got their meds, the pharmacist avoided trouble, and the physician took responsibility.

When pharmacists chose not to dispense, one of the biggest challenges was breaking the news to the patient. Pharmacists feared that patients might become violent. Some had been yelled at or threatened by patients. They knew that they were the one thing standing between the patient and a drug they desperately wanted. The solution? A sidestep. Cynthia, a New Jersey pharmacist admitted: "I may tell them that I don't have the drug in stock or I can't get the drug." Why? "Because it is easier . . . that way when I walk out of here at night no one is waiting for me."

Many pharmacists took the same tack. By saying that the drug was out of stock, they made it seem like the choice was out of their hands. This left the patient with no one to blame and, the pharmacist hoped, prevented them from coming back. Note that pharmacists' fears do not necessarily reflect actual patients' behavior. Most patients who are addicted to or diverting opioids are not violent, but a bad experience or two was enough to put pharmacists on edge.

Juggling all of this information and initiating difficult conversations with doctors and patients took a toll on busy pharmacists. It is easy to understand why pharmacists found the monitoring program a tremendous relief. It untangled a chaotic process and made policing easy.

Pharmacy routines became more efficient with the PDMP. Pharmacists today don't need to go searching for information to decide who deserves care. All they have to do is hit a few computer keys to get a PDMP report that offers detailed evidence of a patient's behavior. They can see the number of clinics, hospitals, and pharmacies from which the patient has acquired opioids. They can see the types of opioids and the dose. If they are lucky enough to work in a state with an algorithmically sophisticated PDMP, they can even get a risk score. Of course, these decisions are still not easy. Pharmacists do not rely on PDMP reports alone to make choices about patient care, but PDMPs do compile critical information they could not easily access before. PDMP reports clarify an opaque process and help pharmacists navigate a risky practice environment rife with uncertainty. Pharmacists think that PDMPs provide them with data necessary to make dispensing decisions quickly and correctly, so they feel more comfortable policing patients with the PDMP in hand.

One might imagine that if pharmacists checked the database for every patient every time, PDMP use could disrupt the discriminatory practices that pharmacists engaged in before they had access. However, pharmacists are still time-strapped, so most do not check on everyone. They have two choices to make: whether to check the monitoring program and whether to dispense.

Most pharmacists only check the database for patients they consider "suspicious," so PDMP use tends to reinforce instead of counter discriminatory practices. Pharmacists still use red flags and gut feelings to identify suspicious patients, but now they also use them to decide whether to check the monitoring program. Like many pharmacists, Paul checks the PDMP for specific categories of patients; these include new patients and patients who have a high-volume prescription. "Any new client that enters, we look at the CURES system [California's PDMP]. Any client that gets a large quantity, we might just do a spot check on them." Stories that don't add up drive pharmacists to the database. Paul says he consults it "any time we get an unusual call like 'I lost my written prescription' or 'I lost my medicine.' . . . Those are the signals—the red flag goes up."

PDMPs also help pharmacists find patients who would have previously flown under the radar and reassures them about patients whom they previously doubted. Minh, a chain pharmacist in Missouri, was surprised to find that "all these patients that I thought were following the rules . . . were actually trying to divert." Meanwhile, "some people I thought might've been abusing, they're actually getting it on time."

Pharmacists feel more confident in their decisions when they use the PDMP. Information found there either confirms or refutes the pharmacist's initial impression, so they can dispense or refuse with a clear conscience. Still, sometimes pharmacists are not so sure. They come across prescriptions that may or may not be legitimate and they can't get enough information from the PDMP. In those cases, they protect themselves from law enforcement by closely documenting interactions with patients and physicians, a practice I call *defensive pharmacy*. Akin to defensive medicine,[26] the goal is to protect the healthcare provider, even if it undermines patient care.

Pharmacists practice defensive pharmacy when they document interactions with physicians and patients as if they are gathering evidence for an investigation. At the extreme end of documentation, pharmacists require considerable information from patients and closely track any dispensing exceptions made on their behalf. For example, if a patient wants an early prescription because they are traveling, Diego, who staffs an independent pharmacy near Miami, requires the patient to show him travel tickets or hotel reservations. He copies these and files them in their chart before dispensing the medication in case he gets audited. Eduardo, another Florida pharmacist, keeps track of conversations he has with physicians to protect himself from the DEA: "If we get audited, the DEA comes in, or if, God forbid, the patient goes and overdoses, I have that documented conversation."

Pharmacists communicate with patients differently too. PDMP use emboldens them to stand up to patients in ways they previously had not—their policing practices, once hidden, become explicit. Some pharmacists share

PDMP data with patients to let them know they are being watched and to discourage them from returning to the pharmacy. They own their professional discretion by telling patients that they are actively refusing instead of hiding behind the lie that the drug is out of stock.

Laura, a chain pharmacist in Southern California, explains how her approach to refusal changed once she had the PDMP: "We look at their CURES, we're just like, 'Oh, I'm sorry. I can't fill this for you.' And now, eight out of ten times, they know it. They'll just be like, 'Okay. Thanks.'" She takes the prescription away because now she has proof of wrongdoing. "Before, it was more like, 'I'm not comfortable.' 'Well, why aren't you comfortable?' And now we're like, 'Well, because you just went to two other doctors, you filled it at this independent pharmacy, you filled it at this other retail pharmacy,' and then I'll be like, 'You know, within 30 days, you filled 480 tablets. That's a little too much.'" Patients confronted with evidence don't push back, Laura says. "Now they're like, 'Okay.'"

Pharmacists are less concerned about patient confrontation or violence because they now have adequate proof of the patient's behavior. Pharmacists report that after taking this proactive approach, they have fewer patients who are addicted to or diverting opioids. In sum, PDMPs afford new kinds of routines that bring pharmacists deeper into policing territory.

Relationships

Technology use also reconfigures pharmacists' relationships with other professionals. Pharmacists who use PDMPs to police patients find new ways to interact with physicians and law enforcement, professionals who exercise significant power over them. Before the PDMP, pharmacists subtly resisted physicians' power and avoided law enforcement out of fear. Now, pharmacists openly challenge physicians and ally with law enforcement.

Pharmacists are stuck in an interprofessional hierarchy that dates to the early 1900s when allopathic physicians gained power and pushed pharmacists, midwives, chiropractors, and nurses to the fringes of medical practice. Allopathic medicine became mainstream and other professionals were either subordinated to physicians (nurses and pharmacists) or thrust out (chiropractors and midwives).[27] This explains why pharmacy work depends on medical work. Pharmacists can only do their main job—filling prescriptions—when a physician writes the script. Pharmacists might be important for keeping patients safe, but physicians do not always see it that way.

Years ago, when pharmacists relied on gut feelings to make dispensing decisions, calling the doctor was difficult. They had little to go on, and physicians were hard to reach and unhappy to hear from them. Pharmacists who dared question physicians' prescriptions faced hostility—doctors did not hesitate to remind pharmacists where they belonged. A chain pharmacist in San Francisco says a physicians told him, "I'm the doctor, you're the pharmacist; do whatever I say." Not all doctors behaved this way, but just a few negative interactions made pharmacists think twice about calling. Physicians were receptive to calls about fraudulent prescriptions because those threatened their medical license, but they chafed at calls about high-volume prescriptions.

This left pharmacists in an untenable position—required to monitor uncooperative physicians. Pharmacists coped by developing subtle but powerful resistance tactics. Pharmacists decided that if physicians were uncooperative or were overprescribing opioids, they simply would not dispense their prescriptions. They put those physicians' names on a blacklist and used the chainwide electronic system to warn other pharmacists. One Northern California chain pharmacist described these physicians as those who "prescribe a lot and often. And their patients come in, they're all cash-paying patients. There's no question about it." When patients came to the pharmacy with a prescription bearing those doctors' signatures, pharmacists either told the patients that they did not dispense for this physician or used their old trick—telling them that the drug was out of stock.

Pharmacists didn't want their colleagues to get in trouble, either, so they repurposed the notes section in the physician profile of their stores' electronic systems to write coded messages. They dubbed these physicians "candy doctors" because they doled out opioids like candy. Laura flags doctors in the system like this: "We have a little comment section at the bottom. It just basically says, 'Verify all controls.'" She is careful about terminology. "We don't really say 'candy doctor,' but we have our own little way of speaking to other pharmacists like starring after the physician's name, just asterisks, anything that's out of the norm makes a pharmacist look at it closer." Physician blacklists and intra-chain communication allowed pharmacists to police physicians but avoid confrontation. These tactics reinforced the medical hierarchy and kept physicians' power intact even as pharmacists subtly claimed power when possible. The PDMP helped pharmacists challenge physicians directly.

Pharmacists gained power vis-à-vis physicians because of two factors: PDMPs gave pharmacists more patient information than ever before, and enormous legal settlements against pharmacies like Walgreens required pharmacists to scrutinize opioid prescriptions very closely. In 2013, Walgreens reached an $80 million settlement with federal authorities on the condition that it create a "good faith dispensing" protocol that requires pharmacists to call physicians and gather detailed information on opioid patients.[28] Physicians resisted—they said pharmacists were interfering with the practice of medicine[29]—but to no avail. Since then, these practices have only grown more common.

Required to use the PDMP by their employers, what had once been anathema to pharmacists—questioning physicians' prescribing practices—became routine. Traci, a Southern California chain pharmacist, explains how using the PDMP changed her interactions with physicians. When she first started calling to get more information about patients, doctors were confused. "What is this?" they asked. "I've never seen this. Why are you asking so many questions?" She would explain that the pharmacy now required documentation of what regimens the patient tried and failed, when the patient was last seen, and other supporting information. She concludes, "So now they're kind of used to it. . . . But yeah, they were pretty hostile."

Plagued by concerns about crime, pharmacists now question whether the physician's treatment plan is appropriate. A pharmacist who works at a chain in Saint Louis noted the shift: "Before the PDMP, it was lots of determining the legitimacy of the prescription, determining fraudulent prescriptions or altered prescriptions. With the rise of additional training, it's moved more to the legitimacy of the therapy itself, which has been a major change." He embraces this new responsibility. It is evident in how he describes his work: "Part of my professional judgment and corresponding responsibility is evaluating the doctor's chosen therapy."

Pharmacists are still attuned to power dynamics, so they tread carefully. They rarely accuse physicians of wrongdoing; instead, they gently ask if they are aware of the patient's behavior or note potential problems with the prescription. Pharmacists are most likely to call physicians who are unknown to them, who work far away from the pharmacy, and who are not connected to a university system or cancer center.

Kevin, who works at an independent pharmacy across the bay from Tampa, Florida, calls physicians on each new opioid prescription. He also contacts physicians who prescribe an opioid alongside a benzodiazepine. Both drugs are sedatives that slow a person's breathing, so together they increase the risk of overdose death.[30] Kevin avoids angering the doctor by citing the science: "Pain management guidelines really say avoid opioids with benzos," he tells them. "We're seeing a lot of the deaths and overdoses from this combination." His goal is to make the physician aware, but these conversations are also part of defensive pharmacy. "I cover my butt," he says. "It's a due diligence thing." He marks the conversation in a memo to make sure he covers all of the legal bases. "I document everything along the way."

Pharmacists continue to put notes in the chain-wide system to alert other pharmacists of problems with that doctor. A statement in the doctor's profile to "verify all controls" tells other pharmacists to be careful. Even as pharmacists use more overt strategies to police physicians, they retain some covert strategies, especially the physician blacklist. In some stores, the blacklist has become incorporated into chain-wide systems. This removes the choice about dispensing from the pharmacist and puts it in the hands of the pharmacy. One Florida pharmacist explains that his chain tracks physicians for whom pharmacists are unwilling to dispense. Pharmacists can submit a complaint form to the chain and once those complaints pass a threshold, no pharmacists working for the company can dispense for that doctor.

Other chain pharmacies seem to take the opposite tack. Shireen owns her own pharmacy in Southern California. She cut ties with her previous employer—a chain pharmacy—because they couldn't agree about opioids. Shireen, who describes herself as very vigilant, ran into problems when she was "floating," working different shifts at different pharmacies. The regular pharmacist would normally fill the prescription, but she refused because she saw a problem—multiple pharmacies or multiple doctors. Customers complained and her employers wrote her up. They told her to stop being so forthcoming with the patients (she had a habit of telling the patient exactly why she wasn't going to fill) and to "keep the customers happy." The chain had a system that allowed pharmacists to take notes. Shireen and her colleagues would caution others that "the DEA says don't fill for this doctor." Or "this doctor writes cocktails, the holy trinity." They put all kinds of notes in the system like "don't fill for this doctor; be vigilant." The system worked well and was a crucial communication tool for pharmacists. There were a lot of options on the system. But then, "all of sudden, and this was system wide, all of those were wiped out. Clean slate." I asked Shireen what she thought happened. She told me she suspected they didn't want pharmacists to use that information to deny prescriptions, then she clammed up. "I don't want to say anything more about that."

Problems with employers aside, pharmacists report that physicians are far more responsive now. That is partly because physicians better understand the overdose crisis, plus pharmacists have solid evidence courtesy of the PDMP.

PDMP use has also tightened the relationship between pharmacists and law enforcement.

It might seem like the worst thing that can happen to a patient is to be ejected from the pharmacy without their meds, but being arrested is worse. Pharmacists have grown increasingly aligned with law enforcement and more willing to report patients to the police. They also report bad doctors. The relationship between pharmacists and law enforcement is reciprocal. Enforcement agents told me they get some of their best tips from pharmacists. In a way, this makes sense—both pharmacists and enforcement agents use enforcement technology to police patients and physicians. It is no wonder they consider one another allies. However, these new collaborative practices contrast sharply with those prior to the PDMP. Past relationships were saturated with frustration, fear, and futility.

Before PDMPs were commonly used, pharmacists tended to call the police only when they suspected that a prescription was forged or stolen. Most of the time, they called the physician first and then called the police at the physician's request. Things did not always go according to plan, and they wondered if contacting law enforcement was worth it, especially when their efforts went nowhere and stoked fears of patient violence. Often, those arrested were released the next day and pharmacists worried about retaliation. At best, pharmacists were flooded with paperwork; and at worst, they were called to testify for cases that went nowhere.

Exasperated, Ken, who owns his own pharmacy in Northern New Jersey, told me, "We've called the police a number of times and that's very frustrating 'cause you've got to go to court. And you sit in court and the person doesn't show up and you just waste hours and hours of time." A chain pharmacist in Northeast Mississippi, just across the border from Tennessee, agrees. She previously worked for a big box store where she called the police on patients until her employer told her not to. "They actually stopped us from doing that because they want you to testify, and you have a whole lot of red tape that goes along with getting them arrested. Plus, it's dangerous." She resorted to telling the patient the drug was out of stock or saying, "The doctor said this is not valid" (after consulting with the physician); then she destroyed the prescription. These kinds of experiences illustrate why pharmacists found it easier to claim the drug was unavailable than to jump through the hoops necessary to contact law enforcement.

Even pharmacists who convinced law enforcement to take action felt ambivalent. Anthony faxed information about several questionable prescriptions to the DEA from his chain in San Francisco but initially received no response. "I made a phone call. I did online reporting and then, as far as I know, I never was contacted back by anyone." Several months later, though, "there was an investigation, finally, into this particular doctor, and the DEA did visit the pharmacy." The doctor was eventually put out of business, but Anthony spent the meantime agonizing over what to do with that doctor's prescriptions. "I feel like for months people were getting things they probably shouldn't be getting." He tried to be vigilant by calling and verifying the prescription, but doctors were unaccommodating. "Sometimes you would actually get to talk to the doctor, but the doctor would just try to justify it by giving you these diagnoses and they would fax you a pain sheet of all the different diagnoses they had." That left him in a precarious position. "At the end of the day, you have to believe and trust the doctor, but after you are seeing it so often and from so many different patients, flags just go off. This doesn't seem right."

Anthony was especially concerned about the pain patients who relied on this doctor for their meds. "It was tough," he sighed, "because we would see legit patients from the practice, too, patients that you knew were in severe pain and that did need it. So it was like you didn't all of a sudden want to shut down the doctor or stop filling prescriptions for the doctor." Anthony felt torn between policing the physician and caring for his patients.

In rare cases, pharmacists had good rapport with law enforcement. One pharmacist had a DEA agent approach her at her chain pharmacy near Jacksonville, Mississippi, give her his card, and say, "Call me anytime you need me." From then on, she called the DEA when she spotted a fake prescription and worked with them to arrest the patient. "Now, if I get a fake one, I always call the DEA first." The DEA agent tells her if the prescription is legitimate. "If it's fake, I go ahead and fill it. We sell it to the patient. Most times, the DEA is already set up to get the person." She was careful to note that she treats everyone equally. "I don't discriminate. I wouldn't say, 'Okay I'm going to let you go and then call the DEA on another person.' I call on all of them."

She was the exception. Pharmacists generally felt ambivalent about calling the police. Gita, a pharmacist I spoke with in San Francisco in 2009, was conflicted when a patient tried to pass a questionable script at her pharmacy. She wanted verification before dispensing. She told the patient she was waiting to hear from the physician, but the patient didn't want to stick around. "I said, 'Well, if you want to go to another pharmacy, I can call that pharmacy and see if they have this particular medication in stock.'" After the patient left, Gita heard from the physician. He didn't write the script. She called the police and told them where the patient was headed. "By the time she got to the other place, the cops were there. And it is kind of sketchy because she knew who I was, and she could come after me at any point. And here I was a new grad, trying to, like, arrest people."[31] Like Gita, most pharmacists were unconvinced that it was their duty to call the police. Doing so made them feel like "a detective and not a pharmacist."

Pharmacists also stayed away from law enforcement because they were afraid. Pharmacists dispensed opioids with almost no guidance, so they feared that they would be the ones investigated. Recall Richard who struggled to follow the law while bombarded with questionable opioid prescriptions at his tiny Mississippi pharmacy. He was torn. He wanted to do a perfect job, to follow the law to a T, but didn't know how. "If you're not being very careful," he reasoned, "then you're asking to end up in trouble."

Far from inviting law enforcement in, pharmacists struggled to keep law enforcement out. That changed when they got their hands on the PDMP. Pharmacists with access to the monitoring program have little to fear from law enforcement. They feel more confident that their dispensing practices are in legal bounds because they check the database and document their findings. Now, they have nothing to hide. As a result, they feel more inclined to contact law enforcement when they are concerned about a patient or a physician. When asked if they saw law enforcement as allies or adversaries, most pharmacists said allies.

When Shireen worked at a chain pharmacy, she had a good working relationship with the DEA and local law enforcement. "I would report to the DEA if I ever suspected a prescription should not have been filled. And then there was a time that the police officer called me and said, 'If this patient walks in can you let us know?' And I did and they came and arrested the patient." She also relied on the DEA to help her make dispensing decisions. She reached out to the DEA and asked, "Should I fill for this doctor?" They called back and said, "Don't fill," so she didn't.

Minh also collaborates with law enforcement. He once helped catch someone who had written a fraudulent prescription. "We called the police. They said, 'Okay, tell us when exactly she's going to fill it and when she's going to pick it up.'" He put candy instead of opioids in the pill bottle. "When she came up to the window, the cops were right there. We get calls all the time from the police: 'Hey, can you find out if the patient is actually on this?'" Likewise, Minh will call the police if he ever needs assistance, "especially with someone who's jumping from pharmacy to pharmacy or doing something that's illegal.

The cops will come back to me as well, saying, 'Hey, can you check the fill dates for this guy?' or 'Can you check where he's been filling?' They kind of use me as a PDMP resource," meaning that the local police, who do not have access to the PDMP, ask him to share the information, and he complies.

Pharmacists do, however, face pushback from employers who consider patient arrests bad for business. At his chain pharmacy in Kansas City, Carter's employers discourage calling the police. "We've just been flat told a week ago 'do not try to have anyone arrested.' Like, if you want to get law enforcement involved, then I have to call my boss, the market director, and get approval from him." I asked if he knew why. Simple. "They don't want to get sued." He wanted the option, though. "I feel like their logic doesn't add up." He shrugged. "I mean, they trust me with hundreds of thousands of dollars' worth of medication. But they don't trust me to make sure that this is a fake prescription, and getting the police involved is the right course of action. It's frustrating. It's just corporate. It's very corporate."

Enforcement agents want information that pharmacists have. The physician blacklist is especially valuable because it tells them who deserves closer scrutiny. Joe, a sheriff's deputy in California, says that pharmacists are especially helpful "when it comes to a patient doctor shopping." In one incident, "we arrested a lady recently who went to 126 physicians in one year and got over 10,000 Dilaudid pills. We didn't get that tip from a doctor, we got it from a pharmacist who said, 'Hey, I ran a CURES report when she came here to fill the script, it's out of control, you're going to need to look at her.' So we did, and we arrested her for doctor shopping."

In an especially striking example of the pharmacist–law enforcement alliance, a California chain pharmacist noted that one of pharmacists' "primary functions is we are the drug controllers" and explained that, because of this, pharmacists are "partners with the DEA because their whole job is to control all of the drugs, the legal and the non." Pharmacists who police patients and physicians see law enforcement as allies working to achieve a common goal.

Roles

Behavior and identity influence one another. The more that someone engages in a task, the more likely it is that they will see that task as central to their identity. Someone who writes is a writer; someone who teaches is a teacher; and so on. PDMP use has done more than change how pharmacists make decisions and how they interact with other professionals. It has shifted the very core of pharmacy.

Today's pharmacists operate on the cusp of healthcare and law enforcement, where caring and policing blur. Pharmacists are at once asked to be medical and legal gatekeepers. They are supposed to treat patients using the best techniques available and they are supposed to closely monitor patients for signs of illegal activity. Pharmacists once found these roles incompatible. They hesitated to police patients—it was exhausting, time-consuming, and emotionally taxing. Besides, they were healthcare providers, not police officers. Now, they regularly police patients and consider it a core aspect of their job.

They arrive at this conclusion through a cyclical process. Pharmacists use PDMPs to establish new routines. These routines reshape their relationships with physicians and law enforcement. As a result, they adopt new roles that incorporate both medical and legal gatekeeping. These roles make their routines appear even more legitimate—if you identify as police, it makes sense to police patients—and these routines justify newly configured relationships. All of these changes go together.

The process is complicated, and it cannot be attributed to PDMPs alone. Broad cultural factors operate alongside surveillance technology to push healthcare professionals toward policing patients. Popular narratives that blame the healthcare system for the overdose crisis[32] caution pharmacists to be more careful. In response, pharmacists have come to reframe policing patients as patient care and embrace PDMPs as a tool they use for keeping patients safe. Monitoring programs entered the scene at a time when pharmacists were strongly urged to be legal gatekeepers. Pressure from employers and the public helped pharmacists understand why they *should* police patients; the database ensured that they *could*. As a gatekeeper, pharmacists went from reluctant to enthusiastic.

Before PDMPs, pharmacists saw themselves as healthcare providers and thought policing patients clashed with their professional duties. Legal gatekeeping exceeded their training, and beyond that, it was annoying, it seemed dangerous, and they didn't do it well. Trying to live incompatible roles left them with a feeling of dissonance that they could not shake,[33] so pharmacists drew a bright line between medical and legal gatekeeping and banished the latter to the farthest outposts of their professional scope.

As the overdose crisis revved up, the boundaries pharmacists had carefully erected around their professional jurisdiction splintered, and pharmacists faced intense pressure to police patients. This threw them into disequilibrium. Not only did they think policing patients was not part of their jobs, but they lacked the tools necessary to do it. Kansas chain pharmacist Sarah said,

"Although I'm in the business of patient safety, I'm not in the police business. That's the least fun part of my job, feeling like you're a police." A nearby independent pharmacist added, "It can be frustrating because we didn't go to school to manage narcotics for patients. We went to school to learn drugs and counsel patients and run pharmacies. It's not what we were intended to do."

In those days, pharmacists lived a contradiction—they believed that legal gatekeeping lay beyond their professional purview but still did it every day. Pharmacists checked patients in store-wide databases, questioned physicians, and reported patients to the police. However, doing so made them deeply uncomfortable. Pharmacists believed that monitoring patients for illegal activity at best distracted them from their real jobs and at worst undermined patient care. They might cooperate with physicians and the police, but they were convinced that these tasks were better suited to enforcement agents. One exclaimed, "Oh, God, I've caught people—they've been filling fake prescriptions at our pharmacy for four years. We've had people arrested." She didn't feel good about it, though. "It's like I'm constantly surrounded with it, and that is really hard." Before PDMPs, pharmacists were legal gatekeepers, but reluctant ones.

Once pharmacists got PDMPs, they embraced legal gatekeeping, but not immediately. Policing patients routinely and systematically left them distraught. They began to occupy an intermediate space with one foot in medical gatekeeping and one foot in legal gatekeeping. Torn between two roles, pharmacists were uncomfortable. They didn't think that an enforcement tool belonged in healthcare practice. One pharmacist insisted the PDMP is "not healthcare" but rather "enforcement of the law." Pharmacists needed to find a way to reconcile the new routines that monitoring programs made possible with their roles as healthcare providers, those for which they were trained and to which they remained committed.

The stressful experience of being pulled in two directions at once soon gave way to a new, largely subconscious, *reframe and embrace* strategy that allowed them to harmonize competing roles. In the end, pharmacists reframed legal gatekeeping as medical gatekeeping to justify their involvement. They already believed that dispensing opioids to people who did not need them increased the risk of overdose and death, so they reasoned that ensuring the legitimacy of each prescription was a way to protect patients' health. Therefore, using the PDMP was not legal gatekeeping, a role they defined as outside the bounds of their practice; it was medical gatekeeping, a role that fell squarely within their purview. This cognitive shift enabled pharmacists to shed their reluctance and embrace legal gatekeeping.

In my conversations with Minh and Charlotte, both chain pharmacists in Saint Louis, I remarked that checking the PDMP seemed time-consuming.[34] They acknowledged that it slowed them down but thought it was worth it. According to Charlotte, pharmacists like the PDMP "because it helps us fill that prescription legitimately and determine if it's an appropriate prescription for that specific patient." She believes the monitoring program helps her fulfill her ethical obligations. "I mean, a pharmacist took an oath to do no harm just like other medical professionals. So, it helps us prevent causing harm."

Minh echoes Charlotte's sentiment and explains that using the PDMP also protects him from law enforcement. He says he checks the PDMP for every controlled substance prescription, no matter how long he has known the patient or who the prescriber is. "But evaluating that level of care and then protecting my license, there's really no time that I wouldn't spend trying to protect those things, the patient or myself." I asked him what he meant by protecting his license, "Like, what are you concerned could happen if you weren't as diligent as you are?" Law enforcement was top of mind. "Earlier today, the DEA raided five Rite Aids in Ohio on the suspicion of disproportionate opioid prescriptions or usage or whatnot. And for me, that would raise both my licensure and ability to provide." He also fears losing his license or going to prison, so he uses the PDMP "just to protect myself, but also to function at the highest level of my license to assist patients in their medical treatment. I mean, bottom line, that's what I'm supposed to do. That's my profession, that's what I chose to do, and checking PDMP has become one of those things that helps fulfill those requirements."

I point out that when I first started talking with pharmacists, they were resistant to monitoring patients in this way. Minh reiterates that using the PDMP has helped him to be a better pharmacist. "What evaluating opioids has done is reinforced what my education was for and that is achieving the best therapeutic outcome for a patient." That means talking with doctors and nurses more often. "I want the best outcome for patients and if I disagree with the plan and what the doctor's written, then I feel it's my responsibility to have that dialogue with the provider." Reframing his role in this way helps Minh to embrace policing patients and to see it as a way to expand his professional scope.

Most pharmacists thought the same way as Minh and Charlotte. However, some pharmacists were really resistant to the idea that they were policing patients or engaging in enforcement of any kind. Eduardo, an independent pharmacist in South Florida, twisted himself in knots trying to explain why using the PDMP was not policing. I noted that the PDMP and other tools like urine drug screens, pain contracts, and random pill counts might look like enforcement tools to an outsider. I asked if he thought about them as enforcement tools or something else. He told me the tools were surveillance, but definitely not enforcement. "Nobody's trying to actually go and put anybody in jail," he scoffed. "You never wake up in the morning and it's like, 'How many people can I catch today?' You're not trying to play cop. A pharmacist trying to play cop is really out of his depth; he doesn't know what he's doing. He can be investigative, he can be referring, he can be advising." But Eduardo was very clear that checking the PDMP did not feel like policing.

In Eduardo's mind, the difference between surveillance and enforcement is gathering information versus taking measures to put someone "behind bars." He thinks that preventing patients from getting medications helps the patient. "If the doctor filled the prescription too soon and I saw that and I stopped that, that's less pills for a guy that's trying to abuse. How is that tyrannical enforcement?" However, he felt good about surveilling patients. "Surveillance is not wrong if needed. It is needed, don't you think?" I reflected his thoughts back to him. "You're not thinking of it as an enforcement tool. You're thinking of it as a surveillance tool, so it gives you more information that you need in order to make a good decision about whether or not to dispense?" "Yeah," he conceded. "Just to prevent harm."

It is the rare pharmacist who thinks of the PDMP as an enforcement tool. A pharmacist who worked in a chain pharmacy about thirty minutes from Eduardo's had an entirely different take. I asked him the same question about whether PDMPs were enforcement tools. He leapt to defensive pharmacy. "It's CYA. It's just covering your own ass." By that, he meant that he was trying to take care of customers and prevent lawsuits at the same time. In a nutshell, he says, using a PDMP "is really law enforcement. It's not taking care of that patient. It's to prevent them from diverting." It is policing because "you're trying to catch the people that are doing wrong."

Defensive pharmacy and legal gatekeeping go hand in hand. Part of the reason that pharmacists now consider policing patients central to their professional role is because newer pharmacists educated in the shadow of the overdose crisis were trained to prioritize alleviating harm, which, for them, means refusing to dispense opioids. An independent pharmacist who has been practicing in Florida for fewer than ten years explains: "My generation of new pharmacists were trained with these things. . . . We know that we're the gatekeepers. We know this is part of our job. Not only are we making sure that patients are getting what they need, taking care of them, we need to make sure they're not going to be hurt by what they're taking." However, even pharmacists who were practicing before the crisis have begun to consider legal gatekeeping a fundamental role. Older pharmacists have been retrained to accept legal gatekeeping, and newer pharmacists had it woven into their training from the start.

Pharmacists balk at the term "detective" even when they describe using investigatory strategies. When Charlotte explains that checking the PDMP at her chain pharmacy in Missouri gives her more confidence that the prescription is legitimate, she is careful to differentiate between the work of a detective and the work of a pharmacist. "If I do utilize the PDMP, I feel like I have more confidence that I've investigated the script enough to see whether or not it's legitimate." Despite using terms like "investigated," Charlotte insists she is not a cop. "I never went to a detective school and I can't claim that I have any law enforcement background. But as a pharmacist, I legitimately looked at that prescription as an actual prescription and then I investigated the patient." Acting this way protects her from legal consequences. "I would feel comfortable with the way I filled prescriptions if law enforcement wanted to investigate me individually."

Phrases like "investigated the script" and "investigated the patient" reveal that today's pharmacists are oriented around crime and criminality. They police patients while providing care; but they make it clear that they are not police. Instead, they see legal gatekeeping as a way to prevent patient harm. The fact that it protects them from law enforcement helps, too. Pharmacists like Charlotte investigate patients because they want to make decisions that are defensible if they find themselves targets of a law enforcement investigation.

At the same time, pharmacists report that they are not afraid of law enforcement. I asked pharmacists if law enforcement could use the PDMP to surveil them. They hadn't given it much thought, but didn't care if they could. Pharmacists noted that they were already closely monitored by their employers and by the pharmacy board, so one more set of eyes did not matter. Besides, they had already covered their bases—they were checking the PDMP, documenting patient behavior, and refusing to dispense for undeserving patients. Legally, they thought, they were in the clear.

The Brave, New World of Pharmacy

For decades, the federal CSA imposed a policing role on pharmacists that they had had no good way to fulfill. The PDMP enabled them to embody this role, but it placed them in uncomfortable territory that threatened to undermine their role as healthcare providers. They coped with this through doctrinal and semantic sleight of hand: Policing is not policing when it's patient care. Reframing and embracing legal gatekeeping helps pharmacists convince themselves that little had changed.

Monitoring programs have made pharmacy work more efficient, but more efficient at what? PDMPs are surveillance technologies, not healthcare tools, so they do not offer new ways to deal with pain or substance use disorders; they simply empower pharmacists to view patients with suspicion and refuse to treat them. Doing so distances pharmacists from their sworn oath to provide care. Pharmacists believe that using the PDMP improves patient care, but only patient outcomes can determine whether or not that is true.

Policed at the clinic, the hospital, and the pharmacy counter, what happens to patients who don't make the cut? Where do they go when no one will prescribe or dispense their medications? Short answer: they suffer. And the establishment bears how much responsibility? Patients for whom no help is available must fend for themselves, and the data shows a disturbing provider willingness to let this happen. In the opioid prescriber's realm, every decision either exacerbates or eases, hurts or relieves, or both. Or both at the same time. On a good day, the balance tips in the patient's favor. But there aren't nearly enough good days.

6

Arresting Care

PHYSICIANS AND PHARMACISTS who use PDMPs to police patients believe they are doing the right thing. They are obeying the law and restricting access to addictive drugs. What could be wrong with that? However, research shows that turning patients away hurts them. Recall Kristen and Gerard, the physicians who fired their patients for failing to follow a pain contract. Kristen told patients that she couldn't prescribe "in good conscience" because she feared they would die of an overdose, and Gerard thought he might go to jail.

Studies show that some patients who can't get prescription opioids turn to the illegal, unregulated supply. Others give up hope and take steps to end their pain for good.[1] This "routing" patients, or turning them away, occurs because providers lack the tools to help patients with addiction and pain and because they fear law enforcement. Doctors and pharmacists find themselves caught between professional obligations to provide care and legal obligations to police patients. Those doctors and pharmacists who prioritize care place themselves at legal risk. Those who protect themselves cast patients adrift.

A Code of Ethics, a Cloak of White

Shoulder to shoulder in a sea of white, medical students raise their right hands and vow to put their patients first. They recite in unison: "As a member of the medical profession, I solemnly pledge to dedicate my life to the service of humanity. The health and well-being of my patient will be my first consideration." The oath varies, but the sentiment does not: They will treat patients, not diseases; they will do good; they will avoid harm; they will respect their patients' autonomy, treat them fairly, and honor their dignity.[2] Some oaths urge physicians to fight for social justice and to "improve the health of communities, both local and global."[3] Together with their classmates, these doctors-to-be in their new white coats commit to leaving the profession and the world better than they found it.

Started in 1993 at Columbia University by the Gold Foundation, the White Coat Ceremony exists to "emphasize humanism in medicine at the very start of medical education."[4] The ceremony has become so popular that nurses and pharmacists created their own.[5] Pharmacists receive their coats the first year of their PharmD as they vow to make "the welfare of humanity and relief of suffering" their primary concerns and promise to "apply [their] knowledge, experience, and skills to assure optimal outcomes for all patients."[6] The oaths set the ethical standards that physicians and pharmacists are duty bound to uphold.

Ethical principles are the foundation of healthcare practice. Professional codes of ethics reflect the four key principles popularized by philosophers Thomas Beauchamp and James Childress.[7] These are beneficence (do good), nonmaleficence (do no harm), autonomy (let patients make their own choices), and justice (treat patients fairly and equitably). These same four ethical principles are woven into law as well. They are the standards that professional boards use to gauge professional behavior. Those who act unethically can be required to pay a fine, undergo remedial education, or relinquish their license.[8]

Health professions place so much weight on ethical standards because they are professionally obligated to act in another person's best interests. In medicine, this is called a fiduciary relationship; in pharmacy, a covenant.[9] Both relationships acknowledge unequal power between two parties and obligate the more powerful party to prioritize the interests of the less powerful party. Healthcare providers know much more about treatment than their patients do, and they could easily abuse their power by manipulating patients into accepting their desired outcome. Casting the relationship in ethical terms sets standards of behavior from which providers should not deviate.

Ethical obligations apply to the entire doctor–patient relationship, even when it ends. It is unethical for physicians to fire patients without making sure they have somewhere to go. The American Medical Association Code of Ethics requires physicians to inform the patient about any potential roadblocks to ongoing care. It also states: "When considering withdrawing from a case, physicians must: (a) Notify the patient (or authorized decision maker) long enough in advance to permit the patient to secure another physician. (b) Facilitate transfer of care when appropriate."[10] Failing to do so is abandonment.[11]

Recent changes to law and policy untether providers from their ethical obligations and undermine the provider–patient relationship. These changes hinge on the "Guideline for Prescribing Opioids for Chronic Pain" published by the Centers for Disease Control and Prevention (CDC) in 2016.[12] The CDC guidelines sought to rein in opioid prescribing to curb an alarming spike in overdose deaths. They recommend that physicians make sure that benefits of opioid therapy outweigh risks, start with the "lowest effective dose," assess opioid-related harms, use prescription drug monitoring programs (PDMPs) and urine tox screens, and "offer or arrange" buprenorphine or methadone to patients with opioid use disorders. The guidelines also urge physicians to be very cautious about escalating a patient's dose. Ideally, the guidelines state, a patient should stay below 90 morphine milligram equivalents (MME) to avoid an increased risk of overdose. Patients who want to escalate beyond that dose or who are not showing improvement should be referred to a pain specialist.

Written for primary care clinicians, the guidelines were not meant for all opioid patients and were never intended to be hard and fast rules, but that is exactly what they became. Soon after the guidelines were published, state legislatures, insurance companies, clinics, and hospitals used the guidelines to justify new limits on opioid prescribing. State legislatures restricted opioids for acute pain to no more than seven days,[13] insurers and pharmacies like CVS and Express Scripts restricted the maximum dose that they would reimburse or dispense to 90 MME,[14] and several organizations responsible for setting quality standards supported a metric that downrated physicians with patients on more than 120 MME.[15] Physicians felt pressure from employers and medical associations to comply with the guidelines. Failing to do so could result in embarrassment when their high prescribing rates were revealed to their peers or in disciplinary action.

The aggregate amount of opioids prescribed became a litmus test for patient care—the lower the better. Hospitals and clinics complied by tapering patients to lower doses against their will, taking patients off opioids altogether, and refusing to take new patients on opioids. Notably, in 2012, the U.S. Department of Veterans Affairs adopted an aggressive strategy to get veterans off opioids. Eight years later, they celebrated a 64 percent reduction in patients receiving opioids and a 70 percent reduction in patients taking opioids long term.[16] All of these changes created a restrictive treatment environment that made it hard for patients on opioids to find care. What resulted was a game of musical chairs in which patients who lost their provider were unlikely to find another, leaving them with the difficult choice of receiving subpar treatment or no treatment at all. Despite enthusiasm for tapering, research shows that forced tapering often does little good and causes harm. Strong evidence demonstrates that forced tapering is unlikely to improve pain or quality of life[17] and makes patients more likely to overdose and experience mental health crises. Faster tapers make these harms more likely.[18]

Not all tapering is bad, however. Context matters. Tapering can work well when the patient chooses it (without coercion) and when they are tapered slowly with close monitoring in multidisciplinary clinics with the option to reverse the taper.[19] The biggest problem is abrupt, irreversible tapers that force patients down to a standard dose regardless of their needs or desires. As you will see, patient-centered components are missing from the kinds of tapering most physicians provide. Advocates for pain patients are especially concerned about policies and laws that create universal guidelines for all patients. They argue that treatment should be tailored to the needs of each individual patient and that setting the same dose limits for everyone invites harm.

These advocates acknowledge that being on high-dose opioids long term can result in the potential for physiological harm such as compromised respiration, sleep apnea, a higher risk of bacterial infection, constipation, altered bone density, and overdose.[20] However, they insist that those harms must be weighed against the harms of tapering such as overdose, suicide, and mental health crises. Physicians find themselves in the unenviable position of having to weigh one set of harms against another. Physicians who choose to keep patients on high doses must justify that decision to their employers and possibly to boards and federal agencies like the DEA. Quickly tapering a patient, even though it can do harm, does not require the same degree of justification, which may explain why so many physicians do it.

In 2019, a set of thought leaders, physicians, and other stakeholders urged the Department of Health and Human Services (HHS) to act immediately to prevent tapering harms. "Currently, no data exist to support forced, community-based opioid tapering to drastically low levels without exposing patients to potentially life-threatening harms," they wrote in a letter published in the journal *Pain Medicine*.[21] Experts blame policy for failing to deliver patient-centered care and note that "legacy patients," those "treated with long-term opioid therapy," struggle to find a new primary care physician if tapered or fired.[22]

Physicians face a choice between two options: cut off care or hand the patient over to law enforcement. This is routing—a way for providers to dismiss patients they consider difficult or don't know how to help. Cutting patients off is indirect routing, and contacting law enforcement is direct routing. Instead of centering patients' well-being, routing protects providers from law enforcement. Doing so puts the provider's interests above the patient's and undermines their ethical vows.

Indirect Routing

Doctors face a tough legal and regulatory environment. All eyes are on them, these healers turned drug dealers turned cops. They must obey the law, follow CDC guidelines, appease their employers, and meet insurance requirements without losing sight of their ethical obligations. In some ways, medical training does physicians a disservice. It teaches them to practice in an idealized version of the healthcare system instead of the system that exists. This creates ambivalence that makes it hard to do the right thing and results in what bioethicists call "moral distress" or "moral injury."[23] Pharmacists face similar challenges from a different angle.[24] Both types of providers grapple with the mismatch between healthcare as it is and as it should be. This cognitive struggle reveals itself when providers turn patients away with nowhere else to go.

Physicians and pharmacists indirectly route patients by firing existing patients, tapering patients' doses, and rejecting potential patients. These are the same actions described in chapters 5 and 6 as policing patients, but here we revisit providers' behavior with a focus on the consequences it has for patients. Patients must run a gauntlet to prove themselves worthy of opioids. They submit to invasive scrutiny of their bodily fluids and pharmaceutical records. In doing so, they sacrifice privacy for relief.

Providers take these steps because they satisfy some legal or regulatory demand and shield them from consequences. At the same time, these tactics harm patients. Providers manage to ignore those harms by imagining a mythic elsewhere—another doctor, clinic, or hospital that will take the patients they turn away.[25] Even knowing that others are unlikely to take cast-off patients, physicians and pharmacists still insist that patients have options. This illusion of the healthcare system, one that hews most closely to the idealized version they were taught about in school, allows providers to justify their behavior to themselves. Still, motivation for indirect routing ranges from callous to compassionate. Some providers want to get rid of patients who fail to follow their rules, others fear for patients' safety. A few are motivated by both.

The Fired Patient

As explained earlier, physicians use the pain contract to establish rules of engagement. When a urine screen or PDMP report shows that a patient has violated the contract, many physicians fire them. Sometimes they have a conversation first or give the patient a second chance, but most do not tolerate inconsistencies or lies. The problem, from the physician's standpoint, is that the patient has broken the trust that is essential to the doctor–patient relationship. Jessica, the family medicine doctor in Kansas City, explains: "Everybody who is getting opioids in my clinic has a very clear understanding of the rules under which I operate, and if they don't follow the rules, then I will discontinue prescribing and they're welcome to seek care elsewhere." In her pain clinic near Miami, Susan relies heavily on drug screens: "If you're abusing it, if it's not in your urine or something else is in your urine, I don't care what your excuse is. You're out the door because you signed a contract with me."

Nicole, a Kansas City internist, describes what she tells patients who have broken the rules. She relies heavily on the pain contract to justify her choice to discontinue care. "I'm just like, 'I'm not going to be able to prescribe this medication anymore.'" When the patient asks why, she tells them their drug screen was positive. They push back, saying it is a false result. "And I'll be, like, 'Well, that may be true, but unfortunately, this is what's stated in your pain contract.' I try to give patients the benefit of the doubt as much as possible just because it makes them really angry if you call them a liar." She tells them that she understands their situation, but her hands are tied. "This isn't going to continue to work, because you violated the contract."

Some physicians keep patients on but tell them "no more opioids." This is a partial firing, a way for doctors to cordon off care they don't want to provide. Nicole says, "I'm still going to treat you for your diabetes and your hypertension and your COPD, as long you're not constantly hounding me about the narcotics that I'm not going to give you." I asked if she considered her actions a form of patient abandonment. She paused, shrugged, and said, "I don't know. I mean, what am I supposed to do?" Ultimately, she concluded that she isn't abandoning patients so much as taking a modality off the table. Patients who don't like it can go somewhere else. "This isn't McDonald's. We say that all the time. You don't just come in and get whatever you want."

Pharmacists take a similar approach to protecting themselves. They invoke their professional authority to refuse to see a patient. Patients at Mark's independent pharmacy in Saint Louis find themselves closely scrutinized. He checks the PDMP for evidence of "doctor shopping," which, for him, is a dealbreaker. "If they have gotten hydrocodone from three different doctors and gone to three different pharmacies, they're done. There's no reason for that. They're an abuser. 'I can't fill this for you here anymore. Goodbye.'" Some pharmacists explain their choice to fire patients in kinder terms but still draw on stigmatizing images of patients to make their point. Mark doesn't want people who are misusing drugs in his store. Knowing little about them, he fills in their backstory in his mind. "Those people have to get their money somewhere, and they're probably robbing, beating up some old lady for her purse in the city to get it. It destroys neighborhoods."

Mark takes his role as gatekeeper very seriously, especially when it comes to physicians who overprescribe. With respect to physician overprescribing, he says, "Their carefree attitude cannot be our carefree attitude." When I asked him why, he confided that he once had a patient who ended her life with benzodiazepine medications[26] he had dispensed. It happened early in his pharmacy career. "She came in the day before and she was smiling, and I filled the prescription. I started thinking what did I miss? What could I have done? It still bothers me." Patients who are fired for violating the pain contract risk being marked with a red flag that makes them untouchable by other physicians. Physicians unwilling to take the extreme step of firing a patient might taper them instead, an option that pharmacists do not have.

The Tapered Patient

Motivations to taper are complex. Physicians are concerned about overdose, frustrated with patients who are dishonest, worried about insurance companies, and afraid of law enforcement. The result is that patients receive less medication than they want or need. Many physicians taper patients to comply with the CDC guidelines. They aim to get below one of the CDC's thresholds— either 90 MME or 50 MME. Others taper as punishment for breaking the rules—lying, seeing other doctors, or taking illegal drugs. Here, too, the degree of compassion varies.

Patients have no choice in the matter. When physicians decide to force a taper, the patient will receive less medication no matter how well they are doing on their current dose. Kansas City physicians Blake (pain management) and Jessica (family medicine) take somewhat different approaches to tapering. Blake likes to create an illusion of choice to help the patient feel better about the taper. He tells the patient, "I have a goal for you" but admits that "goal" means "mandate." "I want you to be at 50 percent of your current pain medication prescription by such and such a date. Here are some options. Do you want to decrease your Oxycodone 10 mg four times a day to 7.5 four times a day or do you want to decrease to 10, three times a day?' This is like asking a child if they want a whole apple or a sliced apple. The outcome is the same, but the kid feels like she had a choice." Blake says, "I really don't care" what the patient chooses, "I'm getting the same result. I'm decreasing it by 10 mg per day. But you're more willing to work with me because I'm not sitting down with you and saying, 'I'm taking away one of your pain pills.'"

He offers other "choices," too. If the patient is not yet ready to taper, Blake allows them to wait until the next month, but tells them that will result in a faster taper. "You are not going to want to do it all in one month. That's going to be very painful. But by this date we're going to decrease by such and such amount." I asked what he would do if one of the patients he tried to taper had an opioid use disorder since those patients are known to fare poorly on forced tapers.[27] He said there was nowhere to send them.

By contrast, Jessica tapers more slowly. She feels comfortable as long as there is a downward trend. When a patient comes to her on a high MME, she initiates a conversation. "You're at an exceptional risk for overdose[28] and we're going to taper you down. You get to choose the rate at which we do it, but every single time we get a refill it's going to be less than the time before." The outcome? "At this point, either I lose patients because that's not what they want, or they say, 'That sounds good to me. I want to get off of these forever,' and we set a taper timeline and make a spreadsheet." She doesn't care how long it takes. However, if a patient fails to follow the plan, she invites them to leave. "I say, 'Maybe I'm not the best doctor for you because this is what I think is best for your health.'"

The notion that another doctor would take the patient reflects the "mythic elsewhere." Providers say patients can simply go somewhere else but privately acknowledge that such a place does not exist. However, they stress that they are not abandoning their patients. We have already met Kristen, a pain management physician for whom honesty is a top priority. She strictly enforces the pain contract and dismisses patients who don't abide by it, such as those who take pills too early and run out before their next prescription is due. I asked if she considers that abandonment. She said "no" because she tapers them first. "We give them a thirty-day notice, so technically that's not abandonment and we usually counsel them. Like if they're on opioids, I'll usually give them the tapering schedule to get them off their opioids."

Research shows that a thirty-day taper for patients who have been taking large amounts of opioids for a long time can result in excruciating withdrawal. Says bioethicist and opioid researcher Travis Rieder, who endured a quick taper himself, putting these patients on a thirty-day tapering schedule "is basically sentencing them to a month of torture."[29] That is why experts recommend tapering no faster than 5–10 percent per week in standard cases and

5–10 percent per month in complex cases.[30] Kristen, like many physicians, urges the patient to be honest even as she takes steps to prevent other physicians from taking the patient. "You need to be very honest with your new provider as to your behavior," she tells them. The new provider will review her records and Kristen warns the patient that she is "going to document the circumstances that made us go to this decision point so you're going to have to pony up what happened."

Knowing the risk associated with this kind of record, I ask Kristen if new providers will actually take the patient. She admits they probably won't but chalks that up to the patient's behavior. "They consciously chose not to abide by the agreed upon terms [of the pain contract] and, in my opinion it's like, you know, we all make choices in life. If I go and drive drunk, I'm going to have to deal with the consequences of that." She goes on to say, "If I don't write them for you that doesn't necessarily mean that somebody else should. Maybe this is a sign that that's just not the right thing for you." Kristen indicates that she is teaching the patient discipline by setting boundaries, but her approach does not comport with best practices for treating addiction, chronic pain, and withdrawal.[31] Framing the problem in terms of bad choices conflicts with medical understandings of addiction. The Diagnostic and Statistical Manual of Mental Disorders defines opioid use disorder as "a problematic pattern of opioid use leading to clinically significant impairment or distress." Criteria to meet the diagnosis include continued use despite negative consequences in the realm of work, interpersonal relationships, and play.[32] Most people make choices to optimize positive outcomes and minimize negative ones, which is something that people with opioid use disorders, by definition, do not do.

Holding patients accountable is not Kristen's only motivation. She also tapers in anticipation that insurance companies will stop covering high MMEs. She has seen patients suddenly denied coverage. "They just say, 'We're not going to authorize this,' and then we're kind of forced to give them clonidine or something to help with opioid withdrawal and tell them to space out their meds, because their insurance company will not authorize it." She tries to prevent this by staying ahead of the game. She tells patients that their insurance may have a cap on how much medication they will cover, which may be lower than the amount they are currently taking. "And so it'd be better for us to work on doing that ourselves before it becomes an urgent matter than it would be to have your insurance company just drop the hammer on you." She is also afraid of the board. "I think it's very concerning when there is a suggestion that if you prescribe a patient more than a certain amount of opioid, you're going to be subjected to scrutiny by your medical board. I mean, that's very frightening to most physicians." She wants to follow best practices. "I don't want to be told that I'm committing some ethical violation or that I'm a bad doctor because I choose to treat my patients with opioids." Tapered patients are certainly free to seek care somewhere else, but they are unlikely to be successful. They are in a predicament, stuck between providers who taper or fire them and providers who refuse to take them on.

The Rejected Patient

We know from previous chapters that physicians and pharmacists reject new patients who exhibit red flags. Pharmacists like Diego who works at an independent pharmacy in Florida deter specific patients to avoid problems. He used to see a lot of patients he suspected were shopping around. No longer. "We're very picky about our patients, so we hardly get that kind of traffic anymore." It is understandable that providers do not want to take patients who could get them in trouble. At the same time, providers know they should put patients first and without much effort can learn to prescribe and dispense buprenorphine to provide treatment for opioid use disorder. Tension between protecting themselves and helping the patient creates a dilemma. Perhaps this explains why physicians and pharmacists cling to the hope of the mythic elsewhere—it allows them to conjure someone who will take the patients they reject.

Physicians are wary of new patients who ask for opioids. Neil, an internist, said a woman requesting treatment for back pain came to his clinic without records from her previous doctor, "And she just basically told the story of what her opioid needs were and why she was on them. I told her that I was a little uncomfortable prescribing that dose and that medicine to her without knowing more and without trying a few other things first."

Neil did not want to prescribe opioids, and the patient balked at the alternatives. After that, the interaction "got a little contentious," leaving Neil even more convinced that he shouldn't prescribe opioids. "I said, 'Given the conflict that we're experiencing over this, I don't feel like I can take care of you when it comes to opioid therapy.'" He didn't reject the patient entirely. "I'd be happy to take care of her for anything else, diabetes, blood pressure, you name it, but I would be deferring her pain management to anybody but me." The patient left and never came back.

Neil's "anybody but me" encapsulates the mythic elsewhere. He hopes to restrict his practice to those who follow his rules and who don't push back. This makes it easier to follow law and practice guidelines, but more difficult on patients. Many pain patients go through several failed treatments before finding something that works, enduring pain all the while. That might explain why they resist trying something new—it is terrifying to imagine being catapulted into pain instead of receiving relief. This fear, when directed at physicians, can trigger the physician's choice not to prescribe. Unlike many other medical conditions, simply explaining to the physician what has or has not worked is often not enough to convince the physician to continue a course of treatment. This is because patients with pain have been culturally characterized as malingerers and because physicians can't easily tell the difference between a patient who wants opioids to treat pain and a patient who wants opioids to manage an opioid disorder. The threat of patient dishonesty looms large over the doctor–patient relationship and doctors are hyperaware of red flags. Pain patients must manage their emotions to be seen as deserving in physicians' eyes. They have to be open to suggestions, they can't get angry, or they are out the door.

Rejection looks different depending on the setting. Emergency medicine physicians reject patients who are not experiencing emergencies. Jonathan has seen patients come to his emergency department in South Florida with all kinds of conditions. "They have fibromyalgia. They have headache complexes like migraines or things like that, and they insist on opiate pain medicines." Unsure what to do, he started querying the PDMP and asking himself: "Does a normal human being go to ten pharmacies? Does a normal human being have fifteen different prescribers?" and concluding, "I think a normal, rational person would say no."

Jonathan could start a conversation with the patient "to say, 'Well, I think you have a problem,'" but he was never able "to take it that step further to say, 'You know, you're addicted to opiate pain medications. I need to help you. I need to get you into therapy.'" Unable to link patients to care, he might prescribe a short round of pills to get the patient out of the emergency room. He knows that it isn't right, but it is all he has time for and it is what state law allows. Besides, he has only seven minutes with a patient, which is not nearly enough time to address the complexity of chronic pain. He ends up telling patients to go to a primary care physician even though he knows they won't prescribe pain meds. "The hospital is a healthcare safety net that is frequently overrun and does not have adequate resources to help everyone, and at some point, sometimes we are left to say, 'I'm sorry, but that's not really an emergency.'" He feels like he can't do enough. "I didn't solve your problem about why you came in today. I said, 'Go find yourself a primary care physician, and oh, by the way, none of the primary care physicians in this area will prescribe you pain medicine.'" His frustration is palpable. He recognizes that he is referring patients to nowhere, but he lacks time and resources to do anything else.

Pharmacists also reject patients in various ways. One of the more subtle tactics, a holdover from pre-PDMP days, is saying the medication is "out of stock." These are the words Kevin uses in his tiny pharmacy in a Florida strip mall when he wants to avoid conflict. He considers being more direct a time suck. "I could say, 'Hey, I'm not going to fill for you,' and then my corporate gets a call. They'll call their doctor. The doctor calls me. I mean, it's just a waste of time." It's faster and easier to tell the patient he can't get it with the added bonus of placing blame elsewhere.

He has seen patients get very upset if they don't receive their medication and acknowledges that these patients are suffering. "Some of them may be going through withdrawal, or some may be having mental issues, unfortunately." He doesn't want to get involved. "The best way is to say, 'Listen, it's out of my hands. It's on somebody else.'" He encourages patients to "reach out to the DEA. They're the ones who are regulating the stuff. Write your politicians. Write your senators, whatever you want to do. But it's out of my hands here." He knows he is shirking responsibility to make his life easier.

Patients who fail to follow the rules, who are cast as undeserving, find themselves subject to these three kinds of indirect routing. But these patients are not anomalies. In the grand scheme of medicine, it is the rare patient who perfectly adheres to a physician's regimen. Our tendency to do what makes us happy instead of what makes us healthy might frustrate physicians who want us to heal, but failures seldom get us fired. Of course, most physicians do not face legal consequences for their patients' nonadherence, which is what sets pain patients and patients with substance use disorders apart. So does the fact that nonadherence is woven into the very definition of addiction.

Direct Routing

In contrast to indirect routing, which sends patients on a road to nowhere, sometimes physicians and pharmacists send patients straight into the arms of law enforcement. I call this direct routing because healthcare providers intentionally hand patients off to the police. Pharmacists directly route patients more often than physicians, who generally consider calling the cops a Health Insurance Portability and Accountability Act (HIPAA) violation or whose employers discourage them from doing so. Fraud is the most common reason that pharmacists report patients. A handful of pharmacists tell law enforcement when they think a patient is doctor or pharmacy shopping. At her Southern California pharmacy, Shireen admits that "the DEA has a lot of faxes from me. This patient is turning in a fake prescription or this patient is going to multiple doctors or this patient is going to multiple pharmacies." She doesn't expect to hear back but considers it her responsibility to alert them about patients who break the law. "I feel like they have to know if somebody is drug seeking. It is their job to investigate it, not mine."

The rare pharmacist helps cops catch patients. Recall Minh from chapter 6 who worked with police to set up a sting by putting candy in a pill bottle and alerting the police when the patient picked up her meds. Minh considers cases like these clear-cut. "On the forged script, that was really easy, that's totally illegal. We're going to automatically call the police on any type of forged prescription." He also calls if the patient pays with a bad check, but he hesitates if the patient has gone to multiple doctors or pharmacies. In those cases, he calls the doctor, because "I don't want to jump to any conclusions yet." Other pharmacists share his perspective. They call about fraud, nothing else. Kevin doesn't report doctor or pharmacy shopping that he spots in the PDMP because "we don't have enough information at our disposal here in the pharmacy to be making any law enforcement calls outside of a fraudulent prescription." Even with the PDMP, he says, "I don't have enough information to say, 'hey, this is a problem.'"

Relationships between police and providers might be enough to deter patients from seeking care. This is what Stanford sociologist Sarah Brayne calls "system avoidance," which is a general term that refers to "the practice of individuals avoiding institutions that keep formal records" because those records make both surveillance and arrest more likely.[33] Avoided institutions include hospitals, banks, schools, and work. In the pharmacy context, this means that patients might stay away from pharmacies because they are afraid of arrest. System avoidance is one reason why strengthening the bond between healthcare providers and cops can be detrimental to patient care, particularly for minoritized groups and those with a criminal record. The stakes of criminal justice contact are especially high for people of color, who are more likely to be arrested for drug crimes, serve longer sentences, and bear an indelible mark of a criminal record.[34] Providers can't serve two masters.

They can't abide by their ethical commitments to put patients first and work with police to arrest them. Direct routing helps to establish a pipeline between healthcare and law enforcement that may be useful in some cases (like trying to prevent fraudulent scripts) but problematic in others (like going to multiple doctors because the patient is unable to find care). Putting patients first means giving patients the benefit of the doubt and trying to figure out what is motivating their behavior instead of just handing them off to law enforcement.

From Mythic Elsewhere to Toxic Somewhere

What happens to the patients who are fired, tapered, turned away, or handed off to law enforcement? Does their need for opioids disappear when they walk out the door? Can they easily find another provider willing to take them on? Not likely. Research on these spurned patients reveals an unsettling truth: The mythic elsewhere is in fact a toxic somewhere, an illegal drug market where labels have no meaning, fentanyl masquerades as prescription opioids, and the strength of a dose is anyone's guess.

For all of its faults, prescription medication has one thing going—it is tightly regulated. Eighty milligrams of OxyContin is 80 milligrams of oxycodone no matter where you buy it. It has been tested for purity by scientists committed to quality control. This predictability is absent from the illegal drug supply that has become cross-contaminated and full of fentanyl and other risky drugs like xylazine, an animal tranquilizer known as "tranq."[35] Fentanyl now appears in drugs labeled cocaine and benzodiazepines that are sold to people who have never taken opioids before. Taking drugs from the street is a game of Russian roulette—you never know what you are going to get and some of what you get can kill you. Physicians who route patients run the risk of subjecting them to this dangerous game.

Doctors are trained to care for patients, and treating pain and opioid use disorder is well within their purview and professional mission. Interactions with patients who have pain or misuse substances, even when unpleasant, are opportunities to help. But physicians find it much riskier to help their patients when outside forces raise the stakes. They may know the right course of action, but the system makes it hard for them to take it. Patients bear the weight of this struggle.

Lack of access to prescription opioids has had powerful unintended consequences. People with opioid use disorders who can no longer access prescription opioids transition to illegal drugs like heroin and fentanyl. This shift started around 2010 when an era of excessive prescribing yielded to an era of opioid restriction. At the time, Purdue created a version of OxyContin that it said could not be abused and physicians concerned about law enforcement cut back on prescribing. Indeed, misusing the new drug proved more difficult to do—but it was still possible.[36] However, many people hooked on the new drug just took the path of least resistance and opted for other prescription opioids or heroin.[37] According to a *New England Journal of Medicine* article that examined drug use after Purdue made the switch: "[T]here was no evidence that OxyContin abusers ceased their drug abuse as a result of the abuse-deterrent formulation. Rather, it appears that they simply shifted their drug of choice."[38]

A burgeoning market of cheap heroin thrived in the wake of diminishing prescription opioid markets. What resulted was a rash of heroin-involved overdose deaths and the dawning of the second wave of the overdose crisis in which heroin, not pills, posed the greatest threat.[39] The CDC guidelines that came out in 2016 restricted the prescription market even further while more powerful synthetic opioids like fentanyl flooded the drug supply.[40] This helps explain why patients whose physicians cut off opioid access were more likely to turn to heroin and fake pills (those made to look like OxyContin but actually made of heroin or fentanyl) and why overdose rates spiked as a result.[41]

People with opioid use disorders have not traversed this perilous terrain alone. There is a group of pain patients who have spent decades on high doses of opioids. They began to receive opioids at the turn of the century from doctors who prescribed liberally and report that opioids remove the debilitating pain that prevents them from enjoying life. The trouble is that it is hard to find someone to prescribe their current regimen. Norms have changed. Doctors trained in the heyday of opioids who believe that no dose is too high are starting to retire, leaving these "legacy patients" in the hands of more cautious providers. Other doctors refuse to take new patients or have gotten out of the pain management business altogether.[42] Newer physicians, trained in the wake of the overdose crisis, adhere to strict opioid regimens and taper patients down to doses recommended by the CDC.

Think back to Jennifer, the Saint Louis pain management specialist who inherited from a retired physician several patients on opioids she would not have prescribed. Jennifer was committed to tapering even if it made the patient's pain worse. Physicians like Jennifer are pressured to taper, fire, and refuse to accept opioid patients by employers eager to meet new performance metrics set by insurance companies and accrediting bodies. These strict standards make it hard to treat the 50 million Americans who live with chronic pain.[43] One consequence of the new, conservative prescribing regime is the rise of pain deserts where patients cannot find treatment. Sudden loss of opioids brings pain roaring back, leaving these "pain refugees" desperate.[44] With nowhere to turn, some patients take their own life.[45]

Doug Hale had been prescribed opioids since 2001 after he began experiencing bladder inflammation due to a surgery. He tried everything from physical therapy to epidurals to cognitive behavioral therapy before turning to painkillers. Opioids were the only thing that worked. He managed his pain on methadone[46] and OxyContin until his primary care physician insisted that he taper. The doctor said he had to wean off opioids completely within one month.

Doug checked into a detox program where he received 40 milligrams of morphine a day, but it did not touch his pain. He took extra pills, ran out, and found himself exiled by his doctor, who told him, "I'm not going to risk my license for you. The methadone clinic can deal with you." The methadone clinic doctors refused. He was a chronic pain patient and they treated opioid use disorders. He returned to his doctor and begged for help, which he did not receive. The next day, Doug Hale, fifty-three, sat down in his backyard and shot himself in the head. "Can't take the chronic pain anymore," the suicide note read, and he blamed the doctors, whom he saw as "mostly puppets trying to lower expenses" who "(do not accept) any responsibility." His wife of thirty-two years, Tammi, now advocates for people in pain and criticizes physicians' "one-size-fits-all" mentality. She saves special vitriol for the CDC, whose guidelines, she says, "are killing people."[47]

Doug Hale is one of many pain patients who died by suicide in the past 10 years. Thomas Kline, a family physician in North Carolina, keeps track. He runs a website that records the names of patients who have ended their life after being denied pain meds.[48] Kline describes inadequate pain treatment as "one of the worst health care crises in our history" and says that people are "committing suicide for no other reason than being forced to stop opioids for chronic pain." Callousness that has pervaded medicine is to blame, he says. "There are five to seven million people being tortured on purpose."[49]

Like Kline, Stefan Kertesz, an internist and addiction specialist, has sounded the alarm about tapering risks for over a decade. He has critiqued the Department of Veterans Affairs' aggressive tapering strategy and highlighted the consequences such a drastic reduction has for patients.[50] In a talk given to pain specialists in 2020, Kertesz pointed to a study other researchers published in the *American Journal of Preventative Medicine*.[51] The study showed that after the Veterans Health Administration implemented their Opioid Safety Initiative, opioid overdose deaths continued to rise. What changed was a lower likelihood that those patients had received an opioid prescription from the VA three months prior to death. "We have not necessarily altered the course of death . . . but we have reduced the chance that we have touched the patient with a prescription before they are dead," said Kertesz, who finds these results maddening. "Simply removing your fingerprints doesn't make the patient more safe."[52] Kertesz and his colleagues have cautioned other health systems against making the same mistake.[53]

Kate Nicholson is a civil rights attorney who has spent decades in chronic pain due to a botched surgery. She heads the National Pain Advocacy Center, an organization that brings together scientists, clinicians, advocates, and people with lived experience to "advance the health and human rights of people in pain."[54] She is concerned that the CDC pain guidelines that were designed as recommendations have become requirements. In a 2019 op-ed for the *Los Angeles Times*, Nicholson urged the CDC to fight back against the misapplication of its 2016 guidelines. She argued that "tackling the overdose crisis is a vital public policy goal. But chronic pain patients should not become casualties in that fight."[55]

In fact, the CDC did clarify its guidelines in 2019 and updated them in 2022.[56] In an article published in the *New England Journal of Medicine* in June 2019, the drafters of the original guidelines stressed that the guidelines did not support tapering to 90 MME and that tapering could have harmful consequences.[57] The retraction came too late. By that time, insurers, regulators, pharmacies, and state governments had taken the guidelines as gospel.

The CDC took a stronger stance in 2022. It issued a new document that warned health systems and state medical boards not to use the guidelines to create rigid restrictions and cautioned them against creating policies that encouraged rapid tapering or that penalized physicians for taking new patients on opioids.[58] We don't yet know what the impact of the 2022 guidelines will be, but much effort will be needed to overcome the harm done by the 2016 guidelines.

In the meantime, the pressure to taper persists. According to Corey Davis, an attorney and the director of the Harm Reduction Legal Project at the Network for Public Health Law, "states took the CDC's thresholds and turned them into strict limits that were misconstrued or overread by providers who didn't want to get in trouble and didn't want to be hassled." State statutes limited days and doses. State Medicaid programs set limits on opioid quantity and encouraged physicians to taper patients.[59] For example, in 2018, Oregon Medicaid opted to cover prescriptions above 90 MME only for cancer or palliative care. In 2018–2019, South Dakota and Texas reduced the amount of opioids they would cover from 300 MME to 90 MME.[60]

Physicians feel trapped. During our interview, Kristen asked, "What's the liability when somebody gets tapered and then they kill themselves because they're suffering? I mean, you have a situation in which they're getting medication that's potentially harmful but now they've killed themselves." She doesn't want to respond to threats, but she fears losing patients. "We've had people come in here and they'd be like, 'Well, if you don't give me such and such, I'm going to kill myself.' You can't just give them what they want." At the same time, she says "you'd feel horrible if somebody overdosed on your watch, if one of your patients was weaned and then they killed themselves. You just don't know what the right answer is every time." Unraveling the power of the CDC guidelines will take a while, and state leaders may be hesitant to reverse course.[61] Doctors are trapped in old systems and patients can't wait for change.

Alternatives to Routing

Although many doctors are daunted by the complexity of the current healthcare system, I was pleased to find a handful of physicians who navigate these treacherous waters successfully. Three physicians I interviewed have found a way to care for patients despite pressures to police them. They each use different strategies, but all are driven by the importance of relationships. As I talked with them, I was struck by my own reaction to their stories. I walked away from each interview thinking how much I would like to have a doctor like them. I imagine their patients feel the same way.

Megan Wears Many Hats

Megan is a family medicine physician in San Francisco. She works at a Federally Qualified Health Center (FQHC)[62] where her patients are all uninsured or government insured, and most are minorities. Her clinic sees around 11,000 patients and nearly 70 percent of them speak Spanish. Megan takes a holistic approach to medicine. She focuses on the entire patient and on how the patient fits into their family and other social systems. She tells me that this is a hallmark of family medicine. Holistic understanding informs how she treats pain and addiction. Her main strategy is to meet patients where they are. She learns new skills so that she can help her patients the best way possible.

The complexities of pain, both where it comes from and how it presents itself, occupy Megan's thoughts. "Everybody's pain is totally personal and different." She sees all kinds of pain in her practice and has come to understand that a patient's symptoms can obscure their root cause. Careful distinctions need to be made between "the experience of suffering and the experience of physical pain." The difference, as Megan sees it, is this: "There are a lot of people who come in in pain, but when you help them unravel it, there's something else. It's really trauma, it's depression, it's existential loneliness." All kinds of things disguise themselves. One example, she notes, is addiction. "Addiction walks in the door calling itself pain."

Her experience reveals a complicated truth about illness and treatment. It shows that the question that drives many physicians' practices—is this patient in pain, struggling with addiction, or diverting medication?—is not so easy to answer. Most physicians I talked to wanted to answer that question, to neatly separate patients into categories, because it gave them a clear path forward: treat the pain patients (cautiously) and reject the rest. Megan takes a different tack.

She wants to get at the root problem because she wants to know *how* to treat each patient. And what sets her apart is she has the skills to do so. Megan is board certified in addiction medicine, runs a chronic pain group, works with pregnant women who use substances, does prevention and early identification of addiction in adolescence, and has dipped her toe into the world of psychology. Each role brings a unique set of treatment tools.

Megan does not send patients elsewhere if she can treat them herself. "I feel really strongly about getting away from the model where we have to refer to each specialist," she says. And she refuses to respect traditional boundaries among specialties. "I provide addiction care. And I'll provide it straight out of a pain clinic because we feel like we just have to be with the patient where they are and be able to be flexible in that way. I have people I've been treating for addiction for years and I'm their therapist too. We just talk through whatever a psychologist would talk through with them. I really believe in the integrated model where we do this all together, and I'm willing to do your diabetes and your addiction and we can talk about all of that stuff and I can be there for all of it."

She saves referrals for patients who need care she cannot provide. "There are going to be times when it goes outside my scope, right? Something that's too complicated. You develop a psychotic disorder and my first couple of tries are not working or somebody needs a joint surgery for their pain." She tries to hand patients off to providers with whom she has a relationship. "We have all that stuff available in our system."

A main reason that Megan can do all of this is because she works in an FQHC that provides an integrated model of practice. FQHCs are federally funded safety-net clinics for disadvantaged patients that are required to deliver comprehensive primary care services.[63] They tend to have integrated resources that other clinics don't. Working for this kind of organization helps, but Megan has also taken it upon herself to develop the techniques necessary to accommodate as many patients as possible.

Her commitment to helping is why she chafes at the integration of enforcement into healthcare. Regarding opioids, she is concerned that "we are thinking so much about legal issues that we are moving into more black-and-white and less complex thinking." Not everyone she refers to shares her perspective. When Megan encounters colleagues who are committed to policing patients, she tries to steer them in a more compassionate direction. She recalls trying to get a patient a joint replacement from orthopedic surgeons who had cast people who use drugs as undeserving. They had a rule that patients who had used drugs in the past ten years could not get a joint replacement unless they had gone through what they call the "sobriety pathway." Patients had to submit to urine drug testing every two months. After proving themselves sober for one year, they could begin the path toward joint replacement, which required several more visits. Megan thought these rules were "ridiculous," so she offered to help. She would manage the patient's addiction so that they could meet the surgeon's requirements. By building rapport with the surgeons, then gently pushing back, she hoped to achieve her "secret goal," which was to "get them to get rid of this ridiculous policy altogether." It was an uphill battle.

She told me about a patient she had a week earlier who last used cocaine in 2014 and came in for urine drug screens routinely since then. They were all negative. She wrote to the surgeons and said, "Hey, it turns out, he's done a year! Like, he's done your thing. So would you be willing to just do surgery on him? I think he's a great candidate." One of the surgeons wrote back and said, "I guess he can get a little bit of credit for good behavior and time served." Not only did the surgeons use what Megan calls "criminalizing language," but they still wanted to see the patient regularly to build a relationship. "And during that time, we can make it clear all the negative consequences of relapsing to substance abuse and make sure he never does it again." Megan shook her head. "How does this person think using that language can actually be effective at helping somebody not use? Like his monthly talking-tos are what this patient needs." She worried these surgeons would undo all of her good work.

Still, Megan explains, she uses enforcement tools such as PDMPs and urine drug screens in her practice, not in order to remove patients from her care but as diagnostic instruments. Her claim is credible because she actually has the tools to treat patients with substance use disorders. Megan takes some legal risks. "I will do things that, if a DEA agent saw them, they would get mad at me. And then I document in a way that covers myself." For example, she saw a new patient she knew had an opioid use disorder, but she documented it as chronic pain. "I didn't write anywhere in the note that I had made that diagnosis (of OUD)." Her justification? "I just needed a couple of months to get to know him, to start to be able to move him toward treatment." In cases like these, she says, "I will take those couple of months' risk." Megan skirts the law to carve out space for her to develop rapport with the patient and figure out what is really going on.

I asked why the DEA would be upset for what seems like a reasonable delay. "That is malpractice because I'm diagnosing addiction and prescribing a medication that is not approved for the treatment of addiction." She only does this in very special circumstances: "If someone comes in with opioid use disorder, I will not initiate treatment for them with oxycodone or something like that." But when she feels it is warranted, she will take these risks on behalf of the patient because her philosophy is "patient first—then figure out how to keep ourselves protected."

She finds herself under the watchful eye of law enforcement for reasons she considers unjustified. "I prescribe buprenorphine, and as part of prescribing buprenorphine, the DEA comes and visits you. Which is so ironic to me because prescribing buprenorphine is like the safest thing I do for addiction. They should be coming and visiting me about the oxycodone prescriptions, but they don't." Despite attracting additional scrutiny, Megan treats addiction with medications like bupe because she considers it the best thing for her patients.

Khalil Treats Addiction in the Clinic

Across the country at a clinic in Tampa, Florida, Khalil also works in family medicine. His main strategy—prescribing buprenorphine—is less comprehensive than Megan's, but he is motivated by the same desire to help patients. Like most physicians, Khalil received no training on addiction in medical school or in his residency. He chose to get an X-waiver, a special addendum to his DEA registration, that permitted him to prescribe buprenorphine for opioid use disorder when faced with a patient he could not help.[64] He had just started his new job when a patient came in asking for refills on Suboxone[65]—a medication Khalil had never seen before. "I started writing the prescriptions, and then I did some research and realized that without an X-waiver you can prescribe it for pain, but you can't prescribe it for opioid use disorder."

He was in a bind. The patient was driving hours to reach him from another state; "he was trying to stay clean." Khalil referred the patient elsewhere, but the situation unsettled him. "My inability to provide for that patient was what sent me to go get the waiver." He wanted the skills to follow through with his patient's care. "As a family medicine doc, I try to do as much as I possibly can for my patient. I see a really wide scope of things. And that was one of the things that I'm like, 'Hey, you know, I can do this, I'm just not certified to do it.' So I want to get the certification." Like Megan, Khalil expanded his toolkit to help patients instead of passing them off to someone else.

For Khalil, the most important thing is establishing a therapeutic relationship with the patient. I asked him how he differentiates pain from addiction and diversion. "We have a saying," he tells me, "that the patient has the answer to all your questions. So, if I ask the right questions, I can assess their intentions." He compares this to a judge figuring out if someone is guilty by asking the appropriate questions. "Now, can patients lie? Yes. But it's my job to decipher what is going on." He notes that stigma affects how physicians treat patients. "Oftentimes, substance use in general can be put in this category of 'how dare they.'" He takes a different perspective. "I tend to push the view that they are sick just like anyone else with diabetes or high blood pressure, just sick. It's out of their control, and if it were up to them, they probably wouldn't pick to go down this road." This perspective keeps him grounded. "It allows me to provide them the best care I possibly can." Viewing patients as sick instead of manipulative helps him develop the strong connections that are essential to their therapeutic journey. "When I don't have those relationships built, I'm just a prescription pad."

Khalil considers it his duty to prescribe medications to treat opioid use disorder. "It's a personal belief that if I can give you an opioid, I should be able to get you off an opioid. And if I'm not trained to do Suboxone therapy then I should not be prescribing opioids." This is the same responsibility he has with other kinds of care. "If I'm going to do a procedure, I should be able to handle the complications." His sentiment is one bioethicists share. Johns Hopkins professor Travis Rieder, who appeared in chapter 1 and again in chapter 5, had a terrible time finding someone to get him off opioids he was prescribed after a motorcycle accident. His experience motivated him to rethink the separation of pain and addiction treatment. In an article published in *Health Affairs*, he establishes the following moral principle for prescribers: "Each physician has a duty to prescribe only those medications that he or she can responsibly manage for the length of a patient's need, including the treatment of foreseeable side effects." Specifically, "If a physician prescribes a highly addictive medication for pain management, with serious and predictable withdrawal effects, then he or she has a duty to see that patient through the weaning process as safely and comfortably as possible." If the physician can't do that, they must refer the patient to someone who can.[66]

One of Khalil's limitations is that he can only prescribe Suboxone in the university hospital where he sees a middle-class, insured population. He also works at a free clinic where he sees a lower-class, uninsured population and cannot prescribe it there due to company policy. This sets him apart from Megan, who prescribes buprenorphine in her FQHC and indicates how class and race bias is built into addiction treatment.[67]

Khalil also makes use of enforcement tools. He does urine drug screens and has adopted a "three strikes" policy he uses to take patients off Suboxone if he thinks they are diverting. He doesn't fire them—he considers that "abrasive"— he just refuses to prescribe. He also uses the PDMP for all patients on controlled substances because Florida law requires it. Khalil does not like to prescribe opioids for pain with the exception of cancer pain. He admits he plays hot potato sometimes when he has patients on opioids who are not willing to try anything else. "If the patient says, 'Doc, I've been getting my Percocet every day three times a day for the past twenty-five years, you're not going to change it, I don't care what you say,' then that patient should probably go to pain management." However, if patients are open to change, "those are the patients I love to work with."

Khalil especially likes tapering patients off opioids. The reason is personal. His cousin's grandmother, who was like his own grandmother, had taken a variety of opioids, including fentanyl patches and pills. She had gotten so debilitated that she had become a "couch potato." The drugs dulled the pain . . . and her personality. She went from being an active person, involved in her family's lives, to sitting around all day. Khalil suggested that the family talk to her doctor about stopping the meds. When she weaned off, it "changed her whole personality back." Khalil insists that "getting off the medication and starting fresh" was "the best thing we ever did for her." He feels rewarded when his patients undergo a similar transformation. Khalil admits that he does not do everything correctly. But he is doing the best he can, and his efforts put him in a better position to care for patients with opioid use disorder than many other physicians.

Liam Treats Addiction in the Hospital

Liam is an addiction specialist and emergency medicine physician in Saint Louis, Missouri. He provides medications for opioid use disorder in the hospital to prevent relapse and connects patients to care. I asked Liam what he does for patients with opioid use disorders. He tells me that his hospital adopted a program to initiate buprenorphine treatment in the emergency department. That's when things began to change. The program works by starting treatment early, assessing, and then linking the patient to care with an addiction specialist.

It all begins with a conversation that helps the physician figure out what the patient needs. Liam can prescribe something to get them over the hump so that they can move on to care. Timing is key.

If the patient is already experiencing withdrawal symptoms, Liam can start buprenorphine immediately. If the patient is not yet in withdrawal, he sends the patient home to start the medicine on their own with his guidance. He is comfortable with that approach because "in a lot of cases, the patients have used buprenorphine before, so they're somewhat familiar with it."

Liam says this medication-first model—provide medications first, ask questions later—is a "paradigm shift" that has helped physicians like him treat patients more effectively. "We used to think, 'Hey, I need to have a two-hour conversation with you about your use and all this other stuff.' Which is important to have, but it's not important to have in the emergency department." Liam knows that patients are not in a good place to talk when they are in pain and there is no reason for physicians to allow patients to suffer when relief is available. "I always tell people if you've ever had formal gastroenteritis [stomach flu], and you're just trying not to vomit, the last thing you want is someone giving you a lecture. It's the same thing here." When he wants to prescribe buprenorphine to a patient in withdrawal, he keeps the conversation to two minutes, tops, before prescribing the medication and bringing in additional help.

This is a game-changer. "Give them that medication, make them feel better, and now they're in a place where they can actually have a conversation with you." Then he calls in the peer support specialist (also called a "recovery coach")—a person in recovery from a substance use disorder who is embedded in the healthcare team.[68] Peer support specialists are trained and certified to help patients navigate the challenges of accessing and adhering to treatment. They help patients find doctors to treat them long term, provide emotional support, and link patients to resources such as jobs, housing, and community support. Research shows that peer support specialists help keep patients in treatment and decrease the likelihood of overdose as well as provide other benefits.[69] Liam values the work that peer support specialists do, though there are not enough of them to go around. "It would be great if we had recovery coaches in every ED; however, that's not going to happen. But you can do buprenorphine in every ED." Some physicians worry about patients diverting buprenorphine; Liam does not. "Because we're talking about a couple of days' worth of medication, the risk issue with diversion is about as minimal as you're going to get."

Liam has refined his approach over time. "My conversation now with patients who have overdosed is a lot different than what it was when I was a resident," he admits. He realized that yelling at patients, telling them they almost died, does no good. "They're not stupid. They're well aware of what happened." Liam sympathizes with physicians who do that, though. "People generally aren't saying that to be mean. I think they're frustrated and are trying to help." It is counterproductive, though. In his experience, yelling sets up a confrontational situation with the patient that impedes the therapeutic relationship.

Instead, Liam proceeds gently and infuses his statements with a deep concern for the patient. He recognizes that people who just overdosed are miserable. They are going through withdrawals that are extremely painful in a hospital setting. The first thing he says is, "We're not going to hold you here." That eases patients' fears about how long they must endure the withdrawal pain. Next comes the compassion. He says, "Hey, I'm concerned about you. You know you overdosed, and something really bad could have happened to you." He follows this up with an offer of aid. "I'd like to get you help. What do you think about all that?" Then he lets the patient talk. Some patients want help, and others do not. Either way, he talks about harm reduction, developing a plan for how patients can use drugs as safely as possible. Liam does use the PDMP to check the patient's story, especially when they want opioids to treat pain. He conducts urine drug screens in his clinic, but not in the hospital, because most patients are up-front about their drug use and because getting patients to provide urine can take hours.

Liam thinks that opioids have a place in medical care and opposes opioid-free emergency department policies. He has a problem with physicians who say, "We're just not going to treat your pain at all. You're not going to get any prescriptions." He says that there is a way to do right by the majority of patients that involves "really trying to engage them, trying to control their pain, prescribing what seems responsible." Beyond that, physicians should also "help them get access if their pain truly is not controlled." That is, making sure that someone else evaluates them and gets to the root of the problem.

One challenge that Liam faces is continuity of care. He would be open to seeing patients he induces on buprenorphine in the emergency department long term, but many patients are uninsured and cannot afford to get medication, and others have needs he cannot address. He also recognizes that the emergency department is not the best place to receive ongoing care. Therefore, he connects patients to other recovery centers because "they have so many other needs that we're not able to provide in a clinic."

Another challenge is contacting the primary care provider when patients have overdosed. He says he reaches out when he knows their physician. Often, his time with the patient is so brief he doesn't know if they have a primary. But if the patient leaves because they are "angry and upset," he doesn't follow up. "You have other things to do. You don't think to yourself, 'Oh yeah, Mr. and Mrs. Smith just walked off ten minutes ago, I probably should go call their doctor.' No. Because that patient's out of sight, out of mind."

The complicated relationship between race, culture, and medicine also plagues Liam. He is a white physician in a hospital that treats mostly Black patients. He knows that minoritized patients have valid concerns about how they are treated in the healthcare system, especially when it comes to substance use: "If they've had addiction issues in the past, I already know it's been a very negative experience." Liam tries to be sensitive in his conversations with these patients, but it doesn't always work.

He shared one encounter that did not go well. "I had an old lady, years ago, who had cocaine in one of her urine drug screens. So I asked her about her drug use, and she said no. And I'm like, 'So you've never used cocaine before?' She denied it and got very upset that I asked her again. I said, 'I'm asking you because we have a urine drug screen that showed this.'" He left to deal with another emergency and when he came back her son was in the room, very upset. Liam printed off the drug screen and said, "This is why I was asking. This is what the drug screening showed." He thinks that racial tension simmered beneath that interaction. "If I was his same race, I have the feeling that things would have gone differently." Liam's concerns and this incident demonstrate the bigger picture: that doctors must deal with medical problems in a complex ecosystem of racial disparities, drug criminalization, and social tensions that exacerbate problems and make it harder to address patients' needs.

Liam is quick to emphasize that physicians can easily treat patients with buprenorphine in emergency settings. "It doesn't require having a strong addiction medicine background or understanding where this is going for the next three months after this. It's just kind of like treating diabetes or high blood pressure." Liam says he can do far more for patients now than he could before the program was implemented. "In the past it was like, 'Oh no, we can't do anything. You need an addiction specialist.'" Now he can offer patients some relief before getting them into longer-term care.

The strategies that Megan, Khalil, and Liam have adopted—learning new skills and providing buprenorphine in the clinic and the hospital—are the counterbalance to routing. These physicians have altered their practices to keep patients in the healthcare system. They didn't start out with the resources they needed; they listened to their patients and acquired tools to help them. Of course, these physicians are not perfect. They all use urine drug screens and PDMPs to monitor patients. Megan has to skirt the law to help patients the way she sees fit. Khalil refuses to prescribe opioids for pain. And Liam's group cannot help uninsured patients long term. Still, it is a start. These physicians provide a glimpse of what robust treatment could look like. Providers don't have to make patients behave flawlessly; they can meet patients where they are.

Rehabilitating Treatment

Doctors and pharmacists who route patients out of the healthcare system place them in harm's way. Providers are motivated to route because of perceived or real legal risk, but doing so undermines their professional obligations and facilitates overdose death and suicide. These three doctors have found a way to navigate a broken system. However, it is easy to understand why others feel paralyzed. They find themselves in a damned if you do, damned if you don't situation. It was not so long ago that overprescribing opioids hurt patients. The message fueled by pharma and driven by regulators and medical leadership was "use opioids to treat pain." Providers did just that and found themselves responsible for injury and death. Now the message has flipped to "don't use opioids unless absolutely necessary." But following that guidance also contributes to injury and death. Providers with a mandate to care for their patients struggle to find a way forward. They need help. If that help is to be effective, it must arrive in the form of practical and actionable systemic change.

Healthcare providers are not alone in their urge to offload clients elsewhere. "Routing" is a common practice that links nonenforcement fields to the criminal justice system. Teachers and principals call the police on misbehaving students.[70] Mandatory reporters such as teachers, nurses, and social workers refer families to Child Protective Services.[71] Public health workers report to the cops people with HIV/AIDS who may be having unsafe sex.[72] Such routing may be most likely when the frontline worker–enforcer pipeline is firmly established, either when an enforcement worker is in the field (police officers who work in schools) or when the referrals are legally required (mandatory reporters).

To this point, we have focused primarily on how providers make decisions. But we miss crucial parts of the story if we ignore the context in which those decisions are made. What looks like bad behavior seems perfectly reasonable in a healthcare system that is fragmented, expensive, riddled with discrimination, and for the most basic care chronically inaccessible. Add the stigma associated with pain and addiction and the blame assigned physicians for the overdose crisis, and you have a recipe for disaster. Viewing the problem this way still doesn't let providers off the hook. Patients report that there are some cruel providers out there. However, even the kindest, most compassionate provider must traverse a dysfunctional path. How can we escape this harm cycle and create a system that benefits everyone?

7

Rethinking Policy and Practice

FIXING THE HEALTHCARE TOOLKIT

KEVIN DID EVERYTHING IN HIS POWER, but he could not save his daughter. In a conference room at a South Florida hotel, hundreds of law enforcement agents sat rapt as he shared the painful events leading up to her death.[1] Brooke first used drugs as a teenager. She started with pills, then switched to heroin. Her father, a narcotics officer, got her the best care; she cycled in and out. He paid for in-patient treatment, then the facility expelled her for a rules violation. The rule she broke? She had some ibuprofen. Kevin was outraged. "Have you ever heard of a cancer patient kicked out of the hospital for a rules violation? Have you ever heard of a diabetic kicked out for having an ice cream cone?" Brooke went to outpatient treatment that centered on abstinence. After one day sober, she overdosed and was revived with Narcan.

The time came when Kevin felt he had no choice. He called the police, who had previously gone easy on his daughter out of respect for him, and told them to stop extending her professional courtesy. Brooke was sentenced to four months in jail. During that time, she was off drugs, and Kevin caught glimpses of the girl he once knew. "I had my old Brooke back." The reprieve was short-lived. Brooke relapsed on heroin. She was using with friends one night when she started to overdose. Her friends, scared that her cop dad would arrest them, made her leave the house. Weak, she drove to a church parking lot, where she stopped breathing. She was nineteen years old.

Devastated, her dad lashed out. He made it his mission to get every one of Brooke's so-called friends arrested and prosecuted. But her funeral was an epiphany for him. Surrounded by all of those people who loved his daughter, he saw that she was part of a community, a community that was suffering, and he vowed to help them. In 2018, Kevin founded Brooke's House, a sober living home for women, to honor his daughter. The eighteen-bed facility runs a pet salon and junk removal service and teaches skills like chocolate making. They always keep one bed available in case a police officer has a daughter who needs help.[2] With the gentle sounds of crying all around us, Kevin pleaded with his fellow officers: "The next time you deal with a drug addict or you see a girl struggling on the street, know that she has parents, brothers, sisters, even kids. I want you to think of my daughter Brooke. God bless Brooke."

Brooke is one of 100,000 children, friends, siblings, and parents who die each year from drug overdose.[3] Their deaths are not inevitable. They are signs of a broken healthcare system that casts patients aside instead of providing them with the treatment they need. Moreover, they are signs of a frayed social safety net that fails to support people who suffer. Why couldn't Kevin, a police sergeant and pillar of his community, get effective treatment for his daughter? Why were his many attempts unsuccessful? What does Brooke's death tell us about America's capacity to treat addiction and pain?

Inadequate Treatment

The quick answer is there isn't enough high-quality treatment to go around. In an effort to treat addiction like a disease, many states and municipalities have developed or expanded programs to increase referrals into care. These diversionary programs[4] have become especially popular in the criminal justice system and include drug courts and police-assisted diversion programs. Drug courts are programs that allow people who are arrested for drug crimes to go to treatment instead of jail. If participants "complete" treatment to a judge's satisfaction, their criminal records are expunged. However, if participants fail, they must serve time. Police-assisted diversion programs empower police officers to refer people to treatment. People who use drugs can go to the police voluntarily to relinquish their stash and request help, or, during an arrest, police can offer treatment instead of jail.

Drug courts and police-assisted diversion programs are part of a "no wrong door" approach that makes treatment more accessible by creating more pathways in.[5] Responses to these programs are mixed. Some people laud diversionary programs for giving people a second chance to get sober. Others consider them coercive and question why getting access to treatment should require contact with law enforcement. However, opponents agree on one thing: new programs do little good without a corresponding increase in treatment. The "no wrong door" approach loses appeal when it does nothing but create more doors to an overcrowded house. Even with the best intentions, more competition for scarce resources will not upend the crisis.

Another problem is that patients, family members, courts, and police struggle to tell the difference between high- and low-quality care.[6] If asked to define addiction treatment, most people would describe either a twenty-eight-day, inpatient facility whose goal is to help people recover by abstaining from drugs or self-help programs like Alcoholics Anonymous or Narcotics Anonymous that promote abstinence through a series of steps. These programs have captured the American psyche because they are the ones most often featured in popular movies and television shows. Many people would be surprised to learn that they are not the most effective. The gold standard treatments for opioid use disorder are buprenorphine and methadone.[7] Both are opioids that help reduce cravings and withdrawal and block the effects of other opioids like oxycodone and heroin.

In a 2020 study published in *JAMA*, researchers compared 40,885 people with opioid use disorder who received one of six types of addiction treatment: (1) no treatment; (2) detoxification at a hospital or residential facility; (3) intensive treatment in a clinic or partial hospitalization; (4) buprenorphine or methadone; (5) naltrexone (a nonopioid medication for opioid use disorder); or (6) outpatient counseling.[8] They wanted to see how each type of treatment affected overdose and emergency department visits or hospitalization three and twelve months after treatment. Only patients on buprenorphine and methadone had a lower overdose risk at both time periods and were less likely to be seen in the emergency department or admitted to the hospital after three months.

Another study published in *JAMA* showed that patients who received initial doses of buprenorphine in the emergency department were more likely to engage in formal treatment, less likely to use illicit opioids, and less likely to need inpatient addiction treatment services compared to patients who received either a referral to treatment or a brief intervention.[9] However, inpatient abstinence-based treatment and self-help programs are not associated with a lower risk of overdose. Abstinence-based inpatient treatment, in particular, can double the risk of overdose when patients leave the facility.[10] No doubt, abstinence-based programs work for some people and can provide important social support, but medications for opioid use disorder show the most promise for most patients.

The downside is that methadone and buprenorphine are difficult to access. Methadone can only be provided at federally certified opioid treatment programs (OTPs), which exist in only 20 percent of U.S. counties.[11] OTPs are also restrictive in terms of hours and rules; most require patients to line up early each morning to receive a daily dose of methadone. This leaves patients tied to the clinic and makes it difficult to travel or hold down a job, especially if they must go a long distance to access care. This is why some methadone users refer to the medication as "liquid handcuffs."[12]

Buprenorphine is unique because it is the first medication for opioid use disorder to be prescribed or dispensed in physicians' offices.[13] Before 2023, physicians were required to obtain a DATA waiver (also called an X-waiver) to prescribe buprenorphine. This required additional training and capped the number of patients physicians could treat—30 at a time the first year, 100 the second year, and then they could apply to treat as many as 275 the third year.[14] Physicians rarely met those caps. Less than 10 percent of primary care providers had an X-waiver, and 40 percent of U.S. counties lacked a single waivered provider before the waiver was eliminated.[15] Of those with an X-waiver, 43 percent did not list that fact on the Substance Abuse and Mental Health Services Administration (SAMHSA) website designed to help prospective patients find treatment.[16]

To make things worse, inadequate regulation of the treatment industry has bred predatory work-based rehab programs that offer no treatment at all and bear a striking resemblance to prison labor.[17] These programs often leave patients worse off than they found them. Patient advocate Ryan Hampton says, "Treatment centers are only nominally accountable to loosely enforced rules. Unless someone dies and the family makes a huge stink or decides to press charges, the news barely makes a ripple. It's just another dead addict: another free bed, for the next desperate patient."[18]

One thing is clear: Good treatment is hard to find. People who seek care for themselves or their loved ones enter a twisted realm where evidence-based care is sparse and expensive, and readily available treatment can do worse than fail. The world needs better treatment and more of it.

Wrong Stories, Wrong Solutions

The longer answer to why Kevin could not help his daughter is that treatment alone is not enough. Treatment addresses problems after they have occurred. Wouldn't it be better to stop or mitigate suffering ahead of time? This is no simple task. The causes of the overdose crisis are complex and intertwined. The solutions are, too.

There is no easy way out of the overdose crisis, no silver bullet, no miracle cure. We get out when we do the hard work of caring for people and communities, when we repair our social safety net, prevent pain and trauma, and set people up to thrive—a tall order, no doubt, but the only hope we have for escaping this cycle of addiction, pain, and death. That is why prevention and harm reduction should play a critical role in curbing the overdose crisis.

The stories we tell ourselves matter. Stories about what is wrong with our society ultimately guide policy and practice. We must get those stories right. The same way a picture frame encloses an image, the stories we tell about social problems highlight certain elements and eliminate others. The frame we have put around the opioid crisis captures a single compelling story—one of doctors and drug companies peddling an outrageously addictive drug to the American public.[19] But when it comes to finding solutions, this story is far too narrow to do us much good. That is where sociology can help.

The utility of a sociological lens lies in its flexibility. It can zoom in to the fine-grained details of a single doctor making a decision about a single patient and it can zoom out to show the landscape in which the physician practices. It can swing in an arc to trace the historical events leading up to a critical moment in time. It is at its best a complex, multilayered, storytelling device. That is what makes a sociological perspective so useful for understanding social problems like the overdose crisis. Sociologists insist on examining problems in context and understanding problems in relation to one another.

In this book, I have used a sociological lens to show how the fields of healthcare and law enforcement have changed as a result of trying to solve the overdose crisis. Enforcement agents have gotten better at investigating and prosecuting healthcare providers. Physicians and pharmacists have responded by getting better at policing patients. Both changes have been made possible by prescription drug monitoring programs—two-tiered surveillance technologies that help law enforcement monitor providers and help providers monitor patients. Turning providers into cops comes at patients' expense. They find themselves turned away at the hospital, clinic, and pharmacy counter, left without help and without hope. Meanwhile, overdose rates increase each year with no signs of abating.

The stock story about the overdose crisis is so centered on healthcare that it has convinced our leaders that solutions lie there. *If overprescribing opioids got us into this mess, cutting back on prescribing can get us out.* This logic has brought us interventions like PDMPs, opioid-free emergency departments, seven-day limits on acute pain prescriptions, tapering, urine drug screens, and pain contracts. The goal is to make fewer opioids available for overdose.

Opioid prescribing rates have now nearly returned to pre-crisis levels, so if all we cared about was cutting back prescribing, these solutions would be a roaring success. But before you get too excited, remember that the real goal is to reduce overdose deaths and those rates are higher than ever.[20] Research on PDMPs shows that they are associated with lower rates of prescribing, but higher rates of overdose death and heroin use.[21] Our leaders gambled on the idea that reducing prescribing would reduce overdose. They lost.

They failed to foresee that people who could not get prescription opioids would turn to illegal drugs like heroin and fentanyl. These are the drugs that drive our current crisis.[22] Yet lawmakers insist on tackling prescription opioids. No matter how many restrictions are placed on healthcare providers, they will not stop people from overdosing on illegal drugs. Even if every physician stopped prescribing opioids right now, we would still lose at least 70,000 people to overdose each year.[23] Not only that, but without opioids, suicide among pain patients would increase.[24] People whose opioid use disorders who are treated with methadone or buprenorphine (themselves opioids) would lose access to care. Ridding our hospitals, clinics, and pharmacies of prescription opioids will never help because prescription drugs are not to blame. Maligning opioids only deprives doctors and patients of our most powerful painkillers, an essential part of the healthcare toolkit.

Bad pharmaceutical companies are not the sole culprits. Purdue Pharma did irreparable harm, but there will always be those eager to benefit from other people's suffering, and peddling addictive products is extremely profitable. Purdue could not have done so much damage, though, without gatekeepers who swung wide the gates and let them in—the FDA that let them label their drug as less addictive, the legislators who stopped the DEA from taking action, and the doctors who believed their lies.[25] Purdue also did not create the social suffering that makes opioids appealing in the first place. They capitalized on it, and our government let them.

What a tragedy it is to try to make things better and end up making them worse. Before, we had a prescription opioid crisis. Now, we have an illegal fentanyl crisis, alarming rates of suicide among pain patients, a resurging HIV/AIDS crisis, and a mounting hepatitis C outbreak.[26] The message is clear: What we are doing is not working. We can't continue along this path that leads to death and despair, not if we value our lives and the lives of our loved ones.

Where do we go from here? We can learn a lot by extending the frame, by placing the story we know so well in its broader social context. Doing so helps us understand why some strategies to curb the overdose crisis have succeeded while others have failed. Reframing what we think we know is an important first step to telling ourselves a different story—a more comprehensive and accurate story—so we can forge a new path.

We can start by clearly seeing what is before us. Addiction and chronic pain stem from problems that have little to do with healthcare. They lie in trauma, stress, and social decline.[27] They lie in mental health disorders and perpetual racism that cry out for self-medication.[28] They lie in social systems that have skewed punitive.[29] This is the story we haven't heard enough, one that competes with the tale that makes doctors and drug companies its central characters. Untreated pain and trauma cast a pall over people's lives. Many are left behind by social systems designed to sort them into "deserving" and "undeserving" patients. But people with chronic pain and people with addiction are different sides of the same coin, coping the best they can with diseases of despair.[30] Moreover, chronic pain and addiction are ongoing conditions. Doctors can hope to treat them, but not necessarily cure them. The return of pain, the relapse of addiction are not moral failings, but symptoms of persistent illness. People will fall. We need a safety net to catch them when they do.

Our current solutions to the overdose crisis not only fail to create a safety net but further damage the one that exists. Our leaders have misunderstood the problem, devised ill-conceived solutions, provided insufficient resources, and erected legal barriers to access those resources. None of these tactics will resolve the crisis. It is time to learn from our mistakes. We must let a century of failed drug policy catalyze a new era driven by compassion, science, experience, and common sense.

Let's let healers heal again. Let's cast off the blinders of misplaced morality to see suffering through new eyes. Let's harness the strength of healthcare and empower providers to treat patients effectively instead of policing them.

Forging a New Path

Physicians and pharmacists can do some things right now to keep patients safe and help them get healthy. But their efforts will be in vain if they are not accompanied by serious investment in harm reduction and social services that prevent overdose, link people to care, and pull communities out of decline. That is why we need a three-pronged solution centered on treatment, harm reduction, and prevention. A comprehensive approach will be expensive and complex but also robust and sustainable. It ensures that providers have the right tools for the job and helps repair our social fabric to stop people from falling through the gaps. Nothing less will do.

Expand Treatment Capacity

Healthcare providers in this arena face two major barriers: They have the wrong tools for the job, and they practice in an environment that impedes care provision. Partly, these shortcomings have arisen because providers have been told the wrong story. Several of the physicians and pharmacists I interviewed thought they were helping patients by turning them away or handing them over to the police. They still believe that overprescribing and overdispensing opioids fuels the crisis and think that their gatekeeping saves lives. Providers want to help their patients but don't know how.

One of the first things they can do is expand access to buprenorphine. The bar has never been lower. Congress removed the X-waiver in 2022, which means that any physician with a DEA registration can prescribe buprenorphine to treat opioid use disorder.[31] Remember Khalil, who decided to get X-waivered when he couldn't help a patient in recovery? Physicians should take a page out of Khalil's book and get the information necessary to help them feel comfortable prescribing bupe. Doing so puts a useful tool in their toolkits and it could change their responses to information found in the PDMP. Instead of using PDMP reports to justify refusing to care for patients, physicians prepared to treat addiction could care for patients in a new way. This would also disrupt the game of patient hot potato by helping physicians keep patients in their practice instead of referring them elsewhere.

Pharmacists, too, must help. Right now, fewer than half of U.S. pharmacies carry and dispense buprenorphine.[32] That creates a serious impediment to care. Pharmacists should educate themselves on the medication and commit to stocking and dispensing it. This will require a nationwide push. Many pharmacists hesitate to attract people who use drugs to their pharmacies. They worry those patients will argue with them, engage in petty theft, or scare off other patients.[33] Perhaps these fears persist because pharmacists have not seen patients well-managed on buprenorphine. It is also possible that pharmacists do not want to be known as the only pharmacy that provides the medication because they do not want an influx of patients with opioid use disorders. A Mississippi chain pharmacist I interviewed for an earlier project about syringe provision stated: "Not that I want them using a dirty syringe, it's just that I don't really want to be the one affiliated with, 'Oh, I can go buy them and they'll give me whatever needles I need for my fix.' I don't want to be the needle exchange program for the community."[34] Spreading out care across pharmacies could alleviate these concerns. Expanding treatment provision comports nicely with the no-wrong-door approach because it makes the house bigger, prepared to accommodate more people in need.

A second easy strategy is providing syringes and naloxone (the drug that reverses opioid overdose) to people who use drugs. Physicians can prescribe both to their patients with opioid use disorders and can prescribe naloxone to pain patients on high doses of opioids if they need it. Pharmacists are critical here. Even though most states permit pharmacists to dispense naloxone, quite a few pharmacies do not have it in stock.[35] Pharmacies should commit to carrying and dispensing naloxone.

Laws about syringe provision vary by state, but even in states that permit pharmacists to sell syringes, some pharmacists insist that the patient provide evidence that they will use it to inject medication like insulin. Frank, a pharmacy owner in Wichita, Kansas, says that patients sometimes come in asking for syringes for a relative who doesn't have an insulin prescription on file. They tend to come in after hours when the doctors' offices are closed and cannot verify the prescription. That raises red flags, so he will "just kind of interview them" by asking "who the patient is, who the patient's doctor is and what insulin they're on." If they provide satisfactory answers, Frank allows them to "purchase a ten pack, not a whole box, just a ten pack," then follows up with the doctor the next day and documents what he finds. Frank goes to a lot of trouble to stop people who use drugs from getting access to clean syringes. Pharmacists should do the opposite; they should sell syringes to people who request them. Doing so also would reduce the spread of HIV/AIDS and other blood-borne diseases.

A third strategy is creating more hospital-based programs to initiate patients on buprenorphine, like the one Liam described in chapter 6. Access to care is especially important when transitioning out of or between institutions including hospitals, inpatient addiction treatment, prisons, and jails.[36] Providing patients with a few days' worth of buprenorphine and a link to care would help reduce those risks and get people into treatment.[37] It would disrupt the revolving door in and out of the hospital that so frustrates physicians by getting patients into ongoing care.

When it comes to pain, physicians should rightsize treatment. One-size-fits-all regimens like those recommended by the CDC don't work. Doctors are under tremendous pressure to limit opioid prescribing, but ultimately the

CDC guidelines are guidelines and physicians have their own licenses that give them the medical authority to decide what is right for their patients. I don't say that to minimize the power of organizational policy or anxieties about being targeted by law enforcement—those are very real concerns. I say that to urge physicians to reclaim their professional power and autonomy. They are the ones with the medical training, the ones who sit in the room with the patient, see their suffering, and hear their stories, not employers, insurance companies, or law enforcement. It is up to physicians to set the standards of care and fight for their patients. In doing so, physicians will also be fighting for themselves, for the right to act like healers, for the capacity to align their actions with their ethics. When doctors reject reactionary policy and affirm the doctor-patient relationship, everyone wins.

Of course, that does not mean that physicians should prescribe opioids as readily as they did in the late 1990s and early 2000s when so many doctors fell under Purdue's spell. Instead, they should make informed decisions about when an opioid is appropriate and avoid forcing patients off medications that work. Listening to patients and advocating for their needs will help physicians uphold their professional identity as caregivers.

Together, physicians and pharmacists can advocate for policies that would help them make treatment more available. Three steps would go a long way toward achieving this goal: (1) expand telemedicine, (2) move methadone treatment into pharmacies, and (3) allow pharmacists to provide both methadone and buprenorphine in tandem with physicians.

Rules about buprenorphine relaxed during the COVID-19 pandemic. Federal law permitted patients to receive buprenorphine prescriptions via video chat or over the phone. Strong evidence shows that telemedicine increased access to treatment and helped more people stay in treatment. It also removed barriers to care for vulnerable groups such as people who are unhoused.[38] Now that the Biden administration has declared an end to the COVID-19 public health emergency, loosened telehealth restrictions could tighten up again. Doctors and pharmacists should advocate to keep the existing telehealth rules in place. They should also stake a claim on methadone.

Methadone clinics are something of a therapeutic anomaly. Developed in the 1970s to treat veterans who returned from Vietnam hooked on heroin, opioid treatment programs (OTPs) segregate the treatment of opioid use disorder from other kinds of medical care.[39] As noted earlier, those who need access must run a daily gauntlet of surveillance that includes routine drug tests and being observed while urinating and while taking the drug.[40] During

COVID, the federal government kept methadone accessible by expanding take-home options.

Restrictions on methadone provision along with OTPs' punitive bent leads some patients to shy away and others to fight back.[41] There is currently a thriving movement to "free methadone" led by academics, journalists, activists, and people who use drugs.[42] They argue against methadone exceptionalism and insist that OTP doctors should prescribe the medication more liberally, with fewer restrictions, and allow patients to take more medications home with them instead of going to the clinic each day. To make the drugs most accessible, advocates argue, they should be dispensed in pharmacies.[43]

Other powerful leaders agree. Nora Volkow, director of the National Institute on Drug Abuse, has argued that physicians should be able to prescribe methadone to patients and that pharmacists should be able to dispense it.[44] Timothy Fensky, former president of the National Association of Boards of Pharmacy, made it his mission to expand access to medications for opioid use disorder as part of his 2020 presidential initiative.[45]

Significant research supports their positions. Pharmacists and patients report feeling satisfied with pharmacy-based methadone and buprenorphine programs in Canada, Australia, New Zealand, and Western Europe, and pharmacists there have proven themselves capable of providing related clinical care that is confined to OTPs in the United States. Patients appreciate pharmacists' longer hours and accessibility, and all of these countries have lower overdose rates than the United States.[46]

With such powerful advocates, moving methadone into pharmacies seems like a no-brainer. Pharmacies are far more plentiful than OTPs, which means that putting methadone in the hands of pharmacists could expand access exponentially. The sticking point is this: Organizations, like people, have a vested interest in their own survival and will fight mightily to stay alive.[47] OTPs have spent fifty years with a monopoly on methadone provision. The fight has already begun.

In July 2022, the American Association for the Treatment of Opioid Dependence (AATOD), the lobbying arm of OTPs, tried to kill the Opioid Treatment Access Act, a Senate bill whose stated goal was to "expand access to substance use disorder treatment" by permitting physicians and pharmacists to provide methadone.[48] AATOD distributed a fact sheet urging senators to oppose the bill. They argued that methadone belongs in OTPs because it is safer and because treatment involves more than just medication. They concluded, in bold, "OTPs are effective because of all the resources and support provided to each patient. Those resources do not exist in private physician offices and pharmacies."[49]

Proponents, led by University of Pittsburgh medical professor Dr. Paul Joudrey, countered that failing to expand access to methadone contributes to overdose deaths and that other countries successfully provide methadone without additional contingencies. This last point echoes the findings of the National Academy of Sciences, Engineering, and Medicine in 2019.[50] Research indicates that strict clinic requirements may help explain why more than half of methadone patients leave treatment in their first year.[51] In *Filter* magazine, Joudrey said of AATOD: "They cannot cherry pick the science just because they don't want things to change. They should listen to expert groups like the National Academy of Science and Medicine and put patients' needs first."[52] The bill did not advance beyond committee, but representatives introduced a similar bill in 2023.[53]

It remains to be seen whether the days of isolating methadone are coming to an end, but physician and pharmacy groups could use their power to speed up its integration into mainstream medicine. Doing so would also help to medicalize opioid use disorders, treating them like any other medical condition. Of course, the healthcare system also helps to perpetuate stigma and inequality, issues that warrant close attention as mainstream healthcare organizations begin to offer addiction treatment.[54] In addition, pharmacy-based methadone will not be possible unless pharmacy chains make significant changes to pharmacy operations and staffing. Remember that pharmacy is a high-pressure job where it is often down to a single pharmacist and a single technician to juggle calls, texts, walk-ins, and drive-thru patients and somehow also find the time to prepare medications, contact physicians, call insurance companies, and give immunizations. Most pharmacists would balk at adding yet another task to their list (let alone a task that requires them to work with stigmatized patients).

Chain pharmacies must anticipate these concerns and prepare their pharmacists to succeed. That means creating spaces where they can administer methadone and adding additional staff to allow pharmacists sufficient time to care for those patients. Many pharmacies already have private spaces available to provide immunizations. Those could also be used for methadone. Pharmacies must also educate pharmacists, technicians, and other employees about the benefits of methadone and advertise their participation to the public.

You may recall the media frenzy that ensued when CVS took tobacco products out of its stores in 2014. Then-president and CEO Larry J. Merlo proudly declared: "Ending the sale of cigarettes and tobacco products at CVS/pharmacy is the right thing for us to do for our customers and our company to help people on their path to better health."[55] Five years later, Merlo noted that removing tobacco was only the first step. "As a health care company now combined with Aetna, we're taking even bolder steps to transform the consumer health care experience and help lead our customers, patients and the communities we serve on a path to better health."[56] Putting methadone, a lifesaving medication, in the pharmacy is the next logical step to promote public health, one that all pharmacies (not just CVS) should eagerly embrace.

A related step is empowering pharmacists to provide buprenorphine and methadone. On the whole, physicians have made clear that providing medications for opioid use disorder is not a top priority. As mentioned earlier, less than 10 percent of physicians are X-waivered to provide buprenorphine and over half of those with waivers do not make that fact public. It is unclear if these numbers will change now that the X-waiver requirement has been eliminated, but the time to expand access is now and pharmacists should be the agents.

Recent studies in the United States have shown that pharmacists can successfully manage buprenorphine prescriptions. Because pharmacists cannot legally prescribe the medication, they collaborate with a physician who works with several pharmacists to care for their patients. One study in North Carolina, funded by the National Institute on Drug Abuse, shows that patients felt satisfied with the care pharmacists provided and were likely to adhere to treatment regimens.[57] Another study in Rhode Island showed that patients were more likely to stay in treatment in a pharmacy-based program than in standard care.[58] The fact that pharmacists have much longer hours than physicians and are open on weekends means they are the ideal professionals to offer this medication. If more pharmacists provided buprenorphine this way, far more patients would have access.

Schools of medicine and pharmacy need to make education and training on addiction and pain treatment core parts of their curricula. Primary care physicians should be prepared to treat these conditions as a matter of course instead of passing patients off to specialists. Like Megan (see chapter 6), physicians should wear many hats and be equipped with the tools to treat patients, whatever their needs.

Healthcare providers promise to leave the world better than they found it. There are steps they can take individually to help patients, but they must also mobilize to support policies that help patients writ large. They must push back on forces that require them to police. They can do some of that in their daily practice, though much of it requires them to act as a collective by raising their singularly powerful voice. Doing both will pay dividends in lives saved.

These solutions are important, but they are only part of the puzzle. Providers alone did not get us into the opioid crisis, and they alone cannot get us out. For these efforts to make a difference, policymakers must also alter the landscape in which providers practice. That means investing in harm reduction and fortifying the social safety net.

Invest in Harm Reduction and Prevention

One of the best things to come out of the overdose crisis is a stronger, more organized Harm Reduction Movement.[59] The harm reduction philosophy is simple: meet people where they are at and encourage any positive change. This approach cuts against the grain of pervasive ideas about treatment and recovery. You probably already know some of the most popular, such as the notion that families should dole out "tough love" because "hitting rock bottom" is the only thing that will convince a loved one to turn their life around. Then there's the troubling idea that only complete abstinence counts as recovery.

In reality, people don't fail to recover because of lack of will. They fail because effective treatment is not available and drugs are. Punishing people into getting better has never worked. The idea runs counter to the very definition of substance use disorder. People who meet this diagnosis engage in "compulsive use despite negative consequences." That is, they continue to use drugs even though they are being punished for it.[60] Why would heaping on more punishment help?

Harm reductionists reject hateful ideas about people who use drugs and advocate instead for radical empathy. Journalist Maia Szalavitz summarizes: "People with addiction are often homeless, rejected, and marginalized. Many have preexisting mental issues. Nobody wants to see them. So when somebody approaches them with love and no judgment and says, 'Hey, I don't care if you're using drugs, I just want you to stay alive'—that changes everything. When people feel valued, they might value themselves more."[61]

Activists recognize that many of the harms associated with drug use come from factors other than the drug itself, chiefly (1) uncertainty about the drugs purchased on the unregulated market where fentanyl poses as heroin and prescription opioids, and (2) the spread of blood-borne diseases when drugs are used without sterile equipment.[62] That is why they have fought so hard for programs and resources that make drug use safer.[63]

We have harm reductionists to thank for syringe provision programs where people who inject drugs can get sterile syringes, the widespread availability of naloxone, overdose prevention centers where people who use drugs can use them more safely, fentanyl test strips that reveal the amount of fentanyl in a drug, and much more.[64] These approaches have helped reduce overdose and drug use-related harms.

It wouldn't take much to extend harm reduction philosophy to chronic pain sufferers. Doctors should encourage any positive change instead of rejecting patients or forcing them onto strict tapering schedules that put their health and their lives at risk. When physicians taper, they should do so slowly and in concert with the patient, attend closely to signs of distress or reduced quality of life, and adjust the tapering schedule accordingly. There may be no reason to taper at all if patients are well-managed on opioids.[65]

Physicians can repurpose their skills at defensive documentation to help patients—they can tightly document the medical necessity of their decisions to ward off law enforcement and keep patients safe. And they can push back on policies and laws that require them to sacrifice the very soul of medical practice—their ability to heal.

Decades of evidence show the effectiveness of harm reduction interventions, yet these programs are not as widespread or well-funded as they should be. Political ambivalence hamstrings progress. President Joe Biden earned praise from advocates for people who use drugs for championing "harm reduction" in his State of the Union address of March 1, 2022, and for including fentanyl test strips in his drug-control strategy.[66] Eight months later, New York City took harm reduction even further when it became the first city to allow overdose prevention centers (OPCs). OnPoint NYC reports that after one year of operation the centers had intervened in 636 overdoses, served 2,841 unique participants, and kept 435,078 units of hazardous waste from littering parks, streets, and buildings.[67] Despite their success, the city still refuses to fund them, leaving them to scrape together funds from private donors. The city will soon receive almost $100 million for one year's worth of opioid settlement funds, but city officials refuse to use that money for OPCs without matching funds from the state and federal government. Said City Health Commissioner Dr. Ashwin Vasan: "We're out in front. And we've been pioneers in this space, but we need the rest of government to come and follow us."[68] Politicians engage in this one-step-forward, two-steps-back dance while their constituents' lives hang in the balance.

It is past time for lawmakers to go all in on harm reduction. They must fully legalize and fund syringe provision programs, overdose prevention centers, and drug checking, and get naloxone into the hands of people who use drugs. These proven strategies will keep people alive and help link them to treatment if and when they want it. Lawmakers must also stop creating harsher punishments for people who use and sell drugs. In some ways, the tides have turned— hateful rhetoric that stigmatized people who used crack cocaine in the 1980s and 1990s has given way to more compassionate descriptions of people who use drugs as sick people in need of help, not punishment. Of course, the racially disparate approaches to what have been coded as "Black" and "White" crises are glaring. What is even more striking is that the supposedly "kinder and gentler" War on Drugs uses the same playbook that drove up mass incarceration and decimated Black communities.[69]

Two examples drive this point home. One: Police departments nationwide have invested in harm reduction by requiring their officers to carry naloxone. Knowing that people might not want to call the police out of fear of arrest, states and municipalities adopted Good Samaritan laws that prevent police from making an arrest in the case of overdose. However, shortly after these laws were enacted, police began using a new strategy to investigate overdose deaths called "drug-induced homicide."[70] Recall from earlier that these are cases in which investigators trace an overdose back to the person who supplied the drug and hold that person—whether a drug dealer, friend, or doctor—accountable.[71] Drug-induced homicide tactics raised the stakes of getting police involved in overdose at the same time that Good Samaritan laws were enacted to lower them, leaving us no better off than we were before.[72]

Two: Fears about new drugs impede efforts to drive down drug criminalization. U.S. lawmakers have finally reached a tentative bipartisan agreement about punishment for some people who use and sell drugs. In the face of overcrowded prisons and a growing movement for criminal justice reform, the U.S. Sentencing Commission reduced sentences for drug offenses and applied some of those reductions retroactively,[73] and some state's attorneys have refused to prosecute people for low-level drug crimes.[74] At the same time, lawmakers have doubled down on harsh penalties for fentanyl use and sales.[75] These laws help politicians appear tough on crime but they will not stop overdose. They simply feed into the harsh, racially biased cycle of arrest, punishment, and diminished opportunity post-incarceration that make drug criminalization so harmful.

When our leaders govern through fear, they do long-term damage. Americans need to overcome the punitive impulses that hijack our thinking every time a new drug enters the scene and opt for humane approaches that help people and communities thrive. This is large-scale harm reduction. Most importantly, decision makers must involve people who use drugs and people with chronic pain in developing strategies. They know what they need, they know what works and what doesn't, and they are the ones suffering the most from this unending crisis. We must heed the mantra of people who use drugs: "Nothing about us without us."[76]

In the grand scheme, the overdose crisis is a symptom of much larger social problems that cry out for attention and investment. The stock story about the overdose crisis serves us so poorly because it focuses too heavily on drug availability. It is what's known as a "supply side" story, the crux of which is that if drugs were not available, people would not use them. Heavy focus on the drug supply has catalyzed laws that severely punish those who traffic drugs. Supply-side concerns are also why so much attention has been paid to opioid manufacturers, distributors, and prescribers in the contemporary overdose crisis.[77]

These efforts are largely in vain. Drug crises are games of whack-a-mole. Suppress one, and another crops up. Over a forty-year span, the most feared drug has shifted from crack to methamphetamine to prescription opioids to heroin to fentanyl. Focusing narrowly on specific drugs has left us trapped in a vicious cycle with no end in sight.[78] Cracking down on one type of drug tends to let more-dangerous, higher-potency drugs take its place, a process that drug policy experts call the "Iron Law of Prohibition."[79] Under Prohibition in the Roaring Twenties, beer and wine gave way to spirits, which gave way to moonshine. In a subsequent era, laws targeting powder cocaine gave way to crack. In our current crisis, prescription opioids gave way to heroin, which gave way to fentanyl.[80] Not only is shutting down supply an impossible task, but the assumption that drug availability drives drug use is deeply flawed. Truth is, people use drugs for all kinds of reasons, and understanding those motivations holds the key to stopping overdose and improving society writ large.

We must ask ourselves: Why do people use drugs? And how does drug use relate to other kinds of problems our society faces? These sorts of questions help us arrive at a "demand side" story that makes clear why some people use drugs and others don't.[81] The answers reveal that psychological, social, and economic conditions are the biggest drivers of addiction, overdose, and pain.[82] Some people use drugs to feel good, and some people use them to cope with mental or physical pain.[83] What is curious is the variation in how the same drugs affect different people. According to the 2021 National Survey of Drug Use and Health, 9.8 million Americans used heroin or use prescription painkillers nonmedically. However, only 5.6 million people met the criteria for an opioid use disorder.[84] That means that 43 percent of people who used opioids illicitly did not have an opioid use disorder. Similarly, an estimated 5 million to 8 million Americans use prescription opioids to treat chronic pain.[85] They have ongoing exposure to powerful painkillers. Yet most do not have an opioid use disorder.[86]

Shift your gaze to people's life circumstances and patterns begin to emerge. A disproportionate number of people with substance use disorders have corresponding mental, behavioral, or emotional disorders. Of the 44 million adults who had a substance use disorder, almost half also had a mental illness and 15 percent had a serious mental illness.[87] Childhood trauma is also linked to chronic pain.[88] On a grander scale, addiction and chronic pain are symptoms of much larger social diseases like racism, class inequality, violence, homelessness, educational inequality, unemployment and underemployment, food insecurity, and trauma.[89]

Neither police nor healthcare providers can tackle all of these issues alone. Healthcare and criminal justice are vast fields, but they offer blunt tools for addressing social problems that give rise to drug crises. Several of the nation's largest cities spend 40 percent of their general budgets on policing, more than twice that of other social services.[90] Yet many social ills stem from problems that police can't fix. We can't arrest our way out of homelessness, joblessness, or domestic violence, nor can prisons repair mental health. We need to invest in social workers, psychologists, housing specialists, and employment experts who have more refined tools for the job, and we need to devote funds to agencies that provide these kinds of services. Some cities have had success with hotlines for mental health emergencies that send social workers instead of police to help people who are struggling.[91] Movements for a living wage, universal healthcare, and housing also show promise. Bottom line: Investing in healthy communities is an upstream way to prevent drug crises, and it offers the added benefit of tackling other social problems at the same time. Only by expanding our social safety net and ensuring care for all people can we hope to disrupt the cycle of overdose and death.

Eliminating prescription opioids won't solve the opioid crisis, but you wouldn't know that by looking at the steps our lawmakers are taking. Law tends to lag behind social crises. Today's lawmakers are so busy litigating yesterday's problems that they fail to plan for the problems that lie ahead. And law moves at a glacial pace, while social problems are adept and adaptable, changing quickly and without warning. In two decades, the United States went from 17,000 overdose deaths to over 100,000.[92] In four short years, the driver of those deaths went from prescription drugs to heroin to synthetic fentanyl.[93]

Meanwhile, the victory many communities are celebrating is over the pharmaceutical industry.[94]

Today's opioid crisis is just the latest iteration of a cycle of moralized, racialized drug panics that have occurred over the last century.[95] Lawmakers' myopic approaches to drug crises make it difficult to escape these cycles because funding is tied to specific drugs and to narrowly defined outcomes. At the federal level, there is an enormous wave of funding to address the opioid crisis, but the real crisis is not about a class of drugs. It is about tears in our social fabric that leave gaping holes in resources for marginalized communities. It is about the failure to address the psycho-social and economic underpinnings of drug use and its rampant criminalization. Instead of trying to eradicate opioids, we must find a way to dramatically reduce human suffering.

Surveillance Technology as a Conduit of Change

The overdose crisis urges us to think about how technology reshapes professional practice. When boundaries blur between criminal justice and other social fields, vulnerable groups suffer. The research in this book weaves together the shortcomings of the U.S. healthcare system, the logics of social fields, the criminalization of social problems, and technology's unparalleled surveillance capacity.

Placing law enforcement surveillance technology in healthcare fundamentally changes treatment. Thanks to the PDMP, enforcement agents have improved strategies for targeting providers, who now fear arrest and incarceration for doing their jobs. Naturally, they grasp the nearest tool—big data surveillance technology. What they don't realize is that PDMPs usher punitive logics into healthcare without expanding treatment capacity. Punitive logics are invasive—they easily worm their way into locales outside the criminal justice system—and big data surveillance technology ferries them along. In the most optimistic view of PDMPs, we could imagine the same tool being used to punish and to treat. But in practice, PDMPs are surveillance tools regardless of who uses them, and ongoing use has the alarming side effect of turning healthcare providers into enforcement agents.

Of course, the problem is not the technology itself. Technology does not *do* anything. Blaming technology for social ills is like blaming math for a bad economy. Instead, as sociologist Sarah Brayne reminds us, technology is social.[96] What matters most is the context in which technology is implemented and used. The PDMP entered a space where treatment options for pain and addiction were few and where available options were expensive and hard to access. It was also posited as a solution to a social problem with deep roots in social decline and despair, an enormous and complex problem that does not lend itself to quick fixes.[97]

Recall that when I began this project and learned that healthcare and law enforcement were both fighting the opioid crisis, I thought I would find a story of competition.[98] Healthcare and law enforcement bring different worldviews to bear on social problems, and they use different resources and strategies with different goals. Sociologists tell us that professional fields are hungry. They gobble up problems even if they don't have a solution. Workers go to great lengths to protect their territory from would-be competitors.[99] Using this logic, I expected healthcare and law enforcement to fight each other for control of this crisis, to jockey for power over how to define the problem and how to intervene.

Instead, I found a story of resistance, at least at first. Enforcement agents and healthcare providers did not treat this problem like a precious commodity; they blamed each other for starting the crisis and tossed it into the other's territory hoping they would fix it. Today, efforts to collaborate have replaced efforts to hand off responsibility. Strategies that unite healthcare and law enforcement have gained nationwide popularity and receive extensive media attention. These include drug courts, naloxone provision programs, police-assisted recovery programs, and social workers and psychologists embedded into police departments. The collaboration described in this book has received less attention and fewer accolades. Perhaps it is more palatable to witness police officers acting like healthcare providers than to observe healthcare providers acting like cops.

A host of reasons explain why healthcare leaders and public health advocates want law enforcement to curb the opioid crisis. Public health, in particular, is overtaxed and underfunded, eager to tap into law enforcement's wealth. These collaborations offer a comforting image of everyone working together to address a very serious social problem. And yet working together does not mean contributing equally. Law enforcement's outsized power helps it set the agenda. Law enforcement allocates material resources. Law enforcement frames the problems and solutions. And like any other group, law enforcement organizations prioritize survival.[100] Enforcement leaders survive by internalizing healthcare practices, not by relinquishing their funds or prestige to healthcare providers and public health advocates.[101]

Healthcare leaders make a grave error when they adopt enforcement technology without considering how it might impact healthcare work and patient care. Healthcare providers cannot competently surveil and treat their patients at the same time. When they attempt to do both, physicians end up treating patients like criminals or refusing to treat them at all. Pharmacists turn patients away and call it care. Patients find themselves cast out of the healthcare system and thrust into the criminal justice system or left to fend for themselves.

The PDMP alone is not responsible for blurring boundaries between healthcare and law enforcement. For many people, particularly those who belong to minoritized groups, those lines have always been crossed with impunity. In many ways, technological solutions to the opioid crisis are a cautionary tale about much more than the opioid crisis, one that warns against what sociologist Trevor Hoppe calls "the pitfalls of using the criminal justice system to tackle disease."[102]

Theorizing Technology, Work, and Field Change

Today, scholars who work at the medical–legal frontier tackle urgent questions about the consequences of blurring boundaries between healthcare and criminal justice.[103] They ask whether it is wise to erect drug courts where people try to heal with a prison sentence hanging over their heads, where judges, not doctors, call the shots.[104] They reveal what happens when police officers bring patients into emergency departments and how their presence shapes who gets care first.[105] They show how trauma is reinvented as crime.[106] They witness how emergency medical technicians, police, and nurses embrace or eschew responsibility for people in emergency situations.[107] And they warn of the pitfalls of criminalizing disease.[108]

This research constitutes a field of scholarship that examines relationships between criminal justice and other social fields. Painted with broad strokes, studies fall into three main categories: (1) relationships between workers in criminal justice fields and workers in other fields;[109] (2) the placement of criminal justice workers into nonenforcement fields;[110] and (3) the movement of social problems between criminal justice and other fields.[111]

Studies in the first category include Kaaryn Gustafson's classic book on the criminalization of welfare that shows how welfare workers developed close relationships with law enforcement in an effort to root out (practically nonexistent) welfare "cheats."[112] Another example is Kelley Fong's study of how mandatory reporters such as teachers and doctors attempt to help troubled families by calling child protective services but end up subjecting them to heavy surveillance and the frightful risk of family separation.[113] Studies in the second category include Aaron Kupchick's examination of school resource officers that shows how cops in schools transforms the educational environ-ment,[114] and Armando Lara-Millán's research on nursing triage that shows how patients brought into the hospital by a police officer are "rushed" to be seen while others are "delayed."[115] Examples of the third include classic re-search on medicalization and criminalization that shows how the same social problem is treated differently depending on which field is responsible for ad-dressing it[116] as well as Trevor Hoppe's recent work on how public health became oriented toward crime in an effort to combat HIV/AIDS.[117] Together, these studies help us reconsider the cost of softening field boundaries and letting law enforcement in.

Other (seemingly unrelated) scholars focus on the interplay between tech-nology and society and ask what it means to live in the age of digital pana-ceas.[118] Have a social problem? Tech has a solution. Their studies show how intensive surveillance alters work and worsens inequality. Examples include Karen Levy's book on how technology that promised to improve truck drivers' safety undermines their capacity to do the job,[119] Sarah Brayne's research on how new technology transforms police forces, and Virginia Eubanks's study of technological approaches to providing resources for the poor.[120] Princeton sociologist Ruha Benjamin warns that we are experiencing the "new Jim Code" where racial disparities are coded into seemingly neutral technology with devastating impact.[121] Tech has a hard time staying put; once created, tech products tend to creep into other arenas where they are put to new uses.[122] On the whole, this research raises urgent concerns about privacy, work, and inequality as we rush headlong into our digital future.

My research contributes to both lines of inquiry. It offers a Trojan Horse Framework for understanding how the use of a law enforcement technology in healthcare spaces helps to reorient professionals toward surveillance and punishment. This change happens gradually through the ongoing use of tech-nology and results not from the technology alone but the social conditions in which the tech is implemented. I call PDMPs "Trojan horse technologies,"[123] because the main features of that famous story, though of course not all of its details, reveal the timeless human errors of the opioid story. Three things make a technology a Trojan horse: (1) the mismatch between the logics—the under-lying principles—of the field that created it and the field that uses it; (2) the invasiveness of the logics the technology ushers in; and (3) the foothold that the logics associated with the technology already have in the field.

In the case of the opioid crisis, the logics of the field that created the technology are certainly different from the logics of the field in which it is implemented. Law enforcement is oriented around surveillance and punishment, while healthcare is oriented around treatment and care. Law enforcement gave healthcare the technology as a "gift" while harboring ulterior motives. Their goal was not to improve healthcare for healthcare's sake, but rather to systematically gain access to healthcare information and to convince doctors and pharmacists to be more cautious about opioid provision. By enlisting healthcare providers in the project of tamping down on opioids, law enforcement hoped to make their jobs a bit easier. Unaware of these intentions, healthcare providers saw PDMPs as healthcare tools designed to help patients.

Ongoing use of the technology helped reorient physicians and pharmacists toward surveillance and punishment, which they reframed as treatment and embraced as part of their work. These changes are evident in providers' routines, their relationships with law enforcement and other healthcare providers, how they envision their professional roles, and their impetus to route patients out of healthcare. These changes are also evident in how providers set strict limits around care, toss patients from one specialty to another, and ultimately route patients out of the healthcare system. These outcomes result from how invasive enforcement logics are—they initially seem like commonsense approaches to a wide variety of problems. We can best understand them through a gardening metaphor. Like weeds that grow in any kind of soil, invasive logics make their way into other fields and, without constant vigilance, choke out delicate plants that require intensive care. Because they seem so sensible, invasive logics displace other logics that may, in fact, be more appropriate to the field in question. However, even the most invasive logics would struggle to gain traction if they had not already established a foothold in the field. In the opioid case, federal and state law already required physicians and pharmacists to monitor opioids; the fact that the PDMP gave them a sanctioned way to do so made it especially attractive.

At the same time that doctors and pharmacists adopted surveillance technology, three social conditions contributed to change in pain management care: political pressure, efficiency pressure, and inadequate tools. Healthcare providers and administrators faced significant pressure from those outside the field to address the growing social problem of the overdose crisis. Providers were under constant pressure to perform efficiently, which robbed them of time that they could use to devise other solutions.[124] Doctors and pharmacists were also hamstrung by the lack of healthcare tools to address the mounting crisis for which they were blamed. Together, this helps us understand why healthcare providers have so readily adopted enforcement practices. Healthcare is another powerful field whose logics pervade foreign territory. Consider the wide range of problems that have been medicalized, from gambling to weight gain to children's misbehavior. It would be reasonable to anticipate that healthcare logics make their way into enforcement territory and transform criminal justice work. However, it would also be reasonable to expect criminal justice to resist such an intrusion.[125] This question is most appropriate for future research.

It's Time to Look a Gift Horse in the Mouth

A popular proverb warns never to look a gift horse in the mouth, but the proverb has nothing to do with the Trojan horse. In fact, it offers contradictory advice. Horses grow more teeth over time, so their teeth indicate their age and, by extension, their value. A person who looks a gift horse in the mouth is ungrateful for the gift until they know how much it is worth. In today's context, that would be like unwrapping a present, then immediately looking up its price on the Internet, a faux pas indeed.

But imagine if the Trojans had looked their gift horse in the mouth. If, instead of assuming that a horse-shaped wooden sculpture signified their victory and belonged within their city walls, they had mustered a healthy degree of skepticism. If they had asked who sent the horse, for what purpose, and, most importantly, what it contained inside?

This question is broadly relevant today. Fields as wide-ranging as education, finance, law enforcement, and medicine have invited big data technology to pierce their borders. Their leaders delight in technology's gifts while ignoring, on purpose or through naïveté, any strings attached. Big data technology has proliferated through partnerships between government agencies and tech entrepreneurs.[126] Government leaders consider the technology a boon because it makes tasks easier and faster and because it stretches the bounds of possibility. But there's a trade-off: The private companies that create technology have no incentive to disclose how their algorithms work. In fact, immense profits lie in hiding this information. Limited budgets motivate government officials to do more with less, but the technology that makes this possible is a black box of arcane code.[127]

As demonstrated in these pages, that black box injects logics from other fields that become apparent only through daily use. We didn't look our Trojan horse in the mouth, and now the invasive logics of surveillance and punishment have encroached deeply, affecting how we treat patients, teach students, provide aid, and impose penalty.

These social changes amount to a clear warning against the mindless embrace of technology. My research encourages a measured approach to implementation, one that precludes unintended consequences that result in harm. But can we solve social problems without sacrificing the essence of social fields? Through perseverance and best practices, empathy and education, common sense and common ground, this book shows that we most certainly can.

A Field Approach to Qualitative Research

How It All Began

When I was a graduate student in sociology, drug research was the last thing on my mind. Having come from psychology, sociology presented itself as a vast and exciting field, one I vowed to explore to its fullest. Unlike some of my peers whose research agendas were clear from day one, I cycled through many subfields—from social movements to organizational studies to race and ethnicity to gender—before settling into medicine and law. Some sociologists are driven by theory. I am driven by cases, those real-world social problems that pose challenges for people's lives. The case that captivated me through most of graduate school was reproductive justice. I was interested in understanding inequality in abortion access and the interminable debates over reproduction in our homes, religious institutions, and legislatures.

I started graduate school vaguely aware of pharmacists who refused to dispense emergency contraceptive pills (ECPs). Soon after, anti-abortion pharmacists who considered emergency contraception an abortifacient (an abortion-causing agent) captured headlines across the nation. I had so many questions. What struck me was the stark contrast in how groups on opposite sides of the emergency contraception debate framed pharmacy work. NARAL, a pro-choice group, put out an ad that featured a man and woman in bed with only their feet visible. Between them lay the black, rubber-soled shoes of a pharmacist. The copy read: "WHO INVITED THE **PHARMACIST**?"[1] Anti-abortion groups such as Pharmacists for Life International, on the other hand, emphasized that pharmacists were professionals, not automatons. They asserted that pharmacists should not have to leave their personal beliefs at the door just to do their jobs.

Regardless of one's stance on abortion, it is easy to see why pharmacists were more receptive to the idea that they were professionals with decision-making authority than the idea that they were a nuisance standing between the patient and their physician. I began to interview pharmacists at the height of this debate, interested in what factors they took into account when making decisions. Was it just about their personal beliefs, or did law, the politics of their community, and their employers' policies matter, too?

I designed my dissertation research to explore these questions. I created what seemed to me a rather elegant research design. I selected four states with different pharmacists' responsibility laws—one with a "conscience clause" that allowed pharmacists to opt out of providing drugs they morally opposed (Mississippi), one with a "duty to dispense" law that required pharmacists to dispense all prescriptions a doctor prescribed (New Jersey), one with a "refuse and refer" law that allowed the pharmacist to opt out but required them to find someone else to dispense (California), and one with no law (Kansas). Within each state, I used voting records to select one more-liberal and one more-conservative county, and within each county, I selected pharmacists in the widest possible set of organizational settings who dealt with ECPs: inpatient hospital pharmacists working in Catholic and non-Catholic hospitals, and community pharmacists working for large chain drugstores and small independent pharmacies. I traveled to each state, where I recruited just over 100 pharmacists to participate in the study, and I met with them in the back rooms of their pharmacies, in coffee shops, and at their homes to learn how they made decisions about providing ECPs.

I originally created a semi-structured interview instrument that focused exclusively on ECPs, but with the prompting of one my mentors, Francesca Polletta, I added this question: "What would you say are the key ethical issues that pharmacists face in daily practice?" I thought I already knew the answer: ECPs, of course! The contraception battle in pharmacy had received so much media attention that I assumed it was top of mind for pharmacists. I was wrong. I wanted to talk about emergency contraception; they wanted to talk about opioids. Across the board, pharmacists said painkillers were their biggest challenge. Remember, this was 2009, long before the opioid crisis was splashed across the front page of every major newspaper and two years before the federal government took steps to address the crisis. Yet pharmacists faced the issue every day on the frontlines of care.

I became fascinated by pharmacists and their experiences. Sociologists hadn't written much about pharmacists; they preferred to research doctors and nurses (that is still true today). But I learned some important things about pharmacists in my ECP research that helped me better understand healthcare provision. I learned that, contrary to popular belief, pharmacists do not dispense everything that doctors prescribe. They work under their own professional licenses and while they endure pressure from physicians and from employers to behave in certain ways, ultimately decisions about dispensing medications are up to them. In our highly pharmaceuticalized society, that makes pharmacists the ultimate gatekeepers to healthcare and gives them outsized power over patients' lives.

I also learned that pharmacists were suffering from a lack of guidance when it came to opioids. State and federal law gave them a "corresponding responsibility" to ensure that they dispensed opioids for the right reasons—but they could be sued for failing to dispense to someone in need.[2] Pharmacists were on a tightrope, taking careful steps to avoid over- or underprescribing. They also were among the first professionals to encounter the crisis. They were the ones who saw patients who tried to fill forged prescriptions, patients who kept mysteriously losing their medication or having it stolen, and patients who needed their drugs early because they were constantly going out of town. Pharmacists found it nearly impossible to figure out whether patients were taking opioids for physical pain, to feed an addiction, or to sell. And even if they knew patients were struggling with addiction, they had no way to help them. They experienced what Andrew Jameton calls "moral distress," a situation where one knows the right thing to do but institutional circumstances prevent it from happening.[3] Pharmacists may not have known specifically how to treat addicted patients, but they knew help was needed and they had no way to offer it.[4]

By the time I graduated, the opioid crisis was in full swing. The Obama administration had issued a report titled "Epidemic: Responding to America's Prescription Drug Abuse Crisis,"[5] and the prevailing story was of young teenagers whose lives were cut short by opioids that their physicians prescribed. Yet something else was happening that drew less attention. Healthcare and law enforcement leaders were beginning to work together to combat the opioid crisis. They held joint conferences, they devised collaborative strategies, and, most intriguingly, they shared technology. State legislatures adopted prescription drug monitoring programs (PDMPs) in rapid succession so that by 2010, thirty-four states had operational PDMPs.[6] These changes piqued my curiosity. I thought to myself, healthcare and criminal justice are so different.

They want different things and they approach problems in different ways. How can they possibly agree on how to address a nationwide crisis? I decided to find out.

The Anatomy of Research Design

While designing a research study to tackle all of this, I encountered the same kinds of problems that qualitative researchers typically face. First, it is important to know that qualitative researchers want their findings to apply to other cases, but not in the same way that quantitative researchers do. Quantitative researchers aim for "statistical generalizability," meaning they can assume that the findings from their study are applicable to a broad population of interest. If they study patients' decisions about seeking prenatal care, for example, they want to make sure that they have captured a broad enough sample of patients that they can make statements about pregnant patients writ large, not just the patients they surveyed. They also need to make sure that their sample is large enough to accommodate the statistical analyses they want to do.

Qualitative research doesn't work this way. The goal of most qualitative research is "theoretical generalizability," meaning that the theoretical mechanisms the researcher uncovers can be applied to other cases.[7] A qualitative researcher might study how teachers treat students and find that they parse students into categories of "deserving" and "undeserving" and give group members different treatment. They might uncover this process by observing thirty teachers in Minneapolis. Their findings then help other researchers who study police officers or physicians understand how these workers, too, evaluate client deservingness and link these evaluations to treatment. This goal allows the number of observations to be far fewer than those found in quantitative research.

Even if qualitative researchers can collect a smaller sample, they are still concerned about variation and representativeness. Most social science is designed to explain variation. Why does this group behave differently than that group? Why does this group fare worse than that group? So sociologists look for variation that they can try to explain. They need to select cases that differ on some variable. They also need to ensure that their cases somehow represent a broader set of cases and not a total outlier. For example, Reed College in Oregon is known for its unique curriculum that does not provide grades. If a qualitative researcher wanted to understand something broadly about how universities operate, selecting Reed alone would be a poor choice because its standard practices lie far afield of those of typical universities. A researcher might instead compare Reed to the University of Oregon, Portland State University, and Oregon Coast Community College to examine aspects of how different kinds of universities operate. The researcher who did that would control for conditions that vary at the state level—the political leanings of the legislature, the amount of state funding, and so on—and capture the variation she really cares about (maybe prestige, racial composition of the university, or grading strategy).

Returning to the opioid crisis, I was a lone researcher interested in understanding how healthcare and law enforcement worked collaboratively or combatively to address a shared social problem. Even though the opioid crisis was a nationwide phenomenon, it did not affect all Americans the same way. Appalachia, widely regarded as ground zero of the crisis, has many features that make it unique compared to other states. Appalachia spans thirteen states, including Kentucky, Ohio, and West Virginia, and the people who live there are among the poorest in the nation. Appalachians had few resources to combat the crisis, resulting in an incredibly high death rate. Journalists and researchers were drawn to Appalachia to tell this story of social decline, political abandonment, and overall disinvestment that ravaged Appalachian communities. By the time I began my work, some of those stories had already been told. *New York Times* journalist Barry Meier wrote *Painkiller* in 2002. More than decade and a half later, Sam Quinones's *Dreamland* appeared, then Beth Macy's *Dopesick*, and then Chris McGreal's *American Overdose*.

However, I didn't avoid Appalachia because the research field was crowded. I steered clear because it was not the best site to answer my questions. I wanted to know how healthcare leaders and enforcement agents worked together and against each other to address this crisis. That required selecting places where both groups existed. I also wanted to select places where resources to combat the crisis were available. The story of insufficient resources seemed to me an obvious, if important one. I wanted to understand what happened in places rich in resources. People were dying there too. Why?

I designed the original study about pharmacists in the way I described earlier—by gathering what I call a "nested maximum variation sample"[8] based on law, politics, and organization. A maximum variation sample is a technique for selecting the broadest possible set of participants.[9] This is where differences between quantitative and qualitative research again prove informative. Quantitative researchers generally look for the most typical case because they want to generalize their findings to a specific population. Qualitative researchers who use maximum variation sampling do so because they want to capture the most variation possible within a space. That is, they want to understand the broadest possible range on a given variable. A nested maximum variation sample involves gathering maximum variation samples on multiple variables that influence one another (in my case, organizations operate within political environments that operate in legal environments).[10] I had data on pharmacists in California, Kansas, Mississippi, and New Jersey, but Florida and some other states were a better fit for the broader project that involved physicians and law enforcement in addition to pharmacists.

I started the second phase of the project by conducting pilot studies in California, New Jersey, and New York (California because I had extensive connections there and New Jersey and New York out of convenience—I was a postdoc at Princeton at the time). The pilot studies helped me uncover some key sources of variation that would prove useful for my research. I learned about how PDMPs operate and where they are situated in state bureaucracies. I also learned about the wide variety of enforcement agencies involved in tackling the opioid crisis.

I designed a research study that captured a set of nested maximum variation samples across four dimensions: states, counties, organizations, and professions. By this time, I was particularly interested in the use of PDMPs in healthcare and law enforcement. I reasoned that the same technology could look different depending on who controlled it. If criminal justice agencies controlled the PDMP, it probably operated more like an enforcement tool. If healthcare agencies controlled the PDMP, it probably operated more like a healthcare tool. I explored this hunch by selecting three states that varied on the existence and locus of the PDMP—California, whose PDMP is in the Department of Justice; Florida, whose PDMP is in the Board of Health, and Missouri, which did not have a PDMP at the time but later developed a county-based (rather than statewide) system.

I was interested in how enforcement agents targeted providers, so I wondered about how the organization of prosecution in the state might impact what enforcement agents did and, by extension, shape the enforcement environment in which healthcare providers practiced. The three states I selected helped me explore this hunch as well. California and Missouri both have a decentralized system where prosecution varies by county. In contrast, Florida is the only state to have a statewide prosecutor who takes cross-county drug cases. New York has the next closest thing, a Special Narcotics Prosecutor who

TABLE 1. Interview Participants by State

State	Physicians	Pharmacists	Enforcement agents	Other
California	7	63	37	5
Florida	7	8	11	3
Kansas	0	21	5	3
Kentucky	4	11	9	10
Mississippi	0	28	0	0
Missouri	19	10	25	11
New Jersey	0	29	0	0
New York	0	0	7	4
Totals ($n = 337$)	37	170	94	36

oversees cases across the five boroughs of New York City, but Florida is the only state to have that mechanism at the state level.

Within each state, I used voting records to select a more conservative and a more liberal county but ensured that the counties were approximately the same size and had the same types of resources. Within each county, I mapped the field for enforcement agencies and healthcare providers involved in the crisis and selected interview participants who represented each one. Examples of enforcement organizations include the DEA, state and federal fraud investigators, sheriffs' departments, narcotics task forces, boards of medicine and pharmacy, and federal, state, and local prosecutors. Examples of healthcare organizations include hospitals, clinics, and community pharmacies where I interviewed three types of physicians (pain management, emergency medicine, and general practice) and two types of pharmacists (chain and independent). I did not interview many nurses or nurse practitioners because in the states I selected, they could not independently prescribe opioids (table 1).

Once I identified the types of participants I was seeking, I used snowball sampling and cold emails and phone calls to recruit participants. California was the easiest because I already had healthcare and law enforcement contacts there who referred me to their colleagues in California and other states. Pharmacists were the easiest to recruit with cold calls. The overwhelming majority chose to participate—until I got to Florida. Most Florida pharmacists wanted nothing to do with my study. They tended to be concerned about how participation would affect their employment. I suspect this is because Florida was a hotbed of opioid activity in the early 2000s and because Walgreens had reached an enormous settlement with the DEA in Florida in 2013.[11] It also may have been easier to recruit in other states because I did them first, so the research field was not as saturated. Perhaps Florida pharmacists and physicians were suffering from research fatigue. With few contacts in Florida, I gathered physicians' email addresses from the Board of Medicine website. Few responded. One was only interested if she would be paid. I had better luck with physicians who worked for teaching hospitals than with physicians in private practice.

I created three semi-structured interview instruments, one for each type of worker—law enforcement, physician, and pharmacist. I tailored the instrument to each participant's unique experience and to explore ideas that arose in other interviews. From 2009 to 2019, I collected 337 interviews, including from pharmacists, physicians, and enforcement agents. The pharmacy data in California and Kansas was longitudinal—I spoke with thirteen of the same pharmacists before and after the PDMP was in regular use. If the same pharmacist was not available, I recruited a pharmacist at the same pharmacy. If that was not possible, I chose a nearby pharmacy to retain geographic variation. I also reinterviewed eight enforcement agents and one nurse who did pain consults in the hospital.

This nested maximum variation sampling strategy enabled me to overcome one of the key challenges that plague qualitative researchers: I could capture significant variation across providers, organizations, counties, and states as a lone researcher. Although ultimately there were fewer differences across locales than I anticipated, designing the study this way ensured that I could find differences if they were present. This novel approach offers a systematic way for qualitative researchers to capture key sources of variation. Using the field as the unit of analysis also let me consider multiple subfields within a larger field. I could see variation within a single field (for example, organizational differences in chain versus independent pharmacies), across multiple fields (pharmacy to medicine to law enforcement), and within a local field (a single county or state).

So, You've Gathered Some Data—Now What?

I analyzed data using a grounded theory approach, meaning that instead of gathering all of the data and then analyzing it, I analyzed as I went, allowing findings from earlier interviews to inform questions I asked in later ones. After returning from the field, I had interviews professionally transcribed, then I worked with a team of undergraduate research assistants to help code the data using Atlas.ti qualitative coding software. We began by indexing the data,[12] dividing it based on the major interview questions about PDMP use, differentiating pain patients, addicted patients, diverting patients, and so on. Then we ran reports on each of the major questions and analyzed them to develop substantive and theoretical codes. Substantive codes address a particular topic like pain or opioids while theoretical codes address concepts like deservingness or gatekeeping. While coding, we wrote memos to capture our understanding of the data.

We initially met weekly to discuss the codebook and key ideas that were emerging. Later, I divided students into teams based on type of worker, with one team for pharmacists, one for physicians, and one for law enforcement. In the middle of coding, I went on sabbatical to the Radcliffe Institute for Advanced Study at Harvard.[13] There, I recruited undergraduate research partners who worked alongside my Saint Louis University undergrads to code the data. To compare pre- and post-PDMP data for pharmacists, we created a Microsoft Excel spreadsheet that put the same person's accounts of decision-making at each point in time side by side and analyzed the differences. We also did an analysis of the entire pre-PDMP dataset and the post-PDMP dataset.

This book cannot possibly capture all the intricacies we found in the data. However, our analytical strategy ensured that all perspectives were represented and enabled us to compare workers across various categories to arrive at the claims made in the book. My hope is that this nested maximum variation sampling strategy will assist other researchers who want to study large, multipronged social problems.

ACKNOWLEDGMENTS

IT TAKES A VILLAGE TO WRITE A BOOK. This manuscript is the culmination of fifteen years of research and the insights I have received from a wide variety of supporters along the way. I have been so fortunate to engage with such generous people who have shared their experiences and their struggles. The foundation necessary to sustain a writing project is community and I have been fortunate to join several.

Within weeks of starting my Ph.D. program at the University of California, Irvine, I knew I had found my people. My earlier degrees were in psychology, so sociology was unfamiliar territory. I quickly learned that sociologists were asking the kinds of questions that I wanted to ask and were answering them in ways I found compelling. I will be forever grateful to David S. Meyer who recruited me to Irvine and saw that sociology was a great fit before I did. My mentors Ed Amenta, Francesca Polletta, Carroll Seron, and Tracy Weitz nurtured the seed of this idea in its earliest stages and Nina Bandelj, Philip Cohen, Martha Feldman, David Frank, Ann Hironaka, Andrew Penner, Belinda Robnett, and David Snow provided guidance along the way. Most importantly, my dissertation advisor, Cal Morrill, taught me the exciting parts of organizational and socio-legal theories, helped shape the contours of this study, and has tirelessly supported me throughout my career. Thank you, Cal, for everything.

Irvine was a wonderful place to study sociology in no small part due to the generous, engaged students it attracts. I am especially grateful to Ryan Acton, Georgiana Bostean, Steve Boutcher, Catherine Corrigall-Brown, Remy Cross, Erin Evans, Yuki Kato, Jasmine Kerrissey, Kelsy Kretschmer, Diana Pan, Danielle Rudes, Leah Ruppaner, and Megan Thiele, whose friendship made graduate school such a welcoming place. I am also grateful to Alegria Baquero, Connie McGuire, Katie Pine, Graham Rowlands, Ines Viskic, Jaye Austin Williams, and the "Brunch Bunch" for their support.

Much of this project developed while I was a postdoctoral research associate at Princeton University. I am grateful to Betsy Armstrong, Bernadette Atuahene,

Elana Broch, Kelly Cleland, Paul DiMaggio, Michael McCann, Lisa Miller, Paul Starr, Kim Lane Scheppele, James Trussell, and Keith Wailoo, who provided support and mentorship. My fellow postdocs and graduate students made Princeton a rich intellectual home. Thank you to Sarah Brayne, Clayton Childress, Jessica Cooper, Michaela DeSoucey, Kelli Hall, Patrick Ishizuka, Karen Levy, Neda Maghbouleh, Zitsi Mirakhur, Jayanti Owens, David Pedulla, Lauren Senesac, Adam Slez, Beth Sully, Sarah Thébaud, Sal Thorkelson, Sarinnapha Vasunilashorn, Janet Vertesi, and Amy Winter for their engagement with my work then and now. And a special thank you goes to Miranda Waggoner, my officemate and forever friend, thank you for devoting so much time to helping me and providing your brilliant insights. I am so lucky to have you in my life.

Thank you to my wonderful colleagues, administrators, and staff at Saint Louis University who have provided me with the time and resources needed to write this book: Sara Bauman, Doug Boin, David Borgmeyer, Matthew Christian, Ric Colignon, Amy Cooper, Chris Duncan, Monica Eppinger, Keon Gilbert, Scott Harris, Joel Jennings, Donna LaVoie, Mike Lewis, Katie MacKinnon, Adrienne McCarthy, Kate Moran, Ken Olliff, Bruce O'Neill, Jasmin Patel, Fran Pestello, Fred Pestello, and Chris Prener. Thank you also to the amazing scholars at SLU's Health Law Center and Center for Health Care Ethics who have provided me with additional homes on campus, especially Jeff Bishop, Harold Braswell, Kelly Dineen, Jason Eberl, Rob Gatter, Sandy Johnson, Elizabeth Pendo, Amy Sanders, Ana Santos Rutschman, Sidney Watson, Yolonda Wilson, and Ruqaiijah Yearby. A dedicated team of research assistants provided the human power necessary to fuel a project of this magnitude. I thank you all, notably Hiba Al-Ramahi, Maddie Baumgart, Amogh Chariyamane, Abby Lawrence, Ilana Litvak, Emily Lustig, Anika Mazumder, Connor Reis, Elizabeth Salley, Maxine Taylor, and Cameron Wolfram. I am also grateful to scholars at Washington University in Saint Louis who have offered time and feedback to brainstorm this project: Caity Collins, David Cunningham, Jenine Harris, Hedy Lee, Zakiya Luna, Ariela Schachter, and Adia Harvey Wingfield.

I began writing this manuscript as a fellow at the Radcliffe Institute for Advanced Study at Harvard University from 2019–2020. I am grateful to all my fellow fellows who fostered a sense of wonder and helped expand my thinking about the world and to the amazing staff who made the fellowship run so smoothly. Special thanks go to Allan Brandt, Edo Berger, Sharon BrombergLim, Tomiko Brown-Nagin, Paul Chang, Mac Daniel, Todd Dionne, Ivelisse

Estrada, Caleb Gayle, Rebecca Haley, Jane Huber, Every Ocean Hughes, Camara Phyllis Jones, Tali Mendelberg, Heather Min, Khalil Gibran Muhammad, Allison Ney, Gala Porras-Kim, Nina McConigley, Meredith Moss Quinn, Claudia Rizzini, Manisha Sinha, James Sturm, and Colleen Walsh and to Steve Coates, who taught me about campus lore. I am also grateful to Harvard sociologists Jason Beckfield, Sasha Killewald, and David Showalter for sharing their thoughts over coffee and meals and to Tony Jack, who made Cambridge so much fun. My Radcliffe research assistants were extraordinary: Leena Ambady, Taya Cowan, and Reem Omer. Finally, there are no words to express my gratitude to the VPs—Fran Berman, Anne Higonnet, and Alexi Lahav—your deep engagement with my work made this book so much better and your ongoing support helped me through the roughest patches. What a joy it has been to work with you. Nous pouvons, et nous avons pu!

One of the wonderful things about doing research like this is how your community keeps expanding. I discovered such wonderful people in the pharmacy and medical fields early in this work. Thank you John Colaizzi Sr., Don Downing, Trish Freeman, Jim Kuperberg, Helene Lipton, Dan Millspaugh, Lorie Rice, and Ellie Vogt for helping me understand your professions. Thank you to Ted Smith and the city of Louisville for my first opportunity to engage in translational research.

Thank you to my early readers and those who workshopped drafts—Jenny Carlson, Scott Collier, Nicole Gonzalez Van-Cleve, Ruth Horowitz, Anna Marshall, Laura Beth Nielsen, Jenn Oliva, Winnie Poster, Travis Rieder, John Robinson, Fred Rottnek, Joe Soss, Mark Suchman, and Rachel Winograd.

Thank you to all of the scholars whom I met at conferences who chatted over coffee and offered tidbits of advice that turned out to be life-changing: KT Albiston, Denise Anthony, Scott Barclay, Howie Becker, Emilio Castilla, Dan Chambliss, Laurie Edelman, Chuck Epp, Patty Ewick, Michelle Goodwin, Carol Heimer, Kate Kellogg, Brian Kelly, Michael Lipsky, Steven Maynard-Moody, Doug McAdam, Rory McVeigh, Michael Musheno, Bernice Pescosolido, Dorothy Roberts, Susan Silbey, Jonathan Simon, Stefan Timmermans, and Robert Zussman.

I am so grateful to my cadre of legal scholars and social scientists, who produce excellent research and lead by example: Hadar Aviram, Ruha Benjamin, Ellen Berrey, Danielle Bessett, Erin Cech, Renee Cramer, Jeff Dudas, Mary Dudas, Jeanne Flavin, Kelley Fong, Lori Freedman, Kaaryn Gustafson, Keith Guzik, Gitte Sommer Harrits, Helena Hansen, Beth Hoffman, Trevor Hoppe, Tania Jenkins, Joanna Kempner, Katrina Kimport,

Anna Kirkland, Lee Kravetz, Greta Krippner, Aaron Kupchik, Sarah Lageson, Armando Lara-Millán, Sandy Levitsky, Liz McCuskey, Allison McKim, Seema Mohapatra, Christine Morton, Sigrún Ólafsdóttir, Shannon Portillo, Rashawn Ray, Keramet Reiter, Mary Rose, Josh Seim, Lori Sexton, Brad Silberzahn, Michelle Smirnova, Justin Steil, Forrest Stuart, Mary Nell Trautner, Josh Wilson, and the "Powerful Women." Being in your company has made me a better scholar. Thank you to the Law and Society Association and the American Sociological Association for providing me with such rich intellectual homes and for hosting our community each year.

Thanks to Twitter (RIP), I am pleased to have found fellow travelers whose ongoing engagement and advocacy impress me each day: Leo Beletsky, Jef Bratberg, Jennifer Carroll, Corey Davis, Taleed El-Sabawi, Morgan Godvin, Ryan Hampton, Carl Hart, Lucas Hill, Ayana Jordan, Stefan Kertesz, Bill Kinkle, Jeff Little, Ryan Marino, Ryan McNeil, Stephen Murray, Jules Netherland, Kate Nicholson, Brandon del Pozo, Helen Redmond, Zach Siegal, Kim Sue, Maia Szalavitz, Bob Twillman, Sheila Vakharia, Sarah Wakeman, Ingrid Walker, and Claire Zagorski.

Thank you to all the healthcare professionals and enforcement agents who participated in this study. I appreciate your willingness to share candidly the struggles you face and to offer me a glimpse into your daily lives. I cannot name you here because I promised you confidentiality, but I hope that I have honored your contribution in this book. To everyone who is struggling with chronic pain and/or opioid use disorder—your lives matter and you deserve better. To everyone who is trying to create commonsense policies and practices that help those in need—I see you and value your work.

My gratitude goes to the team at Princeton University Press: To Meagan Levinson, my amazing editor who believed in this book from the start and helped transform an idea into a manuscript: I couldn't have done this without you. Thanks also to Erik Beranek, Kathleen Cioffi, Eric Crahan, Jennifer Harris, Rachael Levay, Steve Stillman, and so many others who brought this book into being. Thank you also to John Dycus, who has now edited two generations of Chiarellos—you always find just the right turn of phrase. Note that any errors in this book are mine alone.

Thank you to all of the organizations that supported this project: the American Council of Learned Societies; the Department of Health and Human Services Agency for Healthcare Research and Quality; the National Institute on Drug Abuse's Loan Repayment Program; Princeton's Center for Health and Wellbeing, Law and Public Affairs, and Office of Population Research;

The Radcliffe Institute for Advanced Study at Harvard University; Saint Louis University's College of Arts and Sciences and Office of the Vice President for Research; and UC Irvine's Center for Organizational Research. My tremendous appreciation goes to the National Science Foundation CAREER Programs in Law & Science and Sociology for investing in my research and making this project possible. I also value all of the journalists and media outlets who have invited me to share my work with the public.

On a personal note, much appreciation goes to everyone who nourished my mind and body: Bo Andell, Barb Anderson, Star Craven, Terence Crowley, Liese Rugen, Lisa Smout, Barb Yemm, and especially Sabin Lamson—our journey together changed my life.

I would also like to thank my parents, who encouraged each new endeavor and cheered me on; my dear friends Lindsey Kingston, Fred Trotter, and Susan Trotter for all of your support over the years; and my darling Chris Bethel, whose love has been a sustaining force and who makes me laugh every day. There is no doubt that I have left someone very important off this list. Please know that you are no less appreciated for not being named. I feel so lucky to do the work I do among so many people I admire. Thank you all.

NOTES

Introduction

1. I use the terms "overdose crisis" and "opioid crisis" interchangeably in this book. "Opioid crisis" is a popular term, but it is important to note that opioids themselves do not constitute a crisis; it is the overdose deaths that result from them and other drugs that deserve the most attention.

2. Mann, "More than a Million Americans Have Died from Overdoses during the Opioid Epidemic"; National Institute on Drug Abuse, "Drug Overdose Death Rates," February 9, 2023.

3. Social problems are problems in society.

4. Chiarello, "The War on Drugs Comes to the Pharmacy Counter"; Chiarello, "How Organizational Context Affects Bioethical Decision-Making."

5. Oliva, "Prescription Drug Policing"; Oliva, "Dosing Discrimination."

6. Chiarello, "The War on Drugs Comes to the Pharmacy Counter."

7. Eubanks, *Automating Inequality*; Brayne, *Predict and Surveil: Data, Discretion, and the Future of Policing*; Marx, *Windows into the Soul: Surveillance and Society in an Age of High Technology*; Benjamin, *Race after Technology: Abolitionist Tools for the New Jim Code*.

8. PDMP TTAC, "History of Prescription Drug Monitoring Programs."

9. Centers for Disease Control and Prevention, "Integrating and Expanding Prescription Drug Monitoring Program Data: Lessons from Nine States." 2017. http://www.cdc.gov/drugoverdose/pdf/pehriie_report-a.pdf.

10. National Association of Boards of Pharmacy, "NABP's Role in Combating the Opioid Epidemic."

11. Chiarello, "Trojan Horse Technologies: Smuggling Criminal-Legal Logics into Healthcare Practice."

12. Mintz, *Unruly Bodies: Life Writing by Women with Disabilities*; Foucault, *Discipline and Punish: The Birth of the Prison*; Timmermans and Gabe, "Introduction."

13. Waggoner, *The Zero Trimester: Pre-Pregnancy Care and the Politics of Reproductive Risk*; Armstrong, *Conceiving Risk, Bearing Responsibility: Fetal Alcohol Syndrome and the Diagnosis of Moral Disorder*; Roberts, *Killing the Black Body: Race, Reproduction, and the Meaning of Liberty*; Conrad and Schneider, *Deviance and Medicalization: From Badness to Sickness*.

14. Brayne, "Big Data Surveillance: The Case of Policing," 979.

15. Peripheral neuropathy is nerve damage.

16. Hampton, *American Fix*. This quote has been edited for brevity. The full story can be found on pp. 7–9 of *American Fix*.

17. Centers for Disease Control and Prevention, "Drug Overdose Deaths | Drug Overdose | CDC Injury Center."

18. Centers for Disease Control and Prevention, "Understanding the Epidemic | Drug Overdose | CDC Injury Center."

19. Centers for Disease Control and Prevention, "Understanding the Epidemic | Drug Overdose | CDC Injury Center."

20. National Institute on Drug Abuse, "Overdose Death Rates," January 29, 2021.

21. National Institute on Drug Abuse, "Drug Overdose Death Rates," February 9, 2023.

22. Centers for Disease Control and Prevention, "Coronavirus Disease 2019."

23. Centers for Disease Control and Prevention, "Prescribing Practices | Drug Overdose | CDC Injury Center"; Guy, "Vital Signs."

24. Keefe, Patrick Radden, *Empire of Pain: The Secret History of the Sackler Dynasty*; Meier, *Pain Killer*.

25. Hoffman and Walsh, "Purdue Pharma, Maker of OxyContin, Files for Bankruptcy."

26. Alexander, *The New Jim Crow: Mass Incarceration in the Age of Colorblindness*.

27. Lembke, *Drug Dealer, MD*.

28. Libby, *The Criminalization of Medicine: America's War on Doctors*; Ziegler and Lovrich Jr., "Pain Relief, Prescription Drugs, and Prosecution: A Four-State Survey of Chief Prosecutors."

29. PDMP TTAC, "History of Prescription Drug Monitoring Programs."

30. Allen, "The 'Oxy Express.'"

31. Lipsky, *Street-Level Bureaucracy, 30th Anniversary Edition*; Maynard-Moody and Musheno, *Cops, Teachers, Counselors*; Maynard-Moody and Portillo, "Street-level Bureaucracy Theory"; Buffat et al., *Understanding Street-Level Bureaucracy*; Zacka, *When the State Meets the Street: Public Service and Moral Agency*; Seim, *Bandage, Sort, and Hustle: Ambulance Crews on the Front Lines of Urban Suffering*.

32. Seim, *Bandage, Sort, and Hustle: Ambulance Crews on the Front Lines of Urban Suffering*; Lara-Millán, "Public Emergency Room Overcrowding in the Era of Mass Imprisonment," 2014; Fong, "Getting Eyes in the Home: Child Protective Services Investigations and State Surveillance of Family Life."

33. U.S. Census Bureau, "Health Insurance Coverage in the United States."

34. "Access to Care and Availability of New Patient Appointments."

35. Relman, "The New Medical-Industrial Complex."

36. Berkrot, "Global Prescription Drug Spend Seen at $1.5 Trillion in 2021."

37. Conrad and Muñoz, "The Medicalization of Chronic Pain."

38. American Board of Medical Specialties, "ABMS Officially Recognizes Addiction Medicine as a Subspecialty"; Nunes et al., "Addiction Psychiatry and Addiction Medicine."

39. DiMaggio and Powell, "The Iron Cage Revisited: Institutional Isomorphism and Collective Rationality in Organizational Fields."

40. DiMaggio and Powell, 64.

41. Thornton and Ocasio, "Institutional Logics"; Thornton et al., "The Institutional Logics Perspective"; Edelman, *Working Law: Courts, Corporations, and Symbolic Civil Rights*.

42. Showalter et al., "Bridging Institutional Logics: Implementing Naloxone Distribution for People Exiting Jail in Three California Counties."

43. Gusfield, *Contested Meanings: The Construction of Alcohol Problems.*

44. Kupchik, *Homeroom Security: School Discipline in an Age of Fear*; Beckett and Herbert, *Banished: The New Social Control in Urban America.*

45. Garland, *The Culture of Control: Crime and Social Order in Contemporary Society.*

46. Feeley and Simon, "The New Penology: Notes on the Emerging Strategy of Corrections and Its Implications."

47. The rhetoric of the punitive turn emerged in the 1970s, but substantive changes in prisons did not occur until the 1990s, as Phelps (2011) demonstrates. Gustafson, *Cheating Welfare: Public Assistance and the Criminalization of Poverty*; Gilliom, *Overseers of the Poor: Surveillance, Resistance, and the Limits of Privacy*; Kupchik, *Homeroom Security: School Discipline in an Age of Fear*; Soss et al., *Disciplining the Poor: Neoliberal Paternalism and the Persistent Power of Race.*

48. Simon, *Governing through Crime: How the War on Crime Transformed American Democracy and Created a Culture of Fear.*

49. Simon, *Governing through Crime*, 4.

50. Brayne, *Predict and Surveil: Data, Discretion, and the Future of Policing*, 3. Marx, *Windows into the Soul: Surveillance and Society in an Age of High Technology*; Pasquale, *The Black Box Society*; O'Neil, *Weapons of Math Destruction: How Big Data Increases Inequality and Threatens Democracy.*

51. Bovens and Zouridis, "From Street-Level to System-Level Bureaucracies: How Information and Communication Technology Is Transforming Administrative Discretion and Constitutional Control"; Brayne, *Predict and Surveil: Data, Discretion, and the Future of Policing.*

52. Eubanks, *Automating Inequality.*

53. Benjamin, *Race after Technology: Abolitionist Tools for the New Jim Code.*

54. Brayne, *Predict and Surveil: Data, Discretion, and the Future of Policing*; Lageson, *Digital Punishment: Privacy, Stigma, and the Harms of Data-Driven Criminal Justice.*

55. Zuboff, *The Age of Surveillance Capitalism: The Fight for a Human Future at the New Frontier of Power.*

56. Brayne, *Predict and Surveil: Data, Discretion, and the Future of Policing.*

57. Eubanks, *Automating Inequality.*

58. Marx, *Undercover: Police Surveillance in America*; Innes, "Control Creep"; Nelkin and Andrews, "DNA Identification and Surveillance Creep."

59. Chiarello, "Trojan Horse Technologies: Smuggling Criminal-Legal Logics into Healthcare Practice."

Chapter 1. Criminalizing Care

1. Maria's story is paraphrased from a Human Rights Watch report titled "'Not Allowed to Be Compassionate': Chronic Pain, the Overdose Crisis, and Unintended Harms in the US," https://www.hrw.org/sites/default/files/report_pdf/hhr1218_web.pdf.

2. Human Rights Watch, ii.

3. Centers for Disease Control and Prevention, "CDC Guidelines for Prescribing Opioids for Chronic Pain—United States, 2016."

4. Human Rights Watch, "Not Allowed to Be Compassionate," iii.

5. Human Rights Watch, iv.

6. Human Rights Watch, iv.

7. Meier, *Pain Killer*.

8. Meier; Guy, "Vital Signs."

9. National Institute on Drug Abuse, "Overdose Death Rates," January 29, 2021.

10. Dineen and DuBois, "Between a Rock and a Hard Place"; U.S. Department of Justice, "Cases against Doctors."

11. PDMP TTAC, "History of Prescription Drug Monitoring Programs."

12. Chronic pain is long-lasting pain, compared to acute pain, which has a short duration.

13. Rummell, "Purdue Pharma Strikes $8B Plea Deal over Marketing of OxyContin."

14. O'Hagan, "Patrick Radden Keefe on Exposing the Sackler Family's Links to the Opioid Crisis."

15. Courtwright, *Dark Paradise*; Goode, *Drugs in American Society*.

16. Courtwright, *Dark Paradise*.

17. Provine, *Unequal under Law: Race in the War on Drugs*.

18. Provine *Unequal under Law: Race in the War on Drugs*; Musto, *The American Disease: Origins of Narcotic Control*; Alexander, *The New Jim Crow: Mass Incarceration in the Age of Colorblindness*; Simon, *Governing through Crime: How the War on Crime Transformed American Democracy and Created a Culture of Fear*; Conrad and Schneider, *Deviance and Medicalization: From Badness to Sickness*.

19. Provine, *Unequal under Law: Race in the War on Drugs*.

20. Courtwright, *Dark Paradise*.

21. Courtwright.

22. Musto, *The American Disease: Origins of Narcotic Control*; Hohenstein, "Just What the Doctor Ordered."

23. Conrad and Schneider, *Deviance and Medicalization: From Badness to Sickness*.

24. Provine, *Unequal under Law: Race in the War on Drugs*.

25. Linnemann, "Mad Men, Meth Moms, Moral Panic: Gendering Meth Crimes in the Midwest"; Nieman Reports, "The Superpredator Script."

26. Provine, *Unequal under Law: Race in the War on Drugs*.

27. Alexander, *The New Jim Crow: Mass Incarceration in the Age of Colorblindness*.

28. Travis et al., *The Growth of Incarceration in the United States: Exploring Causes and Consequences*.

29. Kang-Brown et al., "People in Jail and Prison in Spring 2021"; Fair and Walmsley, "World Prison Population List, Thirteenth Edition."

30. Gramlich, "Black Imprisonment Rate in the U.S. Has Fallen by a Third since 2006."

31. Carson, *Prisoners in 2021*.

32. Omori, Marisa. "'Nickel and Dimed' for Drug Crime: Unpacking the Process of Cumulative Racial Inequality"; Alexander, *The New Jim Crow: Mass Incarceration in the Age of Colorblindness*.

33. Netherland and Hansen, "The War on Drugs That Wasn't."

34. NBC News, "How Florida Brothers' 'Pill Mill' Operation Fueled Painkiller Abuse Epidemic."

35. Netherland and Hansen, "The War on Drugs That Wasn't."

36. Lembke, *Drug Dealer, MD*.

37. Conrad and Schneider, *Deviance and Medicalization: From Badness to Sickness*, 36–38; Szalavitz, *Unbroken Brain*.

38. Alexander et al., "Effect of Early and Later Colony Housing on Oral Ingestion of Morphine in Rats."

39. Robins, *The Vietnam Drug User Returns: Final Report, September 1973*; Hall and Weier, "Lee Robins' Studies of Heroin Use among US Vietnam Veterans."

40. Case and Deaton, *Deaths of Despair and the Future of Capitalism*; Shanahan et al., "Does Despair Really Kill?"

41. Khoury et al., "Substance Use, Childhood Traumatic Experience, and Posttraumatic Stress Disorder in an Urban Civilian Population"; Szalavitz, *Unbroken Brain*; SAMHSA, "Key Substance Use and Mental Health Indicators in the United States: Results from the 2019 National Survey on Drug Use and Health."

42. Dineen, "Addressing Prescription Opioid Abuse Concerns in Context."

43. Sinha, "Chronic Stress, Drug Use, and Vulnerability to Addiction"; Dineen, "Addressing Prescription Opioid Abuse Concerns in Context."

44. Brown, "Prescription Opioids Aren't Driving the Overdose Crisis. Illicitly Manufactured Synthetic Opioids Are."

45. National Institute on Drug Abuse. "Drug Overdose Death Rates," February 9, 2023.

46. Jones et al., "Changes in Synthetic Opioid Involvement in Drug Overdose Deaths in the United States, 2010–2016"; CDC, "Other Drugs."

47. Jones et al., "Changes in Synthetic Opioid Involvement in Drug Overdose Deaths in the United States, 2010–2016," 43.

48. SAMHSA, "Key Substance Use and Mental Health Indicators in the United States: Results from the 2021 National Survey on Drug Use and Health."

49. National Institute on Drug Abuse, "Drug Overdose Death Rates," February 9, 2023; Centers for Disease Control and Prevention, "Three Waves of Opioids Overdose Deaths."

50. Note that the percentages add up to more than 100 percent because multiple drugs are often involved in the same overdose death. When that occurs, the death is attributed to both drugs. National Institute on Drug Abuse, "Drug Overdose Death Rates," February 9, 2023.

51. National Institute on Drug Abuse.

52. Kline, "Suicides Associated with Forced Tapering of Opiate Pain Treatments."

53. Darnall et al., "International Stakeholder Community of Pain Experts and Leaders Call for an Urgent Action on Forced Opioid Tapering," March 1, 2019.

54. Netherland and Hansen, "The War on Drugs That Wasn't."

55. Netherland and Hansen.

56. Beckett and Brydolf-Horwitz, "A Kinder, Gentler Drug War?"

57. Hansen et al., *Whiteout: How Racial Capitalism Changed the Color of Opioids in America*.

58. Rates are measured out of 100,000 of the population.

59. Kaiser Family Foundation, "Opioid Overdose Deaths by Race/Ethnicity."

60. James and Jordan, "The Opioid Crisis in Black Communities," 405, 404.

61. James and Jordan.

62. SAMHSA, *The Opioid Crisis and the Black/African American Population: An Urgent Issue*, p. 5.

63. "NIH's HEAL Initiatives Keep Progressing Thanks to Scientists' Ingenuity"; Goodnough, "Overdose Deaths Have Surged during the Pandemic, C.D.C. Data Shows."

64. Beletsky, "America's Favorite Antidote: Drug-Induced Homicide in the Age of the Overdose Crisis."

65. Tiger, *Judging Addicts*, 134.

66. Pager, *Marked: Race, Crime, and Finding Work in an Era of Mass Incarceration*.

67. Tiger, *Judging Addicts*; Paik, *Discretionary Justice*.

68. El-Sabawi, "Carrots, Sticks and Problem Drug Use."

69. El-Sabawi and Carroll, "A Model for Defunding: An Evidence-Based Statute for Behavioral Health Crisis Response," 37.

70. Tiger, *Judging Addicts*; El-Sabawi and Carroll, "A Model for Defunding: An Evidence-Based Statute for Behavioral Health Crisis Response."

71. Beletsky, "Deploying Prescription Drug Monitoring to Address the Overdose Crisis: Ideology Meets Reality"; Oliva, "Dosing Discrimination"; Oliva, "Prescription Drug Policing."

72. Townsend et al., "Did Prescribing Laws Disproportionately Affect Opioid Dispensing to Black Patients?"

73. Smirnova, *The Prescription-to-Prison Pipeline: An Intersectional Analysis of the Medicalization and Criminalization of Pain*.

74. Beckett and Brydolf-Horwitz, "A Kinder, Gentler Drug War?"

75. Provine, *Unequal under Law: Race in the War on Drugs*, 167.

76. U.S. Drug Enforcement Administration, "Drug Scheduling."

77. Centers for Disease Control and Prevention, "Fentanyl | Drug Overdose | CDC Injury Center."

78. National Institute on Drug Abuse, "Overdose Death Rates," January 29, 2021.

79. Goode, *Drugs in American Society*.

80. Case and Deaton, *Deaths of Despair and the Future of Capitalism*.

81. Case and Deaton.

82. Hampton, *American Fix*.

83. Smith et al., "Exploring the Link between Substance Use and Mental Health Status"; Roberts et al., "Psychological Interventions for Post-Traumatic Stress Disorder and Comorbid Substance Use Disorder."

84. Walker, *High: Drugs, Desire, and a Nation of Users*.

85. Hart, *Drug Use for Grown-Ups: Chasing Liberty in the Land of Fear*.

86. Szalavitz, *Unbroken Brain*.

87. Castillo, "The Invisible Majority."

88. Institute of Medicine (US) Committee on Advancing Pain Research, Care, and Education, *Relieving Pain in America*.

89. Treede et al., "A Classification of Chronic Pain for ICD-11."

90. Dineen and Goldberg, "Introduction: Living with Pain in the Midst of the Opioid Crisis."

91. Chiarello, "Where Movements Matter: Examining Unintended Consequences of the Pain Management Movement in Medical, Criminal Justice, and Public Health Fields."

92. Meldrum, "A Capsule History of Pain Management."

93. Saunders, "The Evolution of Palliative Care."

94. Saunders, "The Evolution of Palliative Care"; Roberts, "The History of Hospice: A Different Kind of Health 'Care.'"

95. Chiarello, "Where Movements Matter: Examining Unintended Consequences of the Pain Management Movement in Medical, Criminal Justice, and Public Health Fields."

96. Tompkins et al., "Providing Chronic Pain Management in the 'Fifth Vital Sign' Era"; Scher et al., "Moving beyond Pain as the Fifth Vital Sign and Patient Satisfaction Scores to Improve Pain Care in the 21st Century."

97. Tompkins et al., "Providing Chronic Pain Management in the 'Fifth Vital Sign' Era."

98. Guy, "Vital Signs."

99. Meier, "In Guilty Plea, OxyContin Maker to Pay $600 Million"; Centers for Disease Control and Prevention, "Protect Patients from Opioid Overdose."

100. Burgess et al., "Patient Race and Physician's Decisions to Prescribe Opioids for Chronic Low Back Pain"; Meghani et al., "Time to Take Stock"; Roberts, *Fatal Invention: How Science, Politics, and Big Business Re-Create Race in the Twenty-First Century*; Morales and Yong, "Racial and Ethnic Disparities in the Treatment of Chronic Pain."

101. Frakt and Monkovic, "A 'Rare Case Where Racial Biases' Protected African-Americans."

102. James and Jordan, "The Opioid Crisis in Black Communities."

103. Inquirer, "The Opioid Crisis Shows Why Racism in Health Care Is Always Harmful, Never 'Protective' l Opinion."

104. Jennifer Oliva, e-mail with the author, May 2, 2024.

105. Nicholson, "The Opioid Crackdown Is Hurting People in Pain | Washington Monthly."

106. Szalavitz, "Opinion | What the Opioid Crisis Took from People in Pain."

107. Boekel et al., "Stigma among Health Professionals towards Patients with Substance Use Disorders and Its Consequences for Healthcare Delivery."

108. Goldberg, "Pain, Objectivity and History: Understanding Pain Stigma."

109. Santayana, *The Life of Reason, Or, The Phases of Human Progress: Reason in Society*.

Chapter 2. Trojan Horse Technologies

1. U.S. Drug Enforcement Administration, "Special Agent."

2. U.S. Drug Enforcement Administration, "Diversion Investigator."

3. U.S. Department of Justice and Office of the Inspector General Evaluation and Inspections Division, "Follow-Up Review of the Drug Enforcement Administration's Efforts to Control the Diversion of Controlled Pharmaceuticals."

4. Meier, *Pain Killer*.

5. Sacco, "Drug Enforcement in the United States: History, Policy, and Trends."

6. Each state has its own name for the PDMP. CURES stands for Controlled Substance Utilization Review and Evaluation System.

7. Accessing PDMP information is not this easy for all law enforcement. State laws about access vary, so some enforcement agents can log into PDMPs directly while others must first get a warrant or subpoena. For more on this, see Boustead, "Privacy Protections and Law

Enforcement Use of Prescription Drug Monitoring Databases," and J. D. Oliva et al., *Dosing Discrimination: Regulating PDMP Risk Scores.*

8. U.S. Department of Justice, "Automation of Reports and Consolidated Orders System (ARCOS)."

9. Short for "narcotic," a drug category that includes opioids.

10. Insurance tracks how recently a patient has filled a prescription and will reject those that it deems too early. Patients can get around insurance by paying cash instead, which is why pharmacies consider paying cash a "red flag."

11. Chiarello, "The War on Drugs Comes to the Pharmacy Counter."

12. Kuehn, "CDC"; National Institute on Drug Abuse, "Overdose Death Rates," January 29, 2021.

13. Meier, *Pain Killer*; Lembke, *Drug Dealer, MD.*

14. Experts have begun using the term "misuse" or "nonmedical use," but the term "abuse" is used in the Controlled Substances Act, which is why I use it here.

15. Although several states have legalized marijuana for medical and/or recreational use, it is still federally illegal as of 2023.

16. U.S. Department of Justice, "Controlled Substance Schedules."

17. "State PDMP Profiles and Contacts."

18. "PMP Gateway." Previously called Appris Health.

19. Appriss Health, "Appriss Health and State Governments"; National Association of Boards of Pharmacy, "NABP PMP InterConnect Is the Answer the Government Is Looking For."

20. Sacco et al., "Prescription Drug Monitoring Programs."

21. Prescription Drug Monitoring Program Training and Technical Assistance Center, *History of Prescription Drug Monitoring Programs.*

22. Lee, "Purdue Pharma Offers Two $1 Million Grants to Combat Prescription Drug Abuse."

23. PDMP TTAC, "History of Prescription Drug Monitoring Programs."

24. PDMP TTAC.

25. Doyle et al., "PDMP 3.0: Investigating the Future of Prescription Drug Monitoring Programs."

26. This name was later changed to NarxCare.

27. Oliva, "Dosing Discrimination."

28. Weiner et al., "Advanced Visualizations to Interpret Prescription Drug Monitoring Program Information."

29. Davis et al., "Evolution and Convergence of State Laws Governing Controlled Substance Prescription Monitoring Programs, 1998–2011."

30. Dickson-Gomez et al., "Effects of Implementation and Enforcement Differences in Prescription Drug Monitoring Programs in 3 States."

31. Oliva, "Dosing Discrimination."

32. Pasquale, *The Black Box Society: The Secret Algorithms That Control Money and Information*; Brayne, *Predict and Surveil: Data, Discretion, and the Future of Policing*; Eubanks, *Automating Inequality.*

33. Benjamin, *Race after Technology: Abolitionist Tools for the New Jim Code.*

34. O'Neil, *Weapons of Math Destruction: How Big Data Increases Inequality and Threatens Democracy*.

35. Benjamin, *Race after Technology*; Brayne, *Predict and Surveil*.

36. O'Neil, *Weapons of Math Destruction*; Benjamin, *Race after Technology*; Zuboff, *The Age of Surveillance Capitalism: The Fight for a Human Future at the New Frontier of Power*.

37. Lyon, *Surveillance as Social Sorting: Privacy, Risk, and Digital Discrimination*.

38. Lageson, *Digital Punishment: Privacy, Stigma, and the Harms of Data-Driven Criminal Justice*; Oliva, "Dosing Discrimination"; Lyon, *Surveillance as Social Sorting*; WIRED, "A Drug Addiction Risk Algorithm and Its Grim Toll on Chronic Pain Sufferers."

39. Oliva, "Prescription Drug Policing," February 1, 2019.

40. Oliva.

41. Beletsky, "Deploying Prescription Drug Monitoring to Address the Overdose Crisis: Ideology Meets Reality."

42. Bell and Salmon, "Pain, Physical Dependence and Pseudoaddiction: Redefining Addiction for 'Nice' People?"; Conrad and Muñoz, "The Medicalization of Chronic Pain"; Conrad and Schneider, *Deviance and Medicalization: From Badness to Sickness*; Hampton, *American Fix*.

43. Roberts, *Killing the Black Body: Race, Reproduction, and the Meaning of Liberty*; Goodwin, *Policing the Womb: Invisible Women and the Criminalization of Motherhood*; Gustafson, *Cheating Welfare: Public Assistance and the Criminalization of Poverty*; Glenn, "The Birth of the Crack Baby and the History That 'Myths' Make"; Roberts, *Torn Apart*; Smirnova, *The Prescription-to-Prison Pipeline: An Intersectional Analysis of the Medicalization and Criminalization of Pain*.

44. Roberts, *Torn Apart*; Fong, *Investigating Families: Motherhood in the Shadow of Child Protective Services*.

45. Garland, *The Culture of Control: Crime and Social Order in Contemporary Society*; Pager, *Marked: Race, Crime, and Finding Work in an Era of Mass Incarceration*; Wright and Barber, *The Politics of Punishment: A Critical Analysis of Prisons in America*.

46. Provine, *Unequal under Law: Race in the War on Drugs*; Alexander, *The New Jim Crow: Mass Incarceration in the Age of Colorblindness*.

47. Alexander, *The New Jim Crow*; Provine, *Unequal under Law*.

48. Alexander, *The New Jim Crow*, 56.

49. Alexander.

50. Alexander, 56.

51. Garland, *The Culture of Control*; Phelps, "Rehabilitation in the Punitive Era: The Gap between Rhetoric and Reality in US Prison Programs."

52. Alexander, *The New Jim Crow*.

53. Mauer, *Race to Incarcerate*.

54. Sherry, *The Punitive Turn in American Life: How the United States Learned to Fight Crime Like a War*; Garland, *The Culture of Control*; Phelps, "Rehabilitation in the Punitive Era."

55. OECD member countries generally have more extensive economic infrastructures than non-OECD countries.

56. Prison Policy Initiative, "States of Incarceration."

57. NAACP, "Criminal Justice Fact Sheet | NAACP."

58. Benjamin, *Captivating Technology*; Brayne, *Predict and Surveil*; Eubanks, *Automating Inequality*; Benjamin, *Race after Technology*; Lara-Millán, "Public Emergency Room Overcrowding in the Era of Mass Imprisonment," 2014.

59. Eubanks, *Automating Inequality*; Brayne, *Predict and Surveil*.

60. Brayne, *Predict and Surveil*; Benjamin, *Captivating Technology*.

61. Zuboff, *The Age of Surveillance Capitalism*; O'Neil, *Weapons of Math Destruction*; Pasquale, *The Black Box Society*; Eubanks, *Automating Inequality*; Brayne, *Predict and Surveil*.

62. 21 C.F.R. § 1306.04(a).

63. Chiarello, "The War on Drugs Comes to the Pharmacy Counter."

64. Gast, "Who Defines Legitimate Medical Practice-Lessons Learned from the Controlled Substances Act, Physician-Assisted Suicide and Oregon v. Ashcroft."

65. Abood and Burns, *Pharmacy Practice and the Law*.

66. Macaulay, "Non-Contractual Relations in Business: A Preliminary Study"; Sarat, "Legal Effectiveness and Social Studies of Law: On the Unfortunate Persistence of a Research Tradition."

67. Chiarello, "The War on Drugs Comes to the Pharmacy Counter"; Chiarello, "How Organizational Context Affects Bioethical Decision-Making."

68. Chiarello, "The War on Drugs Comes to the Pharmacy Counter."

69. Unless they have a special exemption to provide opioids to treat substance use disorders, described later in this chapter.

70. Rieder, *In Pain: A Bioethicist's Personal Struggle with Opioids*.

71. National Provider Identifiers are ten-digit numbers unique to each healthcare provider that enable them to complete administrative and financial transactions including insurance billing.

72. Yong et al., "Prevalence of Chronic Pain among Adults in the United States."

73. SAMHSA, "Key Substance Use and Mental Health Indicators in the United States: Results from the 2019 National Survey on Drug Use and Health."

74. Mezei and Murinson, "Pain Education in North American Medical Schools"; Hoffman, "Most Doctors Are Ill-Equipped to Deal with the Opioid Epidemic. Few Medical Schools Teach Addiction."

75. Mezei and Murinson, "Pain Education in North American Medical Schools." These statistics come from a 2011 study, so they may not reflect the current state of medical education. However, there is no evidence to suggest that these statistics have changed much in the past decade. See for example this international study on medical education about pain: Shipton et al., "Systematic Review of Pain Medicine Content, Teaching, and Assessment in Medical School Curricula Internationally."

76. Residency Roadmap, "General Surgery"; Hoffman, "Most Doctors Are Ill-Equipped to Deal with the Opioid Epidemic"; *Pain Management Fellowships*; Macy et al., "Growth and Changes in the Pediatric Medical Subspecialty Workforce Pipeline."

77. National Institute on Drug Abuse, *Common Comorbidities with Substance Use Disorders Research Report*.

78. Rieder, *In Pain: A Bioethicist's Personal Struggle with Opioids*.

79. Meier, *Pain Killer*.

80. McBain et al., "Growth and Distribution of Buprenorphine-Waivered Providers in the United States, 2007–2017."

81. Bell and Salmon, "Pain, Physical Dependence and Pseudoaddiction: Redefining Addiction for 'Nice' People?"

82. Chiarello, "The War on Drugs Comes to the Pharmacy Counter"; Chiarello, "How Organizational Context Affects Bioethical Decision-Making."

83. Kazerouni et al., "Pharmacy-Related Buprenorphine Access Barriers."

84. Meyerson et al., "I Could Take the Judgment If You Could Just Provide the Service"; Chiarello, "Nonprescription Syringe Sales: Resistant Pharmacists' Attitudes and Practices."

85. Saloner et al., "A Public Health Strategy for the Opioid Crisis."

86. Patzer, "Council Post."

87. Larochelle et al., "Opioid Prescribing after Nonfatal Overdose and Association with Repeated Overdose."

88. Larochelle et al.

89. Legal Action Center, "Emergency: Hospitals Are Violating Federal Law by Denying Required Care for Substance Use Disorders in Emergency Departments."

90. Hampton, *American Fix.*

91. Meier, *Pain Killer.*

92. The organization that accredits hospitals. Previously known as the Joint Commission on Accreditation of Healthcare Organizations.

93. Mularski et al., "Measuring Pain as the 5th Vital Sign Does Not Improve Quality of Pain Management"; Tompkins et al., "Providing Chronic Pain Management in the 'Fifth Vital Sign' Era."

94. Centers for Disease Control and Prevention, "CDC Guideline for Prescribing Opioids for Chronic Pain—United States, 2016."

95. Centers for Disease Control and Prevention, "CDC Guideline for Prescribing Opioids for Chronic Pain—United States, 2016." The MME is a measure that standardizes opioid doses by pegging them to morphine.

96. Nicholson and Hellman, "Opioid Prescribing and the Ethical Duty to Do No Harm."

97. Dineen, "Definitions Matter: A Taxonomy of Inappropriate Prescribing to Shape Effective Opioid Policy and Reduce Patient Harm."

98. Nicholson and Hellman, "Opioid Prescribing and the Ethical Duty to Do No Harm."

99. Drug Enforcement Administration, "Walgreens Agrees to Pay a Record Settlement of $80 Million for Civil Penalties under the Controlled Substances Act."

100. U.S. Attorney's Office (USAO), "U.S. Attorney's Office—U.S. Department of Justice."

101. WBUR, "Backlash against Walgreen's New Painkiller Crackdown."

102. Weiner et al., "A Health System–Wide Initiative to Decrease Opioid-Related Morbidity and Mortality"; Sandbrink and Uppal, "The Time for Opioid Stewardship Is Now"; Shoemaker-Hunt and Wyant, "The Effect of Opioid Stewardship Interventions on Key Outcomes."

103. Darnall et al., "International Stakeholder Community of Pain Experts and Leaders Call for an Urgent Action on Forced Opioid Tapering," March 1, 2019.

104. Tarkan, "Moving Toward an (Almost) Opioid-Free Emergency Department"; Medscape, "The Opioid-Free ED."

105. Holmgren and Apathy, "Evaluation of Prescription Drug Monitoring Program Integration with Hospital Electronic Health Records by US County-Level Opioid Prescribing Rates."

106. Hilton, "Medical Misinformation Consequences in Health Care."

107. Conrad and Schneider, *Deviance and Medicalization*; Gusfield, *Contested Meanings*; Hoppe, *Punishing Disease*.

108. Paik, *Discretionary Justice*; Tiger, *Judging Addicts*.

109. El-Sabawi, "Carrots, Sticks, and Problem Drug Use: Law Enforcement's Contribution to the Policy Discourse on Drug Use and the Opioid Crisis."

110. Brennan and Suchman, "Law and Technology in Healthcare Organizations"; Anthony and Stablein, "Privacy in Practice."

111. Brayne, *Predict and Surveil: Data, Discretion, and the Future of Policing*.

112. American Civil Liberties Union, "ACLU Sues to Protect Privacy of Drug Prescriptions"; American Civil Liberties Union, "ACLU Joins Lawsuit to Defend Confidential Medical Records from Warrantless Federal DEA Searches"; Freed Wessler, "ACLU Challenging DEA's Access to Confidential Prescription Records Without a Warrant"; Oliva, "Prescription Drug Policing," February 1, 2019.

Chapter 3. White Coat Crime

1. *Busting Dr. Tseng's Pill Mill* | *American Greed* | *CNBC Prime*.

2. Gerber et al., "California Doctor Convicted of Murder in Overdose Deaths of Patients."

3. Hayden, "'Drug Dealing' California Doctor Arrested after 14 Patients Die from Overdoses."

4. Gerber et al., "California Doctor Convicted of Murder in Overdose Deaths of Patients."

5. Gerber, "Doctor Convicted of Murder for Patients' Drug Overdoses Gets 30 Years to Life in Prison"; Hayden, "'Drug Dealing' California Doctor Arrested after 14 Patients Die from Overdoses."

6. Gerber, "Doctor Convicted of Murder for Patients' Drug Overdoses Gets 30 Years to Life in Prison."

7. Hedegaard et al., "Drugs Most Frequently Involved in Drug Overdose Deaths: United States, 2011–2016."

8. Prosecutors tried physicians with these kinds of charges in the past, but now they are more successful at winning convictions. See for example Hoffmann, "Treating Pain v. Reducing Drug Diversion and Abuse: Recalibrating the Balance in Our Drug Control Laws and Policies," and Libby, *The Criminalization of Medicine: America's War on Doctors*.

9. Hoffmann, "Treating Pain v. Reducing Drug Diversion and Abuse."

10. Jaslow, "Undercover Cop Goes to Doctor with Dog X-Ray and Is Prescribed Painkillers, Doc Arrested."

11. Jaslow, "Doctor Who Prescribed Drugs Based on Dog X-Ray Suspended."

12. Los Angeles County District Attorney's Office, "Outcome of Physician Opioid Case," February 25, 2022.

13. Allen, "The 'Oxy Express'"; Campo-Flores, "Fight over a Fix for Florida 'Pill Mills.'"

14. This refers to names of discs in the back, lumbar 4 and lumbar 5.

15. A weaker opioid than OxyContin.

16. I later learned that similar categories were reflected in the health law literature. See for example Dineen and Dubois, who refer to these categories as the "4D model"—dated, duped, disabled, and dishonest—and advocate for reframing these physicians as careless, corrupt, and compromised. Dineen and DuBois, "Between a Rock and a Hard Place."

17. By "enforcement landscape," I mean the set of laws, rules, enforcement agencies, and enforcement practices that pertain to healthcare practice.

18. Chapter 13 of Title 21 of the United States Code, 21 U.S.C. § 848.

19. Legitimate doctors will sometimes give patients more than one prescription for the same medication, but they write it for different dates so that the patient can fill each prescription when they are finished with the last without having to make another appointment. Three prescriptions written for the same date indicate that the physician knows that the medication is not being used for legal medical purposes.

20. Guidelines for providing good quality care.

21. Eisinger, *The Chickenshit Club: Why the Justice Department Fails to Prosecute Executives.*

22. The DEA also conducts administrative cases, but the tension I describe here is not present in those cases because the criminal and administrative sides of the DEA work together on task forces (recall Brandon and Abby from chapter 3), so they don't "burn" each other's cases in the same way. Their work is more collaborative than contentious.

23. Legal Information Institute, "Beyond a Reasonable Doubt."

24. Coleman, *The Criminal Elite: Understanding White-Collar Crime.*

25. Siegel, "The Opioid Crisis Is About More Than Corporate Greed"; "Automation of Reports and Consolidated Orders System (ARCOS)."

26. Now called the Diversion Control Division.

27. Associated Press, "Opioid Epidemic Shares Chilling Similarities with Past Drug Crises."

28. Beletsky, "America's Favorite Antidote: Drug-Induced Homicide in the Age of the Overdose Crisis."

29. California Narcotic Officers Association (CNOA), "About CNOA."

30. Boustead, "Privacy Protections and Law Enforcement Use of Prescription Drug Monitoring Databases"; Oliva, "Dosing Discrimination."

31. Missouri's PDMP was very rudimentary at the time of my interview with Ken.

32. California's PDMP.

33. A combination of drugs that fetches a high price on the street, has no known medical purpose, and carries a high risk of death.

34. Eisinger, *The Chickenshit Club: Why the Justice Department Fails to Prosecute Executives.*

35. Dineen and DuBois, "Between a Rock and a Hard Place."

36. Some references such as Aviv's New Yorker article call her Linda Atterbury, but I call her Linda Schneider because that is the name used in the lawsuits against her.

37. Aviv, "Prescription for Disaster | The New Yorker."

38. Szalavitz, "Undoing Drugs: The Untold Story of Harm Reduction and the Future of Addiction."

39. Szalavitz.

40. Paraphrased from Szalavitz, p. 247. This is a common strategy that prosecutors use. See also Barkow, *Prisoners of Politics: Breaking the Cycle of Mass Incarceration.*

41. Aviv, "Prescription for Disaster | The New Yorker."

42. Aviv.

43. "Haysville Doctor and Wife Sentenced in Deadly Prescription Overdoses"; Aviv, "Prescription for Disaster | The New Yorker."

44. Szalavitz, "Undoing Drugs: The Untold Story of Harm Reduction and the Future of Addiction."

45. Aviv, "Prescription for Disaster | The New Yorker."

46. Szalavitz, "Undoing Drugs: The Untold Story of Harm Reduction and the Future of Addiction"; Reason.com, "Dr. Feelscared."

47. Term for physicians who write opioids. Another popular term is "scripter."

48. Aviv, "Prescription for Disaster | The New Yorker."

49. Aviv.

50. A geographic area with limited access to pain care.

51. An opioid.

52. For an insightful look at the complexities of the Schneider case, see Aviv, "Prescription for Disaster."

53. Aviv.

54. JRANK, "Criminal Law—Elements of a Crime"; Foster, "Mens Rea: An Overview of State-of-Mind Requirements for Federal Criminal Offenses."

55. *Ruan v. United States*, 142 S. Ct. 2370, 213 L. Ed. 2d 706 (2022).

56. U.S. Department of Justice, "Dr. Couch and Dr. Ruan Sentenced to 240 and 252 Months in Federal Prison for Running Massive Pill Mill."

57. An *amicus brief* or *amicus curiae* is a document written by someone who is not a party to the case to add insights that bear on the case.

58. Brief of Amici Curiae Professors of Health Law and Policy in Support of Petitioner, Ruan v. U.S., No. 20-1410 (U.S. Apr. 7, 2021), 2021 WL 6138180. In the spirit of transparency, note that I am a co-signer on this brief.

59. Jeter, "Opinion."

60. *Ruan v. United States*, 142 S. Ct. 2370, 213 L. Ed. 2d 706 (2022).

61. Jeter, "Opinion."

62. Libby, *The Criminalization of Medicine: America's War on Doctors*; Hoffmann, "Treating Pain v. Reducing Drug Diversion and Abuse: Recalibrating the Balance in Our Drug Control Laws and Policies."

Chapter 4. Surveilling Patients in the Hospital and the Clinic

1. Scott et al., *Institutional Change and Healthcare Organizations: From Professional Dominance to Managed Care.*

2. Rathore, "Physician 'Gag Laws' and Gun Safety"; Grant et al., "The Growing Criminalization of Pregnancy"; Rodriguez, "Lawmakers Push Legislation to Protect Doctors Who Prescribe Ivermectin for COVID-19. Can They Do That?"; Ballentine and Hanna, "Missouri Lawmakers Ban Gender-Affirming Care, Trans Athletes; Kansas City Moves to Defy State | AP News."

3. Freidson, *Profession of Medicine*; Freidson, *Professional Dominance: The Social Structure of Medical Care*; Larson, *The Rise of Professionalism*; Starr, *The Social Transformation of American Medicine*, 2008.

4. Scott et al., *Institutional Change and Healthcare Organizations: From Professional Dominance to Managed Care.*

5. Weiner, *On Becoming a Healer: The Journey from Patient Care to Caring about Your Patients.*

6. Weiner, *On Becoming a Healer.*

7. Maynard-Moody and Musheno, *Cops, Teachers, Counselors.*

8. Fassin, "Compassion and Repression: The Moral Economy of Immigration Policies in France"; Seim, *Bandage, Sort, and Hustle: Ambulance Crews on the Front Lines of Urban Suffering;* Lara-Millán, "Public Emergency Room Overcrowding in the Era of Mass Imprisonment"; Kimport et al., "The Stratified Legitimacy of Abortions."

9. This is not to say that physicians are all-powerful. Their choices are constrained by their organizational settings, the resources available, the law, insurance, and patients' ability to pay. Still, physicians have outsized resources in the healthcare system.

10. American Medical Association, "AMA Code of Medical Ethics Opinions on Patient-Physician Relationships."

11. Chiarello, "The War on Drugs Comes to the Pharmacy Counter"; Chiarello, "How Organizational Context Affects Bioethical Decision-Making."

12. Of course, this is oversimplified, but these are the general steps.

13. Note that Matt conflates tolerance, dependence, and addiction. Tolerance is when a patient gets used to their dose and needs more to have the same effect; dependence means that a person has become reliant on the drug so that if they were to suddenly stop using it, they would go into withdrawal; addiction is a psychological disorder characterized by continued drug use despite negative consequences.

14. Chiarello, "The War on Drugs Comes to the Pharmacy Counter"; Chiarello, "How Organizational Context Affects Bioethical Decision-Making."

15. U.S. Department of Justice, "Title 21 United States Code (USC) Controlled Substances Act—Section 801-971."

16. Rieder, *In Pain: A Bioethicist's Personal Struggle with Opioids.*

17. Meier, *Pain Killer.*

18. Tai-Seale et al., "Electronic Health Record Logs Indicate That Physicians Split Time Evenly between Seeing Patients and Desktop Medicine."

19. American Medical Association, "2021 Overdose Epidemic Report."

20. Kiang et al., "Opioid Prescribing Patterns among Medical Providers in the United States, 2003–17: Retrospective, Observational Study."

21. Rieder, "There's Never Just One Side to the Story."

22. Also known as an "opioid agreement," a "pain treatment agreement," or an "opioid patient provider agreement."

23. National Institute on Drug Abuse, "Sample Patient Agreement Forms."

24. Darnall and Fields, "Clinical and Neuroscience Evidence Supports the Critical Importance of Patient Expectations and Agency in Opioid Tapering"; Fenton et al., "Long-Term Risk of Overdose or Mental Health Crisis after Opioid Dose Tapering."

25. Rieder, *In Pain: A Bioethicist's Personal Struggle with Opioids,* 87–88.

26. Note that at the time I did these interviews, an X-waiver was required to prescribe buprenorphine. The waiver is no longer required as of December 2022.

27. Centers for Disease Control and Prevention, "CDC Guidelines for Prescribing Opioids for Chronic Pain."

28. Centers for Disease Control and Prevention, "CDC Guideline for Prescribing Opioids for Chronic Pain—United States, 2016."

29. AAPC. "What Are Relative Value Units (RVUs)?"

30. Nelson et al., "Opioid Deprescribing in Emergency Medicine—A Tool in an Expanding Toolkit."

31. National Institute on Drug Abuse, "Sample Patient Agreement Forms."

32. American Board of Medical Specialties, "ABMS Officially Recognizes Addiction Medicine as a Subspecialty."

33. MedPage Today Staff, "ACGME a 'Game-Changer' for Addiction Medicine."

34. Goffman, *Stigma: Notes on the Management of Spoiled Identity*.

35. Hampton, *American Fix*.

36. Rieder, *In Pain: A Bioethicist's Personal Struggle with Opioids*.

37. SAMHSA, "Become a Buprenorphine Waivered Practitioner." These rules changed during the COVID-19 pandemic, so now physicians can treat up to 30 patients with buprenorphine without certification or additional training.

38. Wakeman et al., "Comparative Effectiveness of Different Treatment Pathways for Opioid Use Disorder," February 5, 2020.

39. Huhn and Dunn, "Why Aren't Physicians Prescribing More Buprenorphine?"; Berk, "To Help Providers Fight the Opioid Epidemic, 'X the X Waiver' | Health Affairs Forefront."

40. Wakeman et al., "Comparative Effectiveness of Different Treatment Pathways for Opioid Use Disorder," February 5, 2020.

41. A vast body of research on inequality in medicine suggests that physicians' behavior is likely to vary by patient's race or ethnicity, gender, and class, with patients in minoritized groups receiving worse care than those in dominant groups. However, because I did not systematically gather information about patients in this project, an analysis of these forms of inequality is beyond the scope of this book.

Chapter 5. Surveilling Patients at the Pharmacy Counter

1. This is a pseudonym.

2. Xanax is not an opioid, but a benzodiazepine. However, like opioids, it is often used nonmedically, and it is especially dangerous when used in combination with an opioid.

3. National Institute on Drug Abuse, "Overdose Death Rates," January 29, 2021.

4. Executive Office of the President of the United States, "Epidemic."

5. PDMP TTAC, "History of Prescription Drug Monitoring Programs."

6. U.S. Drug Enforcement Administration, "Walgreens Agrees to Pay a Record Settlement of $80 Million for Civil Penalties under the Controlled Substances Act."

7. Gebhart, "Pharmacists Want More Time with Patients."

8. *Jerry Seinfeld—Pharmacists*.

9. Chiarello, "The War on Drugs Comes to the Pharmacy Counter"; Lipsky, *Street-Level Bureaucracy*.

10. Patient Safety Network, "The Pharmacist's Role in Medication Safety."

11. Abood and Burns, *Pharmacy Practice and the Law*; U.S. Department of Justice, "Title 21 United States Code (USC) Controlled Substances Act—Section 801-971."

12. Chiarello, "The War on Drugs Comes to the Pharmacy Counter"; Chiarello, "How Organizational Context Affects Bioethical Decision-Making."

13. Although it may affect their bonuses.

14. Chiarello, "Medical versus Fiscal Gatekeeping: Navigating Professional Contingencies at the Pharmacy Counter."

15. Scheiber, "How Pharmacy Work Stopped Being So Great—The New York Times."

16. NBC News, "Pharmacists Say They're Overworked and Understaffed, Risking Patient Safety."

17. STAT, "Why Drug Prescriptions Should Include Diagnoses."

18. Chiarello, "The War on Drugs Comes to the Pharmacy Counter."

19. Glenn, "The Birth of the Crack Baby and the History That 'Myths' Make"; Roberts, *Killing the Black Body: Race, Reproduction, and the Meaning of Liberty*; Trawalter, "Black Americans Are Systematically Under-Treated for Pain. Why?"; Lara-Millán, "Public Emergency Room Overcrowding in the Era of Mass Imprisonment."

20. Lyon, *Surveillance as Social Sorting*.

21. Chiarello, "The War on Drugs Comes to the Pharmacy Counter."

22. This is a paraphrase, not an exact quote. Certain colors and shapes of drugs have higher street value, as do brand name versus generic drugs.

23. This is a paraphrase.

24. This quotation was originally used in Chiarello, "How Organizational Context Affects Bioethical Decision-Making."

25. A full analysis of racial disparities in pharmacy care is not possible because most of the pharmacists I interviewed did not indicate the race of their patients. However, a growing body of research on race and PDMPs demonstrates that PDMP use is exacerbating racial disparities in opioid treatment. Laws that mandate PDMP use are associated with fewer opioids prescribed to Black patients, but not white patients and with a larger reduction of prescriptions given to sickle cell patients (who are disproportionately Black) compared to bone cancer patients. See Townsend et al., "Did Prescribing Laws Disproportionately Affect Opioid Dispensing to Black Patients"; Kilaru et al., "Prescription Drug Monitoring Program Mandates and Opioids for Acute Pain." Another study found that veterans were more likely to be queried in the database if they were Hispanic. See Andrea et al., "Factors Related to Prescription Drug Monitoring Program Queries for Veterans Receiving Long-Term Opioid Therapy." Though these studies do not specifically focus on pharmacists, they do indicate that racial discrimination could play a major role in which patients are monitored in healthcare.

26. Starr, *The Social Transformation of American Medicine*.

27. Cramer, *Birthing a Movement: Midwives, Law, and the Politics of Reproductive Care*; Starr, *The Social Transformation of American Medicine*.

28. Segall, "Walgreens Secret Checklist Reveals Controversial New Policy on Pain Pills | Journal of Medicine | NAMD."

29. Buckley and Buckley, "Pharmacists Feeling Pain over AMA Resolution."

30. National Institute on Drug Abuse, "Benzodiazepines and Opioids."

31. This quotation was originally used in Chiarello, "Medical versus Fiscal Gatekeeping: Navigating Professional Contingencies at the Pharmacy Counter."

32. Lembke, *Drug Dealer, MD*.

33. Chiarello, "The War on Drugs Comes to the Pharmacy Counter."

34. Elsewhere, I have indicated that PDMP use is fast and efficient. This is true when compared to other strategies like calling the physician, calling other pharmacies, and running prescriptions through insurance. However, it is not so efficient that pharmacists can easily check the database for every patient. Pharmacy is such a fast-paced business that pharmacists still must be careful about how they use their time.

Chapter 6. Arresting Care

1. Binswanger et al., "The Association between Opioid Discontinuation and Heroin Use: A Nested Case-Control Study"; Darnall et al., "International Stakeholder Community of Pain Experts and Leaders Call for an Urgent Action on Forced Opioid Tapering"; Lin et al., "Changing Trends in Opioid Overdose Deaths and Prescription Opioid Receipt among Veterans."

2. PBS.org, "NOVA | Doctors' Diaries | The Hippocratic Oath: Modern Version"; Kao and Parsi, "Content Analyses of Oaths Administered at U.S. Medical Schools in 2000"; Parsa-Parsi, "The Revised Declaration of Geneva."

3. Duke University School of Medicine, "White Coat Ceremony."

4. Arnold P. Gold Foundation, "White Coat Ceremony: Background and Significance."

5. American Association of Colleges of Nursing, "White Coat Ceremony Recipients"; Briceland et al., "The Impact of Pharmacy Student Participation in the White Coat Ceremony on Professionalization."

6. American Association of Colleges of Pharmacy, "Oath of a Pharmacist."

7. Beauchamp and Childress, *Principles of Biomedical Ethics.*

8. Abood and Burns, *Pharmacy Practice and the Law.*

9. American Medical Association, "AMA Code of Medical Ethics Opinions on Patient-Physician Relationships"; Haddad, "Reflections on the Pharmacist-Patient Covenant."

10. American Medical Association, "AMA Code of Medical Ethics Opinions on Patient-Physician Relationships."

11. Fishbain et al., "Alleged Medical Abandonment in Chronic Opioid Analgesic Therapy"; Jung and McDowell, "Abandonment."

12. Hereafter, "the CDC guidelines." The guidelines were revised in 2022, as I explain later, but the 2016 guidelines played a major role in changing professional behavior.

13. Kertesz et al., "Opioid Prescription Control"; National Conference of State Legislatures, "Prescribing Policies: States Confront Opioid Overdose Epidemic"; Zezima, "With Drug Overdoses Soaring, States Limit the Length of Painkiller Prescriptions."

14. Anson, "CVS to Limit Opioid Prescriptions."

15. Kertesz et al., "Opioid Prescription Control."

16. Office of Public and Intergovernmental Affairs, "VA Reduces Prescription Opioid Use by 64% during Past Eight Years."

17. Frank et al., "Patient Outcomes in Dose Reduction or Discontinuation of Long-Term Opioid Therapy."

18. Agnoli et al., "Association of Dose Tapering with Overdose or Mental Health Crisis among Patients Prescribed Long-Term Opioids"; Larochelle et al., "Comparative Effectiveness of Opioid Tapering or Abrupt Discontinuation vs No Dosage Change for Opioid Overdose or Suicide for Patients Receiving Stable Long-Term Opioid Therapy."

19. Frank et al., "Patient Outcomes in Dose Reduction or Discontinuation of Long-Term Opioid Therapy"; Kertesz et al., "Nonconsensual Dose Reduction Mandates Are Not Justified Clinically or Ethically."

20. Coluzzi et al., "The Effect of Opiates on Bone Formation and Bone Healing"; Bateman et al., "Understanding and Countering Opioid-Induced Respiratory Depression"; Walker et al., "Chronic Opioid Use Is a Risk Factor for the Development of Central Sleep Apnea and Ataxic Breathing"; Kotlińska-Lemieszek and Żylicz, "Less Well-Known Consequences of the Long-Term Use of Opioid Analgesics."

21. Darnall et al., "International Stakeholder Community of Pain Experts and Leaders Call for an Urgent Action on Forced Opioid Tapering," March 1, 2019.

22. Lagisetty et al., "Access to Primary Care Clinics for Patients with Chronic Pain Receiving Opioids"; Larochelle et al., "Opioid Tapering Practices—Time for Reconsideration?"

23. Berger, "Moral Distress in Medical Education and Training"; Čartolovni et al., "Moral Injury in Healthcare Professionals"; Jameton, "Nursing Practice: The Ethical Issues"; Lamiani et al., "When Healthcare Professionals Cannot Do the Right Thing."

24. Sporrong et al., "Measuring Moral Distress in Pharmacy and Clinical Practice."

25. The term "mythic elsewhere" is occasionally used in culture and film studies to describe a "never, never land" that transcends personal limitations or a place where unwanted groups can be exiled. Lyndgaard, "Landscapes of Removal and Resistance: Edwin James's Nineteenth-Century Cross-Cultural Collaborations"; Thomson, "The Work of Art in the Age of Electronic (Re)Production." Here, I am using it to describe an imagined healthcare system where unwanted patients can get the care they need.

26. Benzodiazepines are not opioids. They are depressants that are usually used to treat anxiety. Examples include Valium, Xanax, and Klonopin.

27. Larochelle et al., "Comparative Effectiveness of Opioid Tapering or Abrupt Discontinuation vs No Dosage Change for Opioid Overdose or Suicide for Patients Receiving Stable Long-Term Opioid Therapy."

28. It is true that the 2016 CDC guidelines state that people above 90 MME are at higher risk of overdose, but later research shows that tapering patients actually presents a greater overdose risk than keeping patients on a high dose. See Kertesz et al., "Nonconsensual Dose Reduction Mandates Are Not Justified Clinically or Ethically"; Larochelle et al., "Comparative Effectiveness of Opioid Tapering or Abrupt Discontinuation vs No Dosage Change for Opioid Overdose or Suicide for Patients Receiving Stable Long-Term Opioid Therapy."

29. Travis Rieder, e-mail with the author, March 8, 2023.

30. Darnall et al., "Patient-Centered Prescription Opioid Tapering in Community Outpatients with Chronic Pain"; Dowell et al., "Patient-Centered Reduction or Discontinuation of Long-Term Opioid Analgesics: The HHS Guide for Clinicians."

31. Darnall et al., "Patient-Centered Prescription Opioid Tapering in Community Outpatients with Chronic Pain"; Dowell et al., "Patient-Centered Reduction or Discontinuation of Long-Term Opioid Analgesics: The HHS Guide for Clinicians"; Wakeman et al., "Comparative Effectiveness of Different Treatment Pathways for Opioid Use Disorder," February 5, 2020.

32. American Psychiatric Association, Diagnostic and Statistical Manual of Mental Disorders, 5th Edition.

33. Brayne, "Surveillance and System Avoidance."

34. Alexander, *The New Jim Crow: Mass Incarceration in the Age of Colorblindness*; Beckett and Brydolf-Horwitz, "A Kinder, Gentler Drug War?"; Pager, *Marked: Race, Crime, and Finding Work in an Era of Mass Incarceration*; Provine, "Race and Inequality in the War on Drugs."

35. Bebinger, "They Call It 'Tranq'—And It's Making Street Drugs Even More Dangerous"; Joseph, "In Philadelphia, 'Tranq' Is Leaving Drug Users with Horrific Wounds. Other Communities Are Bracing for the Same."

36. Cicero et al., "Effect of Abuse-Deterrent Formulation of OxyContin."

37. Cicero et al.; Mars et al., "Every 'Never' I Ever Said Came True."

38. Cicero et al., "Effect of Abuse-Deterrent Formulation of OxyContin," 189.

39. Ciccarone, "The Triple Wave Epidemic"; Manchikanti et al., "Fourth Wave of Opioid (Illicit Drug) Overdose Deaths and Diminishing Access to Prescription Opioids and Interventional Techniques: Cause and Effect."

40. National Institute on Drug Abuse, "Overdose Death Rates," January 29, 2021.

41. Coffin et al., "Illicit Opioid Use Following Changes in Opioids Prescribed for Chronic Non-Cancer Pain."

42. Dineen and DuBois, "Between a Rock and a Hard Place"; Hoffman, "Were These Doctors Treating Pain or Dealing Drugs?"

43. Dahlhamer, "Prevalence of Chronic Pain and High-Impact Chronic Pain among Adults—United States, 2016."

44. Goldstone, "The Pain Refugees: The Forgotten Victims of America's Opioid Crisis"; Rubin, "Limits on Opioid Prescribing Leave Patients with Chronic Pain Vulnerable."

45. Szalavitz, "Opinion | What the Opioid Crisis Took from People in Pain."

46. Methadone is used to treat pain, not only opioid use disorder.

47. Anson, "Chronic Pain Patient Abandoned by Doctor Dies"; Kertesz and Satel, "Some People Still Need Opioids"; McKend, "Chronic Pain Patients Push Back against New Opioid Rules."

48. Kline, "Suicides Associated with Forced Tapering of Opiate Pain Treatments."

49. Llorente, "As Doctors Taper or End Opioid Prescriptions, Many Patients Driven to Despair, Suicide | Fox News."

50. Kertesz and Gordon, "A Crisis of Opioids and the Limits of Prescription Control."

51. Lin et al., "Changing Trends in Opioid Overdose Deaths and Prescription Opioid Receipt among Veterans."

52. *Dr. Stefan Kertesz | Perspective on Opioids | #PainAB2020.*

53. Kertesz et al., "Nonconsensual Dose Reduction Mandates Are Not Justified Clinically or Ethically"; Kertesz et al., "Opioid Prescription Control"; Kertesz and Satel, "Some People Still Need Opioids."

54. National Pain Advocacy Center, "National Pain Advocacy Center."

55. Nicholson, "The Clampdown on Opioid Prescriptions Is Hurting Pain Patients—Los Angeles Times."

56. Centers for Disease Control and Prevention, "What's New, What's Changed"; Dowell, "CDC Clinical Practice Guideline for Prescribing Opioids for Pain"; Dowell et al., "No Shortcuts to Safer Opioid Prescribing."

57. Dowell et al., "No Shortcuts to Safer Opioid Prescribing."

58. Centers for Disease Control and Prevention, "What's New, What's Changed."

59. Vestal, "States Likely to Resist CDC Proposal Easing Opioid Access."

60. Human Rights Watch, "Not Allowed to Be Compassionate."

61. Vestal, "States Likely to Resist CDC Proposal Easing Opioid Access."

62. FQHC Associates, "What Is a Federally Qualified Health Center (FQHC)?"

63. FQHC Associates.

64. X-waivers were required for physicians to prescribe buprenorphine until Congress eliminated the requirement on December 29, 2022.

65. A brand-name drug that combines buprenorphine and naloxone.

66. Rieder, "In Opioid Withdrawal, with No Help in Sight."

67. Hansen and Roberts, "Two Tiers of Biomedicalization: Buprenorphine, Methadone, and the Biopolitics of Addiction Stigma and Race"; Hansen and Skinner, "From White Bullets to Black Markets and Greened Medicine."

68. Magidson et al., "Peer Recovery Coaches in General Medical Settings."

69. SAMHSA, "Peers Supporting Recovery from Substance Use Disorders"; Magidson et al., "Peer Recovery Coaches in General Medical Settings"; Eddie et al., "Lived Experience in New Models of Care for Substance Use Disorder"; Orme et al., "Cost and Cost Savings of Navigation Services to Avoid Rehospitalization for a Comorbid Substance Use Disorder Population."

70. Kupchik, *Homeroom Security: School Discipline in an Age of Fear*; Nolan, "Policing Student Behavior."

71. Fong, "Getting Eyes in the Home: Child Protective Services Investigations and State Surveillance of Family Life"; Fong, *Investigating Families: Motherhood in the Shadow of Child Protective Services.*

72. Hoppe, *Punishing Disease.*

Chapter 7. Rethinking Policy and Practice: Fixing the Healthcare Toolkit

1. I heard Kevin's story at a law enforcement conference I attended in 2019. Most of this story comes from my fieldnotes on the talk he gave there. However, I filled in a few missing details using this article in *The Atlantic*, https://www.theatlantic.com/politics/archive/2018/11/narcotics-cop-loses-his-daughter-heroin-overdose/575425/,and the website for Brooke's House, https://brookeshouse.org/.

2. Brooke's House. "Home." Accessed January 20, 2023. https://brookeshouse.org/.

3. Centers for Disease Control and Prevention, "Vital Statistics Rapid Release—Provisional Drug Overdose Data."

4. Note that the term "diversion" is being used differently here than it is in other places in this book. That is because law enforcement uses the term "diversion" to refer to the movement of legal drugs to illegal markets and also uses the term "diversion" to refer to "diversionary programs" like drug courts that "divert" people who would otherwise have received jail time into treatment instead.

5. Wen and Warren, "Combatting the Opioid Epidemic"; High et al., "State Targeted Response to the Opioid Crisis Grants (Opioid STR) Program: Preliminary Findings from Two Case Studies and the National Cross-Site Evaluation."

6. Hampton, *American Fix.*

7. Drug Policy Alliance, "Opioid Agonist Treatment (OAT)."

8. Wakeman et al., "Comparative Effectiveness of Different Treatment Pathways for Opioid Use Disorder," February 5, 2020.

9. D'Onofrio et al., "Emergency Department–Initiated Buprenorphine/Naloxone Treatment for Opioid Dependence."

10. Pierce et al., "Impact of Treatment for Opioid Dependence on Fatal Drug-Related Poisoning."

11. Pew Charitable Trusts, "Overview of Opioid Treatment Program Regulations by State."

12. Frank et al., "It's Like 'Liquid Handcuffs'"; *Liquid Handcuffs: A Documentary to Free Methadone.*

13. SAMHSA, "Buprenorphine."

14. SAMHSA, "Understanding the Final Rule for a Patient Limit of 275."

15. McBain et al., "Growth and Distribution of Buprenorphine-Waivered Providers in the United States, 2007–2017"; Huhn and Dunn, "Why Aren't Physicians Prescribing More Buprenorphine?"; U.S. Department of Health and Human Services and Office of Inspector General, "Geographic Disparities Affect Access to Buprenorphine Services for Opioid Use Disorder." In 2022, Congress removed the X-waiver, which made it legal for all physicians with a DEA registration to prescribe buprenorphine to treat opioid use disorder: https://www.samhsa.gov/medication-assisted-treatment/removal-data-waiver-requirement.

16. Ali et al., "Public Listing Status of Data-Waivered Providers."

17. Letson, "American Rehab."

18. Hampton, *American Fix*, 91.

19. Macy, *Dopesick*; Keefe, *Empire of Pain: The Secret History of the Sackler Dynasty*; Meier, *Pain Killer: An Empire of Deceit and the Origin of America's Opioid Epidemic*; Lembke, *Drug Dealer, MD.*

20. Centers for Disease Control and Prevention, "Vital Statistics Rapid Release—Provisional Drug Overdose Data."

21. Cerdá et al., "Measuring Relationships between Proactive Reporting State-Level Prescription Drug Monitoring Programs and County-Level Fatal Prescription Opioid Overdoses"; Gugelmann et al., "Windmills and Pill Mills"; Martins et al., "Prescription Drug Monitoring Programs Operational Characteristics and Fatal Heroin Poisoning"; Davis et al., "Overdose Epidemic, Prescription Monitoring Programs, and Public Health"; Davis et al., "Opioid Prescribing Laws Are Not Associated with Short-Term Declines in Prescription Opioid Distribution."

22. Ciccarone, "The Triple Wave Epidemic."

23. National Institute on Drug Abuse, "Overdose Death Rates," January 29, 2021.

24. Manchikanti et al., "Fourth Wave of Opioid (Illicit Drug) Overdose Deaths and Diminishing Access to Prescription Opioids and Interventional Techniques: Cause and Effect."

25. Meier, *Pain Killer: An Empire of Deceit and the Origin of America's Opioid Epidemic*; Keefe, *Empire of Pain: The Secret History of the Sackler Dynasty*; Macy, *Dopesick.*

26. Webster, "Pain and Suicide"; Department of Health and Human Services, Office of Infectious Disease and HIV/AIDS, "Viral Hepatitis in the United States"; Reardon, "The U.S. Opioid Epidemic Is Driving a Spike in Infectious Diseases"; Ciccarone, "The Triple Wave Epidemic."

27. Szalavitz, "Undoing Drugs: The Untold Story of Harm Reduction and the Future of Addiction"; Case and Deaton, *Deaths of Despair and the Future of Capitalism.*

28. Smirnova, *The Prescription-to-Prison Pipeline: An Intersectional Analysis of the Medicalization and Criminalization of Pain*.

29. Simon, *Governing through Crime: How the War on Crime Transformed American Democracy and Created a Culture of Fear*; Gustafson, *Cheating Welfare: Public Assistance and the Criminalization of Poverty*; Hoppe, *Punishing Disease*.

30. Case and Deaton, *Deaths of Despair and the Future of Capitalism*.

31. SAMHSA, "Removal of DATA Waiver (X-Waiver) Requirement."

32. Law, "Many Pharmacies Don't Carry Life-Saving Addiction Drug"; Hill et al., "Availability of Buprenorphine/Naloxone Films and Naloxone Nasal Spray in Community Pharmacies in Texas, USA."

33. Chiarello, "Nonprescription Syringe Sales: Resistant Pharmacists' Attitudes and Practices."

34. Chiarello.

35. Hill et al., "Availability of Buprenorphine/Naloxone Films and Naloxone Nasal Spray in Community Pharmacies in 11 U.S. States"; Graves et al., "Naloxone Availability and Pharmacy Staff Knowledge of Standing Order for Naloxone in Pennsylvania Pharmacies"; Guadamuz et al., "Availability and Cost of Naloxone Nasal Spray at Pharmacies in Philadelphia, Pennsylvania, 2017."

36. Waddell et al., "Reducing Overdose after Release from Incarceration (ROAR)"; Walley et al., "Association between Mortality Rates and Medication and Residential Treatment after In-patient Medically Managed Opioid Withdrawal"; Peterson et al., "US Hospital Discharges Documenting Patient Opioid Use Disorder without Opioid Overdose or Treatment Services, 2011–2015."

37. Christian et al., "Hospital Buprenorphine Program for Opioid Use Disorder Is Associated with Increased Inpatient and Outpatient Addiction Treatment"; Bottner et al., "The Development and Implementation of a 'B-Team' (Buprenorphine Team) to Treat Hospitalized Patients with Opioid Use Disorder."

38. Lin et al., "Impact of COVID-19 Telehealth Policy Changes on Buprenorphine Treatment for Opioid Use Disorder"; Hailu et al., "Telemedicine Use and Quality of Opioid Use Disorder Treatment in the US during the COVID-19 Pandemic"; Harris et al., "Utilizing Telemedicine during COVID-19 Pandemic for a Low-Threshold, Street-Based Buprenorphine Program"; Wang et al., "Telemedicine Increases Access to Buprenorphine Initiation during the COVID-19 Pandemic."

39. Wyse et al., "Medications for Opioid Use Disorder in the Department of Veterans Affairs (VA) Health Care System."

40. Brico, "Witnessed Urine Screens in Drug Treatment."

41. Meyerson et al., "Nothing Really Changed"; O'Byrne and Jeske Pearson, "Methadone Maintenance Treatment as Social Control"; Woo et al., "Don't Judge a Book by Its Cover"; Joudrey et al., "Methadone for Opioid Use Disorder—Decades of Effectiveness but Still Miles Away in the US."

42. *Liquid Handcuffs: A Documentary to Free Methadone*; Redmond, "There Has to Be a Better Way to Free Methadone."

43. Joudrey et al., "Methadone for Opioid Use Disorder—Decades of Effectiveness but Still Miles Away in the US."

44. Facher, "Top U.S. Addiction Researcher Calls for Broad Deregulation of Methadone."

45. National Association of Boards of Pharmacy, "Presidential Initiative | Medication-Assisted Treatment."

46. Joudrey et al., "Methadone Access for Opioid Use Disorder during the COVID-19 Pandemic within the United States and Canada"; Jeantaud et al., "Substitution Treatment for Opiate Dependence"; Soares et al., "A Survey to Assess the Availability, Implementation Rate, and Remuneration of Pharmacist-Led Cognitive Services throughout Europe"; Luger et al., "Involvement of Community Pharmacists in the Care of Drug Misusers"; Lea et al., "Consumer Satisfaction with Opioid Treatment Services at Community Pharmacies in Australia"; Uosukainen et al., "First Insights into Community Pharmacy Based Buprenorphine-Naloxone Dispensing in Finland"; Sheridan et al., "Community Pharmacies and the Provision of Opioid Substitution Services for Drug Misusers"; Chaar et al., "Factors Influencing Pharmacy Services in Opioid Substitution Treatment."

47. Scott and Davis, *Organizations and Organizing: Rational, Natural and Open Systems Perspectives.*

48. Markey, S.3629—117th Congress (2021–2022): Opioid Treatment Access Act of 2022.

49. Knopf, "AATOD Fact-Checks Methadone/Buprenorphine Bills."

50. National Academies of Sciences, Engineering, and Medicine, *Medications for Opioid Use Disorder Save Lives.*

51. Reisinger et al., "Premature Discharge from Methadone Treatment."

52. Redmond, "Methadone Clinics Step Up Their Backlash against Reform."

53. H.R. 1359—118th Congress (2023–2024): Modernizing Opioid Treatment Access Act.

54. Roberts, *Fatal Invention: How Science, Politics, and Big Business Re-Create Race in the Twenty-First Century*; Washington, *Medical Apartheid: The Dark History of Medical Experimentation on Black Americans from Colonial Times to the Present*; Matthew, *Just Medicine: A Cure for Racial Inequality in American Health Care.*

55. Landau, "CVS Stores to Stop Selling Tobacco | CNN."

56. CVS Health, "Tobacco-Free for Five Years."

57. Wu et al., "Buprenorphine Physician–Pharmacist Collaboration in the Management of Patients with Opioid Use Disorder."

58. Green et al., "Physician-Delegated Unobserved Induction with Buprenorphine in Pharmacies."

59. Szalavitz, "Undoing Drugs: The Untold Story of Harm Reduction and the Future of Addiction."

60. Szalavitz, "Drug Addiction Should Be Treated Like a Learning Disorder—Not a Crime."

61. Ouellette, "First, Do No Harm."

62. Drug Policy Alliance, "Harm Reduction."

63. Urban Survivors Union, "Home | Urban Survivors Union"; Drug Policy Alliance, "Drug Policy Alliance"; National Harm Reduction Coalition, "National Harm Reduction Coalition."

64. Szalavitz, "Undoing Drugs: The Untold Story of Harm Reduction and the Future of Addiction"; Drug Policy Alliance, "Harm Reduction." For a comprehensive history of harm reduction, see Maia Szalavitz's book *Undoing Drugs.*

65. Frank et al., "Patient Outcomes in Dose Reduction or Discontinuation of Long-Term Opioid Therapy"; Agnoli et al., "Association of Dose Tapering with Overdose or Mental Health

Crisis among Patients Prescribed Long-Term Opioids"; Darnall et al., "International Stakeholder Community of Pain Experts and Leaders Call for an Urgent Action on Forced Opioid Tapering," March 1, 2019.

66. White House, "Remarks of President Joe Biden—State of the Union Address as Prepared for Delivery"; Hoffman and Rios, "Fentanyl Test Strips Highlight Rift in Nation's Struggle to Combat Drug Deaths."

67. Gibson et al., "OnPoint NYC: A Baseline Report."

68. Lewis, "Supervised Injection Sites in NYC Have Saved Lives. But Officials Won't Provide Funds."

69. Collins and Vakharia, "Criminal Justice Reform in the Fentanyl Era."

70. Beletsky, "America's Favorite Antidote."

71. Godvin, "My Friend and I Both Took Heroin. He Overdosed. Why Was I Charged with His Death?"

72. Collins and Vakharia, "Criminal Justice Reform in the Fentanyl Era."

73. Collins and Vakharia, 5.

74. Hodge and Flingai, "What Happened When Boston Stopped Prosecuting Nonviolent Crimes"; Johns Hopkins Bloomberg School of Public Health, "Baltimore's No-Prosecution Policy for Low-Level Drug Possession and Prostitution Finds Almost No Rearrests for Serious Offenses."

75. Collins and Vakharia, "Criminal Justice Reform in the Fentanyl Era."

76. Belle-Isle, "'Nothing about Us, without Us': The Inclusion of People with Lived Experience in Harm Reduction Decisions—Matters of Substance."

77. Ciccarone, "The Triple Wave Epidemic."

78. Szalavitz, "Opinion | The Most Important Question about Addiction."

79. Cowan, "How the Narcs Created Crack"; Beletsky and Davis, "Today's Fentanyl Crisis."

80. Filter, "Infographic: The 'Iron Law of Prohibition.'"

81. Ciccarone, "The Triple Wave Epidemic."

82. Szalavitz, "Undoing Drugs: The Untold Story of Harm Reduction and the Future of Addiction"; Smirnova, *The Prescription-to-Prison Pipeline: An Intersectional Analysis of the Medicalization and Criminalization of Pain*; Ciccarone, "The Triple Wave Epidemic"; Sue, *Getting Wrecked: Women, Incarceration, and the American Opioid Crisis*; Case and Deaton, *Deaths of Despair and the Future of Capitalism*.

83. Hart, *Drug Use for Grown-Ups: Chasing Liberty in the Land of Fear*; Walker, *High: Drugs, Desire, and a Nation of Users*; Smirnova, *The Prescription-to-Prison Pipeline: An Intersectional Analysis of the Medicalization and Criminalization of Pain*; Szalavitz, "Undoing Drugs: The Untold Story of Harm Reduction and the Future of Addiction"; Case and Deaton, *Deaths of Despair and the Future of Capitalism*.

84. SAMHSA, "Key Substance Use and Mental Health Indicators in the United States: Results from the 2021 National Survey on Drug Use and Health."

85. Kroenke et al., "Challenges with Implementing the Centers for Disease Control and Prevention Opioid Guideline."

86. Szalavitz, "Opinion | What the Opioid Crisis Took from People in Pain."

87. SAMHSA, "Key Substance Use and Mental Health Indicators in the United States: Results from the 2021 National Survey on Drug Use and Health."

88. Felitti et al., "Relationship of Childhood Abuse and Household Dysfunction to Many of the Leading Causes of Death in Adults: The Adverse Childhood Experiences (ACE) Study."

89. Case and Deaton, *Deaths of Despair and the Future of Capitalism*; Alexander, *The New Jim Crow: Mass Incarceration in the Age of Colorblindness*; Smirnova, *The Prescription-to-Prison Pipeline: An Intersectional Analysis of the Medicalization and Criminalization of Pain*; Berwick, "The Moral Determinants of Health."

90. Hoff, "8 Charts That Show How Major US Cities Spend Taxpayer Dollars on Police versus Social Programs"; Buchholz, "How Much Do U.S. Cities Spend on Policing?"

91. Glauser, "Why Some Doctors Want to Defund the Police"; El-Sabawi and Carroll, "A Model for Defunding: An Evidence-Based Statute for Behavioral Health Crisis Response."

92. Centers for Disease Control and Prevention, "Vital Statistics Rapid Release—Provisional Drug Overdose Data"; National Institute on Drug Abuse, "Overdose Death Rates," January 29, 2021.

93. Ciccarone, "The Triple Wave Epidemic."

94. "Executive Summary—National Opioids Settlement"; Mann and Bebinger, "Purdue Pharma, Sacklers Reach $6 Billion Deal with State Attorneys General."

95. Provine, "Race and Inequality in the War on Drugs"; Alexander, *The New Jim Crow: Mass Incarceration in the Age of Colorblindness*; Courtwright, *A Century of American Narcotic Policy*.

96. Brayne, *Predict and Surveil: Data, Discretion, and the Future of Policing*.

97. Case and Deaton, *Deaths of Despair and the Future of Capitalism*.

98. Heimer, "Competing Institutions."

99. Conrad, *The Medicalization of Society: On the Transformation of Human Conditions into Treatable Disorders*; Conrad and Schneider, *Deviance and Medicalization: From Badness to Sickness*; Heimer, "Competing Institutions"; Abbott, *The System of Professions*.

100. Scott and Davis, *Organizations and Organizing: Rational, Natural and Open Systems Perspectives*.

101. El-Sabawi, "Carrots, Sticks, and Problem Drug Use: Law Enforcement's Contribution to the Policy Discourse on Drug Use and the Opioid Crisis."

102. Hoppe, *Punishing Disease*, 12.

103. Brayne, "Surveillance and System Avoidance"; Lara-Millán, *Redistributing the Poor: Jails, Hospitals, and the Crisis of Law and Fiscal Austerity*; Seim, *Bandage, Sort, and Hustle: Ambulance Crews on the Front Lines of Urban Suffering*; Hoppe, *Punishing Disease*; Fong, "Getting Eyes in the Home: Child Protective Services Investigations and State Surveillance of Family Life"; Morse, "Legal Mobilization in Medicine"; Rowen, "Worthy of Justice: A Veterans Treatment Court in Practice"; Tiger, *Judging Addicts*; McKim, *Addicted to Rehab: Race, Gender, and Drugs in the Era of Mass Incarceration*; Howard, "The Pregnancy Police: Surveillance, Regulation, and Control"; Chiarello, "The War on Drugs Comes to the Pharmacy Counter"; Michelle Smirnova, *The Prescription-to-Prison Pipeline: An Intersectional Analysis of the Medicalization and Criminalization of Pain*; Timmermans and Gabe, "Introduction."

104. Tiger, *Judging Addicts*; Tiger, "Drug Courts and the Logic of Coerced Treatment"; McKim, "'Getting Gut-Level' Punishment, Gender, and Therapeutic Governance"; Castellano, "The Politics of Benchcraft: The Role of Judges in Mental Health Courts."

105. Lara-Millán, "Public Emergency Room Overcrowding in the Era of Mass Imprisonment," 2014.

106. Smirnova, *The Prescription-to-Prison Pipeline: An Intersectional Analysis of the Medicalization and Criminalization of Pain*.

107. Seim, *Bandage, Sort, and Hustle: Ambulance Crews on the Front Lines of Urban Suffering*; Seim, "The Ambulance: Toward a Labor Theory of Poverty Governance."

108. Hoppe, *Punishing Disease*.

109. Fong, "Getting Eyes in the Home: Child Protective Services Investigations and State Surveillance of Family Life"; Seim, "The Ambulance: Toward a Labor Theory of Poverty Governance"; Gustafson, *Cheating Welfare: Public Assistance and the Criminalization of Poverty*.

110. Kupchik, *Homeroom Security: School Discipline in an Age of Fear*; Lara-Millán, "Public Emergency Room Overcrowding in the Era of Mass Imprisonment."

111. Conrad and Schneider, *Deviance and Medicalization: From Badness to Sickness*; Conrad, *The Medicalization of Society: On the Transformation of Human Conditions into Treatable Disorders*; Hoppe, *Punishing Disease*.

112. Gustafson, *Cheating Welfare: Public Assistance and the Criminalization of Poverty*.

113. Fong, "Getting Eyes in the Home: Child Protective Services Investigations and State Surveillance of Family Life"; Fong, *Investigating Families: Motherhood in the Shadow of Child Protective Services*.

114. Kupchik, *Homeroom Security: School Discipline in an Age of Fear*.

115. Lara-Millán, "Public Emergency Room Overcrowding in the Era of Mass Imprisonment."

116. Conrad and Schneider, *Deviance and Medicalization: From Badness to Sickness*; Conrad and Muñoz, "The Medicalization of Chronic Pain"; Jenness, "Explaining Criminalization: From Demography and Status Politics to Globalization and Modernization."

117. Hoppe, *Punishing Disease*.

118. Brayne, *Predict and Surveil: Data, Discretion, and the Future of Policing*; Benjamin, *Race after Technology: Abolitionist Tools for the New Jim Code*; Pasquale, *The Black Box Society*; O'Neil, *Weapons of Math Destruction: How Big Data Increases Inequality and Threatens Democracy*; Eubanks, *Automating Inequality: How High-Tech Tools Profile, Police, and Punish the Poor*; Lageson, *Digital Punishment: Privacy, Stigma, and the Harms of Data-Driven Criminal Justice*; Levy, *Data Driven: Truckers, Technology, and the New Workplace Surveillance*.

119. Levy, *Data Driven: Truckers, Technology, and the New Workplace Surveillance*.

120. Brayne, *Predict and Surveil*; Eubanks, *Automating Inequality: How High-Tech Tools Profile, Police, and Punish the Poor*.

121. Benjamin, *Race after Technology: Abolitionist Tools for the New Jim Code*.

122. Innes, "Control Creep."

123. Chiarello, "Trojan Horse Technologies: Smuggling Criminal-Legal Logics into Healthcare Practice."

124. Weiner, *On Becoming a Healer: The Journey from Patient Care to Caring about Your Patients*.

125. Baumgart-McFarland et al., "Reluctant Saviors: Professional Ambivalence, Cultural Imaginaries, and Deservingness Construction in Naloxone Provision"; El-Sabawi, "Carrots, Sticks, and Problem Drug Use: Law Enforcement's Contribution to the Policy Discourse on Drug Use and the Opioid Crisis."

126. Soss et al., *Disciplining the Poor: Neoliberal Paternalism and the Persistent Power of Race*; Wacquant, *Punishing the Poor: The Neoliberal Government of Social Insecurity*; Eubanks, *Automating Inequality: How High-Tech Tools Profile, Police, and Punish the Poor*.

127. Pasquale, *The Black Box Society*.

Appendix. A Field Approach to Qualitative Research

1. Caps and emphasis in original.

2. Abood and Burns, *Pharmacy Practice and the Law*.

3. Jameton, "Dilemmas of Moral Distress."

4. Chiarello, "How Organizational Context Affects Bioethical Decision-Making"; Chiarello, "The War on Drugs Comes to the Pharmacy Counter."

5. Executive Office of the President of the United States, "Epidemic."

6. State PDMP Profiles and Contacts, "State PDMP Profiles and Contacts."

7. Charmaz, *Constructing Grounded Theory: A Practical Guide through Qualitative Analysis*; Strauss and Corbin, *Grounded Theory in Practice*; Timmermans and Tavory, "Theory Construction in Qualitative Research."

8. Chiarello, "How Organizational Context Affects Bioethical Decision-Making."

9. Lofland et al., *Analyzing Social Settings: A Guide to Qualitative Observation and Analysis*.

10. Chiarello, "How Organizational Context Affects Bioethical Decision-Making"; Chiarello, "The War on Drugs Comes to the Pharmacy Counter."

11. U.S. Drug Enforcement Administration, "Walgreens Agrees to Pay a Record Settlement of $80 Million for Civil Penalties under the Controlled Substances Act."

12. Deterding and Waters, "Flexible Coding of In-Depth Interviews: A Twenty-First-Century Approach."

13. Now called the Harvard Radcliffe Institute.

REFERENCES

AAPC. "What Are Relative Value Units (RVUs)?" Accessed June 15, 2022. https://www.aapc
.com/practice-management/rvus.aspx.

Abbott, Andrew. *The System of Professions: An Essay on the Division of Expert Labor.* Chicago:
University of Chicago Press, 1988.

Abood, Richard R., and Kimberly A. Burns. *Pharmacy Practice and the Law.* 8th ed. Burlington,
MA: Jones & Bartlett Learning, 2015.

Agnoli, Alicia, Guibo Xing, Daniel J. Tancredi, Elizabeth Magnan, Anthony Jerant, and Joshua
J. Fenton. "Association of Dose Tapering with Overdose or Mental Health Crisis among
Patients Prescribed Long-Term Opioids." *JAMA* 326, no. 5 (August 3, 2021): 411. https://doi
.org/10.1001/jama.2021.11013.

Alexander, Bruce K., Barry L. Beyerstein, Patricia F. Hadaway, and Robert B. Coambs. "Effect
of Early and Later Colony Housing on Oral Ingestion of Morphine in Rats." *Pharmacology
Biochemistry and Behavior* 15, no. 4 (October 1, 1981): 571–76. https://doi.org/10.1016/0091
-3057(81)90211-2.

Alexander, Michelle. *The New Jim Crow: Mass Incarceration in the Age of Colorblindness.* New
York: New Press, 2010.

Ali, Mir M., Robin Ghertner, Laurel Fuller, and Joel Dubenitz. "Public Listing Status of Data-
Waivered Providers: Data Brief." U.S. Department of Health and Human Services, Office of
the Assistant Secretary for Planning and Evaluation, June 2, 2019. https://aspe.hhs.gov
/reports/public-listing-status-data-waivered-providers-data-brief-0.

Allen, Greg. "The 'Oxy Express': Florida's Drug Abuse Epidemic." *NPR*, March 2, 2011, sec. Health.
https://www.npr.org/2011/03/02/134143813/the-oxy-express-floridas-drug-abuse-epidemic.

American Association of Colleges of Nursing. "White Coat Ceremony Recipients." Accessed
December 12, 2022. https://www.aacnnursing.org/White-Coat-Ceremonies.

American Association of Colleges of Pharmacy. "Oath of a Pharmacist," 2021. https://pharmacy
.auburn.edu/about/pp/pharmacist-oath.pdf.

American Board of Medical Specialties (ABMS). "ABMS Officially Recognizes Addiction Medicine as a Subspecialty," March 14, 2016. https://www.abms.org/newsroom/abms-officially
-recognizes-addiction-medicine-as-a-subspecialty/.

American Civil Liberties Union (ACLU). "ACLU Joins Lawsuit to Defend Confidential Medical Records from Warrantless Federal DEA Searches." Accessed December 21, 2021. https://
www.aclu.org/press-releases/aclu-joins-lawsuit-defend-confidential-medical-records
-warrantless-federal-dea.

———. "ACLU Sues to Protect Privacy of Drug Prescriptions." Accessed December 21, 2021. https://www.aclu.org/press-releases/aclu-sues-protect-privacy-drug-prescriptions.

American Medical Association (AMA). "2021 Overdose Epidemic Report," 2021. https://www .ama-assn.org/system/files/ama-overdose-epidemic-report.pdf.

———. "AMA Code of Medical Ethics Opinions on Patient-Physician Relationships." Accessed June 14, 2022. https://www.ama-assn.org/system/files/code-of-medical-ethics-chapter-1 .pdf.

American Psychiatric Association (APA). "Diagnostic and Statistical Manual of Mental Disorders, 5th Edition" 21 (2013): 591–643.

Amstislavski, Philippe, Ariel Matthews, Sarah Sheffield, Andrew R. Maroko, and Jeremy Weedon. "Medication Deserts: Survey of Neighborhood Disparities in Availability of Prescription Medications." International Journal of Health Geographics 11, no. 1 (November 9, 2012): 48. https://doi.org/10.1186/1476-072X-11-48.

Andrea, Sarah B., Tess A. Gilbert, Benjamin J. Morasco, Somnath Saha, and Kathleen F. Carlson. "Factors Related to Prescription Drug Monitoring Program Queries for Veterans Receiving Long-Term Opioid Therapy." Pain Medicine 22, no. 7 (July 1, 2021): 1548–58. https://doi.org /10.1093/pm/pnaa386.

Anson, Pat. "Chronic Pain Patient Abandoned by Doctor Dies." Pain News Network. Accessed October 19, 2022. https://www.painnewsnetwork.org/stories/2016/12/22/chronic-pain -patient-abandoned-by-doctor-dies.

———. "CVS to Limit Opioid Prescriptions." Pain News Network. Accessed October 20, 2022. https://www.painnewsnetwork.org/stories/2017/9/22/cvs-to-limit-opioid-prescriptions.

Anthony, Denise L., and Timothy Stablein. "Privacy in Practice: Professional Discourse about Information Control in Health Care." Edited by Aoife M. McDermott and Anne Reff Pedersen. Journal of Health Organization and Management 30, no. 2 (January 1, 2016): 207–26. https://doi.org/10.1108/JHOM-12-2014-0220.

Appriss Health. "Appriss Health and State Governments." 2021. https://apprisshealth.com/who -we-help/state-governments/.

———. "PMP Gateway." Accessed November 24, 2021. https://apprisshealth.com/solutions /pmp-gateway/.

Armstrong, Elizabeth M. Conceiving Risk, Bearing Responsibility: Fetal Alcohol Syndrome and the Diagnosis of Moral Disorder. Baltimore: Johns Hopkins University Press, 2003.

Arnold P. Gold Foundation. "White Coat Ceremony: Background and Significance." Accessed December 12, 2022. https://www.gold-foundation.org/programs/white-coat-ceremony /background-and-significance/.

Associated Press. "Opioid Epidemic Shares Chilling Similarities with Past Drug Crises," October 29, 2017. https://www.statnews.com/2017/10/29/opioid-epidemic-shares-chilling -similarities-with-past-drug-crises/.

Aviv, Rachel. "Prescription for Disaster." New Yorker, April 28, 2014. https://www.newyorker .com/magazine/2014/05/05/prescription-for-disaster.

Ballentine, Summer, and John Hanna. "Missouri Lawmakers Ban Gender-Affirming Care, Trans Athletes; Kansas City Moves to Defy State." Associated Press, May 10, 2023. https://apnews .com/article/transgender-nonbinary-hormone-puberty-missouri-lawmakers-5a8922430ff ab9e43cf9b7ce254bff9f.

Barkow, Rachel Elise. *Prisoners of Politics: Breaking the Cycle of Mass Incarceration*. Cambridge, MA: Belknap Press, 2019. https://www.amazon.com/Prisoners-Politics-Breaking-Cycle -Incarceration/dp/0674919238.

Bateman, Jordan T., Sandy E. Saunders, and Erica S. Levitt. "Understanding and Countering Opioid-Induced Respiratory Depression." *British Journal of Pharmacology* 180, no. 7 (2023): 813–28. https://doi.org/10.1111/bph.15580.

Baumgart-McFarland, Madison, Elizabeth Chiarello, and Tayla Slay. "Reluctant Saviors: Professional Ambivalence, Cultural Imaginaries, and Deservingness Construction in Naloxone Provision." *Social Science and Medicine* 309 (2022): 115230.

Beauchamp, Tom L., and James F. Childress. *Principles of Biomedical Ethics*. New York: Oxford University Press, 2001.

Bebinger, Martha. "They Call It 'Tranq'—And It's Making Street Drugs Even More Dangerous." *Kaiser Health News*, August 11, 2022. https://khn.org/news/article/xylazine-tranq-drugs -dangerous/.

Beckett, Katherine, and Marco Brydolf-Horwitz. "A Kinder, Gentler Drug War? Race, Drugs, and Punishment in 21st Century America." *Punishment and Society* 22, no. 4 (October 1, 2020): 509–33. https://doi.org/10.1177/1462474520925145.

Beckett, Katherine, and Steve Herbert. *Banished: The New Social Control in Urban America*. New York: Oxford University Press, 2009.

Beletsky, Leo. "America's Favorite Antidote: Drug-Induced Homicide in the Age of the Overdose Crisis." *Utah Law Review* 4, no. 4 (2019): 833.

———. "Deploying Prescription Drug Monitoring to Address the Overdose Crisis: Ideology Meets Reality." *Indiana Health Law Review* 15 (2018): 139.

Beletsky, Leo, and Corey S. Davis. "Today's Fentanyl Crisis: Prohibition's Iron Law, Revisited." *International Journal of Drug Policy* 46 (August 1, 2017): 156–59. https://doi.org/10.1016/j .drugpo.2017.05.050.

Bell, Kirsten, and Amy Salmon. "Pain, Physical Dependence, and Pseudoaddiction: Redefining Addiction for 'Nice' People?" *International Journal of Drug Policy* 20, no. 2 (2009): 170–78.

Belle-Isle, Lynne. "'Nothing about Us, without Us': The Inclusion of People with Lived Experience in Harm Reduction Decisions—Matters of Substance." *Matters of Substance, Canadian Institute for Substance Use Research* (blog), March 13, 2014. https://onlineacademiccommunity .uvic.ca/carbc/2014/03/13/nothing-about-us-without-us-the-inclusion-of-people-with -lived-experience-in-harm-reduction-decisions/.

Benjamin, Ruha, ed. *Captivating Technology: Race, Carceral Technoscience, and Liberatory Imagination in Everyday Life*. Durham, NC: Duke University Press, 2019.

———. *Race after Technology: Abolitionist Tools for the New Jim Code*. Medford, MA: Polity Press, 2019.

Berger, Jeffrey T. "Moral Distress in Medical Education and Training." *Journal of General Internal Medicine* 29, no. 2 (February 1, 2014): 395–98. https://doi.org/10.1007/s11606-013 -2665-0.

Berk, Justin. "To Help Providers Fight the Opioid Epidemic, 'X the X Waiver'" | Health Affairs Forefront." Accessed June 16, 2022. https://www.healthaffairs.org/do/10.1377/forefront .20190301.79453/full/.

Berkrot, Bill. "Global Prescription Drug Spend Seen at \$1.5 Trillion in 2021: Report." *Reuters*, December 6, 2016. https://www.reuters.com/article/us-health-pharmaceuticals-spending-idUSKBN13V0CB.

Berwick, Donald M. "The Moral Determinants of Health." *JAMA* 324, no. 3 (July 21, 2020): 225–26. https://doi.org/10.1001/jama.2020.11129.

Binswanger, Ingrid A., Jason M. Glanz, Mark Faul, Jo Ann Shoup, LeeAnn M. Quintana, Jennifer Lyden, Stan Xu, and Komal J. Narwaney. "The Association between Opioid Discontinuation and Heroin Use: A Nested Case-Control Study." *Drug and Alcohol Dependence* 217 (2020): 108248.

Boekel, Leonieke C. van, Evelien P. M. Brouwers, Jaap van Weeghel, and Henk F. L. Garretsen. "Stigma among Health Professionals towards Patients with Substance Use Disorders and Its Consequences for Healthcare Delivery: Systematic Review." *Drug and Alcohol Dependence* 131, no. 1 (July 1, 2013): 23–35. https://doi.org/10.1016/j.drugalcdep.2013.02.018.

Bottner, Richard, Jillian B. Harvey, Amber N. Baysinger, Kirsten Mason, Snehal Patel, Alanna Boulton, Nicholaus Christian, Blair Walker, and Christopher Moriates. "The Development and Implementation of a 'B-Team' (Buprenorphine Team) to Treat Hospitalized Patients with Opioid Use Disorder." *Healthcare* 9, no. 4 (December 1, 2021): 100579. https://doi.org/10.1016/j.hjdsi.2021.100579.

Boustead, Anne E. "Privacy Protections and Law Enforcement Use of Prescription Drug Monitoring Databases." *Law and Policy* 43, no. 3 (2021): 229–61. https://doi.org/10.1111/lapo.12174.

Bovens, Mark, and Stavros Zouridis. "From Street-Level to System-Level Bureaucracies: How Information and Communication Technology Is Transforming Administrative Discretion and Constitutional Control." *Public Administration Review* 62, no. 2 (April 2002): 174–84. https://doi.org/10.1111/0033-3352.00168.

Brayne, Sarah. "Big Data Surveillance: The Case of Policing." *American Sociological Review*, 82, no. 5 (2017): 977–1008. https://doi.org/10.1177/000312241772586.

———. *Predict and Surveil: Data, Discretion, and the Future of Policing*. New York: Oxford University Press, 2020.

———. "Surveillance and System Avoidance: Criminal Justice Contact and Institutional Attachment." *American Sociological Review* 79, no. 3 (2014): 367–91. https://doi.org/10.1177/0003122414530398.

Brennan, Elizabeth, and Mark C. Suchman. "Law and Technology in Healthcare Organizations." In *Research Handbook on Socio-Legal Studies of Medicine and Health*, ed. M.-A. Jacob and A. Kirkland, 169–90. Northampton, MA: Edward Elgar Publishing, 2020.

Briceland, Laurie L., Jeffrey M. Brewer, and Angela Dominelli. "The Impact of Pharmacy Student Participation in the White Coat Ceremony on Professionalization." *American Journal of Pharmaceutical Education* 84, no. 3 (March 2020): 7689. https://doi.org/10.5688/ajpe7689.

Brico, Elizabeth. "Witnessed Urine Screens in Drug Treatment: Humiliating and Harmful." *Filter*, October 28, 2019. https://filtermag.org/urine-screen-drug-treatment/.

Brooke's House. "Home." Accessed January 20, 2023. https://brookeshouse.org/.

Brown, Ethan. 2022. "Prescription Opioids Aren't Driving the Overdose Crisis. Illicitly Manufactured Synthetic Opioids Are." Garrison Project. February 15, 2022. https://thegarrisonproject.org/prescription-opioids-overdose/.

Buchholz, Katharina. "How Much Do U.S. Cities Spend on Policing?" *Statista Infographics*, February 6, 2023. https://www.statista.com/chart/10593/how-much-do-us-cities-spend-on-policing/.

Buckley, Bruce, and Joan Buckley. "Pharmacists Feeling Pain over AMA Resolution." *Pharmacy Practice News*, August 7, 2013.

Buffat, Aurélien, Michael Hill, and Peter Hupe. *Understanding Street-Level Bureaucracy*. Chicago: Policy Press, 2015.

Burgess, Diana Jill, Megan Crowley-Matoka, Sean Phelan, John F. Dovidio, Robert Kerns, Craig Roth, Somnath Saha, and Michelle van Ryn. "Patient Race and Physician's Decisions to Prescribe Opioids for Chronic Low Back Pain." *Social Science and Medicine* 67, no. 11 (2008): 1852–60. https://doi.org/10.1016/j.socscimed.2008.09.009.

Busting Dr. Tseng's Pill Mill | American Greed | CNBC Prime, March 7, 2017. https://www.youtube.com/watch?v=arpRPk5gGOM.

California Narcotic Officers Association (CNOA). "About CNOA." Accessed January 11, 2022. https://www.cnoa.org/about.

Campo-Flores, Arian. "Fight over a Fix for Florida 'Pill Mills.'" *Wall Street Journal*, February 19, 2011, sec. Business. https://www.wsj.com/articles/SB10001424052748703961104576148753447131080.

Carson, E. Ann. 2022. "Prisoners in 2021—Statistical Tables." *Bureau of Justice Statistics*.

Čartolovni, Anto, Minna Stolt, P. Anne Scott, and Riitta Suhonen. "Moral Injury in Healthcare Professionals: A Scoping Review and Discussion." *Nursing Ethics* 28, no. 5 (August 1, 2021): 590–602. https://doi.org/10.1177/0969733020966776.

Case, Anne, and Angus Deaton. *Deaths of Despair and the Future of Capitalism*. Princeton, NJ: Princeton University Press, 2020.

Castellano, Ursula. "The Politics of Benchcraft: The Role of Judges in Mental Health Courts." *Law and Social Inquiry* 42, no. 2 (2017): 398–422.

Castillo, Tessie. "The Invisible Majority: People Whose Drug Use Is Not Problematic." *Filter*, September 25, 2018. https://filtermag.org/the-invisible-majority-people-whose-drug-use-is-not-problematic/.

Centers for Disease Control and Prevention (CDC). "CDC Guidelines for Prescribing Opioids for Chronic Pain." Centers for Disease Control and Prevention, n.d. https://www.cdc.gov/drugoverdose/pdf/guidelines_at-a-glance-a.pdf.

———. "CDC Guidelines for Prescribing Opioids for Chronic Pain—United States, 2016." *MMWR Recommendations and Reports* 65, no. 1 (2016): 1–49.

———. "Coronavirus Disease 2019," December 21, 2020. https://www.cdc.gov/media/releases/2020/p1218-overdose-deaths-covid-19.html.

———. "Drug Overdose Deaths | Drug Overdose | CDC Injury Center," March 25, 2021. https://www.cdc.gov/drugoverdose/data/statedeaths.html.

———. "Fentanyl | Drug Overdose | CDC Injury Center," April 28, 2021. https://www.cdc.gov/drugoverdose/opioids/fentanyl.html.

———. "Integrating and Expanding Prescription Drug Monitoring Program Data: Lessons from Nine States." Accessed August 21, 2017.. http://www.cdc.gov/drugoverdose/pdf/pehriie_report-a.pdf.

———. "Other Drugs." Centers for Disease Control and Prevention, January 26, 2021. https://www.cdc.gov/drugoverdose/data/otherdrugs.html.

———. "Prescribing Practices | Drug Overdose | CDC Injury Center," August 20, 2019. https://www.cdc.gov/drugoverdose/data/prescribing/prescribing-practices.html.

———. "Protect Patients from Opioid Overdose." Centers for Disease Control and Prevention, July 6, 2017. https://www.cdc.gov/vitalsigns/opioids/infographic.html.

———. "Three Waves of Opioids Overdose Deaths." *Centers for Disease Control and Prevention*, March 17, 2021. https://www.cdc.gov/drugoverdose/epidemic/index.html.

———. "Understanding the Epidemic | Drug Overdose | CDC Injury Center," March 17, 2021. https://www.cdc.gov/drugoverdose/epidemic/index.html.

———. "Vital Statistics Rapid Release—Provisional Drug Overdose Data," January 5, 2023. https://www.cdc.gov/nchs/nvss/vsrr/drug-overdose-data.htm.

———. "What's New, What's Changed." Center for Disease Control, November 3, 2022. https://www.cdc.gov/opioids/healthcare-professionals/prescribing/guideline/changes.html.

Cerdá, Magdalena, William Ponicki, Nathan Smith, Ariadne Rivera-Aguirre, Corey S. Davis, Brandon D. L. Marshall, David S. Fink, et al. "Measuring Relationships between Proactive Reporting State-Level Prescription Drug Monitoring Programs and County-Level Fatal Prescription Opioid Overdoses." *Epidemiology* 31, no. 1 (January 2020): 32–42. https://doi.org/10.1097/EDE.0000000000001123.

Chaar, Betty B., Holly Wang, Carolyn A. Day, Jane R. Hanrahan, Adam R. Winstock, and Romano Fois. "Factors Influencing Pharmacy Services in Opioid Substitution Treatment." *Drug and Alcohol Review* 32, no. 4 (2013): 426–34. https://doi.org/10.1111/dar.12032.

Charmaz, Kathy. *Constructing Grounded Theory: A Practical Guide through Qualitative Analysis.* Thousand Oaks, CA: Sage, 2006.

Chiarello, Elizabeth. "How Organizational Context Affects Bioethical Decision-Making: Pharmacists' Management of Gatekeeping Processes in Retail and Hospital Settings." *Social Science and Medicine* 98 (December 2013): 319–29. https://doi.org/10.1016/j.socscimed.2012.11.041.

———. "Medical versus Fiscal Gatekeeping: Navigating Professional Contingencies at the Pharmacy Counter." *Journal of Law, Medicine and Ethics* 42, no. 4 (2014): 518–34.

———. "Nonprescription Syringe Sales: Resistant Pharmacists' Attitudes and Practices." *Drug and Alcohol Dependence* 166 (2016): 45–50.

———. "Trojan Horse Technologies: Smuggling Criminal-Legal Logics into Healthcare Practice." *American Sociological Review* 88, no. 6 (2023): 1131–60. https://doi.org/10.1177/00031224231209445.

———. "The War on Drugs Comes to the Pharmacy Counter: Frontline Work in the Shadow of Discrepant Institutional Logics." *Law and Social Inquiry* 40, no. 1 (2015): 86–122. https://doi.org/10.1111/lsi.12092.

———. "Where Movements Matter: Examining Unintended Consequences of the Pain Management Movement in Medical, Criminal Justice, and Public Health Fields." *Law and Policy* 40, no. 1 (2018): 79–109.

Christian, Nicholas, Richard Bottner, Amber Baysinger, Alanna Boulton, Blair Walker, Victoria Valencia, and Christopher Moriates. "Hospital Buprenorphine Program for Opioid

Use Disorder Is Associated with Increased Inpatient and Outpatient Addiction Treatment." *Journal of Hospital Medicine* 16, no. 6 (2021): 345–48. https://doi.org/10.12788/jhm .3591.

Ciccarone, Daniel. "The Triple Wave Epidemic: Supply and Demand Drivers of the U.S. Opioid Overdose Crisis." *International Journal of Drug Policy* 71 (September 1, 2019): 183–88. https:// doi.org/10.1016/j.drugpo.2019.01.010.

Cicero, Theodore J., Matthew S. Ellis, and Hilary L. Surratt. "Effect of Abuse-Deterrent Formulation of OxyContin." *New England Journal of Medicine* 367, no. 2 (July 12, 2012): 187–89. https://doi.org/10.1056/NEJMc1204141.

Coffin, Phillip O., Christopher Rowe, Natalie Oman, Katie Sinchek, Glenn-Milo Santos, Mark Faul, Rita Bagnulo, Deeqa Mohamed, and Eric Vittinghoff. "Illicit Opioid Use Following Changes in Opioids Prescribed for Chronic Non-Cancer Pain." *PLOS ONE* 15, no. 5 (May 4, 2020): e0232538. https://doi.org/10.1371/journal.pone.0232538.

Coleman, James William. *The Criminal Elite: Understanding White-Collar Crime*. New York: Worth Publishers, 2005.

Collins, Michael, and Sheila Vakharia. "Criminal Justice Reform in the Fentanyl Era: One Step Forward, Two Steps Back," 2020. https://drugpolicy.org/resource/criminal-justice-reform -fentanyl-era-one-step-forward-two-steps-back.

Coluzzi, Flaminia, Maria Sole Scerpa, and Marco Centanni. "The Effect of Opiates on Bone Formation and Bone Healing." *Current Osteoporosis Reports* 18, no. 3 (June 1, 2020): 325–35. https://doi.org/10.1007/s11914-020-00585-4.

Conrad, Peter. *The Medicalization of Society: On the Transformation of Human Conditions into Treatable Disorders*. Vol. 14. Baltimore: Johns Hopkins University Press, 2007.

Conrad, Peter, and Vanessa Lopes Muñoz. "The Medicalization of Chronic Pain." *Tidsskrift for Forskning i Sygdom Og Samfund* 7, no. 13 (2010).

Conrad, Peter, and Joseph Schneider. *Deviance and Medicalization: From Badness to Sickness*. Philadelphia: Temple University Press, 1992. https://www.amazon.com/Deviance -Medicalization-Sickness-Peter-Conrad/dp/0877229996.

Contextualizing Care. "Podcast." Accessed April 4, 2023. https://www.contextualizingcare.org /podcast-2/.

Courtwright, David T. *A Century of American Narcotic Policy*. Edited by Dean R. Gerstein and Henrick J. Harwood. *Treating Drug Problems: Volume 2: Commissioned Papers on Historical, Institutional, and Economic Contexts of Drug Treatment*. Washington, DC: National Academies Press, 1992. https://www.ncbi.nlm.nih.gov/books/NBK234755/.

———. *Dark Paradise*. Cambridge, MA: Harvard University Press, 1982.

Cowan, Richard. "How the Narcs Created Crack." *National Review* 38, no. 23 (1986): 26–31.

Cramer, Renée Ann. *Birthing a Movement: Midwives, Law, and the Politics of Reproductive Care*. Redwood City, CA: Stanford University Press, 2021.

CVS Health. "Tobacco-Free for Five Years." September 3, 2019. https://www.cvshealth.com /news/community/tobacco-free-for-five-years.html.

Dahlhamer, James. "Prevalence of Chronic Pain and High-Impact Chronic Pain among Adults—United States, 2016." *MMWR: Morbidity and Mortality Weekly Report* 67 (2018). https://doi.org/10.15585/mmwr.mm6736a2.

Darnall, Beth D., and Howard L. Fields. "Clinical and Neuroscience Evidence Supports the Critical Importance of Patient Expectations and Agency in Opioid Tapering." *Pain* 163, no. 5 (2022): 824.

Darnall, Beth D., David Juurlink, Robert D. Kerns, Sean Mackey, Brent Van Dorsten, Keith Humphreys, Julio A. Gonzalez-Sotomayor, et al. "International Stakeholder Community of Pain Experts and Leaders Call for an Urgent Action on Forced Opioid Tapering." *Pain Medicine* 20, no. 3 (March 1, 2019): 429–33. https://doi.org/10.1093/pm/pny228.

Darnall, Beth D., Maisa S. Ziadni, Richard L. Stieg, Ian G. Mackey, Ming-Chih Kao, and Pamela Flood. "Patient-Centered Prescription Opioid Tapering in Community Outpatients with Chronic Pain." *JAMA Internal Medicine* 178, no. 5 (May 1, 2018): 707–8. https://doi.org/10.1001/jamainternmed.2017.8709.

Davis, Corey S., Jill E. Johnston, and Matthew W. Pierce. "Overdose Epidemic, Prescription Monitoring Programs, and Public Health: A Review of State Laws." *American Journal of Public Health* 105, no. 11 (November 2015): 9–11. https://doi.org/10.2105/AJPH.2015.302856.

Davis, Corey S., Matthew Pierce, and Nabarun Dasgupta. "Evolution and Convergence of State Laws Governing Controlled Substance Prescription Monitoring Programs, 1998–2011." *American Journal of Public Health* 104, no. 8 (August 2014): 1389–95. https://doi.org/10.2105/AJPH.2014.301923.

Davis, Corey S., Brian J. Piper, Alex K. Gertner, and Jason S. Rotter. "Opioid Prescribing Laws Are Not Associated with Short-Term Declines in Prescription Opioid Distribution." *Pain Medicine* 21, no. 3 (March 1, 2020): 532–37. https://doi.org/10.1093/pm/pnz159.

Deterding, Nicole M., and Mary C. Waters. "Flexible Coding of In-Depth Interviews: A Twenty-First-Century Approach." *Sociological Methods and Research* 50, no. 2 (2021): 708–39.

Dickson-Gomez, Julia, Erika Christenson, Margaret Weeks, Carol Galletly, Jennifer Wogen, Antoinette Spector, Madelyn McDonald, and Jessica Ohlrich. "Effects of Implementation and Enforcement Differences in Prescription Drug Monitoring Programs in 3 States: Connecticut, Kentucky, and Wisconsin." *Substance Abuse: Research and Treatment* 15 (January 1, 2021): 1178221821992349. https://doi.org/10.1177/1178221821992349.

DiMaggio, Paul J., and Walter W. Powell. "The Iron Cage Revisited: Institutional Isomorphism and Collective Rationality in Organizational Fields." *American Sociological Review* 48, no. 2 (1983): 147–60. https://doi.org/10.2307/2095101.

Dineen, Kelly K. "Addressing Prescription Opioid Abuse Concerns in Context: Synchronizing Policy Solutions to Multiple Complex Public Health Problems Contributed Articles." *Law and Psychology Review* 40 (2016): 1–80.

———. "Definitions Matter: A Taxonomy of Inappropriate Prescribing to Shape Effective Opioid Policy and Reduce Patient Harm." *Kansas Law Review* 67 (n.d.): 53.

Dineen, Kelly K., and James M. DuBois. "Between a Rock and a Hard Place: Can Physicians Prescribe Opioids to Treat Pain Adequately While Avoiding Legal Sanction?" *American Journal of Law and Medicine* 42, no. 1 (2016): 7–52.

Dineen, Kelly K., and Daniel S. Goldberg. "Introduction: Living with Pain in the Midst of the Opioid Crisis." *Narrative Inquiry in Bioethics* 8, no. 3 (2018): 189–93.

D'Onofrio, Gail, Patrick G. O'Connor, Michael V. Pantalon, Marek C. Chawarski, Susan H. Busch, Patricia H. Owens, Steven L. Bernstein, and David A. Fiellin. "Emergency Department–

Initiated Buprenorphine/Naloxone Treatment for Opioid Dependence: A Randomized Clinical Trial." *JAMA* 313, no. 16 (April 28, 2015): 1636–44. https://doi.org/10.1001/jama.2015.3474.

Dowell, Deborah. "CDC Clinical Practice Guideline for Prescribing Opioids for Pain." *MMWR Recommendations and Reports* 71 (2022). https://doi.org/10.15585/mmwr.rr7103a1.

Dowell, Deborah, Wilson M. Compton, and Brett P. Giroir. "Patient-Centered Reduction or Discontinuation of Long-Term Opioid Analgesics: The HHS Guide for Clinicians." *JAMA* 322, no. 19 (2019): 1855–56.

Dowell, Deborah, Tamara Haegerich, and Roger Chou. "No Shortcuts to Safer Opioid Prescribing." *New England Journal of Medicine* 380, no. 24 (June 13, 2019): 2285–87. https://doi.org/10.1056/NEJMp1904190.

Doyle, Sheri, Jaya Tripathi, Gillian Leichtling, and Scott Weiner. "PDMP 3.0: Investigating the Future of Prescription Drug Monitoring Programs." Rx Drug Abuse and Heroin Summit, Atlanta, Georgia, April 23, 2019.

Dr. Stefan Kertesz | Perspective on Opioids | #PainAB2020. 2021. https://www.youtube.com/watch?v=4qjGksj8N6o.

Drug Policy Alliance. "Drug Policy Alliance." Accessed February 8, 2023. https://drugpolicy.org/.

———. "The Drug War, Mass Incarceration and Race." Accessed June 14, 2021. https://drugpolicy.org/sites/default/files/drug-war-mass-incarceration-and-race_01_18_0.pdf.

———. "Harm Reduction." Accessed February 8, 2023. https://drugpolicy.org/issues/harm-reduction.

———. "Opioid Agonist Treatment (OAT): The Gold Standard for Opioid Use Disorder Treatment," February 23, 2021. https://drugpolicy.org/resource/opioid-agonist-treatment-oat-gold-standard-opioid-use-disorder-treatment.

Duke University School of Medicine. "White Coat Ceremony." Duke University, n.d. https://medschool.duke.edu/education/health-professions-education-programs/doctor-medicine-md-program/student-experience-0.

Eddie, David, Lauren Hoffman, Corrie Vilsaint, Alexandra Abry, Brandon Bergman, Bettina Hoeppner, Charles Weinstein, and John F. Kelly. "Lived Experience in New Models of Care for Substance Use Disorder: A Systematic Review of Peer Recovery Support Services and Recovery Coaching." *Frontiers in Psychology* 10 (June 13, 2019). https://doi.org/10.3389/fpsyg.2019.01052.

Edelman, Lauren B. *Working Law: Courts, Corporations, and Symbolic Civil Rights*. Chicago: University of Chicago Press, 2016.

Eisinger, Jesse. *The Chickenshit Club: Why the Justice Department Fails to Prosecute Executives*. New York: Simon & Schuster, 2017.

El-Sabawi, Taleed. "Carrots, Sticks, and Problem Drug Use: Law Enforcement's Contribution to the Policy Discourse on Drug Use and the Opioid Crisis." *Ohio State Law Journal* 80, no. 4 (2019). https://doi.org/10.2139/ssrn.3474469.

El-Sabawi, Taleed, and Jennifer J. Carroll. "A Model for Defunding: An Evidence-Based Statute for Behavioral Health Crisis Response." *Temple Law Review* 94 (2021): 1.

Emergency Medicine Residents Association (EMRA). *Pain Management Fellowships*. Accessed December 17, 2021. http://www.emra.org/books/fellowship-guide-book/18-pain-management/.

Eubanks, Virginia. *Automating Inequality: How High-Tech Tools Profile, Police, and Punish the Poor.* New York: St. Martin's Press, 2018.

Executive Office of the President of the United States. "Epidemic: Responding to America's Prescription Drug Abuse Crisis." American Psychological Association, 2011. https://doi.org/10.1037/e580312012-001.

"Executive Summary—National Opioids Settlement." Accessed February 8, 2023. https://nationalopioidsettlement.com/executive-summary/.

Facher, Lev. "Top U.S. Addiction Researcher Calls for Broad Deregulation of Methadone." *STAT*, November 16, 2022. https://www.statnews.com/2022/11/16/nora-volkow-nida-broad-deregulation-methadone/.

Fair, Helen, and Roy Walmsley. "World Prison Population List, Thirteenth Edition," 2021. *World Prison Brief.* https://www.prisonstudies.org/sites/default/files/resources/downloads/world_prison_population_list_13th_edition.pdf}

Fassin, Didier. "Compassion and Repression: The Moral Economy of Immigration Policies in France." *Cultural Anthropology* 20, no. 3 (2005): 362–87.

Federal Bureau of Investigation (FBI). "Haysville Doctor and Wife Sentenced in Deadly Prescription Overdoses." Accessed January 3, 2022. https://www.fbi.gov/kansascity/press-releases/2010/kc102010a.htm.

Feeley, Malcolm M., and Jonathan Simon. "The New Penology: Notes on the Emerging Strategy of Corrections and Its Implications." *Criminology* 30, no. 4 (1992): 449–74.

Felitti, Vincent J., Robert F. Anda, Dale Nordenberg, David F. Williamson, Alison M. Spitz, Valerie Edwards, and James S. Marks. "Relationship of Childhood Abuse and Household Dysfunction to Many of the Leading Causes of Death in Adults: The Adverse Childhood Experiences (ACE) Study." *American Journal of Preventive Medicine* 14, no. 4 (1998): 245–58.

Fenton, Joshua J., Elizabeth Magnan, Irakis Erik Tseregounis, Guibo Xing, Alicia L. Agnoli, and Daniel J. Tancredi. "Long-Term Risk of Overdose or Mental Health Crisis after Opioid Dose Tapering." *JAMA Network Open* 5, no. 6 (June 13, 2022): e2216726. https://doi.org/10.1001/jamanetworkopen.2022.16726.

Filter. "Infographic: The 'Iron Law of Prohibition,'" October 3, 2018. https://filtermag.org/infographic-the-iron-law-of-prohibition/.

Fishbain, David A., John E. Lewis, Jinrun Gao, Brandly Cole, and Rennee Steele Rosomoff. "Alleged Medical Abandonment in Chronic Opioid Analgesic Therapy: Case Report." *Pain Medicine* 10, no. 4 (2009): 722–29. https://doi.org/10.1111/j.1526-4637.2009.00620.x.

Fong, Kelley. "Getting Eyes in the Home: Child Protective Services Investigations and State Surveillance of Family Life." *American Sociological Review* 85, no. 4 (2020): 610–38.

———. *Investigating Families: Motherhood in the Shadow of Child Protective Services.* Princeton, NJ: Princeton University Press, 2023.

Foster, Michael A. "Mens Rea: An Overview of State-of-Mind Requirements for Federal Criminal Offenses." Congressional Research Service, July 7, 2021. https://crsreports.congress.gov/product/pdf/R/R46836.

Foucault, Michel. *Discipline and Punish: The Birth of the Prison.* New York: Vintage Books, 1975.

FQHC Associates. "What Is a Federally Qualified Health Center (FQHC)?" FQHC Associates. Accessed December 15, 2022. https://www.fqhc.org/what-is-an-fqhc.

Frakt, Austin, and Toni Monkovic. "A 'Rare Case Where Racial Biases' Protected African-Americans." *New York Times*, November 25, 2019, sec. The Upshot. https://www.nytimes.com/2019/11/25/upshot/opioid-epidemic-blacks.html.

Frank, David, Pedro Mateu-Gelabert, David C. Perlman, Suzan M. Walters, Laura Curran, and Honoria Guarino. "It's Like 'Liquid Handcuffs': The Effects of Take-Home Dosing Policies on Methadone Maintenance Treatment (MMT) Patients' Lives." *Harm Reduction Journal* 18, no. 1 (August 14, 2021): 88. https://doi.org/10.1186/s12954-021-00535-y.

Frank, Joseph W., Travis I. Lovejoy, William C. Becker, Benjamin J. Morasco, Christopher J. Koenig, Lilian Hoffecker, Hannah R. Dischinger, Steven K. Dobscha, and Erin E. Krebs. "Patient Outcomes in Dose Reduction or Discontinuation of Long-Term Opioid Therapy." *Annals of Internal Medicine* 167, no. 3 (August 2017): 181–91. https://doi.org/10.7326/M17-0598.

Freed Wessler, Nathan. "ACLU Challenging DEA's Access to Confidential Prescription Records without a Warrant." American Civil Liberties Union, January 25, 2013. https://www.aclu.org/blog/privacy-technology/medical-and-genetic-privacy/aclu-challenging-deas-access-confidential.

Freidson, Eliot. *Professional Dominance: The Social Structure of Medical Care*. New Brunswick, NJ: Transaction Publishers, 1970.

———. *Profession of Medicine*. Chicago: University of Chicago Press, 1970. https://press.uchicago.edu/ucp/books/book/chicago/P/bo3634980.html.

Garland, David. *The Culture of Control: Crime and Social Order in Contemporary Society*. Chicago: University of Chicago Press, 2012.

Gast, Scott. "Who Defines Legitimate Medical Practice-Lessons Learned from the Controlled Substances Act, Physician-Assisted Suicide, and Oregon v. Ashcroft." *Virginia Journal of Social Policy and the Law* 10 (2002): 261.

Gebhart, Fred. "Pharmacists Want More Time with Patients." *Drug Topics Journal* 163, no. 3 (March 18, 2019). https://www.drugtopics.com/view/pharmacists-want-more-time-patients.

Gerber, Marisa. "Doctor Convicted of Murder for Patients' Drug Overdoses Gets 30 Years to Life in Prison." *Los Angeles Times*, February 5, 2016, sec. California. https://www.latimes.com/local/lanow/la-me-ln-doctor-murder-overdose-drugs-sentencing-20160205-story.html.

Gerber, Marisa, Lisa Girion, and James Queally. "California Doctor Convicted of Murder in Overdose Deaths of Patients." *Los Angeles Times*, October 30, 2015. https://www.latimes.com/local/lanow/la-me-ln-doctor-prescription-drugs-murder-overdose-verdict-20151030-story.html.

Gibson, Brent, Kailin See, Brittney Vargas Estrella, and Sam Rivera. "OnPoint NYC: A Baseline Report on the Operation of the First Recognized Overdose Prevention Centers in the United States," December 2023. https://onpointnyc.org/wp-content/uploads/2023/12/ONPOINTNYC_OPCREPORT_small-web1.pdf.

Gilliom, John. *Overseers of the Poor: Surveillance, Resistance, and the Limits of Privacy*. Chicago: University of Chicago Press, 2001.

Glauser, Wendy. "Why Some Doctors Want to Defund the Police." *CMAJ* 192, no. 48 (November 30, 2020): 1644–45. https://doi.org/10.1503/cmaj.1095905.

Glenn, Jason E. "The Birth of the Crack Baby and the History That 'Myths' Make." *Journal of Health Politics, Policy and Law*, 2006.

Godvin, Morgan. "My Friend and I Both Took Heroin. He Overdosed. Why Was I Charged with His Death?" *Washington Post*, November 26, 2019. https://www.washingtonpost.com /outlook/my-friend-and-i-both-took-heroin-he-overdosed-why-was-i-charged-for-his -death/2019/11/26/33ca4826-d965-11e9-bfb1-849887369476_story.html.

Goffman, Erving. *Stigma: Notes on the Management of Spoiled Identity*. New York: Simon & Schuster, 2009.

Goldberg, Daniel S. "Pain, Objectivity and History: Understanding Pain Stigma." *Medical Humanities* 43, no. 4 (2017): 238–43. https://doi.org/doi:10.1136/medhum-2016-011133.

Goldstone, Brian. "The Pain Refugees: The Forgotten Victims of America's Opioid Crisis." *Harper's Magazine*, April 1, 2018. https://harpers.org/archive/2018/04/the-pain-refugees/.

Goode, Erich. *Drugs in American Society*. 9th ed. New York: McGraw Hill, 2015.

Goodnough, Abby. "Overdose Deaths Have Surged during the Pandemic, C.D.C. Data Shows." *New York Times*, April 14, 2021, sec. Health. https://www.nytimes.com/2021/04/14/health /overdose-deaths-fentanyl-opiods-coronaviurs-pandemic.html.

Goodwin, Michele. *Policing the Womb: Invisible Women and the Criminalization of Motherhood*. New York: Cambridge University Press, 2020.

Gramlich, John. "Black Imprisonment Rate in the U.S. Has Fallen by a Third since 2006." Pew Research Center, 2020. https://www.pewresearch.org/short-reads/2020/05/06/share-of -black-white-hispanic-americans-in-prison-2018-vs-2006/.

Grant, Melissa Gira. "The Growing Criminalization of Pregnancy." *New Republic*, May 5, 2022. https://newrepublic.com/article/166312/criminalization-abortion-stillbirths-miscarriages.

Graves, Rachel L., Elena Andreyeva, Jeanmarie Perrone, Frances Shofer, Raina M. Merchant, and Zachary F. Meisel. "Naloxone Availability and Pharmacy Staff Knowledge of Standing Order for Naloxone in Pennsylvania Pharmacies." *Journal of Addiction Medicine* 13, no. 4 (2019): 272–78. https://doi.org/10.1097/ADM.0000000000000492.

Green, Traci C., Rachel Serafinski, Seth A. Clark, Josiah D. Rich, and Jeffrey Bratberg. "Physician-Delegated Unobserved Induction with Buprenorphine in Pharmacies." *New England Journal of Medicine* 388, no. 2 (2023): 185–86.

Guadamuz, Jenny S., G. Caleb Alexander, Tanya Chaudhri, Rebecca Trotzky-Sirr, and Dima M. Qato. "Availability and Cost of Naloxone Nasal Spray at Pharmacies in Philadelphia, Pennsylvania, 2017." *JAMA Network Open* 2, no. 6 (June 7, 2019). https://doi.org/10.1001/jamanet workopen.2019.5388.

Gugelmann, Hallam, Jeanmarie Perrone, and Lewis Nelson. "Windmills and Pill Mills: Can PDMPs Tilt the Prescription Drug Epidemic?" *Journal of Medical Toxicology* 8, no. 4 (December 2012): 378–86. https://doi.org/10.1007/s13181-012-0273-8.

Gusfield, Joseph R. *Contested Meanings: The Construction of Alcohol Problems*. Madison, WI: University of Wisconsin Press, 1996.

Gustafson, Kaaryn S. *Cheating Welfare: Public Assistance and the Criminalization of Poverty*. New York: NYU Press, 2011.

Guy, Gery P. "Vital Signs: Changes in Opioid Prescribing in the United States, 2006–2015." *MMWR Morbidity and Mortality Weekly Report* 66 (2017). https://doi.org/10.15585/mmwr .mm6626a4.

Haddad, Amy M. "Reflections on the Pharmacist–Patient Covenant." *American Journal of Pharmaceutical Education* 82, no. 7 (September 2018): 6806. https://doi.org/10.5688/ajpe6806.

Hailu, Ruth, Ateev Mehrotra, Haiden A. Huskamp, Alisa B. Busch, and Michael L. Barnett. "Telemedicine Use and Quality of Opioid Use Disorder Treatment in the US during the COVID-19 Pandemic." *JAMA Network Open* 6, no. 1 (January 24, 2023): e2252381. https://doi.org/10.1001/jamanetworkopen.2022.52381.

Hall, Wayne, and Megan Weier. "Lee Robins' Studies of Heroin Use among US Vietnam Veterans." *Addiction* 112, no. 1 (January 2017): 176–80. https://doi.org/10.1111/add.13584.

Hampton, Ryan. *American Fix: Inside the Opioid Addiction Crisis—and How to End It.* New York: All Points Books, 2018.

Hansen, Helena, Jules Netherland, and David Herzberg. *Whiteout: How Racial Capitalism Changed the Color of Opioids in America.* Oakland: University of California Press, 2023.

Hansen, Helena, and Samuel Roberts. "Two Tiers of Biomedicalization: Buprenorphine, Methadone, and the Biopolitics of Addiction Stigma and Race." *Advances in Medical Sociology* 14, no. 2012 (2012): 79–102.

Hansen, Helena, and Mary E. Skinner. "From White Bullets to Black Markets and Greened Medicine: The Neuroeconomics and Neuroracial Politics of Opioid Pharmaceuticals." *Annals of Anthropological Practice* 36, no. 1 (2012): 167–82. https://doi.org/10.1111/j.2153-9588.2012.01098.x.

Harris, Robert, Amanda Rosecrans, Meredith Zoltick, Catherine Willman, Ronald Saxton, Margaret Cotterell, Joy Bell, Ingrid Blackwell, and Kathleen R. Page. "Utilizing Telemedicine during COVID-19 Pandemic for a Low-Threshold, Street-Based Buprenorphine Program." *Drug and Alcohol Dependence* 230 (January 1, 2022): 109187. https://doi.org/10.1016/j.drugalcdep.2021.109187.

Hart, Carl L. *Drug Use for Grown-Ups: Chasing Liberty in the Land of Fear.* New York: Penguin, 2021.

Hayden, Aly Vander. "'Drug Dealing' California Doctor Arrested after 14 Patients Die from Overdoses." *Oxygen Official Site*, September 25, 2020. https://www.oxygen.com/license-to-kill/crime-news/doctor-hsiu-ying-lisa-tseng-convicted-patient-deaths.

Hedegaard, Holly, Brigham A. Bastian, James P. Trinidad, Merianne Spencer, and Margaret Warner. "Drugs Most Frequently Involved in Drug Overdose Deaths: United States, 2011–2016," 2018.

Heimer, Carol A. "Competing Institutions: Law, Medicine, and Family in Neonatal Intensive Care." *Law and Society Review* 33, no. 1 (1999): 17–66. https://doi.org/10.2307/3115095.

High, Patrick M., Katherine Marks, Vestena Robbins, Rachel Winograd, Teresa Manocchio, Thomas Clarke, Claire Wood, and Mark Stringer. "State Targeted Response to the Opioid Crisis Grants (Opioid STR) Program: Preliminary Findings from Two Case Studies and the National Cross-Site Evaluation." *Journal of Substance Abuse Treatment* 108 (2020): 48–54.

Hill, Lucas G., Lindsey J. Loera, Kirk E. Evoy, Mandy L. Renfro, Sorina B. Torrez, Claire M. Zagorski, Joshua C. Perez, Shaun M. Jones, and Kelly R. Reveles. "Availability of Buprenorphine/Naloxone Films and Naloxone Nasal Spray in Community Pharmacies in Texas, USA." *Addiction* 116, no. 6 (2021): 1505–11. https://doi.org/10.1111/add.15314.

Hill, Lucas G., Lindsey J. Loera, Sorina B. Torrez, Talia Puzantian, Kirk E. Evoy, Daniel J. Ventricelli, Heidi N. Eukel, et al. "Availability of Buprenorphine/Naloxone Films and Naloxone Nasal Spray in Community Pharmacies in 11 U.S. States." *Drug and Alcohol Dependence* 237 (August 1, 2022). https://doi.org/10.1016/j.drugalcdep.2022.109518.

Hilton, Lisette. "Medical Misinformation Consequences in Health Care," December 9, 2021. https://www.drugtopics.com/view/prescription-drug-monitoring-programs-benefit-pharmacists.

HMP Global Learning Network. "NIH's HEAL Initiatives Keep Progressing Thanks to Scientists' Ingenuity." Accessed June 15, 2021. https://www.hmpgloballearningnetwork.com/site/addiction/article/nihs-heal-initiatives-keep-progressing-thanks-scientists-ingenuity.

Hodge, Jamila, and Seleeke Flingai. "What Happened When Boston Stopped Prosecuting Nonviolent Crimes." Vera Institute of Justice, April 2, 2021. https://www.vera.org/news/what-happened-when-boston-stopped-prosecuting-nonviolent-crimes.

Hoff, Madison. "8 Charts That Show How Major US Cities Spend Taxpayer Dollars on Police versus Social Programs." *Business Insider*, June 19, 2020. https://www.businessinsider.com/police-spending-compared-to-other-expenditures-us-cities-2020-6.

Hoffman, Jan. "Most Doctors Are Ill-Equipped to Deal with the Opioid Epidemic. Few Medical Schools Teach Addiction." *New York Times*, September 10, 2018, sec. Health. https://www.nytimes.com/2018/09/10/health/addiction-medical-schools-treatment.html.

———. "Were These Doctors Treating Pain or Dealing Drugs?" *New York Times*, February 28, 2022, sec. Health. https://www.nytimes.com/2022/02/28/health/doctors-painkillers-supreme-court.html.

Hoffman, Jan, and Desiree Rios. "Fentanyl Test Strips Highlight Rift in Nation's Struggle to Combat Drug Deaths." *New York Times*, October 1, 2022, sec. Health. https://www.nytimes.com/2022/10/01/health/fantanyl-test-strips.html.

Hoffman, Jan, and Mary Williams Walsh. "Purdue Pharma, Maker of OxyContin, Files for Bankruptcy." *New York Times*, September 16, 2019, sec. Health. https://www.nytimes.com/2019/09/15/health/purdue-pharma-bankruptcy-opioids-settlement.html.

Hoffmann, Diane E. "Treating Pain v. Reducing Drug Diversion and Abuse: Recalibrating the Balance in Our Drug Control Laws and Policies." *Saint Louis University Journal of Health Law and Policy* 1 (2007): 231.

Hohenstein, Kurt. "Just What the Doctor Ordered: The Harrison Anti-Narcotic Act, the Supreme Court, and the Federal Regulation of Medical Practice, 1915–1919." *Journal of Supreme Court History* 26 (December 17, 2002): 231–56. https://doi.org/10.1111/1059-4329.00027.

Holmgren, A. Jay, and Nate C. Apathy. "Evaluation of Prescription Drug Monitoring Program Integration with Hospital Electronic Health Records by US County-Level Opioid Prescribing Rates." *JAMA Network Open* 3, no. 6 (June 29, 2020): e209085. https://doi.org/10.1001/jamanetworkopen.2020.9085.

Hoppe, Trevor. *Punishing Disease: HIV and the Criminalization of Sickness*. Oakland: University of California Press, 2018.

Howard, Grace. "The Pregnancy Police: Surveillance, Regulation, and Control." *Harvard Law and Policy Review* 14 (2019): 347.

Huhn, Andrew S., and Kelly E. Dunn. "Why Aren't Physicians Prescribing More Buprenorphine?" *Journal of Substance Abuse Treatment* 78 (July 1, 2017): 1–7. https://doi.org/10.1016/j.jsat.2017.04.005.

Human Rights Watch (HRW). "'Not Allowed to Be Compassionate': Chronic Pain, the Overdose Crisis, and Unintended Harms in the US." Human Rights Watch, December 18, 2018.

https://www.hrw.org/report/2018/12/18/not-allowed-be-compassionate/chronic-pain
-overdose-crisis-and-unintended-harms-us.

Innes, Martin. "Control Creep." *Sociological Research Online* 6, no. 3 (2001): 13–18.

Inquirer. "The Opioid Crisis Shows Why Racism in Health Care Is Always Harmful, Never
'Protective' | Opinion." Accessed June 28, 2021. https://www.inquirer.com/health/expert
-opinions/opioid-crisis-racism-healthcare-buprenorphine-20191223.html.

Institute of Medicine (US) Committee on Advancing Pain Research, Care, and Education.
*Relieving Pain in America: A Blueprint for Transforming Prevention, Care, Education, and Re-
search.* The National Academies Collection: Reports Funded by National Institutes of
Health. Washington, DC: National Academies Press, 2011. http://www.ncbi.nlm.nih.gov
/books/NBK91497/.

James, Keturah, and Ayana Jordan. "The Opioid Crisis in Black Communities." *Journal of Law,
Medicine and Ethics* 46, no. 2 (2018): 404–21. https://doi.org/10.1177/1073110518782949.

Jameton, A. "Dilemmas of Moral Distress: Moral Responsibility and Nursing Practice."
AWHONN's Clinical Issues in Perinatal and Women's Health Nursing 4, no. 4 (January 1,
1993): 542–51. https://pubmed.ncbi.nlm.nih.gov/8220368/.

Jameton, Andrew. *Nursing Practice: The Ethical Issues.* Englewood Cliffs, NJ: Prentice-Hall 1984.

Jaslow, Ryan. "Undercover Cop Goes to Doctor with Dog X-Ray and Is Prescribed Painkillers,
Doc Arrested." CBS News, July 13, 2012. Accessed December 29, 2021. https://www.cbsnews
.com/news/undercover-cop-goes-to-doctor-with-dog-x-ray-and-is-prescribed-painkillers
-doc-arrested/.

Jeantaud, I., F. Haramburu, and B. Bégaud. "Substitution Treatment for Opiate Dependence:
Survey of Community Pharmacies in Aquitaine." *Therapie* 54, no. 2 (March 1, 1999):
251–55.

Jenness, Valerie. "Explaining Criminalization: From Demography and Status Politics to Globalization and Modernization." *Annual Review of Sociology* 2004, 147–71.

Jerry Seinfeld—Pharmacists, 2017. https://www.youtube.com/watch?v=rtC2Qb3Qk14.

Jeter, Lisa. "Opinion: Ruan v. United States, 20-1410." National Association of Attorneys General, July 7, 2022. https://www.naag.org/attorney-general-journal/opinion-ruan-v-united
-states-20-1410/.

Johns Hopkins Bloomberg School of Public Health. "Baltimore's No-Prosecution Policy for
Low-Level Drug Possession and Prostitution Finds Almost No Rearrests for Serious Offenses," October 19, 2021. https://publichealth.jhu.edu/2021/baltimores-no-prosecution
-policy-for-low-level-drug-possession-and-prostitution-finds-almost-no-rearrests-for
-serious-offenses.

Jones, Christopher M., Emily B. Einstein, and Wilson M. Compton. "Changes in Synthetic
Opioid Involvement in Drug Overdose Deaths in the United States, 2010–2016." *JAMA* 319,
no. 17 (May 1, 2018): 1819. https://doi.org/10.1001/jama.2018.2844.

Joseph, Andrew. "In Philadelphia, 'Tranq' Is Leaving Drug Users with Horrific Wounds. Other
Communities Are Bracing for the Same." *STAT*, December 2, 2022. https://www.statnews
.com/2022/12/02/tranq-xylazine-drug-users-wounds-philadelphia/.

Joudrey, Paul, Zoe M. Adams, Paxton Bach, Sarah Van Buren, Jessica A. Chaiton, Lucy Ehren-
feld, Mary Elizabeth Guerra, et al. "Methadone Access for Opioid Use Disorder during the
COVID-19 Pandemic within the United States and Canada." *JAMA* 4, no. 7 (July 23, 2021).

https://jama.jamanetwork.com/article.aspx?doi=10.1001/jamanetworkopen.2021.18223 &utm_campaign=articlePDF%26utm_medium=articlePDFlink%26utm_source=article PDF%26utm_content=jamanetworkopen.2021.18223.

Joudrey, Paul J., E. Jennifer Edelman, and Emily A. Wang. "Methadone for Opioid Use Disorder—Decades of Effectiveness but Still Miles Away in the US." *JAMA Psychiatry* 77, no. 11 (November 1, 2020): 1105. https://doi.org/10.1001/jamapsychiatry.2020.1511.

JRANK. "Criminal Law—Elements of a Crime: Mens Rea and Actus Reus." Accessed January 3, 2022. https://law.jrank.org/pages/22506/Criminal-Law-Elements-Crime-Mens-Rea-Actus -Reus.html.

Jung, Saendy, and Rachel H. McDowell. "Abandonment." *StatPearls*. Treasure Island, FL: Stat-Pearls Publishing, 2022. http://www.ncbi.nlm.nih.gov/books/NBK563285/.

Kaiser Family Foundation. "Opioid Overdose Deaths by Race/Ethnicity." *Kaiser Family Foundation*, March 16, 2021. https://www.kff.org/other/state-indicator/opioid-overdose-deaths-by -raceethnicity/.

Kang-Brown, Jacob, Chase Montagnet, and Jasmine Heiss. *People in Jail and Prison in Spring 2021*. New York: Vera Institute of Justice, 2021.

Kansas City Health Department. "Prescription Drug Monitoring Program | Jackson County, MO." Accessed May 5, 2021. https://www.jacksongov.org/859/Prescription-Drug-Monitoring -Program.

Kao, A. C., and K. P. Parsi. "Content Analyses of Oaths Administered at U.S. Medical Schools in 2000." *Academic Medicine* 79, no. 9 (2004): 882–87.

Kazerouni, Neda J., Adriane N. Irwin, Ximena A. Levander, Jonah Geddes, Kirbee Johnston, Carly J. Gostanian, Baylee S. Mayfield, Brandon T. Montgomery, Diana C. Graalum, and Daniel M. Hartung. "Pharmacy-Related Buprenorphine Access Barriers: An Audit of Pharmacies in Counties with a High Opioid Overdose Burden." *Drug and Alcohol Dependence* 224 (July 1, 2021): 108729. https://doi.org/10.1016/j.drugalcdep.2021.108729.

Keefe, Patrick Radden. *Empire of Pain: The Secret History of the Sackler Dynasty*. New York: Knopf Doubleday, 2021.

Keisler-Starkey, Katherine, and Lisa N. Bunch. "U.S. Census Bureau Current Population Reports, P60-271." *Health Insurance Coverage in the United States: 2019*. Washington, DC: U.S. Government Publishing Office, 2020.

Kertesz, Stefan G., and Adam J. Gordon. "A Crisis of Opioids and the Limits of Prescription Control: United States." *Addiction* 114, no. 1 (2019): 169–80. https://doi.org/10.1111/add.14394.

Kertesz, Stefan G., Adam J. Gordon, and Ajay Manhapra. "Nonconsensual Dose Reduction Mandates Are Not Justified Clinically or Ethically: An Analysis." *Journal of Law, Medicine, and Ethics* 48, no. 2 (June 2020): 259–67. https://doi.org/10.1177/1073110520935337.

Kertesz, Stefan G., Adam J. Gordon, and Sally L. Satel. "Opioid Prescription Control: When the Corrective Goes Too Far." *Health Affairs Forefront*. Accessed December 13, 2022. https:// doi.org/10.1377/forefront.20180117.832392.

Kertesz, Stefan, and Sally Satel. "Some People Still Need Opioids." *Slate*, August 17, 2017. https:// slate.com/technology/2017/08/cutting-down-on-opioids-has-made-life-miserable-for -chronic-pain-patients.html.

Khoury, Lamya, Yilang L. Tang, Bekh Bradley, Joe F. Cubells, and Kerry J. Ressler. "Substance Use, Childhood Traumatic Experience, and Posttraumatic Stress Disorder in an Urban

Civilian Population." *Depression and Anxiety* 27, no. 12 (December 2010): 1077–86. https://doi.org/10.1002/da.20751.

Kiang, Mathew V., Keith Humphreys, Mark R. Cullen, and Sanjay Basu. "Opioid Prescribing Patterns among Medical Providers in the United States, 2003–17: Retrospective, Observational Study." *BMJ* 368 (2020).

Kilaru, Austin, Yuhua Bao, Hao Zhang, and Zachary Meisel. "Prescription Drug Monitoring Program Mandates and Opioids for Acute Pain." *Penn Leonard Davis Institute of Health Economics* (blog), June 16, 2021. https://ldi.upenn.edu/our-work/research-updates/prescription-drug-monitoring-program-mandates-affect-use-of-opioids-to-treat-acute-severe-pain/.

Kimport, K., T. A. Weitz, and L. Freedman. "The Stratified Legitimacy of Abortions." *Journal of Health and Social Behavior* 57, no. 4 (December 2016): 503–16. https://doi.org/10.1177/0022146516669970.

Kline, Thomas. "Suicides Associated with Forced Tapering of Opiate Pain Treatments." *Medium*, August 29, 2019. https://thomasklinemd.medium.com/opioidcrisis-pain-related-suicides-associated-with-forced-tapers-c68c79ecf84d.

Knopf, Alison. "AATOD Fact-Checks Methadone/Buprenorphine Bills." *Alcoholism and Drug Abuse Weekly* 34, no. 44 (2022): 4–5. https://doi.org/10.1002/adaw.33616.

Kotlińska-Lemieszek, Aleksandra, and Zbigniew Żylicz. "Less Well-Known Consequences of the Long-Term Use of Opioid Analgesics: A Comprehensive Literature Review." *Drug Design, Development and Therapy* 16 (December 31, 2022): 251–64. https://doi.org/10.2147/DDDT.S342409.

Kroenke, Kurt, Daniel P. Alford, Charles Argoff, Bernard Canlas, Edward Covington, Joseph W. Frank, Karl J. Haake, et al. "Challenges with Implementing the Centers for Disease Control and Prevention Opioid Guideline: A Consensus Panel Report." *Pain Medicine* 20, no. 4 (April 1, 2019): 724–35. https://doi.org/10.1093/pm/pny307.

Kuehn, Bridget M. "CDC: Major Disparities in Opioid Prescribing among States: Some States Crack Down on Excess Prescribing." *JAMA* 312, no. 7 (August 20, 2014): 684–86. https://doi.org/10.1001/jama.2014.9253.

Kupchik, Aaron. *Homeroom Security: School Discipline in an Age of Fear.* New York: NYU Press, 2010.

Lageson, Sarah Esther. *Digital Punishment: Privacy, Stigma, and the Harms of Data-Driven Criminal Justice.* New York: Oxford University Press, 2020.

Lagisetty, Pooja A., Nathaniel Healy, Claire Garpestad, Mary Jannausch, Renuka Tipirneni, and Amy S. B. Bohnert. "Access to Primary Care Clinics for Patients with Chronic Pain Receiving Opioids." *JAMA Network Open* 2, no. 7 (July 3, 2019): e196928. https://doi.org/10.1001/jamanetworkopen.2019.6928.

Lamiani, Giulia, Lidia Borghi, and Piergiorgio Argentero. "When Healthcare Professionals Cannot Do the Right Thing: A Systematic Review of Moral Distress and Its Correlates." *Journal of Health Psychology* 22, no. 1 (July 27, 2015): 51–67. https://doi.org/10.1177/1359105315595120.

Landau, Elizabeth. "CVS Stores to Stop Selling Tobacco." *CNN Health*, February 5, 2014. https://www.cnn.com/2014/02/05/health/cvs-cigarettes/index.html.

Lara-Millán, Armando. "Public Emergency Room Overcrowding in the Era of Mass Imprisonment." *American Sociological Review* 79, no. 5 (2014): 866–87.

———. *Redistributing the Poor: Jails, Hospitals, and the Crisis of Law and Fiscal Austerity*. New York: Oxford University Press, 2021.

Larochelle, Marc, Pooja A. Lagisetty, and Amy S. B. Bohnert. "Opioid Tapering Practices—Time for Reconsideration?" *JAMA* 326, no. 5 (August 3, 2021): 388–89. https://doi.org/10.1001/jama.2021.11118.

Larochelle, Marc R., Jane M. Liebschutz, Fang Zhang, Dennis Ross-Degnan, and J. Frank Wharam. "Opioid Prescribing after Nonfatal Overdose and Association with Repeated Overdose: A Cohort Study." *Annals of Internal Medicine* 164, no. 1 (January 5, 2016): 1. https://doi.org/10.7326/M15-0038.

Larochelle, Marc R., Sara Lodi, Shapei Yan, Barbara A. Clothier, Elizabeth S. Goldsmith, and Amy S. B. Bohnert. "Comparative Effectiveness of Opioid Tapering or Abrupt Discontinuation vs No Dosage Change for Opioid Overdose or Suicide for Patients Receiving Stable Long-Term Opioid Therapy." *JAMA Network Open* 5, no. 8 (August 12, 2022): e2226523. https://doi.org/10.1001/jamanetworkopen.2022.26523.

Larson, Magali Sarfatti. *The Rise of Professionalism: A Sociological Analysis*. Berkeley: University of California Press, 1979.

L.A. Times Blogs—L.A. NOW. "Doctor Who Prescribed Drugs Based on Dog X-Ray Suspended," August 16, 2012. https://latimesblogs.latimes.com/lanow/2012/08/doctor-suspended-dog-xray.html.

Law, Tara. "Many Pharmacies Don't Carry Life-Saving Addiction Drug." *TIME*, June 10, 2022. https://time.com/6186319/buprenorphine-overdoses-pharmacy-drug-treatment/.

Lea, Toby, Janie Sheridan, and Adam Winstock. "Consumer Satisfaction with Opioid Treatment Services at Community Pharmacies in Australia." *Pharmacy World and Science* 30, no. 6 (December 1, 2008): 940–46. https://doi.org/10.1007/s11096-008-9257-9.

Lee, Richard. "Purdue Pharma Offers Two $1 Million Grants to Combat Prescription Drug Abuse." Accessed November 24, 2021. https://www.stamfordadvocate.com/business/article/Purdue-Pharma-offers-two-1-million-grants-to-1084791.php.

Legal Action Center. "Emergency: Hospitals Are Violating Federal Law by Denying Required Care for Substance Use Disorders in Emergency Departments," 2021. https://www.lac.org/assets/files/LAC-Report-Final-7.19.21.pdf.

Legal Information Institute (LII). "Beyond a Reasonable Doubt." Accessed January 5, 2022. https://www.law.cornell.edu/wex/beyond_a_reasonable_doubt.

Lembke, Anna. *Drug Dealer, MD: How Doctors Were Duped, Patients Got Hooked, and Why It's So Hard to Stop*. Baltimore: Johns Hopkins University Press, 2016.

Letson, Al. "American Rehab." *Reveal*. Accessed February 7, 2023. https://revealnews.org/american-rehab/.

Levy, Karen. *Data Driven: Truckers, Technology, and the New Workplace Surveillance*. Princeton, NJ: Princeton University Press, 2022.

Lewis, Caroline. "Supervised Injection Sites in NYC Have Saved Lives. But Officials Won't Provide Funds." *NPR*, June 4, 2022, sec. National. https://www.npr.org/2022/06/04/1103114131/supervised-injection-sites-in-nyc-have-saved-lives-but-officials-wont-provide-fu.

Libby, Ronald T. *The Criminalization of Medicine: America's War on Doctors*. Westport, CT: Greenwood Publishing Group, 2008.

Lin, Lewei (Allison), Talya Peltzman, John F. McCarthy, Elizabeth M. Oliva, Jodie A. Trafton, and Amy S. B. Bohnert. "Changing Trends in Opioid Overdose Deaths and Prescription Opioid Receipt among Veterans." *American Journal of Preventive Medicine* 57, no. 1 (July 2019): 106–10. https://doi.org/10.1016/j.amepre.2019.01.016.

Lin, Lewei, Lan Zhang, Hyungjin Myra Kim, and Madeline C. Frost. "Impact of COVID-19 Telehealth Policy Changes on Buprenorphine Treatment for Opioid Use Disorder." *American Journal of Psychiatry* 179, no. 10 (2022): 740–47.

Linnemann, Travis. "Mad Men, Meth Moms, Moral Panic: Gendering Meth Crimes in the Midwest." *Critical Criminology* 18, no. 2 (2010): 95–110.

Lipsky, Michael. *Street-Level Bureaucracy, 30th Anniversary Edition: Dilemmas of the Individual in Public Service.* New York: Russell Sage Foundation, 2010.

Liquid Handcuffs: A Documentary to Free Methadone. Accessed February 5, 2023. https://www.liquidhandcuffsdoc.com/.

Llorente, Elizabeth. "As Doctors Taper or End Opioid Prescriptions, Many Patients Driven to Despair, Suicide." Accessed December 14, 2022. https://www.foxnews.com/health/as-opioids-become-taboo-doctors-taper-down-or-abandon-pain-patients-driving-many-to-suicide.

Lofland, John, David Snow, Leon Anderson, and Lyn H. Lofland. *Analyzing Social Settings: A Guide to Qualitative Observation and Analysis.* Long Grove, IL: Waveland Press, 2022.

Los Angeles County District Attorney's Office. "Outcome of Physician Opioid Case," February 25, 2022.

Luger, Lisa, Nirlas Bathia, Ron Alcorn, and Robert Power. "Involvement of Community Pharmacists in the Care of Drug Misusers: Pharmacy-Based Supervision of Methadone Consumption." *International Journal of Drug Policy* 11, no. 3 (May 1, 2000): 227–34. https://doi.org/10.1016/S0955-3959(00)00047-5.

Lyndgaard, Kyhl. "Landscapes of Removal and Resistance: Edwin James's Nineteenth-Century Cross-Cultural Collaborations." *Great Plains Quarterly* 30, no. 1 (2010): 37–52.

Lyon, David. *Surveillance as Social Sorting: Privacy, Risk, and Digital Discrimination.* London: Psychology Press, 2003.

Macaulay, Stewart. "Non-Contractual Relations in Business: A Preliminary Study." In *Stewart Macaulay: Selected Works*, 361–77. Cham: Springer, 1963.

Macy, Beth. *Dopesick.* Boston, MA: Little Brown and Company, 2018.

Macy, Michelle L., Laurel K. Leslie, Adam Turner, and Gary L. Freed. "Growth and Changes in the Pediatric Medical Subspecialty Workforce Pipeline." *Pediatric Research* 89, no. 5 (April 2021): 1297–1303. https://doi.org/10.1038/s41390-020-01311-7.

Magidson, Jessica F., Susan Regan, Elizabeth Powell, Helen E. Jack, Grace E. Herman, Christopher Zaro, Martha T. Kane, and Sarah E. Wakeman. "Peer Recovery Coaches in General Medical Settings: Changes in Utilization, Treatment Engagement, and Opioid Use." *Journal of Substance Abuse Treatment* 122 (March 2021): 108248. https://doi.org/10.1016/j.jsat.2020.108248.

Manchikanti, Laxmaiah, Vanila Mathur Singh, Peter S. Staats, Andrea M. Trescot, John Prunskis, Nebojsa Nick Knezevic, Amol Soin, et al. "Fourth Wave of Opioid (Illicit Drug) Overdose Deaths and Diminishing Access to Prescription Opioids and Interventional Techniques: Cause and Effect." *Pain Physician* 25, no. 2 (2022): 97.

Mann, Brian. "More than a Million Americans Have Died from Overdoses during the Opioid Epidemic." *NPR*, December 30, 2021, sec. National. https://www.npr.org/2021/12/30/1069062738/more-than-a-million-americans-have-died-from-overdoses-during-the-opioid-epidemi.

Mann, Brian, and Martha Bebinger. "Purdue Pharma, Sacklers Reach $6 Billion Deal with State Attorneys General." *NPR*, March 3, 2022, sec. Health. https://www.npr.org/2022/03/03/1084163626/purdue-sacklers-oxycontin-settlement.

Markey, Senator Edward J. (D-MA). S.3629—117th Congress (2021–2022): Opioid Treatment Access Act of 2022. http://www.congress.gov/.

Mars, Sarah G., Philippe Bourgois, George Karandinos, Fernando Montero, and Daniel Ciccarone. "'Every "Never" I Ever Said Came True': Transitions from Opioid Pills to Heroin Injecting." *International Journal on Drug Policy* 25, no. 2 (March 2014): 257–66. https://doi.org/10.1016/j.drugpo.2013.10.004.

Martins, Silvia S., William Ponicki, Nathan Smith, Ariadne Rivera-Aguirre, Corey S. Davis, David S. Fink, Alvaro Castillo-Carniglia, Stephen G. Henry, Brandon D. L. Marshall, and Paul Gruenewald. "Prescription Drug Monitoring Programs Operational Characteristics and Fatal Heroin Poisoning." *International Journal of Drug Policy* 74 (2019): 174–80.

Marx, Gary T. *Undercover: Police Surveillance in America*. Oakland: University of California Press, 1988.

———. *Windows into the Soul: Surveillance and Society in an Age of High Technology*. Chicago: University of Chicago Press, 2016.

Matthew, Dayna Bowen. *Just Medicine: A Cure for Racial Inequality in American Health Care*. New York: NYU Press, 2018.

Mauer, Marc. *Race to Incarcerate*. New York: New Press, 2006.

Maynard-Moody, Steven, and Shannon Portillo. "Street-level Bureaucracy Theory," 2010.

Maynard-Moody, Steven Williams, and Michael Craig Musheno. *Cops, Teachers, Counselors: Stories from the Front Lines of Public Service*. Ann Arbor: University of Michigan Press, 2003.

McBain, Ryan K., Andrew Dick, Mark Sorbero, and Bradley D. Stein. "Growth and Distribution of Buprenorphine-Waivered Providers in the United States, 2007–2017." *Annals of Internal Medicine* 172, no. 7 (January 7, 2020): 504–6. https://doi.org/10.7326/M19-2403.

McKend, Eva. "Chronic Pain Patients Push Back against New Opioid Rules." Accessed October 19, 2022. https://www.wcax.com/content/news/Chronic-pain-patients-push-back-against-new-opioid-rules-439714273.html.

McKim, Allison. *Addicted to Rehab: Race, Gender, and Drugs in the Era of Mass Incarceration*. New Brunswick, NJ: Rutgers University Press, 2017.

———. "'Getting Gut-Level' Punishment, Gender, and Therapeutic Governance." *Gender and Society* 22, no. 3 (2008): 303–23.

MedPage Today Staff. "ACGME a 'Game-Changer' for Addiction Medicine," April 17, 2018. https://www.medpagetoday.com/meetingcoverage/asam/72392.

Medscape. "The Opioid-Free ED: Coming Soon to a Hospital Near You." Accessed December 21, 2021. http://www.medscape.com/viewarticle/840689.

Meghani, Salimah H., Eeeseung Byun, and Rollin M. Gallagher. "Time to Take Stock: A Meta-Analysis and Systematic Review of Analgesic Treatment Disparities for Pain in the United

States." *Pain Medicine* 13, no. 2 (February 1, 2012): 150–74. https://doi.org/10.1111/j.1526 -4637.2011.01310.x.

Meier, Barry. "In Guilty Plea, OxyContin Maker to Pay $600 Million." *New York Times,* May 10, 2007. https://www.nytimes.com/2007/05/10/business/11drug-web.html.

———. *Pain Killer: An Empire of Deceit and the Origin of America's Opioid Epidemic.* New York: Random House, 2018.

Meldrum, Marcia L. "A Capsule History of Pain Management." *JAMA* 290, no. 18 (November 12, 2003): 2470. https://doi.org/10.1001/jama.290.18.2470.

Meyerson, Beth E., Keith G. Bentele, Danielle M. Russell, Benjamin R. Brady, Missy Downer, Roberto C. Garcia, Irene Garnett, et al. "Nothing Really Changed: Arizona Patient Experience of Methadone and Buprenorphine Access during COVID." *PLOS ONE* 17, no. 10 (October 25, 2022): e0274094. https://doi.org/10.1371/journal.pone.0274094.

Meyerson, Beth E., Carrie A. Lawrence, Summer Dawn Cope, Steven Levin, Christopher Thomas, Lori Ann Eldridge, Haley B. Coles, Nina Vadiei, and Amy Kennedy. "I Could Take the Judgment if You Could Just Provide the Service: Non-Prescription Syringe Purchase Experience at Arizona Pharmacies, 2018." *Harm Reduction Journal* 16, no. 1 (September 18, 2019): 57. https://doi.org/10.1186/s12954-019-0327-1.

Mezei, Lina, and Beth B. Murinson. "Pain Education in North American Medical Schools." *Journal of Pain* 12, no. 12 (December 1, 2011): 1199–1208. https://doi.org/10.1016/j.jpain.2011 .06.006.

Mintz, Susannah B. *Unruly Bodies: Life Writing by Women with Disabilities.* Chapel Hill, NC: University of North Carolina Press, 2007.

Morales, Mary E., and R. Jason Yong. "Racial and Ethnic Disparities in the Treatment of Chronic Pain." *Pain Medicine* 22, no. 1 (January 1, 2021): 75–90. https://doi.org/10.1093/pm /pnaa427.

Morse, Jaimie. "Legal Mobilization in Medicine: Nurses, Rape Kits, and the Emergence of Forensic Nursing in the United States since the 1970s." *Social Science and Medicine* 222 (February 1, 2019): 323–34. https://doi.org/10.1016/j.socscimed.2018.12.032.

Mularski, Richard A., Foy White-Chu, Devorah Overbay, Lois Miller, Steven M. Asch, and Linda Ganzini. "Measuring Pain as the 5th Vital Sign Does Not Improve Quality of Pain Management." *Journal of General Internal Medicine* 21, no. 6 (June 1, 2006): 607. https://doi .org/10.1111/j.1525-1497.2006.00415.x.

Musto, David F. *The American Disease: Origins of Narcotic Control.* New York: Oxford University Press, 1999.

NAACP. "Criminal Justice Fact Sheet." May 24, 2021. https://naacp.org/resources/criminal -justice-fact-sheet.

National Academies of Sciences, Engineering, and Medicine. *Medications for Opioid Use Disorder Save Lives.* Washington, DC: National Academies Press, 2019. https://nap.nationala cademies.org/catalog/25310/medications-for-opioid-use-disorder-save-lives.

National Association of Boards of Pharmacy (NABP). "NABP PMP InterConnect Is the Answer the Government Is Looking For," November 24, 2020. https://nabp.pharmacy/news /blog/nabp-pmp-interconnect-is-the-answer-the-government-is-looking-for/.

———. "NABP's Role in Combating the Opioid Epidemic." Accessed May 5, 2021. https://nabp .pharmacy/wp-content/uploads/2021/01/NABP-Combat-Opioid-Epidemic.pdf.

———. "Presidential Initiative | Medication-Assisted Treatment." Accessed March 8, 2021. https://nabp.pharmacy/about/presidential-initiative/.

National Conference of State Legislatures (NCSL). "Prescribing Policies: States Confront Opioid Overdose Epidemic," June 30, 2019. https://www.ncsl.org/research/health/prescribing-policies-states-confront-opioid-overdose-epidemic.aspx.

National Harm Reduction Coalition. "National Harm Reduction Coalition." Accessed February 8, 2023. https://harmreduction.org/.

National Institute on Drug Abuse (NIDA). "Benzodiazepines and Opioids," April 21, 2022. https://nida.nih.gov/research-topics/opioids/benzodiazepines-opioids.

———. *Common Comorbidities with Substance Use Disorders Research Report*. Bethesda, MD: National Institute on Drug Abuse, 2020. http://www.ncbi.nlm.nih.gov/books/NBK571451/.

———. "Drug Overdose Death Rates." National Institute on Drug Abuse, February 9, 2023. http://nida.nih.gov/research-topics/trends-statistics/overdose-death-rates.

———. "Overdose Death Rates." National Institute on Drug Abuse, January 29, 2021. https://www.drugabuse.gov/drug-topics/trends-statistics/overdose-death-rates.

———. "Sample Patient Agreement Forms." Accessed June 15, 2022. https://nida.nih.gov/sites/default/files/SamplePatientAgreementForms.pdf.

National Pain Advocacy Center. "National Pain Advocacy Center." Accessed December 14, 2022. https://nationalpain.org/about-us.

———. "Pain Stories: Quána Madison." Accessed May 5, 2021. https://nationalpain.org/community/pain-stories-quana-madison.

NBC News. "How Florida Brothers' 'Pill Mill' Operation Fueled Painkiller Abuse Epidemic," May 7, 2012. http://www.nbcnews.com/news/world/how-florida-brothers-pill-mill-operation-fueled-painkiller-abuse-epidemic-flna757480.

———. "Pharmacists Say They're Overworked and Understaffed, Risking Patient Safety." Accessed June 17, 2022. https://www.nbcnews.com/health/health-care/overworked-understaffed-pharmacists-say-industry-crisis-puts-patient-safety-risk-n1261151.

Nelkin, Dorothy, and Lori Andrews. "DNA Identification and Surveillance Creep." *Sociology of Health and Illness* 21, no. 5 (1999): 689–706.

Nelson, Lewis S., Maryann Mazer-Amirshahi, and Jeanmarie Perrone. "Opioid Deprescribing in Emergency Medicine—A Tool in an Expanding Toolkit." *JAMA Network Open* 3, no. 3 (March 25, 2020): e201129. https://doi.org/10.1001/jamanetworkopen.2020.1129.

Netherland, Julie, and Helena B. Hansen. "The War on Drugs That Wasn't: Wasted Whiteness, 'Dirty Doctors,' and Race in Media Coverage of Prescription Opioid Misuse." *Culture, Medicine, and Psychiatry* 40, no. 4 (December 1, 2016): 664–86. https://doi.org/10.1007/s11013-016-9496-5.

Nicholson, Kate M. "The Clampdown on Opioid Prescriptions Is Hurting Pain Patients—Los Angeles Times." *Los Angeles Times*, January 18, 2019. https://www.latimes.com/opinion/op-ed/la-oe-nicholson-opioids-20190118-story.html.

———. "The Opioid Crackdown Is Hurting People in Pain." *Washington Monthly*, June 15, 2021. https://washingtonmonthly.com/2021/06/15/the-opioid-crackdown-is-hurting-people-in-pain/.

Nicholson, Kate M., and Deborah Hellman. "Opioid Prescribing and the Ethical Duty to Do No Harm." *American Journal of Law and Medicine* 46, nos. 2–3 (2020): 297–310.

Nieman Reports. "The Superpredator Script." Accessed June 14, 2021. https://niemanreports .org/articles/the-superpredator-script/.

Nolan, Kathleen. "Policing Student Behavior: Roles and Responsibilities." In *The Palgrave International Handbook of School Discipline, Surveillance, and Social Control*, edited by Jo Deakin, Emmeline Taylor, and Aaron Kupchik, 309–26. New York: Palgrave Macmillan Cham, 2018. https://doi.org/10.1007/978-3-319-71559-9_16.

NPR.org. "The 'Oxy Express': Florida's Drug Abuse Epidemic." Accessed May 5, 2021. https:// www.npr.org/2011/03/02/134143813/the-oxy-express-floridas-drug-abuse-epidemic.

Nunes, Edward V., Kevin Kunz, Marc Galanter, and Patrick G. O'Connor. "Addiction Psychiatry and Addiction Medicine: The Evolution of Addiction Physician Specialists." *American Journal on Addictions* 29, no. 5 (September 2020): 390–400. https://doi.org/10 .1111/ajad.13068.

O'Byrne, Patrick, and Courtney Jeske Pearson. "Methadone Maintenance Treatment as Social Control: Analyzing Patient Experiences." *Nursing Inquiry* 26, no. 2 (2019): e12275. https://doi .org/10.1111/nin.12275.

Office of Public and Intergovernmental Affairs. "VA Reduces Prescription Opioid Use by 64% during Past Eight Years." News, July 30, 2020. https://www.va.gov/opa/pressrel/pressrelease .cfm?id=5492.

O'Hagan, Sean. "Patrick Radden Keefe on Exposing the Sackler Family's Links to the Opioid Crisis." *Observer*, February 27, 2022, sec. US news. https://www.theguardian.com/us-news /2022/feb/27/empire-of-pain-patrick-radden-keefe-sackler-opioid-crisis-oxycontin.

Oliva, Jennifer D. "Dosing Discrimination: Regulating PDMP Risk Scores." SSRN Scholarly Paper. Rochester, NY: Social Science Research Network, January 18, 2021. https://doi.org /10.2139/ssrn.3768774.

———. "Prescription Drug Policing: The Right to Health Information Privacy Pre- and Post-Carpenter." *Duke Law Journal* 775 (February 1, 2019). https://dx.doi.org/10.2139/ssrn .3225000.

Omori, Marisa. 2019. "'Nickel and Dimed' for Drug Crime: Unpacking the Process of Cumulative Racial Inequality." *Sociological Quarterly* 60, no. 2: 287–313.

O'Neil, Cathy. *Weapons of Math Destruction: How Big Data Increases Inequality and Threatens Democracy*. New York: Crown, 2016.

Orme, Stephen, Gary A. Zarkin, Laura J. Dunlap, Courtney D. Nordeck, Robert P. Schwartz, Shannon G. Mitchell, Christopher Welsh, Kevin E. O'Grady, and Jan Gryczynski. "Cost and Cost Savings of Navigation Services to Avoid Rehospitalization for a Comorbid Substance Use Disorder Population." *Medical Care* 60, no. 8 (August 1, 2022): 631–35. https://doi.org /10.1097/MLR.0000000000001743.

Ouellette, Jennifer. "First, Do No Harm: An Argument for a Radical New Paradigm for Treating Addiction." *Ars Technica*, December 26, 2021. https://arstechnica.com/science/2021/12 /first-do-no-harm-an-argument-for-a-radical-new-paradigm-for-treating-addiction/.

Pager, Devah. *Marked: Race, Crime, and Finding Work in an Era of Mass Incarceration*. Chicago: University of Chicago Press, 2008.

Paik, Leslie. *Discretionary Justice*. New Brunswick, NJ: Rutgers University Press, 2011.

Parsa-Parsi, Ramin Walter. "The Revised Declaration of Geneva: A Modern-Day Physician's Pledge." *JAMA* 318, no. 20 (November 28, 2017): 1971–72. https://doi.org/10.1001/jama .2017.16230.

Pasquale, Frank. *The Black Box Society*. Cambridge, MA: Harvard University Press, 2015.

Patient Safety Network (PSNET). "The Pharmacist's Role in Medication Safety." Accessed June 17, 2022. https://psnet.ahrq.gov/primer/pharmacists-role-medication-safety.

Patzer, Aaron. "Council Post: Why a Lack of Interoperability in Healthcare Is a Detriment to Patients." *Forbes*. Accessed December 17, 2021. https://www.forbes.com/sites/forbestech council/2020/03/02/why-a-lack-of-interoperability-in-healthcare-is-a-detriment-to -patients/.

PBS.org. "NOVA | Doctors' Diaries | The Hippocratic Oath: Modern Version | PBS." Accessed December 12, 2022. https://www.pbs.org/wgbh/nova/doctors/oath_modern.html.

Peterson, Cora, Likang Xu, Christina A. Mikosz, Curtis Florence, and Karin A. Mack. "US Hospital Discharges Documenting Patient Opioid Use Disorder without Opioid Overdose or Treatment Services, 2011–2015." *Journal of Substance Abuse Treatment* 92 (September 1, 2018): 35–39. https://doi.org/10.1016/j.jsat.2018.06.008.

Pew Charitable Trusts. "Overview of Opioid Treatment Program Regulations by State," September 19, 2022. https://pew.org/3Qw8g8c.

Phelps, Michelle S. "Rehabilitation in the Punitive Era: The Gap between Rhetoric and Reality in US Prison Programs." *Law and Society Review* 45, no. 1 (2011): 33–68.

Pierce, Matthias, Sheila M. Bird, Matthew Hickman, John Marsden, Graham Dunn, Andrew Jones, and Tim Millar. "Impact of Treatment for Opioid Dependence on Fatal Drug-Related Poisoning: A National Cohort Study in England." *Addiction* 111, no. 2 (2016): 298–308. https://doi.org/10.1111/add.13193.

Prescription Drug Monitoring Program Training and Technical Assistance Center (PDMP TTAC). *History of Prescription Drug Monitoring Programs*. Brandeis University: Heller School for Social Policy and Management, 2018. https://www.pdmpassist.org/pdf/PDMP_admin /TAG_History_PDMPs_final_20180314.pdf.

Prison Policy Initiative. "States of Incarceration: The Global Context 2018." Accessed December 16, 2021. https://www.prisonpolicy.org/global/2021.html.

Provine, Doris Marie. "Race and Inequality in the War on Drugs." *Annual Review of Law and Social Science* 7, no. 1 (December 2011): 41–60. https://doi.org/10.1146/annurev-lawsocsci -102510-105445.

———. *Unequal under Law: Race in the War on Drugs*. Chicago: University of Chicago Press, 2008.

Rathore, Mobeen H. "Physician 'Gag Laws' and Gun Safety." *AMA Journal of Ethics* 16, no. 4 (April 1, 2014): 284–88. https://doi.org/10.1001/virtualmentor.2014.16.4.pfor2-1404.

Reardon, Sara. "The U.S. Opioid Epidemic Is Driving a Spike in Infectious Diseases." *Scientific American*, September 12, 2019. https://www.scientificamerican.com/article/the-u-s-opioid -epidemic-is-driving-a-spike-in-infectious-diseases/.

Reason.com. "Dr. Feelscared," August 1, 2004. https://reason.com/2004/08/01/dr-feelscared-2/.

Redmond, Helen. "Methadone Clinics Step Up Their Backlash against Reform." *Filter*, August 2, 2022. https://filtermag.org/methadone-clinic-reform-backlash/.

———. "There Has to Be a Better Way to Free Methadone." *Filter Magazine*, March 9, 2022. https://filtermag.org/methadone-clinic-system/.

Reisinger, Heather Schacht, Robert P. Schwartz, Shannon Gwin Mitchell, James A. Peterson, Sharon M. Kelly, Kevin E. O'Grady, Erica A. Marrari, Barry S. Brown, and Michael H. Agar.

"Premature Discharge from Methadone Treatment." *Journal of Psychoactive Drugs* 41, no. 3 (September 2009): 285–96.

Relman, Arnold S. "The New Medical-Industrial Complex." *New England Journal of Medicine* 303, no. 17 (1980): 963–70.

Residency Roadmap. "General Surgery." Accessed December 17, 2021. https://residency.wustl .edu/choosing-a-specialty/specialty-descriptions/general-surgery/.

Rieder, Travis N. "In Opioid Withdrawal, with No Help in Sight." *Health Affairs* 36, no. 1 (January 1, 2017): 182–85. https://doi.org/10.1377/hlthaff.2016.0347.

———. *In Pain: A Bioethicist's Personal Struggle with Opioids.* New York: HarperCollins, 2019.

———. "There's Never Just One Side to the Story: Why America Must Stop Swinging the Opioid Pendulum." *Narrative Inquiry in Bioethics* 8, no. 3 (2018): 225–31. https://doi.org/10 .1353/nib.2018.0071.

Roberts, Dorothy. *Fatal Invention: How Science, Politics, and Big Business Re-Create Race in the Twenty-First Century.* New York: New Press / ORIM, 2011.

———. *Killing the Black Body: Race, Reproduction, and the Meaning of Liberty.* New York: Vintage, 1999.

———. *Torn Apart: How the Child Welfare System Destroys Black Families—and How Abolition Can Build a Safer World.* New York: Basic Books, 2022.

Roberts, Neil P., Pamela A. Roberts, Neil Jones, and Jonathan I. Bisson. "Psychological Interventions for Post-Traumatic Stress Disorder and Comorbid Substance Use Disorder: A Systematic Review and Meta-Analysis." *Clinical Psychology Review* 38 (June 1, 2015): 25–38. https://doi.org/10.1016/j.cpr.2015.02.007.

Roberts, Nicole F. "The History of Hospice: A Different Kind of Health 'Care.'" *Forbes,* June 22, 2018. https://www.forbes.com/sites/nicolefisher/2018/06/22/the-history-of-hospice-a -different-kind-of-health-care/?sh=7f7d210e660c.

Robert Wood Johnson Foundation (RWJF). "Access to Care and Availability of New Patient Appointments." April 7, 2014. https://www.rwjf.org/en/library/research/2014/04/access -to-care-and-availability-of-new-patient-appointments.html.

Robins, Lee N. *The Vietnam Drug User Returns: Final Report, September 1973.* Washington, DC: U.S. Government Printing Office, 1974.

Rodriguez, Adrianna. "Lawmakers Push Legislation to Protect Doctors Who Prescribe Ivermectin for COVID-19. Can They Do That?" USA TODAY. Accessed April 4, 2023. https:// www.usatoday.com/story/news/health/2022/03/10/covid-ivermectin-bill-dozens-states -push-laws-protect-doctors/9356967002/.

Rowen, Jamie. "Worthy of Justice: A Veterans Treatment Court in Practice." *Law and Policy* 42, no. 1 (2020): 78–100.

Rubin, Rita. "Limits on Opioid Prescribing Leave Patients with Chronic Pain Vulnerable." *JAMA* 321, no. 21 (2019): 2059–62.

Rummell, Nick. "Purdue Pharma Strikes $8B Plea Deal over Marketing of OxyContin." *Courthouse News Service,* October 21, 2020. https://www.courthousenews.com/purdue-pharma -strikes-8b-plea-deal-over-marketing-of-oxycontin/.

Sacco, Lisa N. *Drug Enforcement in the United States: History, Policy, and Trends.* Vol. 7. Washington, DC: Congressional Research Service, 2014.

Sacco, Lisa N., Johnathan H. Duff, and Amanda K. Sarata. "Prescription Drug Monitoring Programs." Congressional Research Service, May 24, 2018. https://sgp.fas.org/crs/misc/R42593.pdf.

Saloner, Brendan, Emma E. McGinty, Leo Beletsky, Ricky Bluthenthal, Chris Beyrer, Michael Botticelli, and Susan G. Sherman. "A Public Health Strategy for the Opioid Crisis." *Public Health Reports* 133, no. 1_suppl (November 1, 2018): 24S–34S. https://doi.org/10.1177/0033354918793627.

Sandbrink, Friedhelm, and Raj Uppal. "The Time for Opioid Stewardship Is Now." *Joint Commission Journal on Quality and Patient Safety* 45, no. 1 (January 1, 2019): 1–2. https://doi.org/10.1016/j.jcjq.2018.10.004.

Santayana, George. *The Life of Reason, Or, The Phases of Human Progress: Reason in Society*. Vol. 2. New York: C. Scribner's Sons, 1905.

Sarat, Austin. "Legal Effectiveness and Social Studies of Law: On the Unfortunate Persistance of a Research Tradition." *Legal Studies Forum* 9 (1985): 23.

Saunders, Cicely. "The Evolution of Palliative Care." *Journal of the Royal Society of Medicine* 94, no. 9 (September 2001): 430–32. https://doi.org/10.1177/014107680109400904.

Scheiber, Noam. "How Pharmacy Work Stopped Being So Great." *New York Times*, August 20, 2022. https://www.nytimes.com/2022/08/20/business/economy/pharmacists-job-inflation.html.

Scher, Clara, Lauren Meador, Janet H. Van Cleave, and M. Carrington Reid. "Moving Beyond Pain as the Fifth Vital Sign and Patient Satisfaction Scores to Improve Pain Care in the 21st Century." *Pain Management Nursing* 19, no. 2 (April 2018): 125–29. https://doi.org/10.1016/j.pmn.2017.10.010.

Scott, W. Richard, and Gerald F. Davis. *Organizations and Organizing: Rational, Natural and Open Systems Perspectives*. New York: Routledge, 2015.

Scott, W. Richard, Martin Ruef, Peter J. Mendel, and Carol A. Caronna. *Institutional Change and Healthcare Organizations: From Professional Dominance to Managed Care*. Chicago: University of Chicago Press, 2000.

Segall, Bob. "Walgreens Secret Checklist Reveals Controversial New Policy on Pain Pills." *Journal of Medicine*, National Association of Medical Doctors (NAMD). Accessed June 20, 2022. https://www.namd.org/journal-of-medicine/1632-walgreens-secret-checklist-reveals-controversial-new-policy-on-pain-pills.html.

Seim, Josh. "The Ambulance: Toward a Labor Theory of Poverty Governance." *American Sociological Review* 82, no. 3 (2017): 451–75.

———. *Bandage, Sort, and Hustle: Ambulance Crews on the Front Lines of Urban Suffering*. Oakland: University of California Press, 2020.

Shanahan, Lilly, Sherika N. Hill, Lauren M. Gaydosh, Annekatrin Steinhoff, E. Jane Costello, Kenneth A. Dodge, Kathleen Mullan Harris, and William E. Copeland. "Does Despair Really Kill? A Roadmap for an Evidence-Based Answer." *American Journal of Public Health* 109, no. 6 (June 2019): 854–58. https://doi.org/10.2105/AJPH.2019.305016.

Sheridan, Janie, Victoria Manning, Gayle Ridge, Soraya Mayet, and John Strang. "Community Pharmacies and the Provision of Opioid Substitution Services for Drug Misusers: Changes in Activity and Attitudes of Community Pharmacists across England 1995–2005." *Addiction* 102, no. 11 (2007): 1824–30. https://doi.org/10.1111/j.1360-0443.2007.02016.x.

Sherry, Michael S. *The Punitive Turn in American Life: How the United States Learned to Fight Crime Like a War*. Chapel Hill: University of North Carolina Press Books, 2020.

Shipton, E. E., F. Bate, R. Garrick, C. Steketee, E. A. Shipton, and E. J. Visser "Systematic Review of Pain Medicine Content, Teaching, and Assessment in Medical School Curricula Internationally." *Pain Therapy* 7 (2018): 139–61. https://doi.org/10.1007/s40122-018-0103-z.

Shoemaker-Hunt, Sarah J., and Brandy E. Wyant. "The Effect of Opioid Stewardship Interventions on Key Outcomes: A Systematic Review." *Journal of Patient Safety* 16, no. 3 (September 2020): S36. https://doi.org/10.1097/PTS.0000000000000710.

Showalter, David, Lynn D. Wenger, Barrot H. Lambdin, Eliza Wheeler, Ingrid Binswanger, and Alex H. Kral. "Bridging Institutional Logics: Implementing Naloxone Distribution for People Exiting Jail in Three California Counties." *Social Science and Medicine* 285 (2021): 114293.

Siegel, Zachary. "The Opioid Crisis Is about More Than Corporate Greed." *New Republic*, July 30, 2019. https://newrepublic.com/article/154560/opioid-crisis-corporate-greed.

Simon, Jonathan. *Governing through Crime: How the War on Crime Transformed American Democracy and Created a Culture of Fear*. New York: Oxford University Press, 2007.

Sinha, Rajita. "Chronic Stress, Drug Use, and Vulnerability to Addiction." *Annals of the New York Academy of Sciences* 1141 (October 2008): 105–30. https://doi.org/10.1196/annals.1441.030.

Smirnova, Michelle. *The Prescription-to-Prison Pipeline: An Intersectional Analysis of the Medicalization and Criminalization of Pain*. Durham, NC: Duke University Press, 2023.

Smith, L. Lerissa, Fengxia Yan, Mikayla Charles, Kamal Mohiuddin, Dawn Tyus, Oluwatoyosi Adekeye, and Kisha B. Holden. "Exploring the Link between Substance Use and Mental Health Status: What Can We Learn from the Self-Medication Theory?" *Journal of Health Care for the Poor and Underserved* 28, no. 2 (2017): 113–31. https://doi.org/10.1353/hpu.2017.0056.

Soares, Inês Branco, Tamara L. Imfeld-Isenegger, Urska Nabergoj Makovec, Nejc Horvat, Mitja Kos, Isabell Arnet, Kurt E. Hersberger, and Filipa A. Costa. "A Survey to Assess the Availability, Implementation Rate and Remuneration of Pharmacist-Led Cognitive Services throughout Europe." *Research in Social and Administrative Pharmacy* 16, no. 1 (January 1, 2020): 41–47. https://doi.org/10.1016/j.sapharm.2019.02.002.

Soss, Joe, Richard C. Fording, and Sanford F. Schram. *Disciplining the Poor: Neoliberal Paternalism and the Persistent Power of Race*. Chicago: University of Chicago Press, 2011.

Sporrong, Sofia Kälvemark, Anna T. Höglund, and Bengt Arnetz. "Measuring Moral Distress in Pharmacy and Clinical Practice." *Nursing Ethics* 13, no. 4 (2006): 416–27.

Starr, Paul. *The Social Transformation of American Medicine: The Rise of a Sovereign Profession and the Making of a Vast Industry*. New York: Basic Books, 2008.

STAT. "Why Drug Prescriptions Should Include Diagnoses," March 1, 2021. https://www.statnews.com/2021/03/01/why-drug-prescriptions-should-include-diagnoses/.

State PDMP Profiles and Contacts. "State PDMP Profiles and Contacts." Accessed November 24, 2021. https://www.pdmpassist.org/State.

Strauss, Anselm, and Juliet M. Corbin. *Grounded Theory in Practice*. New York: Sage, 1997.

Substance Abuse and Mental Health Services Administration (SAMHSA). "Become a Buprenorphine Waivered Practitioner." Accessed June 16, 2022. https://www.samhsa.gov/medication-assisted-treatment/become-buprenorphine-waivered-practitioner.

———. "Buprenorphine." Accessed January 24, 2023. https://www.samhsa.gov/medication-assisted-treatment/medications-counseling-related-conditions/buprenorphine.

———. "Key Substance Use and Mental Health Indicators in the United States: Results from the 2019 National Survey on Drug Use and Health," September 2020, 114.

———. "Key Substance Use and Mental Health Indicators in the United States: Results from the 2021 National Survey on Drug Use and Health," 2022. https://www.samhsa.gov/data/sites/default/files/reports/rpt39443/2021NSDUHFFRRev010323.pdf.

———. *The Opioid Crisis and the Black/African American Population: An Urgent Issue.* 2020.

———. "Peers Supporting Recovery from Substance Use Disorders," 2017. https://www.samhsa.gov/sites/default/files/programs_campaigns/brss_tacs/peers-supporting-recovery-substance-use-disorders-2017.pdf.

———. "Removal of DATA Waiver (X-Waiver) Requirement," 1–25 / 23. https://www.samhsa.gov/medications-substance-use-disorders/removal-data-waiver-requirement.

———. "Understanding the Final Rule for a Patient Limit of 275." Accessed February 7, 2023. https://www.samhsa.gov/sites/default/files/programs_campaigns/medication_assisted/understanding-patient-limit275.pdf.

Sue, Kim. *Getting Wrecked: Women, Incarceration, and the American Opioid Crisis.* Oakland: University of California Press, 2019.

Szalavitz, Maia. "Drug Addiction Should Be Treated Like a Learning Disorder—Not a Crime." *Guardian*, April 5, 2016, sec. US news. https://www.theguardian.com/commentisfree/2016/apr/05/drug-addiction-treatment-learning-disorders.

———. "Opinion | The Most Important Question about Addiction." *New York Times*, September 29, 2022, sec. Opinion. https://www.nytimes.com/2022/09/29/opinion/opiate-fentanyl-epidemic.html.

———. "Opinion | What the Opioid Crisis Took from People in Pain." *New York Times*, March 7, 2022, sec. Opinion. https://www.nytimes.com/2022/03/07/opinion/opioid-crisis-pain-victims.html.

———. *Unbroken Brain: A Revolutionary New Way of Understanding Addiction.* New York: St. Martin's Publishing Group, 2016.

———. *Undoing Drugs: The Untold Story of Harm Reduction and the Future of Addiction.* New York: Hachette, 2021.

Tai-Seale, Ming, Cliff W. Olson, Jinnan Li, Albert S. Chan, Criss Morikawa, Meg Durbin, Wei Wang, and Harold S. Luft. "Electronic Health Record Logs Indicate That Physicians Split Time Evenly between Seeing Patients and Desktop Medicine." *Health Affairs* 36, no. 4 (April 2017): 655–62. https://doi.org/10.1377/hlthaff.2016.0811.

Tarkan, Laurie. "Moving Toward an (Almost) Opioid-Free Emergency Department." Practical Pain Management. Accessed December 21, 2021. https://www.practicalpainmanagement.com/treatments/interventional/moving-toward-almost-opioid-free-emergency-department.

Thomson, Douglass. "The Work of Art in the Age of Electronic (Re)Production." *Romanticism on the Net*, no. 10 (1998). https://doi.org/10.7202/005805ar.

Thornton, Patricia H., and William Ocasio. "Institutional Logics." *Sage Handbook of Organizational Institutionalism* 840, no. 2008 (2008): 99–128.

Thornton, Patricia H., William Ocasio, and Michael Lounsbury. "The Institutional Logics Perspective." In *Emerging Trends in the Social and Behavioral Sciences: An Interdisciplinary,*

Searchable, and Linkable Resource, ed. Robert A. Scott and Stephen M. Kosslyn, 1–22. New York: Wiley Online, 2015.

Tiger, Rebecca. "Drug Courts and the Logic of Coerced Treatment." *Sociological Forum* 26, no. 1 (2011): 169–82. https://www.jstor.org/stable/23027286.

———. *Judging Addicts: Drug Courts and Coercion in the Justice System.* New York: New York University Press, 2013.

Timmermans, Stefan, and Jonathan Gabe. "Introduction: Connecting Criminology and Sociology of Health and Illness." *Sociology of Health and Illness* 24, no. 5 (2002): 501–16. https://doi.org/10.1111/1467-9566.00306.

Timmermans, Stefan, and Iddo Tavory. "Theory Construction in Qualitative Research: From Grounded Theory to Abductive Analysis." *Sociological Theory* 30, no. 3 (September 1, 2012): 167–86. https://doi.org/10.1177/0735275112457914.

Tompkins, D. Andrew, J. Greg Hobelmann, and Peggy Compton. "Providing Chronic Pain Management in the 'Fifth Vital Sign' Era: Historical and Treatment Perspectives on a Modern-Day Medical Dilemma." *Drug and Alcohol Dependence* 173 (April 2017): S11–21. https://doi.org/10.1016/j.drugalcdep.2016.12.002.

Townsend, Tarlise N., Amy S. B. Bohnert, Pooja Lagisetty, and Rebecca L. Haffajee. "Did Prescribing Laws Disproportionately Affect Opioid Dispensing to Black Patients?" *Health Services Research* 57, no. 3 (2022): 482–96. doi: 10.1111/1475-6773.13968.

Travis, Jeremy, Bruce Western, and F. Stevens Redburn. *The Growth of Incarceration in the United States: Exploring Causes and Consequences.* Washington, DC: National Academies Press, 2014.

Trawalter, Sophie. "Black Americans Are Systematically Under-Treated for Pain. Why?" *Frank Batten School of Leadership and Public Policy,* June 30, 2020. https://batten.virginia.edu/about/news/black-americans-are-systematically-under-treated-pain-why.

Treede, Rolf-Detlef, Winfried Rief, Antonia Barke, Qasim Aziz, Michael I. Bennett, Rafael Benoliel, Milton Cohen, et al. "A Classification of Chronic Pain for ICD-11." *Pain* 156, no. 6 (June 2015): 1003–7. https://doi.org/10.1097/j.pain.0000000000000160.

Uosukainen, Hanna, J. Simon Bell, Kirsti Laitinen, Ulrich Tacke, Jenni Ilomäki, and Juha H. O. Turunen. "First Insights into Community Pharmacy Based Buprenorphine-Naloxone Dispensing in Finland." *International Journal of Drug Policy* 24, no. 5 (September 1, 2013): 492–97. https://doi.org/10.1016/j.drugpo.2013.02.004.

Urban Survivors Union (USU). "Home | Urban Survivors Union." Accessed February 8, 2023. https://www.druguservoice.org.

U.S. Attorney's Office (USAO). "U.S. Attorney's Office—U.S. Department of Justice." Accessed December 17, 2021. https://www.justice.gov/archive/usao/co/news/2008/October08/10_2_08.html.

U.S. Census Bureau. "Health Insurance Coverage in the United States: 2019." United States Census Bureau. Accessed May 6, 2021. https://www.census.gov/library/publications/2020/demo/p60-271.html.

U.S. Department of Health and Human Services (HHS) and Office of Inspector General (OIG). "Geographic Disparities Affect Access to Buprenorphine Services for Opioid Use Disorder," January 2020. https://oig.hhs.gov/oei/reports/oei-12-17-00240.pdf.

U.S. Department of Justice (DOJ). "Automation of Reports and Consolidated Orders System (ARCOS)." Accessed November 24, 2021. https://www.deadiversion.usdoj.gov/arcos/index.html.

———. "Cases against Doctors." Accessed June 8, 2021. https://apps2.deadiversion.usdoj.gov /CasesAgainstDoctors/spring/main?execution=e1s1.

———. "Controlled Substance Schedules." Accessed November 24, 2021. https://www .deadiversion.usdoj.gov/schedules/.

———. "Dr. Couch and Dr. Ruan Sentenced to 240 and 252 Months in Federal Prison for Running Massive Pill Mill," May 26, 2017. https://www.justice.gov/usao-sdal/pr/dr-couch -and-dr-ruan-sentenced-240-and-252-months-federal-prison-running-massive-pill#:~:text =Couch%20and%20Dr.-,Ruan%20Sentenced%20to%20240%20and%20252%20 Months%20In,For%20Running%20Massive%20Pill%20Mill.

U.S. Department of Health and Human Services (HHS), Office of Infectious Disease and HIV/ AIDS. "Viral Hepatitis in the United States: Data and Trends." April 20, 2016. https://www .hhs.gov/hepatitis/learn-about-viral-hepatitis/data-and-trends/index.html.

———. "Title 21 United States Code (USC) Controlled Substances Act—Section 801-971." 21 USC Codified CSA, 1988. https://www.deadiversion.usdoj.gov/21cfr/21usc/.

U.S. Department of Justice (DOJ) and Office of the Inspector General (OIG) Evaluation and Inspections Division. "Follow-up Review of the Drug Enforcement Administration's Efforts to Control the Diversion of Controlled Pharmaceuticals." July 2006. https://oig.justice.gov /reports/DEA/e0604/final.pdf.

U.S. Drug Enforcement Administration (DEA). "Diversion Investigator." Accessed November 24, 2021. https://www.dea.gov/careers/diversion-investigator.

———. "Drug Scheduling." Accessed May 17, 2021. https://www.dea.gov/drug-information /drug-scheduling.

———. "Special Agent." Accessed November 24, 2021. https://www.dea.gov/careers/special -agent.

———. "Walgreens Agrees to Pay a Record Settlement of $80 Million for Civil Penalties under the Controlled Substances Act." June 11, 2013. https://www.dea.gov/press-releases/2013/06 /11/walgreens-agrees-pay-record-settlement-80-million-civil-penalties-under.

Vestal, Christine. "States Likely to Resist CDC Proposal Easing Opioid Access." *Stateline*, March 1, 2022. https://pew.org/3sxOMHt.

Wacquant, Loïc. *Punishing the Poor: The Neoliberal Government of Social Insecurity.* Durham, NC: Duke University Press, 2009.

Waddell, Elizabeth Needham, Robin Baker, Daniel M. Hartung, Christi J. Hildebran, Thuan Nguyen, Deza'Rae M. Collins, Jessica E. Larsen, and Erin Stack. "Reducing Overdose after Release from Incarceration (ROAR): Study Protocol for an Intervention to Reduce Risk of Fatal and Non-Fatal Opioid Overdose among Women after Release from Prison." *Health and Justice* 8 (July 10, 2020): 18. https://doi.org/10.1186/s40352-020-00113-7.

Waggoner, Miranda R. *The Zero Trimester: Pre-Pregnancy Care and the Politics of Reproductive Risk.* Oakland: University of California Press, 2017.

Wakeman, Sarah E., Marc R. Larochelle, Omid Ameli, Christine E. Chaisson, Jeffrey Thomas McPheeters, William H. Crown, Francisca Azocar, and Darshak M. Sanghavi. "Comparative Effectiveness of Different Treatment Pathways for Opioid Use Disorder." *JAMA Network Open* 3, no. 2 (February 5, 2020): e1920622. https://doi.org/10.1001/jamanetworkopen.2019.20622.

Walker, Ingrid. *High: Drugs, Desire, and a Nation of Users.* Seattle: University of Washington Press, 2017.

Walker, James M., Robert J. Farney, Steven M. Rhondeau, Kathleen M. Boyle, Karen Valentine, Tom V. Cloward, and Kevin C. Shilling. "Chronic Opioid Use Is a Risk Factor for the Development of Central Sleep Apnea and Ataxic Breathing." *Journal of Clinical Sleep Medicine* 3, no. 5 (2007): 455–61.

Walley, Alexander Y., Sara Lodi, Yijing Li, Dana Bernson, Hermik Babakhanlou-Chase, Thomas Land, and Marc R. Larochelle. "Association between Mortality Rates and Medication and Residential Treatment after In-Patient Medically Managed Opioid Withdrawal: A Cohort Analysis." *Addiction* 115, no. 8 (2020): 1496–1508. https://doi.org/10.1111/add.14964.

Wang, Linda, Jeffrey Weiss, Elizabeth Bogel Ryan, Justine Waldman, Stacey Rubin, and Judy L. Griffin. "Telemedicine Increases Access to Buprenorphine Initiation during the COVID-19 Pandemic." *Journal of Substance Abuse Treatment* 124 (May 2021): 108272. https://doi.org/10.1016/j.jsat.2020.108272.

Washington, Harriet A. *Medical Apartheid: The Dark History of Medical Experimentation on Black Americans from Colonial Times to the Present.* New York: Doubleday Books, 2006.

WBUR. "Backlash against Walgreen's New Painkiller Crackdown." Accessed December 17, 2021. https://www.wbur.org/news/2013/08/12/walgreens-painkiller-crackdown.

Webster, Lynn R. "Pain and Suicide: The Other Side of the Opioid Story." *Pain Medicine* 15, no. 3 (March 1, 2014): 345–46. https://doi.org/10.1111/pme.12398.

Weiner, Saul J. *On Becoming a Healer: The Journey from Patient Care to Caring about Your Patients.* Baltimore: Johns Hopkins University Press, 2020.

Weiner, Scott G., Christin N. Price, Alev J. Atalay, Elizabeth M. Harry, Erika A. Pabo, Rajesh Patel, Joji Suzuki, Shelly Anderson, Stanley W. Ashley, and Allen Kachalia. "A Health System–Wide Initiative to Decrease Opioid-Related Morbidity and Mortality." *Joint Commission Journal on Quality and Patient Safety* 45, no. 1 (January 1, 2019): 3–13. https://doi.org/10.1016/j.jcjq.2018.07.003.

Weiner, Scott G., Karen M. Sherritt, Zoe Tseng, and Jaya Tripathi. "Advanced Visualizations to Interpret Prescription Drug Monitoring Program Information." *Drug and Alcohol Dependence* 201 (August 1, 2019): 260–65. https://doi.org/10.1016/j.drugalcdep.2019.03.034.

Wen, Leana S., and Katherine E. Warren. "Combatting the Opioid Epidemic: Baltimore's Experience and Lessons Learned." *Journal of Public Health* 40, no. 2 (June 1, 2018): e107–11. https://doi.org/10.1093/pubmed/fdx093.

White House. "Remarks of President Joe Biden—State of the Union Address as Prepared for Delivery." White House, March 2, 2022. https://www.whitehouse.gov/briefing-room/speeches-remarks/2022/03/01/remarks-of-president-joe-biden-state-of-the-union-address-as-delivered/.

WIRED. "A Drug Addiction Risk Algorithm and Its Grim Toll on Chronic Pain Sufferers." Accessed December 6, 2021. https://www.wired.com/story/opioid-drug-addiction-algorithm-chronic-pain/.

Woo, Julia, Anuja Bhalerao, Monica Bawor, Meha Bhatt, Brittany Dennis, Natalia Mouravska, Laura Zielinski, and Zainab Samaan. "'Don't Judge a Book by Its Cover': A Qualitative Study of Methadone Patients' Experiences of Stigma." *Substance Abuse: Research and Treatment* 11 (January 1, 2017): 1178221816685087. https://doi.org/10.1177/1178221816685087.

Wright, Erik Olin, and Robert Barber. *The Politics of Punishment: A Critical Analysis of Prisons in America.* New York: Harper & Row, 1973.

Wu, Li-Tzy, William S. John, Udi E. Ghitza, Aimee Wahle, Abigail G. Matthews, Mitra Lewis, Brett Hart, et al. "Buprenorphine Physician–Pharmacist Collaboration in the Management of Patients with Opioid Use Disorder: Results from a Multisite Study of the National Drug Abuse Treatment Clinical Trials Network." *Addiction*, January 11, 2021, add. 15353. https://doi.org/10.1111/add.15353.

Wyse, Jessica J., Adam J. Gordon, Steven K. Dobscha, Benjamin J. Morasco, Elizabeth Tiffany, Karen Drexler, Friedhelm Sandbrink, and Travis I. Lovejoy. "Medications for Opioid Use Disorder in the Department of Veterans Affairs (VA) Health Care System: Historical Perspective, Lessons Learned, and Next Steps." *Substance Abuse* 39, no. 2 (2018): 139–44. https://doi.org/10.1080/08897077.2018.1452327.

Yong, R. Jason, Peter M. Mullins, and Neil Bhattacharyya. "Prevalence of Chronic Pain among Adults in the United States." *PAIN*, December 10, 2021. https://doi.org/10.1097/j.pain.0000000000002291.

Zacka, Bernardo. *When the State Meets the Street: Public Service and Moral Agency*. Cambridge, MA: Harvard University Press, 2017.

Zezima, Katie. "With Drug Overdoses Soaring, States Limit the Length of Painkiller Prescriptions." *Washington Post*, August 9, 2017, sec. Politics. https://www.washingtonpost.com/politics/with-drug-overdoses-soaring-states-limit-the-length-of-painkiller-prescriptions/2017/08/09/4d5d7e0c-7d0f-11e7-83c7-5bd5460f0d7e_story.html.

Ziegler, Stephen J., and Nicholas P. Lovrich Jr. "Pain Relief, Prescription Drugs, and Prosecution: A Four-State Survey of Chief Prosecutors." *Journal of Law, Medicine and Ethics* 31, no. 1 (2003): 75–100.

Zuboff, Shoshana. *The Age of Surveillance Capitalism: The Fight for a Human Future at the New Frontier of Power*. New York: PublicAffairs, 2019.

INDEX

A NOTE ON THE TYPE

This book has been composed in Arno, an Old-style serif typeface in the classic Venetian tradition, designed by Robert Slimbach at Adobe.